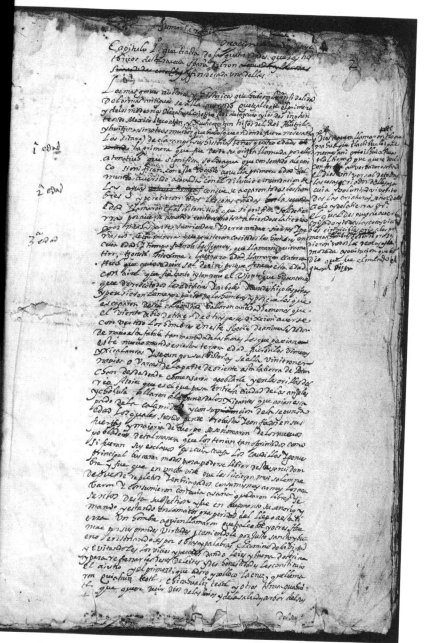

Page 1 of the *Historia de la nación chichimeca*, taken from the digitalized *Códice Chimalpahin*, located in the Biblioteca Nacional de Antropología e Historia, Mexico City. Courtesy of INAH.

The Legacy of Rulership in Fernando d

Ixtlilxochitl's *Historia de la nación chi*

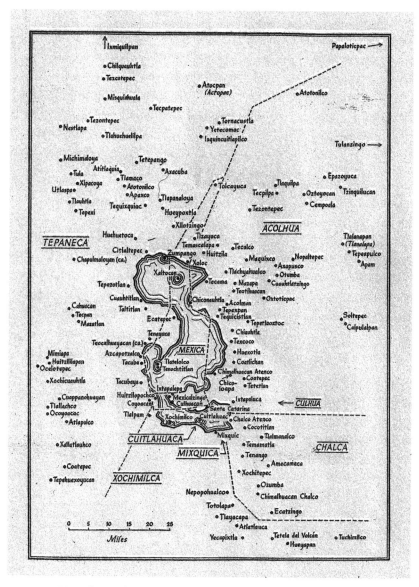

Map of central Mexico before the conquest. From Gibson, *Aztecs Under Spanish Rule*. Courtesy of Stanford University Press.

The Legacy of Rulership in
Fernando de Alva Ixtlilxochitl's
Historia de la nación chichimeca

❦

LEISA A. KAUFFMANN

University of New Mexico Press ✢ Albuquerque

Library of Congress Cataloging-in-Publication Data
Names: Kauffmann, Leisa (Leisa A.), 1969– author.
Title: The legacy of rulership in Fernando de Alva Ixtlilxochitl's
Historia de la nación chichimeca / Leisa A. Kauffmann.
Description: Albuquerque: University of New Mexico Press,
2019. | Includes bibliographical references and index. |
Identifiers: LCCN 2018059039 (print) | LCCN 2019000770 (e-book) | ISBN
9780826360380 (e-book) | ISBN 9780826360373 (printed case: alk. paper)
Subjects: LCSH: Alva Ixtlilxochitl, Fernando de, 1578–1650. Historia chichimeca. |
Alva Ixtlilxochitl, Fernando de, 1578–1650—Criticism and interpretation. | Alva
Ixtlilxochitl, Fernando de, 1578–1650—Influence. | Aztecs—Kings and rulers—
Historiography. | Nezahualcoyotl, King of Texcoco, 1402–1472. | Christianity
and politics—Mexico—Historiography. | Mexico—Kings and rulers—
Historiography. | Nahuas—Historiography. | Chichimecs—Historiography.
Classification: LCC F1219.73. A47 (e-book) | LCC F1219.73.
A47 K38 2019 (print) | DDC 972/.02092—dc23
LC record available at https://lccn.loc.gov/2018059039

Cover illustrations by Marta Esquivel-León
Cover designed by Lila Romero
Composed in Minion Pro

For José Antonio, Dad, Mom, Heidi, and tía Miriam

Contents

Acknowledgments

᠕ AS I BRING THIS PROJECT TO ITS CONCLUSION, I AM ACUTELY AWARE of the fact that it is in reality just a beginning, despite its having been spawned many years ago, in a seminar I took as a first-semester graduate student in the Program in Comparative and World Literature at the University of Illinois, Urbana-Champaign. Taught by Michael Palencia-Roth and filled with fellow students whose friendship continues to this day, the class marked the beginning of my interest in colonial Latin America, Mexico in particular. During my time as a student, I eventually received two Foreign Language and Area Studies fellowships to study Nahuatl at Yale University in the summers of 1999 and 2001, classes that enriched my understanding of that world and its texts. My first thanks, therefore, must go to my professors from the University of Illinois at Urbana-Champaign for the teaching and scholarship that continues to influence me, especially to Idelber Avelar, Nancy Blake, Leon Chai, Dorothy Figueira, Michael Palencia-Roth, Cynthia Radding, and Janet Smarr. Jonathan Amith also deserves my heartfelt thanks for all of his exacting but patient and good-humored teaching of Nahuatl.

Next, from my days as a graduate student, I owe a huge debt of gratitude to Néstor Quiroa and Nicanor Domínguez, whose bibliographies and conversation continue to make me a better scholar, thinker, and person, and to everyone else from those long and lively Friday lunches at La Salsa in Champaign. This includes (but is not limited to!) Rosana Díaz-Zambrana and María Isabel Silva Iturralde, whose company, humor, and solidarity on the journey lightened the load, as well as Angelina Cotler, Jahl Dulanto, and Ángel Viera; Ruth Quiroa Crowell, Lily Quiroa, Carolina Quiroa, and Emmalucía Quiroa couldn't make it to La Salsa, but they opened their home to many impromptu, delicious, and heartwarming evening meals. From the Program in Comparative and World Literature and beyond, I also owe an enormous thank-you to Elise Bartosik, Sriparna Basu, Rini Battacharya, Kevin Carollo, Deirdre Casey,

Mónica de Pedro, Kazuhiro Doki, Rita Faulkner, Swagato Ganguly, Steve Gardner, Yana Hashamova, Waïl Hassan, Beth Hawkins, Stephanie Hilger, Natsumi Ito, Regina Kirtley, Amber Landis, Jade Lee, Marina Mannetti, Margaret Mount, Jyoti Panjwani, Zoé Robles, Ryan Szpiech, Jay Twomey, Valerie Wilhite, and Helen Yeh. From all of you I learned something about the art of living well, about how much joy there is in study and reflection, and about how, in the company of good friends, the line between work and play becomes blurred.

My time in graduate school culminated in a grant from the National Endowment for the Humanities to participate in a 2004 Summer Institute, "Mesoamerica and the Southwest: A New History for an Ancient Land," led by George L. Scheper and Laraine Fletcher. This was an invaluable opportunity to see the region and many of its magnificent archaeological sites in the company of experts, right before beginning my first teaching job in Monmouth, Illinois. To my friends and colleagues at Monmouth College special thanks are owed, especially to Marlo Belschner, Heather Brady, Kathleen Fannin, Arthur Fowler, Monie Hayes, Susan Holm, Anne Mamary, Shigeko Mato, and Hannah Schell.

Here at Wayne State University, I am deeply grateful for the institutional space and support for my research, provided for this project in the form of a University Research Grant, a Humanities Center Scholar in Residence program, and two sabbatical leaves. I am also indebted to all of my friends and colleagues in Classical and Modern Languages, Literatures, and Cultures (aka CMLLC) and other departments. Thanks go especially to Jaqueline Adams, Cathy Barrette, Cyndi Campbell-Jones, Eugenia Casielles, Sarika Chandra, Alina Cherry, Jorge Chinea, Jorgelina Corbatta, José Cuello, Vanessa de Giffis, Fiona Dixon, Amanda Donigian, Anne Duggan, Mohamed El-Sharkawi, Marta Esquivel-León, Muhammed Faisal, Víctor Figueroa, Hernán García, Michael Giordano, Sangeetha Gopalakrishnan, Connie Green, Annie Higgins, Francisco Higuero, Keith Klemm, Haiyong Liu, Jackie Moeller, Paula Oliva-Fiori, Esperanza Ordoñez, Jeri Pajor, Elena Past, Terrie Pickering, Luísa Quintero, Kevin Rashid, Marilynn Rashid, José Antonio Rico-Ferrer, Michelle Ronnick, Anne Rothe, Pam Saenz, Don Schurlknight, Jennifer Sheridan Moss, Donald Spinelli, Eyda Vaughn, Hélène Weldt-Bassan, Dean Western, Sara Wiercinski, Margaret Winters, and Roxana Zúñiga.

Along the journey that writing this book entailed, many scholars of colonial Mexico provided unstinting help and perspective on various issues. In particular, I wish to thank Amber Brian, Galen Brokaw, Pablo García Loaeza,

Jongsoo Lee, Jerry Offner, Javier Eduardo Ramírez López, Camilla Townsend, and Gordon Whittaker. A version of chapter 3 of this book first appeared in the *Colonial Latin American Review* (April 2014) as "Alva Ixtlilxochitl's Colonial Mexican Trickster Tale: Nezahualcoyotl and Tezcatlipoca in the *Historia de la nación chichimeca*," used herein with permission of the publishers, Taylor & Francis. I am likewise grateful to the anonymous reviewers at University of New Mexico Press who gave detailed feedback on the manuscript and to Clark Whitehorn for his help, patience, and understanding throughout the process. Sandra Spicher, copyeditor extraordinaire, deserves a huge thanks, as does Marta Esquivel-León for the cover drawings and Lila Romero for the design. Without these people, this book would not be a reality. Its errors and weaknesses, of course, are all my own.

Finally, to two people who have been friends from the moment I left home and who have provided necessary sanity and fresh thinking when I can't seem to come up with it on my own: Denise Mitsuma and Gaywynn Walton. And to my family, whose forbearance has been unending: I know this has been a long time coming and is way past due. Loving thanks to my parents, Sharon and Norman Kauffmann, my sister Heidi, and my aunt Miriam (who corrected not just one, but two earlier versions of this book!) for their steadfast support. And to Sonia Olaechea, Percy Peralta Sr., and Julia Tacza Rosales for the constant encouragement and good wishes sent from a little further away. Last, but not least, to my longtime partner, José Antonio Peralta, for the unwavering love and wisdom, and also, of course, to Maguita, sweet but fierce canine sister to my beloved Amapola and Lucy, who make sure to remind me when it's time to get up and go for a walk, lest I forget.

Introduction

⁓⧉⁓

⁓ IN EARLY SEVENTEENTH-CENTURY NEW SPAIN, FERNANDO DE ALVA
Ixtlilxochitl (b. ca. 1578–d. 1650), a direct descendent of famous pre-Hispanic
rulers from the region known as Acolhuacan, located in Mexico's central
valley, wrote of his predecessors, "Llamar a un rey, chichimeco, era como
decirle la más suprema palabra que se puede decir" ([1975–1977] 1985, 1:290;
To call a king Chichimeca was to address him with the most sublime praise
that it is possible to utter).¹ A few lines later, still in elegiac mode, he notes
that even in his own day one could hear songs dedicated to their honor and
memory, "donde se echa de ver ser la nación [chichimeca] de más alta y pro-
sapia generación y valerosa de cuantos hay en la Nueva España, ni hubo"
(290–91; where one can see that the [Chichimeca] nation was of the highest
and most worthy lineage and descent of all that there are and ever were in
New Spain). Although the title of the work in which he expresses this sentiment, the *Sumaria relación de todas las cosas que han sucedido en esta Nueva
España*, lacks the specificity of the title eventually given to his longer text and
most famous history, the *Historia de la nación chichimeca*,² there is no question that both—indeed that his entire body of work—have as one of their
most significant raisons d'être to establish the glory of the Tetzcoca rulership
for all time.

This book supplements and complicates the commonplace vision of
Alva Ixtlilxochitl as a writer concerned mainly or even solely with presenting

1

a "respectable" and "Christianized" image of the pre-Hispanic past, of his Acolhua ancestors in particular, to a European audience.[3] It suggests, rather, that this is only the most visible aspect of his historiographical aesthetic. Consciously reading his work within the context of the early colonial Nahua myth-historical tradition, it regards Alva Ixtlilxochitl as a *translator* of Nahua tradition, a bilingual and, in some sense, a bicultural scholar— one of many "indios ladinos"[4] who, as intermediaries in the colonial system, worked to relay elements of indigenous thought and expression into the hegemonic forms of the Spanish language and peninsular and European culture.

In actuality, Fernando de Alva Ixtlilxochitl was of mostly Spanish descent—a privileged *castizo* in the system of racial hierarchies that evolved in New Spain from its roots in the Iberian concept of *limpieza de sangre* (Martínez 2008). While the presence of "Indian blood" in the family tree came to be regarded as a negative quality in the late sixteenth century and early seventeenth century (Martínez 2004, 483), for Alva Ixtlilxochitl, his Nahua ancestors were a source of prestige.[5] This was not only because of their "royal" status, but also because of the role that they played in the conquest: one of his great-great grandfathers on his mother's side was a man named Ixtlilxochitl, eventually baptized as Fernando Cortés Ixtlilxochitl, who helped Hernán Cortés defeat the Mexica and their allies at Tenochtitlan. Moreover, at least as Alva Ixtlilxochitl's histories make a point of asserting, without this distant ancestor's aid and allegiance, Cortés's party would have met certain defeat and the Spanish mission as a whole would have been seriously imperiled. Thus, while his mostly Spanish heritage ensured his participation in the society and quotidian privileges of the white ruling classes, his particular Acolhua ancestry made his background exceptional in both world-historical and personal-economic terms.

Because of this ancestral connection to Nahua (Acolhua) nobility, Alva Ixtlilxochitl's family held wealth in the form of a colonial *cacicazgo*, extensive land holdings that were derived from territories formerly associated with pre-Hispanic rulers or *tlatoque* (singular *tlatoani*). It also indirectly provided Alva Ixtlilxochitl with various kinds of employment in the colonial bureaucracy. In 1612, the colonial viceroyalty granted him an appointment as a *juez gobernador* (judge governor) in the town of Tetzcoco.[6] In his exhaustive introduction to Alva Ixtlilxochitl's collected works, Edmundo O'Gorman ([1975–1977] 1985, 1:25) notes that the official *nombramiento*,[7] or document appointing him to the post, states that he was chosen for the job by the "principales y común" (the nobles and commoners) of the town because he was "propincuo y legítimo sucesor de los reyes que fueron de la dicha ciudad y ser persona capaz y suficiente para este ministerio" (close [relative] and legitimate successor of those who were the kings of this city and a capable and qualified person for this task).[8] In 1616, Alva Ixtlilxochitl went on to occupy the post in the town of Tlalmanalco, a post he held through 1620, when he was appointed to the same position in Chalco, which, as O'Gorman points out (28), he probably continued to occupy in 1622.

In 1620 King Philip III also issued a *cédula real* (royal order) granting the viceroy's petition (which specified Alva Ixtlilxochitl's connection to Tetzcoco's rulers and their aid to Cortés) to appoint Alva Ixtlilxochitl to "oficios calificados conforme a su calidad y méritos" (O'Gorman [1975–1977] 1985, 1:27; official duties commensurate with his status and merits).[9] By 1640 (and probably for some time before that date) Alva Ixtlilxochitl was working as an interpreter in the Juzgado General de Indios (29; General Indian Court), following in the footsteps of his Spanish grandfather, who interpreted for the Real Audiencia (Royal Audience).[10] Indeed, with his direct ties to indigenous nobility, and (most crucially, perhaps) his knowledge of Nahuatl, Alva Ixtlilxochitl, also closely linked to Spanish and creole elite, was thus the perfect Crown candidate—an ideal mediator—for the bureaucratic positions he occupied.[11]

In his capacity as juez gobernador, Alva Ixtlilxochitl certainly gained valuable education in and experience with the laws, precepts, and procedures relating to the viceroyalty's legislation of the affairs of the *república de indios* (the Indian Republic), the world of indigenous pueblos that were in theory to be kept segregated legally and socially from Spanish society, the *república de españoles* (the Spanish Republic). This was knowledge that in some respect already would have been part of his family's legacy, however, derived from its long experience in the courts. From the earliest days of the cacicazgo, Alva Ixtlilxochitl's great-grandfather and his descendents had to establish and protect their status as legitimate inheritors and to prevent cacicazgo holdings from being broken up and usurped. The legal challenges came from all sectors and a wide range of interests. These included relatives, nobles or *principales* of San Juan Teotihuacan, Spanish settlers, and even the *encomenderos*,[12] who received the tributes from the economic activities overseen by Alva Ixtlilxochitl's great-grandfather but still (unsuccessfully) tried to usurp one of the cacicazgo's largest pre-Hispanic palaces and its associated lands (Brian 2016, 54–60; Lee 2016, 123–29; O'Gorman [1975–1977] 1985, 1:9–36; Münch 1976, 11–27; Pérez-Rocha and Tena 2000b, 23–26, 45–47, 64–65).[13]

In 1611, Alva Ixtlilxochitl took over for his father in the effort to secure a viceregal confirmation of his mother's rights to the cacicazgo. In response to his father's petition, the viceroy requested specific documentation—a *probanza* (legal inquiry or questionnaire)—from the townspeople abetting the family's claims. Alva Ixtlilxochitl secured and presented the required documents, and in addition requested a translation of his great-grandfather's *testamento* (last will and testament) from 1563, the key document listing the possessions of the cacicazgo (O'Gorman [1975–1977] 1985, 1:24). He then petitioned the viceroy once again for the requested legal confirmation and, after it was granted, asked to be allowed to keep the originals of the documents pertaining to the case (24–25). In 1614 the confirmation was renewed once again by the viceroy (Diego Fernández de Córdoba, the Marquis of Guadalcázar) (25).

Near the end of his life, in 1643, however, Alva Ixtlilxochitl finds himself once again on the front lines of legal battles involving the cacicazgo. In one of the viceregal decrees renewing the original confirmations of his mother's inheritance of the entailed estate, the viceroy adds a provision barring the holdings from ever being measured by the *juez de medidas*[14] (O'Gorman [1975–1977] 1985, 1:32; 1975–1977, 2:354–69; legal surveyor). Münch (1976, 24) notes that this was a means of minimizing or preventing legal disputes over lands on the part of those who were encroaching upon them. However, not only did the order need to be reissued various times in the month of September, at the end of the month *labradores* (workers) on the cacicazgo presented a document to Andrés de Urbina, the *juez de medidas de tierras del rey* (legal surveyor for the king). In it, they ask for documents to prove his mother's title to the estate, calling her a "Spaniard," and for the lands to be measured (Brian 2016, 54–60; Lee 2016, 123–29; O'Gorman [1975–1977] 1985, 1:32–34; 1975–1977, 2:350–69). After the early rounds of what must have been a tiresome case, Diego de Yebra, a brother-in-law to Alva Ixtlilxochitl, takes over. At one point, however, he cannot present the proper titles because Alva Ixtlilxochitl had them in his possession (O'Gorman [1975–1977] 1985, 1:33). Although the documentation is lacking, eventually, notes O'Gorman (34), the case must have been resolved in favor of the Alva y Cortés family.

As this brief history makes clear, and as many scholars (e.g., Benton 2014; Lee 2008, 2016; Schwaller 2014; Velazco 2003; Villella 2014; Whittaker 2016) have noted, Alva Ixtlilxochitl's formation as a historian of pre-Hispanic Mexico can be directly tied to his need to prove his connection to the dynastic lineages of Tetzcoco and Teotihuacan. As a key aspect of his positions in the viceregal administration and of the defense of the cacicazgo and promotion of his family's economic interests, Alva Ixtlilxochitl needed, and needed to be able to understand and interpret, the many kinds of documents—histories, maps, and wills—that described the history of Tetzcoco and its royal lineage(s) and his family's relationship to them. His historical discourse, notes Villella (2014), has its roots in the language and forms elaborated by the descendents of Native nobility seeking the protection of the Crown and thus the preservation of their rights and privileges after the conquest, most particularly in the genre of the *memorial de méritos y servicios* (account of merits and services).

Given this personal background, it is hardly surprising that Alva Ixtlilxochitl described his Tetzcoca ancestry in such idealistic terms, and that rulership itself, with the Acolhua ancestors at the center, played such a predominant role in his historical narratives. Yet both the intensity of the emotion with which he expresses his pride in these ancestors, evident not only in the quote above but throughout his writing, and the depth of Alva Ixtlilxochitl's *career* as a historian indicate that his dedication to the pre-Hispanic past of New Spain went beyond a preoccupation with his family's vested interests, implying a concern with posterity itself. Indeed, if economic circumstance explains *in part* why he wrote and researched to begin with, it also explains only *in part* why he wrote as he did.

The documentary corpus that comprised Alva Ixtlilxochitl's sources for his histories and those which lay in his family's archives were carefully created and maintained in the context of serving in the long-standing and ongoing legal efforts of the communities (and noble families) that created them.[15] Yet the texts also respond to and form part of a historical tradition that reaches back into preconquest days. Alva Ixtlilxochitl's histories, despite their well-deserved reputation as heavily "Europeanized" renditions of those and other Nahua texts and stories, also form part of that tradition.

Historical documentation within the pre-Hispanic *altepetl*, a principal Nahua political entity (a kind of ethnic state or polity),[16] was a valued and important cultural institution, a high-status practice that was closely tied to the altepetl elite and its rulers.[17] In "Pictorial Documents and Visual Thinking in Postconquest Mexico," Elizabeth Hill Boone (1998, 165) notes that the creation of manuscripts "was always an elite enterprise directed upward toward or used by those in authority." Susan Schroeder (2006), writing on the role of the *amoxtli* (book) in pre-Hispanic and colonial Nahua society, provides a glimpse into this "enterprise":

> It is apparent that each royal family had a designated individual within the lineage who not only inherited the texts but was responsible for preserving them, keeping them current, and then making certain that they passed to the proper heir. Elite status and literacy were dual imperatives. . . .
>
> A term crucial for understanding the relationship of the altepetl, the royal house, and the archives is *pialli*, trust. It connotes the essence or legacy of the state as it was known from the ancient oral and pictorial reports as they were told and recorded over the centuries. (18)

Moreover, she writes,

> According to tradition, the ancient texts were passed from father to son. . . . Thus, there was a person of very high rank[18] within each *altepetl* who was keeper—both interpreter and author—of the precious records. This person likely held the office of *tlamachtiani*, teacher, or sage, a position of such intellectual capability and prestige that succession to rulership was not a consideration. (19–20)

In *Stories in Red and Black*, Boone (2000, 26) reiterates this idea regarding the teacher or sage, writing that the *tlamatini* was considered to be a "highly literate individual and a scholar, an embodiment of wisdom contained in the painted books," and that as "owner of books and possessor of knowledge, . . . [the tlamatini was a person] to whom others turned for advice and guidance. They were counselors to the rulers."[19] Serge Gruzinski (2007, 17), moreover, citing the work of Miguel León Portilla on the pre-Hispanic meaning of the *tlapializtli*, emphasizes its connection to the elite (the *pipiltin*, in Nahuatl) and specifies its cultural function and significance. He writes,

> Los *pipiltin* legitimaban sus poderes y concebían el mundo en el que vivían con apoyo en los conocimientos que conservaban celosamente. Aquel saber señalaba modos de vida, tradiciones por mantener, herencias por transmitir, y todo aquello que, de una manera general, puede designar la palabra náhuatl *tlapializtli*. Al cosmos, se pensaba que esos

conocimientos le conferían una norma, una medida y una estabilidad. A la sociedad la proveían de un orden, una orientación y un sentido. . . . Patrimonio antiguo, conservado y aplicado escrupulosamente, transmitido de un pueblo a otro, aquel saber daba origen a un sistema educativo con un desarrollo único. Templos-escuela reservados para los hijos de los *pipiltin* preparaban a los futuros dirigentes.

The pipiltin legitimated their powers and conceived of the world in which they lived with recourse to this learning that they zealously preserved. This knowledge dictated their ways of life, the traditions to be maintained, the legacies to be handed down, and everything that, in a general sense, can be designated with the Nahuatl word *tlapializtli*. It was thought that this knowledge conferred a standard, a measure, and stability to the cosmos. It gave order, direction, and meaning to society. . . . An ancient patrimony, scrupulously conserved and carried out, and transmitted from one pueblo to another, this knowledge spawned a one-of-a-kind educational system. Temple-schools reserved for the children of the elite prepared its future leaders.

Indeed, as Gruzinski specifies, a formal education in these schools had important social implications:

Además del nacimiento, aquella educación distinguía a los nobles de los plebeyos—los *macehuales*—, haciendo de ellos seres intelectual y moralmente superiores, aquellos "hijos de la gente", "cabello" y "uñas de la gente", que estaban destinados sin excepción y desde el principio a las funciones de mando. (18)

In addition to birth, this education distinguished the nobility from the commoners—the macehuales—, making them intellectually and morally superior beings, those "sons of the people," "hair" and "nails of the people," who were destined without exception and from the beginning to leadership roles.

Although Schroeder (2006) bases her observations of the tradition of the pialli on the work of the great Nahuatl language annalist from Chalco, Domingo Francisco de San Antón Muñón Chimalpahin Quauhtlehuanitzin, and Fernando Alvarado Tezozomoc of Tenochtitlan (both contemporaries of

Alva Ixtlilxochitl), there is a parallel with the work of Alva Ixtlilxochitl. He was part of the ancient dynastic lineage of San Juan Teotihuacan but was not in line to inherit the rulership—one of the requirements of the keeper of the trust noted by Schroeder (20). Moreover, he carried out the major requirements of that role in the context of his own family and for the greater Acolhua region (and beyond), beginning to write shortly after inheriting properties in San Juan Teotihuacan willed to him by his maternal grandmother, the granddaughter of Fernando Cortés Ixtlilxochitl (Alva Ixtlilxochitl 1975–1977, 2:289). For Alva Ixtlilxochitl, writing about the history of Tetzcoco and its rulers and defending his family's cacicazgo were, as Brian (2016, 41–62) has emphasized, simultaneous and mutually complementary endeavors.[20]

According to the analytical bibliography and timeline constructed by Edmundo O'Gorman ([1975–1977] 1985, 1:197–233), which I follow in a very general sense, Alva Ixtlilxochitl's first prose histories[21]—the *Sumaria relación de todas las cosas que han sucedido en esta Nueva España* (Alva Ixtlilxochitl [1975–1977] 1985, 1:259–381), the *Relación sucinta en forma de memorial* (396–413), and the *Compendio histórico del reino de Texcoco* (415–521)—were likely redacted in the early years of the seventeenth century and certainly close to 1608, the date borne on documents from the indigenous town councils of Otumba and San Salvador Cuautlacingo affirming the veracity of the *Compendio* against the backdrop of their own historical knowledge and the old histories that Alva Ixtlilxochitl used to compose his narrative (O'Gorman [1975–1977] 1985, 1:197–233, especially 201, 229–31; see also O'Gorman [1975–1977] 1985, 1:21, 23; and Whittaker 2016, 57–66).[22] It is at this point—after 1608—that Alva Ixtlilxochitl begins to act on behalf of his parents in the legal affairs of the cacicazgo and is given the appointment as juez gobernador of Tetzcoco.

Taken together, these early texts cover the entire history of the central Mexican region from the creation of the world through the Spanish siege of Tenochtitlan and into the early colonial period, with the *Relación sucinta en forma de memorial* representing, in O'Gorman's ([1975–1977] 1985, 1:231) estimation, a summary account of the initial text, the *Sumaria relación de todas las cosas que han sucedido en esta Nueva España*, and its annexed documents.[23] For O'Gorman, this longer first work and the *Compendio histórico del reino de Texcoco* (belonging more clearly to the memorial de servicios (account of merits) genre than Alva Ixtlilxochitl's other, more purely historical, texts) formed the groundwork for a projected definitive history (divided into nine books, one for each Tetzcoco ruler) that never materialized (211,

229–31). Assuming that this general chronology (three early works and two later texts) is correct, the only narrative histories in his known oeuvre that he had not written at this point were what is, in fact, his most extensive work—a de facto magnum opus[24]—the *Historia de la nación chichimeca* (Alva Ixtlilxochitl 1975–1977, 2:7–263) and an extremely short text, the *Sumaria relación de la historia general* ([1975–1977] 1985, 1:529–49).

The *Historia de la nación chichimeca* presents Acolhua-focused central Mexican history from the time of creation through the reign of (Fernando Cortés) Ixtlilxochitl in ninety-five chapters (the last of which remains incomplete) that follow the lineage and recount the lives of Tetzcoco's rulers. The *Sumaria relación de la historia general* reads somewhat like a condensed version of the same basic material—a sumaria or "summary relation" of the longer historical narrative (although it contains some original material as well) and is the only piece not divided into separate chapters or relaciones (accounts).[25] Although incomplete, the *Historia de la nación chichimeca* represents the most extensive, synthetic, personal, and intentional vision of Acolhua history of his historical corpus, as O'Gorman ([1975–1977] 1985, 1:217–18) so incisively observed, and for this reason it is the focal point of this study.[26]

As a historian, Alva Ixtlilxochitl gathered a trove of documents from all over central Mexico, which he then bequeathed to his son, who in turn entrusted them to his friend (and great intellectual of his day), the Jesuit creole Carlos de Sigüenza y Góngora (1645–1700).[27] His methods for engaging in historical research, moreover, described in detail at various points throughout his corpus, exactly mirror those described by Schroeder (2006) for Chimalpahin: "a rigorous process of information collection, corroboration, and synthesis" (20) wherein the corroboration process implies a careful comparison of various sources from different perspectives to be followed by interviews with "the books' owners and other townspeople" (23). As Boone (1998, 190–91) puts it, "The same motivations that drove the painters of postconquest histories compelled the later indigenous historians writing in words." Alva Ixtlilxochitl, she writes, "was cognizant of his position as inheritor of the old histories and of the ancient historical traditions" (191).

Whether officially named, or self-appointed as a keeper of the pialli—trust or historical documents—of his family and of the greater Tetzcoco altepetl (and beyond), Alva Ixtlilxochitl certainly made it a significant part of his life's work. Not only did his methods of research mirror those described by Schroeder for people in such positions, we know that he was consulted on linguistic matters by his brother, Bartolomé—himself a bilingual writer and

translator who worked with the famous Jesuit scholar of the Nahuatl language, Horacio Carochi (Schwaller 1994a; 1994b, 392–94; 1999; 2014; Whittaker 2016, 52–53)—and that the *Compendio* earned the official approval of
the indigenous town councils of San Salvador Cuautlacingo and Otumba
(O'Gorman [1975–1977] 1985, 1:23, 517–21). Most importantly, however, his
own writing as well as the texts he copied and collected—some of the most
significant extant primary sources on Mexican history—survive to this day.

Yet only recently is it possible to engage in a serious effort to identify
and explore some of the historical themes, modes, and paradigms of the
Nahua tradition that inform his writing and to explore the ways in which
they intersect with the (more obvious) dynamics that his work owes to European thought and history. This is due to the increasing number of studies
on Nahua and Nahuatl language texts, including Alva Ixtlilxochitl's principal pictorial source texts, the *Codex Xolotl*, the Mapa Tlotzin, and the Mapa
Quinatzin (e.g., Douglas 2010; Lesbre 2012);[28] the publication of important
primary documents on the indigenous elite, including various documents
from San Juan Teotihuacan (Pérez-Rocha and Tena 2000b, 201–10, 261–79,
379–404); and the publication of important studies discussing his specific
intellectual heritage and cultural milieu (e.g., Benton 2014, 2017; Brian 2010,
2014a, 2014b; Lee 2008, 2016; Lesbre 1995, 1999a, 2004, 2010, 2012; O'Gorman
1985; Schwaller 1999, 2014; Townsend 2014; Velazco 2003; Villella 2014, 2016).

In viewing Alva Ixtlilxochitl as an inheritor and guardian of the legacy of his ancestral dynastic community, San Juan Teotihuacan, and of the
great Acolhua altepetl centered on Tetzcoco, of which it was a constituent
part, it is possible to approach his work in the same way that José Antonio
Mazzotti, in his book *Coros mestizos del Inca Garcilaso* (1996), approached
the *Comentarios reales* of Garcilaso. In the introduction to his study, Mazzotti references the many (and necessary) examinations of the *Comentarios'*
indebtedness to the intellectual milieu of Renaissance Spain, but proposes
that what were then recent trends in literary studies had begun to complicate
the great writer's image as a highly acculturated European(ized) intellectual.
He writes,

> Considerando nuevas tendencias y aportes dentro de los estudios lit-
> erarios coloniales, empieza a socavarse la idea del autor únicamente
> renacentista y por lo tanto aculturado con respecto a su origen indiano
> y quechuahablante. Por el contrario, los estudios recientes establecen
> la posibilidad de encontrar en los *Comentarios* diversas muestras de

un subtexto altamente nutrido de simbología cuzqueña, que siempre cabe revisar a la luz de los aportes brindados por un sector de la antropología, la etnohistoria y la iconografía andinas en los últimos años. El viejo tópico de un Garcilaso hispanizado y de un Waman Puma genuino representante del pensamiento indígena parece derrumbarse simplemente en función de un nuevo aparato conceptual capaz de hacer frente a los textos respetando su especificidad y complejidad precisamente como lo que son: textos. (28–29)

In considering new tendencies and contributions within colonial literary studies, the idea of a solely Renaissance and therefore completely acculturated author with respect to his indigenous and Quechua-speaking origins, begins to erode. On the contrary, recent studies establish the possibility of finding within the *Comentarios* various examples of a subtext highly informed by Cuzqueñan symbolism that can be analyzed in light of the contributions provided by a certain sector of Andean anthropology, ethnohistory and iconography in the last few years. The old refrain of a hispanized Garcilaso and a genuine Guaman Poma, representative of indigenous thought, appears to fall apart simply in the face of a new conceptual apparatus designed to approach texts respecting the specificity and complexity of what they are: texts.

For Mazzotti, the *Comentarios reales* reflect the clear influence of Garcilaso's literary and cultural education in Cusco before the death of his father and his departure for Madrid in 1560. It is a text that responds to and integrates an awareness of the Cuzqueñan hypotexts (in Gérard Genette's formulation, those anterior texts whose presence or influence is felt in the manifest narrative or hypertext), which become part of the carefully crafted subtext of the narrative (17–20, 29–34). This results in and from an assumption of an implicit reader who would have shared Garcilaso's bilingual and bicultural knowledge base, that is, it assumes that Garcilaso would have striven to write a text that his fellow Cuzqueños from the Andean world he portrayed would recognize and authorize as their own (21–22). Mazzotti therefore dedicates himself to revealing the Andean, particularly Cuzqueñan, subtext of the *Comentarios reales*, bringing to light oral forms, symbolism, and implied meanings that an examination of the work from the exclusive point of view of Renaissance Europe would leave out (31–40).

Despite commonalities and congruities with Garcilaso's work (some of which are shared more broadly within the wider group of "indio ladino" historians, as Adorno (1994) has pointed out), Alva Ixtlilxochitl's writing calls for a different interpretative and methodological approach, given the distinct cultural and socioeconomic context of his work and upbringing. Nevertheless, in assuming that Alva Ixtlilxochitl's implicit readership included those with his own bilingual and bicultural awareness, I share one aspect of Mazzotti's interpretative standpoint. In relating Alva Ixtlilxochitl to the world of Nahua semiosis and historiography, moreover, as Mazzotti did for Garcilaso in the Andean context, the overarching goal of our studies is the same: to situate the text in its relationship to the historical and literary world of the indigenous communities whose histories they portray and to which the authors themselves were connected within their respective colonial contexts.

As Brian (2014, 97) has demonstrated, Alva Ixtlilxochitl's writing did not "take place in a vacuum." While his upbringing certainly included some education in Spanish and exposure to texts and knowledge of the humanist tradition of the day,[29] his personal and family background suggests strong interest in Nahuatl and Nahua writing and history. Although Benton (2014, 42) and Villella (2016, 120) note that Alva Ixtlilxochitl was raised in Mexico City, Schwaller (1994a, 96) states that he was likely born in San Juan Teotihuacan and that the family's ties to that town remained strong, moreover, as they maintained and looked after the economic affairs of the cacicazgo (95–96). Alva Ixtlilxochitl indeed seems to have spent a significant amount of time there in his youth and throughout his life as he looked after the interests of his mother's estate. In his lengthy discussion of his sources placed after the narrative of Tolteca history in one of his early texts, the *Sumaria relación de todas las cosas que han sucedido en la Nueva España*, Alva Ixtlilxochitl ([1975–1977] 1985, 1:287–288) writes that he grew up with Nahuatl and Nahuatl speakers and had connections to elders and distinguished Nahuas of his time.[30] His grandfather, moreover, although Spanish in origin, spoke Nahuatl and was an interpreter in the Real Audiencia. In addition, his much younger brother, Bartolomé, as we have seen, a beneficed cleric ordained partly on the basis of his excellent command of Nahuatl, also had a strong interest in the world of Nahuatl letters (Schwaller 1994a, 96; 1999, 6; Whittaker 2016, 50–53). In 1634, he published a confessionary tract in Nahuatl and Spanish aimed at helping other priests identify and eradicate idolatrous beliefs, and later translated three Spanish plays—by Pedro Calderón de la Barca, Antonio Mira de Améscua, and Lope de Vega Carpio (Schwaller 1994a; 1994b, 392–94; 1999; 2014).

Establishing the nature and extent of Alva Ixtlilxochitl's direct ties to and concrete communication with other Nahua historians of his day is a difficult task. In her study of Alva Ixtlilxochitl's manuscripts, however, Brian (2014b, 85) notes how the bound volumes containing them (formerly the British and Foreign Bible Society Manuscript 374) reflect his common cause with other members of the indigenous elite during a period in which they struggled to "maintain their privileged status and make sense of their patrimony within the viceregal state of New Spain, especially as the stories of the Indian past were fading from memories." Alva Ixtlilxochitl's writings, she observes, are interspersed not only with texts of Diego Muñoz Camargo (1529–1599) and Chimalpahin but with other works that were written in the context of legal and administrative proceedings engaged in by indigenous nobility in defense of their rights (87–95). Examples include royal decrees regarding the properties of Isabel Moteucçoma, a description of the torture of a Tarascan ruler, Tangaxoan (or Calzonci), that was created for a legal proceeding brought against his torturer, Nuño de Guzmán, and some of the papers of this ruler's grandson, named Constantino Bravo Huitzimengari, a personal friend of Alva Ixtlilxochitl's who served as a gobernador in indigenous pueblos. Though not all of the texts were directly used within Alva Ixtlilxochitl's own histories, Brian concludes from their presence that "The miscellaneous documents contained in [former] BSMS 374 point to a network of Indian intellectuals, and litigants, who sought to retain their family's histories and maintain their precarious positions of power in colonial Mexico" (94).

In addition, Susan Schroeder (1991, 14–15) and Patrick Lesbre (2004) have discussed in depth some connections, or probable connections, between Alva Ixtlilxochitl and Chimalpahin. The connections remain circumstantial but compelling: geographical connections to the Chalco region; third parties that both knew; a mention of Alva Ixtlilxochitl's grandfather, Juan Grande (the interpreter in the Real Audiencia), in Chimalpahin's *Diario*;[31] indications of common source texts (Lesbre 2004, 248–53), and the fact that some of Chimalpahin's original holographic manuscripts are bound together with those of Alva Ixtlilxochitl in the volumes from the Sigüenza y Góngora collection (the *Códice Chimalpahin*). Thus, while it is not certain, it would not be improbable that the two historians knew of each other and had crossed paths at some point in time.

Neither should we overlook the fact that Alva Ixtlilxochitl ([1975–1977] 1985, 1:285–288) himself explains his participation in a network of indigenous scholars and historians, making it clear that there were many elders and members of the indigenous elite scattered across central Mexico who, like himself, worked to preserve and transmit the stories of their ancestors, and that these contacts willingly provided him with information and sources for his work. There is no doubt that from a young age Alva Ixtlilxochitl was aware of, and took a keen interest in, the Nahua world and its cultural and literary traditions, as he claims (525).[32] Although he shared sources and probably also his own narratives with the great Franciscan historian Juan de Torquemada (ca. 1562–1624)—whose work will provide a counterpoint to this study—and began to reference a wider array of European and non-Acolhua-based Nahua texts possibly due to the latter's influence (Townsend 2014, 6–7), even his later writing as a whole consciously[33] and overwhelmingly references only the Nahua texts on which it relies, despite the strong implicit presence and indeed often heavy handed use of biblical and classical themes, motifs, and personages. Looking past—or, more precisely, within—these glaring European influences, however, I show how the *Historia de la nación chichimeca* remains rooted within Nahua tradition and tied to the Nahua sources that he used and interpreted.

As noted above, the *Historia de la nación chichimeca* is Alva Ixtlilxochitl's most synthetic and polished history and seems to represent the culmination of his career as a historian. It is in this text where, against the backdrop of his earlier work, we see the emergence of a singular vision of the lands and peoples of pre-Hispanic New Spain, a vision that would be appropriated by later historians (García Loaeza 2001, 2006, 2007, 2009; Villella 2016, 119–27) and have an indelible—and distorting—impact on Mexican history, as García Loaeza (2006, 2007, 2009), Lee (2008), and Villella (2016) have demonstrated. Yet while his work lent itself to this appropriation, the story it tells is not—or not only—the story that Mariano Fernández de Echeverría y Veytia (1718–1780), Francisco Clavijero (1731–1787) and Carlos María de Bustamante (1774–1848), for example, picked up on. For Alva Ixtlilxochitl's vision is unlike those of these later historians, or, as I shall show, of his (slightly older) contemporary and colleague, friar Juan de Torquemada. The particular characteristics of Alva Ixtlilxochitl's writing become most visible, in fact, in the ways that the major histories of these two closely related figures diverge, in their distinct approaches to conveying the past of the region in the genre of the Renaissance universal history.[34]

Torquemada's history, whose shortened title reads *Los veinte y un libros rituales y Monarquía indiana*, most often referred to simply as the *Monarquía indiana*, was first published in Seville in 1615, and the *Historia de la nación chichimeca* mentions the work and its writer with great respect on two occasions, most prominently in chapter 49 (1975–1977, 2:137), where he calls Torquemada the "diligentísimo y primer descubridor de la declaración de las pinturas y cantos" (very assiduous and first discoverer of what of the paintings and songs declare).[35] Torquemada does not mention Alva Ixtlilxochitl as a source, but there are several passages that are very similar to those in Alva Ixtlilxochitl's early histories, particularly the *Relación sucinta en forma de memorial*. Because of these correspondences, scholars conclude that the two collaborated in some way, with Alva Ixtlilxochitl turning over his materials to Torquemada and/or by working together to interpret Tetzcoco's iconic-script texts on which their histories rely as primary sources.[36]

For centuries, during his own lifetime and after, Torquemada's work (and his reputation as a historian) suffered under charges of plagiarism. As Miguel León Portilla ([1969] 1975, vii–x), his principal biographer and the editor of the most thorough and up-to-date critical edition of his works, points out, however, the accusation does not account for the fact that the work as a whole is a product of Torquemada's own historical vision and that he worked and wrote in a time when the idea of the historical "author"—as opposed to the medieval, monastic tradition of the historian as copyist and chronicler—was just coming into its own. His work, as León Portilla puts it, is a "crónica de crónicas" ([1969] 1975, 7; 2010, under "Presentación"; chronicle of chronicles). Moreover, in bringing together large sections of texts from indigenous and Spanish ethnohistorical and historical sources, the *Monarquía indiana* today is the most direct source for a great deal of work, such as that of fray Andrés de Olmos, that otherwise would be lost to posterity.

Indeed, Torquemada's vision of the history of New Spain (especially the early history) is to a significant extent both directly and indirectly derived from the early colonial Tetzcoca accounts of the pre-Hispanic and conquest periods of the region. Directly through histories such as those of Alva Ixtlilxochitl and his Tetzcoca sources, the principal and still-surviving iconic-script texts mentioned above (the *Codex Xolotl*, the Mapa Tlotzin, and the Mapa Quinatzin) or the now-lost work of don Alonso de Axayacatl or others (Lesbre 1995), and indirectly through Tetzcoco's influence on the ethnohistorical work of Torquemada's forebearers in the Franciscan order, specifically, Andrés de Olmos (1485?–1571), Toribio de Benavente (Motolinía) (1482–1568), Gerónimo de Mendieta (1525–1604), and Bernardino de Sahagún (1499–1590). The Franciscans' ties to Tetzcoco, as evidenced by Georges Baudot (1995, 256–57) and as I discuss in chapter 1, were early and strong, and it was these early historians whose millennialist-inspired missionary zeal[37] and interest in indigenous cultures and languages influenced Torquemada's formation as a young friar.

By the time Torquemada entered the Franciscan order as a young man, around 1579–1580, according to León Portilla's biography (1983b, 21, 27, 30–31), this first generation of Franciscan arrivals to New Spain had already established methods and founded the key institutions—such as the famous school for sons of indigenous nobility at Santiago Tlatelolco[38]—for accomplishing their missionary task and ministering to their proselytes. Torquemada was taught theology by friar Juan Bautista Viseo (1555–?) and Nahuatl by Antonio Valeriano (1531–1605), one of the Franciscan-trained Nahua scholars and linguists, a descendent of Mexica royalty (Castañeda de la Paz 2011, par. 25–29) who participated in the ethnohistorical work spearheaded by Bernardino de Sahagún and eventually served as juez gobernador of Tenochtitlan (León Portilla 1983b, 23). After Torquemada's ordination as a Franciscan priest in 1587 or 1588 (21, 24) not only did he spend many years doing missionary work in various indigenous provinces (and learning their languages), he showed an early interest in historical scholarship, writing a biography of Sebastián de Aparicio (1502–1600), a prominent (and later beatified) Franciscan of New Spain, that was published at the Santiago Tlatelolco monastery in 1602 (31). From 1591 onward, moreover, as León Portilla states, he began to copy and compile "toda clase de informes y documentos sobre la historia del antiguo mundo indígena" (28; all kinds of reports and documents about the history of the ancient indigenous world.)

In 1603, after serving as guardian in various monasteries around New Spain, Torquemada returned to exercise this post at the Santiago Tlatelolco monastery, which by that time was in a period of decline (León Portilla 1983b, 31–32). From 1603 to 1612, he oversaw the reconstruction of the church's dome and altarpiece, with the indigenous laborers on the project filing a lawsuit and providing testimony against him for such violent behavior and abuse that it nearly resulted in one worker's death. The outcome of the lawsuit is unknown, although Torquemada seems to have continued with his affairs without interruption (36–38). After the flooding that devastated Mexico City in 1604, he was appointed to oversee the reconstruction of some of the city's causeways (32–34), and it is possible that during this time he had contact with Alva Ixtlilxochitl's father, Juan Navas Pérez de Peralada, who was then serving as the *maestro de obras* (general overseer) of the rebuilding projects (Townsend 2014, 6).

Although he had begun to collect and research historical materials of New Spain around 1591, on April 6, 1609, Torquemada was named official chronicler of his order in New Spain and charged with the task of writing a history so that, as León Portilla notes, "aprovechando los trabajos de otros autores y los materiales que había reunido continuara y diera término a la elaboración de la copiosa obra que tenía entre manos" (1983b, 35; taking advantage of the work of other authors and the materials that he had collected, he might continue and bring to a conclusion the copious project on which he was working). It was to be a history that presented both the ancient past of the peoples of New Spain before the arrival of the Spanish and the work of the Franciscans in establishing Christianity therein afterward (León Portilla [1969] 1975, xvi). Having proven himself as a historian and with all of his experience—his intimate ties to the Church at Santiago Tlatelolco and his knowledge of the ethnohistoriographical work of his Franciscan elders (having personally known Olmos, Mendieta, Sahagún, and others such as the Tetzcoca ruler Antonio de Pimentel [León Portilla 1983b, 27])—he set about his task in earnest, finishing the history by 1612, when it was approved by the censors of the Inquisition. Later, he went to Spain in order to oversee its publication, which was done in the shop of Mathías Clavijo in Seville in 1615. As a history, the *Monarquía indiana* embodies the classicism and knowledge of languages that were the hallmark of the best early modern scholarship while, as we shall see in chapters 1 and 2, its structure reflects and remains faithful to the values of the Franciscan order and its vision of purpose in New Spain.

This emphasis on the missionary purpose of the Franciscans explains why, despite the ironically more appropriate title of Torquemada's history, it is in the *Historia de la nación chichimeca*, not the *Monarquía indiana*, that rulership becomes the structural backbone and thematic centerpiece of the historical narrative. Indeed, a full illumination of Alva Ixtlilxochitl as a writer and historian necessarily strives to account for not only the centrality of rulership in his narrative, but for its particular contours and characteristics as well. Through its characterization of individual rulers and organization of ruling lines, the *Historia de la nación chichimeca* establishes an affiliation with both Nahua and European historiographical chronotopes[39] and conceptions of rulership, specifically regarding the relationship between rulers and the divine or "supernatural" world that founds and authorizes their power. Unlike the work of Torquemada, Alva Ixtlilxochitl's narrative incarnates a distinctively Nahua historicity, or conception of history.

In his introduction to his edited collection, *Histories and Historicities in*

Amazonia (2003, x–xi), Neil Whitehead defines historicities as the "cultural schema and subjective attitudes that make the past meaningful" in different cultural contexts, or the "culturally particular methodology of how the past may be written or otherwise expressed." He reminds us that, because historical time and the meaning of the past are themselves cultural constructs, the interpretation of texts must take them into account. "Ethnohistory," he writes, "must also practice the ethnography of historical consciousness" (x). In the case of Alva Ixtlilxochitl, like that of Garcilaso, we must take into consideration the fact that he was working with texts and within contexts in which two (or more) historicities were operative and/or influential. Indeed, as Eduardo de J. Douglas (2003) has pointed out with respect to the *tlacuilo* (painter or scribe) of the Mapa Quinatzin (one of Alva Ixtlilxochitl's major iconic-script source texts), the *Historia de la nación chichimeca* is best understood in the light of the dual cultural legacy of which Alva Ixtlilxochitl was heir. A fuller understanding of his work, therefore, must account for what Douglas, citing Barbara Mundy and Elizabeth Boone, has called "the range of cultural forms and ideological perspectives brought into being by the meeting of the 'Old' and 'New' Worlds . . . ," and it must "read in terms of the indigenous systems of meaning . . . [while] attending to the very public, primarily Spanish, context of production" (282). As Tom Cummins and Joanne Rappaport (2012) write in *Beyond the Lettered City*,

> Native literacies emerging out of the colonial context were richer than mere adaptations to European practices of reading and viewing; they also transformed them, spawning intertextual readings that interacted with indigenous forms of recording and representation, including knot records (khipus), textiles, and sacred geography. That is, literacy is not always—nor ever was—a passive process in which forms of authority and power are reproduced through mechanical everyday practice. . . . All eyes may be focused on the same image, but what is being seen is not the same. (9–10)

Indeed, although seemingly a purely European and Europeanized production, the *Historia de la nación chichimeca* marks its "discontinuity" (Mignolo 1992a, 1992b, 1995)[40] with that colonial tradition, and in so doing is a testament to the heterogeneity[41]—to use Antonio Cornejo Polar's term—of literary and historical production in New Spain.

Like the one described by Cornejo Polar (2011, 75–83) in *Escribir en el aire* for the *Comentarios reales* of Garcilaso, Alva Ixtlilxochitl's historical discourse is a discourse of homogeneity, a discourse that seeks to harmonize or create sutures between the Spanish and (in Alva Ixtlilxochitl's case) the Nahua world. In his analysis, Cornejo Polar points out how Garcilaso's narrative and discourse is full of moments in which the unbridgeable aporias between the two worlds bubble to the surface. These moments lend the text a tragic sensibility wherein the attempt to create a mestizo text, a syncretic, blissful union of worlds, dissolves in the face of what is ultimately an "armonía imposible" (impossible harmony). In Garcilaso, he writes,

> La imagen de armonía que trabajosamente construye el discurso mestizo del Inca se aprecia más como el doloroso e inútil remedio de una herida nunca curada que como la expresión de un gozoso sincretismo de lo plural. . . . [El mestizaje entonces en su obra] termina por reinstalarse . . . en su condición equívoca y precaria, densamente ambigua, que no convierte la unión en armonía sino—al revés—en convivencia forzosa, difícil, dolorosa y traumática. (82)

> The image of harmony that the mestizo discourse of the Inca arduously constructs is better understood as a painful and ineffective remedy for an incurable wound rather than as the joyful expression of a beautiful syncretism of the plural. . . . [The mestizaje of his work thus] ends up reinstating itself in its equivocal and precarious condition, densely ambiguous, that does not convert the union into harmony but into its opposite—into a forced, difficult, painful, and traumatic coexistence.

Unlike what Cornejo Polar sees in the *Comentarios reales*, however, the *Historia de la nación chichimeca* manifests no sense of tragedy in the face of the aporias and contradictions that defined the world out of which Alva Ixtlilxochitl wrote and that he also necessarily confronted. There is no symbolic trace of cultural incommensurability in his discourse, a discourse that, at every turn, posits an ideal, harmonious union between two worlds that were, as the story goes, destined to come together. In the *Historia de la nación chichimeca*, there is no impossibility suddenly emerging from out of the semiotic web of the narrative to lace its grand vision of *mestizaje* with a sense of nostalgia, regret, and bitterness.

On the contrary, the narrative of Alva Ixtlilxochitl, writing as a colonial (indigenous) elite familiar with Nahuatl and Nahua semiosis as well as early modern European learning, exudes throughout a blissful and uninterrupted convergence, a convergence broken only by its own historically constructed interruption in the form of the idolatrous and human-sacrificing Mexica (Lee 2008, 191–209). In the *Historia de la nación chichimeca*'s narrative, historico-literary negotiation of the cross-cultural encounter does indeed reflect the colonial conditions of Cornejo Polar's "totalidad contradictoria" (contradictory totality), but it does so mostly in a larger sense—in its presentation in the Castilian language, its alphabetic body, its reliance on and appropriation of European/colonial concepts to reinstitute Nahua forms, and its suppression of many Nahua forms, symbols, and concepts and its reanalysis of others. All of these characteristics of Alva Ixtlilxochitl's writing necessarily exclude a significant indigenous audience, yet at no point is the harmonious state of affairs of the *Historia de la nación chichimeca* interrupted or undermined for either a Spanish or a bilingual/biliterate reader on the level of the narrative discourse itself.[42]

The blissful harmony goes on, in fact, until the enlightened reader, looking at the image with different eyes (Cummins and Rappaport 2012, 9–10), suddenly realizes that it has the potential to be something quite different from what the hegemonic discourse of the public Spanish world of its production suggests. At that moment, one realizes that the terms and conditions and even the very nature of that convergence has been exclusively determined by the colonial(ist) framework only to the extent that it determines the Eurocentric and political context that shapes the reader's understanding. If a sense of tragedy defines the textual effect of the symbolization of cultural incommensurability, the "armonía imposible" of the *Comentarios reales*, a sense of comedy defines that of the *Historia de la nación chichimeca*, taking the reader into the realm of the ludic and leaving behind the aftertaste of the kind of laughter that comes from knowing that one has managed to subvert the system behind its back.

This kind of laughter is entirely in keeping with the tradition of the trickster, and, as we shall see, the connections between the gods, the trickster, the ruler, and the writer lie at the base of the double-towered pyramid that constitutes Alva Ixtlilxochitl's narrative aesthetic in the *Historia de la nación chichimeca*. Like the work of Garcilaso as discussed by Mazzotti, the *Historia de la nación chichimeca* elaborates an authoritative version of events for an audience that, like the historian, is bilingual and biliterate. My analysis of

Alva Ixtlilxochitl's history, unlike that of Mazzotti for Garcilaso, however, is less a story of palimpsest, which remains to be told, than of a carefully plotted structural and symbolic diglossia that relies on—and indeed develops—some of the very transformations that the Nahua historical tradition underwent through the influence of the early Franciscans (Baudot 1995; Gruzinski 2007 [1991]; Lesbre 1995, 1999a, 2000, 2010). It is by means of this diglossia and double-voicing[43] that the *Historia de la nación chichimeca* (re)articulates significant modes of conceiving of history, rulers, and their relationship to the gods that have been associated with the Nahua tradition and found in Nahua myth-historical texts from pre-Hispanic and colonial times.

Martin Lienhard's (1991, 95–129) appropriation of the terms *diglossia* and *resemanticization* from the field of linguistics to describe the coexistence of two culturally distinct and autonomous signifying spheres captures the essence of the narrative aesthetic of the *Historia de la nación chichimeca*. The two realms remain distinct, although also mutually implicated (and in that sense inseparable) signifying structures, with the Nahua sphere in this case being the clearly unmarked or subtextual system aimed at or comprehensible to a secondary audience of bilingual and biliterate savants like Alva Ixtlilxochitl himself. In its comic interlacing of both European and Nahua historiographical and literary-cultural traditions, the *Historia de la nación chichimeca* embodies an unmistakable resistance to Spanish colonial monoculture, although not to its values or systems of belief or its fundamental political structure. At the same time that the text preserves elements of the Nahua historical tradition (although this is not necessarily its "orality," as Lienhard and others describe it), it works toward and for the colonial processes of resemanticization (or the appropriation and resignification of the Nahua past). To the extent that it is a diglossic text, however, it does not represent a relapse into the neutered sense of the transcultural, unwittingly reinstituting the mestizo "desconflictivizado" (Cornejo Polar 2011, 81; neutralized or made unconflictual) in another guise and erasing the colonial violence or the "malestar" (malaise) (in Lienhard's term) that plagues colonial writing. It is not a single text produced from two parts, but a single text that manifests two different structures in one, with elements of Nahua historicity retaining their autonomy—and doing so through an appropriation of the very hegemonic structure into which it was originally (and ever after) subsumed, as Lienhard (1991, 123) has suggested. In the gap between these structures lie the aporias that accompany colonial violence and its processes of segregation and dehumanization.

The four chapters of this book lay out the diglossic, double-voiced aesthetic of the *Historia de la nación chichimeca* in something of a circular fashion. Chapters 1 and 4 are dedicated to showing the way in which the text articulates with its context of production, while chapters 2 and 3 undertake textual analysis and a close reading of the history. The context of chapter 1 focuses on Alva Ixtlilxochitl's family and the changing definitions of rulership in the colonial period, while the context of chapter 4 is dedicated to a more specific examination of the colonial politics that rocked the tenure (1621–1624) of Viceroy Diego Carrillo de Mendoza y Pimentel, the Marquis of Gelves. The literary analysis of chapter 2 concentrates on the question of genre, specifically the idea of the narrative configuration or emplotment of the historical work, while the third chapter analyzes the portrayal of Alva Ixtlilxochitl's central character, the great Acolhua ruler Nezahualcoyotl. In the conclusion, I take up the topic of the trickster—present throughout, but especially in chapters 1 and 3—and the connection between tricksters and rhetors, returning to the question of the politics of writing and the nature, effects, and implications of Alva Ixtlilxochitl's historiographical aesthetic.

Chapter 1 argues that to grasp the full significance of the role of rulership in the *Historia de la nación chichimeca* it is necessary to look at the struggles and declining fortunes of the traditional tlatoque and their heirs—the old ruling lineages—in the early colonial period. There are, in fact, two parts to the story, only one of which, so far, has been well documented. The part that is directly documented and verifiable is the material or political-economic history of the transition from the altepetl ruled by a tlatoani to the encomienda system[44] with its affiliated tlatoque, now called caciques. These caciques held as private properties lands formerly associated with specific aspects of the former altepetl, continued to receive exemptions and tributes, and were charged with ensuring the smooth transfer of tribute goods and labor to the proper authorities. The more nebulous (and thus much more difficult to study) aspect of the transition is the evolution and destiny of its nonmaterial significance, the fate of the old *tlatocayotl*, or institution of rulership, as a cultural institution, a story that must take into account the imposition of Christianity and its effect on the religious or ritual aspects of rulership that were so important to its authority and practices in pre-Hispanic times.

This is the story that, I argue, the *Historia de la nación chichimeca*—as opposed to Torquemada's *Monarquía indiana*—tells, in part, if we know how to look for it. If we do not read the history in the context of the existing scholarship on the pre-Hispanic Nahua world and the role of the ruler in preconquest society, however, even that small part of the story will remain out of our reach. In his seminal study of colonial Nahua society, *The Nahuas after the Conquest*, James Lockhart (1992, 25) notes that Alva Ixtlilxochitl seems to have been

> far less well informed than Chimalpahin and Tezozomoc [about the nature of pre-Hispanic rulership and altepetl organization] and obscured things further by writing in Spanish; he expressed himself in terms of kings and vast empires, with rulers "giving" regions to the subordinates and allies. Ixtlilxochitl paid little attention to and even perhaps had little grasp of the polity-specific nature of central Mexican rulership or of the importance of a fixed complex of constituent parts.

As we will see, however, if Alva Ixtlilxochitl was unaware of the specific nature of Acolhua social and political organization, or preferred to portray it in European terms, he does not seem to have lost track of the grandeur, importance, and some of the particular Nahua symbolism associated with the office of rulership, symbolism that both connected it to its sources of power in the nonterrestrial realms of the deities and affirmed its place in the larger cosmic order.

While the first two sections of chapter 1 thus present an overview of the pre-Hispanic tlatocayotl and follow its implications in and through the actions and documents of Francisco Verdugo Quetzalmamalitzin Huetzin, Alva Ixtlilxochitl's great-grandfather, the final section opens up a discussion of the universal history as a humanist-influenced genre (the topic of chapter 2) by examining the connection established by Alva Ixtlilxochitl between rulers and writers. In this act whereby Alva Ixtlilxochitl implicitly fashions himself as the true son of his Nahua forefathers, we learn something of the deeper stakes of his scholarly enterprise. A brief comparison of the different ways that he and Torquemada treat Nahua literacy—a matter of emphasis, not content—reveals the rift between the guardian of a patrimonial history (and historical patrimony)[45] and the historian of a colonial missionary endeavor.

Chapter 2 focuses on one of the most distinguishing aspects of the humanist-influenced history—the importance of narrative, what Rolena Adorno ([1986] 2000), quoting Walter Mignolo, has referred to as "assertive formally executed discourse." It begins by outlining Paul Ricoeur's notion, in *Time and Narrative* ([1984] 1990), of the function of a plot, both literary and historical, as that which is organized around the gap between what he refers to as "human time" and "cosmic time." While the former aesthetic, he argues, highlights the gap, the historical narrative—based on social institutions such as the calendar, the passing of the generations, and the trace (the relic or ruin)—strives to bridge it. It then proceeds to compare and analyze distinct features of the narratives of the *Historia de la nación chichimeca* and the *Monarquía indiana*. Having discussed their different attitudes toward their source texts in the previous chapter, I now turn to a discussion of some of the specifics of their (re)presentation of them.

Notwithstanding their apparent collaboration and shared source texts, the two authors produce very different histories, with separate goals and emplotments of their narratives. They have distinct manners of perceiving and relating their principal subjects to the stream of "cosmic" time imagined in the Christian tradition, and they confront in different ways some of the essential and urgent questions that plagued all Christian historians, rooted in the cosmographies of Herodotus and Pliny, since the European discovery of the "New" World: given ultimate unity of "man" kind, where is the trace of those peoples and the lands they inhabited in the classical and biblical texts? How did they get there (Jiménez 2001, 193)? Most significantly, they express different versions of Christian providentialism, of the ultimate (sacred) meaning and purpose of the discovery and conquest. While Torquemada is exclusively concerned with placing the discovery, conquest, and work of the Franciscan missionaries within the framework of "cosmic" time regarded from the point of view of Christian eschatology, the *Historia de la nación chichimeca* presents (itself as) a diglossic and double-voiced chronotope,[46] responding to the imperatives of the Christian reader at the same time that it satisfies the requirements implied in the Nahua stories of creation and Tolteca histories, a sense of time (and place) built around cyclical revolutions of the sun and moon in the twenty-four-hour day, and manifested in the relationship between the rival twins and creator deities Quetzalcoatl and Tezcatlipoca (Graulich 1981).

Because of its outsized role in hinging the Nahua and Christian chronotopes in Alva Ixtlilxochitl's history, the figure (or figures) of Quetzalcoatl receive(s) most of the attention in the second half of chapter 2. After a brief comparison of the representations of Quetzalcoatl figures in the *Monarquía indiana* and the *Historia de la nación chichimeca*, this section is dedicated to unraveling the linear and cyclical emplotment of the latter text, to demonstrating the way in which the textual substructure relies on—appropriates and exploits—the very distorting colonial images of his persona; for example, his association with an apostle-like figure and the idea of a preevangelization of the region. Thus, I show how Alva Ixtlilxochitl's work in the *Historia de la nación chichimeca* is one of innovation and transculturation in which some ancient Nahua forms, structures, thoughts, and ideas survive in new (con) texts. It is Quetzalcoatl's anterior resemanticization within the context of missionary activities and ethnographies—the texts of Motolinía and Olmos as well as Torquemada and the Dominican friar Diego Durán—that becomes a vehicle for enabling this disguised and surreptitious return.

To be sure, this innovation by no means negates the lasting impression that many aspects of Alva Ixtlilxochitl's work—major themes of a "poet-king" and "civilized law giver" discussed by Jongsoo Lee (2008)—left upon Mexican national history. In addition to its distorting effect vis-à-vis the pre-Hispanic world as we (think) we understand its functioning in an anthropological and ethnohistorical sense—and it should be remembered that none of these ideas were invented by Alva Ixtlilxochitl but built up through time in Acolhua historiography (e.g., Douglas 2010, 162; Lesbre 1995, 2000, 2010)—is its purposeful and conscious suppression of significant but taboo aspects of Acolhua religiosity and rulership (Lesbre 1999a; Inoue Okuko 2007, 69–70). Censorship, as Douglas (2010, 12–14, 130–34, 154, 162) points out, would have been especially prevalent in Nahua (Acolhua) historiography in the years after the Tetzcoca lord don Carlos Ometochtzin was burned at the stake for idolatry in 1539. While the iconic-script texts that were created shortly after that time (and became important primary sources of Acolhua history) censor obvious rites such as human sacrifice, however, they do not entirely give up on important symbolic features that indicated rulers' direct connections with sources of power in the nonterrestrial realms, as many scholars have noted (e.g. Douglas 2010; Lesbre 1999b).

Chapter 3 takes a close look at the representation of the single most important persona of Alva Ixtlilxochitl's narrative, the great Acolhua ruler Nezahualcoyotl. Nezahualcoyotl is a common figure in colonial central Mexican historical narratives, especially in the Acolhua tradition. Yet little research done on him in any context discusses what I view to be his major attribute, present across all of his stories and in the *Historia de la nación chichimeca*. Given the consistency with which Nezahualcoyotl and his son and heir, Nezahualpilli, are associated with typical traits of the trickster—wit, cunning, magical powers, challenge to authority, and deceit (masking and unmasking)—it is surprising that they have so rarely been analyzed in terms of their relationship to the patron deity of Tetzcoco, the great trickster and kingmaker himself, Tezcatlipoca. After a discussion of Tezcatlipoca's major attributes, I show how Nezahualcoyotl embodies these characteristics as principal features of his character. In addition, I show how his representation is ultimately inseparable from the physical, sacred landscape through which he moves and in the extremely allegorical nature of the stories and tales in which he appears as an actor.

While there is never any explicit mention of Tezcatlipoca in the *Historia de la nación chichimeca*, Alva Ixtlilxochitl describes him and his importance as an ancestor (and trickster) in the Tetzcoco ruling line in earlier texts. Although it is impossible to know for certain, it seems highly unlikely that these associations in the *Historia de la nación chichimeca* would have been relayed and represented without his awareness.[47] The result is thus a doubly encoded characterization of the hero: on the one hand, Nezahualcoyotl's direct, explicit, and linearly structured connection to "Quetzalcoatl" as a Christian-like apostle figure and, on the other, an implicit symbolism identifying him with the trickster deity. When examined in light of the cyclical dynamic in which the Christianized Quetzalcoatl figure operates, this latter identification opens up yet another venue in which the basic cosmogonic structure is enacted and put into motion, with important implications for understanding the text's representation of the nature and meaning of conquest, the role of Acolhua rulers therein, and their relationship to the colonial regime afterward.

It is this colonial regime and Alva Ixtlilxochitl's own relationship to it to during his lifetime that constitutes the topic of chapter 4. If chapter 1 deals with Alva Ixtlilxochitl's defense of Nahua writing and his establishment of authority and legitimacy as a writer (and therefore the true heir of his Nahua forbearers), and chapter 2 discusses the *Historia de la nación chichimeca* as New World humanist history and the importance of authorship and of history as a narrative art, chapter 4 discusses the all-important didactic functions of the history in the Renaissance, the popular Ciceronian idea of history as philosophy by example, or *historia magistra vitae*. For Alva Ixtlilxochitl's Acolhua rulers are nothing if they are not model, exemplary, Christian princes. Although it has been much more common to associate Alva Ixtlilxochitl's work with the Memorial de méritos y servicios, in many respects, as Brian (2007; 2016, 96–99, 106) notes, the *Historia de la nación chichimeca* reads like a mirror of princes, with Alva Ixtlilxochitl constructing Nezahualcoyotl in the image of the ideal Counter-Reformation and anti-Machiavellian prince.

The potential affront to colonial ideals that the portraying of an indigenous, pagan "Christian prince" represents is, of course, neutralized by Nezahualcoyotl's biblical, David-like resonances and parallels (Velazco 2003; Lee
2008) and his celebration and support of the arrival of Cortés and the "ley
evangélica" (Christian or New Testament Law). Yet there are moments in
the narrative when the line between past and present blurs, and the mirror's
reflection seems to be aimed directly at the immediate colonial circumstances,
becoming a not-so-veiled critique of the Spanish colonial viceregal administration. In these scenes, centered on rulers' reactions to human catastrophes set off by natural disaster—events familiar in the region from both
preconquest and colonial periods—Nezahualcoyotl acts in ways that Spanish authorities should have. In real life, moreover, around the time that Alva
Ixtlilxochitl was probably composing the *Historia de la nación chichimeca*,
the viceroy, the Marquis of Gelves, special agent of the Count-Duke of Olivares, was making or had made himself extremely unpopular among the creole
elite of New Spain and their interested peninsular allies. In the unfolding of
the story, the archbishop, Juan Pérez de la Serna, to whom Alva Ixtlilxochitl
possibly addresses the "Dedicatoria" (dedication) associated with the *Historia
de la nación chichimeca*, is expelled and, on his way out, takes refuge in the
church of San Juan Teotihuacan.

What were the underlying politics of the revolt that eventually saw the
archbishop enter Mexico City in triumph and the viceroy flee for his life?
How does this story relate to the exemplary actions of Nezahualcoyotl in Alva
Ixtlilxochitl's text? These are questions that have no certain answer but that
must be considered in order to do justice to the importance of the concept of
rulership in the narrative. Alva Ixtlilxochitl's dedication of his manuscript to
an important religious figure, possibly the archbishop (maximum religious
authority of the viceroyalty), suggests that at this early date Alva Ixtlilxochitl
perceived the secular church and the close alliance (but not necessarily identification) between creole society and indigenous elites as a more hospitable
environment for his historical endeavors.

According to a marginal note in the burial records of the Church of Santa
Catarina Mártir in Mexico City (O'Gorman 1975–1977, 2:370), Alva Ixtlilxochitl died in 1650, intestate and without leaving behind money for masses
to be given for his soul.[48] The lack of a last will and testament is perplexing,
as Frederick Schwaller (1994a, 98) has commented, given his role as colonial bureaucrat and the importance of the genre to his own family history. It

suggests, however, that he must have had few direct resources—aside from his trove of historical documents and writings—to pass on to his family. According to Vásquez Galicia (2013, 140–42), however, the burial of both Alva Ixtlilxochitl and his wife in Mexico City's Church of Santa Catarina, and more particularly in the chapel of the Preciosa Sangre de Cristo (the Precious Blood of Christ), implies that at one time, at least, they must have had the financial means and/or the social status to be accepted in the circles of the Spanish and creole elite who founded both the church (in 1568) and the *cofradía* (brotherhood) associated with the chapel, to which they almost certainly belonged.[49] Aside from these clues, the end of Alva Ixtlilxochitl's life, like that of the *Historia de la nación chichimeca* (which trails off midway through the conquest of Mexico), remains a mystery. As such, however, it is an ending entirely in keeping with the spirit of the controversial tradition of the (non)deaths of his illustrious forbearers: Topiltzin, Nezahualcoyotl, and Nezahualpilli.

CHAPTER ONE

From Tlatoque to Caciques

Nahua-Christian Rulership in Deed and Word

⤝ IN LAYING THE GROUNDWORK FOR THE STUDY OF THE HISTORICO-
literary aesthetic of the *Historia de la nación chichimeca* in chapters 2 and 3,
this chapter undertakes a variety of different but related tasks aimed at providing an overview of the work's context of production. Because rulership
constitutes both the structural backbone and the thematic focus of the narrative, this context is necessarily centered on assessing the nature, history,
and economic and cultural implications of Alva Ixtlilxochitl's ties to the pre-
Hispanic Tetzcoca nobility whose story he tells. Moreover, although little is
known about the specific intellectual milieu that influenced Alva Ixtlilxochitl's work, it is important to consider what we do know and to attempt to
put together as complete of a picture as possible about the way in which his
work articulates with its context of production.

Beyond the emphasis on rulership in the Nahua tradition and therefore
in his source material, I suggest that the roots of Alva Ixtlilxochitl's representation of the Acolhua rulers can be found in the transformation of colonial
Nahua rulership in the sixteenth century. More specifically, they can be seen
in the life of his great-grandfather, first cacique and then cacique and gobernador of the cacicazgo of San Juan Teotihuacan. Don Francisco Verdugo Quetzalmamalitzin Huetzin was named after his forebearers Quetzalmamalitzin

and Huetzin, heroes of the founding and recovery of Acolhua rule at Teotihuacan in the fifteenth century (Alva Ixtlilxochitl [1975–1977] 1985 1:406; Pérez-Rocha and Tena 2000b, 382–83; Münch 1976, 7–10, 58) and, later, after the Spanish conquistador who became encomendero of the San Juan Teotihuacan region, Francisco Verdugo. He was the last cacique to rule at San Juan Teotihuacan before its institution of the cabildo, a town council system of local governance practiced in Spain that broke the traditional link between the practice of governing and the wealth and status that had accrued to the title of cacique and the realm of the cacicazgo under Spanish rule (Haskett 1991, 4).

One of the fourteen major subsidiary *altepeme* (singular altepetl) of the pre-Hispanic Acolhua federation centered in Tetzcoco, San Juan Teotihuacan was one of few colonial indigenous towns to experience a long period of stable rulership in the aftermath of the violence of the conquest period. Francisco Verdugo Quetzalmamalitzin Huetzin was born in 1518 on the eve of the Spanish conquest and died in 1563. The fact that he was educated and came to power in the early years of the colony and lived a relatively long life enabled him to negotiate colonial politics to the advantage of his family and likely to that of the town as well.[1] The usual challenges to rulership and the threats of breakup and usurpation of the cacicazgo's lands were by and large not successful either in Francisco Verdugo Quetzalmamalitzin Huetzin's day or, because of his foresight, in the years to come. Historians of the San Juan Teotihuacan cacicazgo invariably note it as a rare example of survival into the time of independence (Münch 1976; Pérez-Rocha and Tena 2000b, 26, 46–47).

By the time Alva Ixtlilxochitl was researching and writing his first historical works in the late sixteenth and early seventeenth centuries, however, the indigenous population of New Spain was at its nadir, and the formal recognition and economic and political privileges granted to the indigenous nobility in the early colonial period had been vastly reduced and largely phased out (Gibson 1964, 153–65, 200–19; Pérez-Rocha and Tena 2000b, 24–26; Romero Galván 2003, 28–73). In addition, the Crown had only recently begun to let up on decades of trying to prohibit and sequester work on indigenous languages and cultures done under the auspices of the religious orders whose authority and projects it had initially supported. In Georges Baudot's (1995, 491–526) view, it did so only because by the second decade of the seventeenth century there was no longer any possibility that a reconstituted indigenous nobility and (potentially powerful) autonomous república de indios might eventually be able to seriously infringe upon the ever-expanding interests of Spanish society in New Spain.

In spite of the population decline and the Crown's earlier hostility, in fact, writing in indigenous traditions in the late sixteenth and early seventeenth centuries, as Matthew Restall (1997, 250) has pointed out, experienced something of a golden age—an indication, perhaps, of the extent of the urgency to keep a record of times past in order to safeguard the memory and interests of the indigenous pueblos in the present.[2] Like most colonial writing in the Nahua tradition, the texts from this period reflect, and were ultimately a product of, the early missionary work of the religious orders, especially that of the Franciscans, and what Louise Burkhart (1989) has called the "Nahua-Christian moral dialogue." In Alva Ixtlilxochitl's case, it is possible to trace in his work some of the results of this dialogue, of the long-standing *connection* and *interaction* between the Acolhua nobility and the Franciscan missionaries and educators who established themselves in Tetzcoco in the very earliest days after the conquest and made it a center of their ethnographic research. It is in this sense, therefore, that an examination of the life of Francisco Verdugo Quetzalmamalitzin Huetzin *as well as* a side-by-side analysis of the *Historia de la nación chichimeca* and the *Monarquía indiana* is particularly instructive. Friar Juan de Torquemada (author of the latter history) was a contemporary and collaborator of Alva Ixtlilxochitl and the direct, officially appointed successor to the work of friars Andrés de Olmos, Toribio de Benavente or "Motolinía," Gerónimo de Mendieta, and Bernardino de Sahagún, his Franciscan forebearers in historical and cultural research aimed at rooting out idolatry.[3] His history and that of Alva Ixtlilxochitl are written in the form of the European universal history or *historia general* but are in large part based on sources written in the Nahua historical tradition, some of which they appear to have shared and jointly interpreted. The authors are thus a kind of late and final living example of the cultural and intellectual interaction and collaboration between Acolhua nobility and Franciscan friars.

Part One. From Tlatoque to Caciques: Colonial Rulership and the Cacicazgo of San Juan Teotihuacan

EARLY FAMILY HISTORY

As stated in the introduction to this book, three of Alva Ixtlilxochitl's grandparents were Spanish while his mother's mother, colonial *cacica* (the feminine form of cacique) of the town of San Juan Teotihuacan, was a direct descendent of Acolhua *huey tlatoque* (great rulers) centered in Tetzcoco. Nezahualcoyotl, the most famous Acolhua huey tlatoani, is the centerpiece of the *Historia de la nación chichimeca* and of Acolhua historiography in general. He died forty-seven years before the arrival of Cortés on the Gulf Coast of Mexico in 1519, and his son and successor on the throne, Nezahualpilli, died only four years before that event. Nezahualpilli's son, Ixtlilxochitl, as Alva Ixtlilxochitl's own narratives assert, however, was not originally named to succeed his father as Tetzcoco's tlatoani. Instead, the Mexica (who held imperial sway over the Acolhua and thus had influence in the decision) had tapped his half-brother, Cacama, for the job because of their ties to his mother. Thus, when the Spanish arrived, Ixtlilxochitl joined with them to defeat the Mexica.[4] After becoming baptized, Ixtlilxochitl took the name don Fernando Cortés Ixtlilxochitl, the "don" indicating his noble status, and married a woman named Beatriz Papantzin, who was the widow of Cuitlahuac, the short-lived tlatoani of Tenochtitlan who replaced Motecuhzoma. The daughter of Fernando Cortés Ixtlilxochitl and Beatriz Papantzin was named doña Ana Cortés Ixtlilxochitl. She married Francisco Verdugo Quetzalmamalitzin Huetzin.

Born a year before the beginning of Cortés's initial foray into Tenochtitlan, Francisco Verdugo Quetzalmamalitzin Huetzin would almost certainly have been educated in Nahua ways, but also—very likely under Franciscan authority—in Christianity and in the new ways of the Iberian colonizers. His father, Xiuhtototzin, as Ixtlilxochitl's chief military general (or *capitán general*), fought alongside Nezahualpilli and then for the Spanish in the wars of conquest and died in the Noche Triste (Alva Ixtlilxochitl 1975–1977, 2:145, 231; Münch 1974, 9–10).[5] Mamalitzin,[6] Francisco Verdugo Quetzalmamalitzin Huetzin's older brother, succeeded Xiuhtototzin as ruler and also participated in the conquest of Mexico, dying in 1525 (Münch 1976, 10). Francisco Verdugo Quetzalmamalitzin Huetzin was only seven years old at the time, and, although he was the legitimate successor to the San Juan Teotihuacan rulership (at least under Spanish rules of succession), his cousin, Juan Tlazolyaotzin, took over. The latter ruled until 1533, when, after his death, the officials of San Juan Teotihuacan, following pre-Hispanic tradition, took Francisco Verdugo Quetzalmamalitzin Huetzin to Tetzcoco to be installed as the new ruler by Pedro Tetlahuehuetzquititzin, the Tetzcoco cacique (Pérez-Rocha and Tena 2000, 45, 388).[7] Due to his still-tender age (he was only fifteen years old at the time), his appointment, as Pérez-Rocha and Tena point out, had to be confirmed by the Real Audiencia.[8] Decades later, in the mid-sixteenth century, when the Spanish-style cabildo system of governance was instituted in indigenous communities, he served as both cacique and gobernador of the town until his death in 1563 (Münch 1976, 11, 14; Pérez-Rocha and Tena 2000, 45–47).

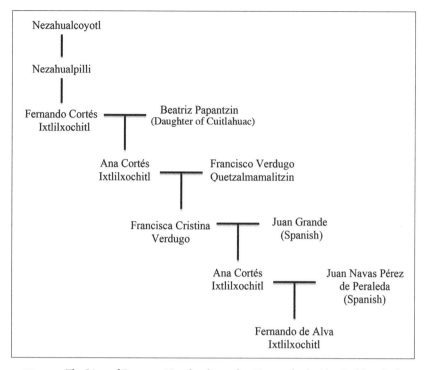

Figure 1. The Line of Descent: Nezahualcoyotl to Fernando de Alva Ixtlilxochitl.

From the documents published thus far it is clear that Francisco Verdugo Quetzalmamalitzin Huetzin managed his position as cacique with unusual diplomacy, skill, and foresight, at least as far as his own familial interests were concerned. In his work on the history of the cacicazgo of San Juan Teoti-huacan, Münch (1976) emphasizes its transition from indigenous altepetl to a cacicazgo that by the mid-seventeenth century resembled in every practical way the typical hacienda of the epoch, a transition whose foundation Francisco Verdugo Quetzalmamalitzin Huetzin laid. In this sense, it follows a pattern described by Charles Gibson (1964) in which the power of those relatively few colonial cacicazgos that did not experience breakup and decline "depended only indirectly upon [the owners'] position as caciques." As Gibson notes,

> Where caciques were still powerful, their power rested upon forms of economic and social domination common to all ruling families regardless of origin. Whereas in the sixteenth century caciques had imitated Spaniards, in the eighteenth century "caciques" and "Spaniards" might

both be mestizos, and if they remained successful they managed their lands, rents, agricultural production, and mode of life after the manner of all hacendados and rancheros. Their properties were enlarged by methods that cannot be meaningfully distinguished from the methods of the propertied class in general. (163)

Left unanswered, however, is the very important (but also very intangible and difficult to answer) question of what happened to the family's participation in the traditional Nahua cultural-religious-symbolic matrix in which the ruler's power and authority was vested, and from which it was derived. That is, what was their relationship to the altepetl's tlatocayotl, its institution of rulership, as conceived and understood in San Juan Teotihuacan over time, and by don Francisco Verdugo Quetzalmamalitzin Huetzin and his heirs, especially as the ruler and ruling line became permanently sidelined from official political functions? What imprint, if any, did the tlatocayotl leave on Alva Ixtlilxochitl's writing?

The documents that helped support the material survival of the cacicazgo throughout the colonial period, including Francisco Verdugo Quetzalmamalitzin Huetzin's 1563 testamento (O'Gorman 1975–1977, 2:281–86; Pérez-Rocha and Tena 2000a, 261–79), and a 1558 probanza (Pérez-Rocha and Tena 2000a, 203–9; legal questionnaire) testifying to his service to the Spanish Crown, open up important, but still partial, vistas onto his means of embodying and negotiating these less recognizable, more symbolic, aspects of Nahua rulership, aspects tied more closely to its significance vis-à-vis the pueblo of San Juan Teotihuacan. Before embarking on that discussion, however, I provide a brief overview of preconquest Nahua rulership as it has been understood and represented in scholarship based on evidence from both preconquest and colonial period sources.

TLATOCAYOTL: NAHUA RULERSHIP BEFORE AND AFTER CONQUEST

In *The Nahuas after the Conquest*, James Lockhart (1992, 94–117) roots his discussion of rulership in the differentiation between nobles (pipiltin, singular *pilli*) and commoners (*macehualtin*, singular *macehualli*) in Nahua society before and after the conquest. The distinction, and the social system built around it, he notes, resembled in many ways the one that existed in Spain at the time of the conquest, especially with respect to the variations in social levels and statuses existing within each group (94–95). Such were the variations in the Nahua world, he writes, that the most certain criteria for determining who could be considered pipiltin (nobles) relied not on specific individual qualities (related to lineage) but on membership in a little understood "noble and patrimonial" (98) institution, called in some cases (in eastern regions of central Mexico such as Tlaxcala), a *teccalli* or "lord-house" (102).[9] This institution or complex, notes Lockhart, appears to have been the sole means by which the pipiltin (who did not participate in the *coatequitl*, or the rotational labor system) had access to both land and retainers or dependents (also part of the macehualtin) who serviced the household and worked the land and thus helped the pipiltin to fulfill their in-kind tribute obligations to the *teuhctli*, or lord, who was in charge of the institution (102–3). Thus, in its purest sense, writes Lockhart, the primary *social* distinction was not between macehualtin (a word whose meaning tended toward the common or general sense of "people") and pipiltin, but between macehualtin and *teteuhctin* (singular teuhctli) or lords (102).[10]

In what Lockhart identified as the "cellular or modular" (1992, 15) formation of the Nahua social and political world, the teteuhctin were in turn members of a larger polity, known as a *calpulli* (meaning "big-house"), that, together with a set number of other calpulli, formed the building blocks of the yet larger-scale entity or ethnic polity known as the altepetl (15–20). The leader of one of these calpulli (its teuhctli or principal teuhctli) served as the tlatoani or principal ruler of the confederated calpulli that made up the altepetl. (And, as mentioned earlier, there was such a thing as confederated or complex altepetl, whose principal rulers were known as huey tlatoque or "great rulers" (20–28).) "In a sense," writes Lockhart, "nothing more needs to be said about a tlatoani than that he was a large-scale teuhctli at the altepetl level" (109). In summary, Lockhart defines the altepetl—the fundamental preconquest entity upon which colonial institutions such as the encomienda based themselves—as an "organization of people holding sway over a given territory" (38) that had three essential parts: first, territory or land; second, people, divided into constituent parts or groupings (the calpulli); and third, a dynastic ruler or tlatoani (15–16).[11]

As both Lockhart (1992, 103) and Schroeder (1991, xvi, 5, 41–44, 163–69, 209–12) make clear, however, it was the institution or office of rulership, the tlatocayotl, apart from the operating individual tlatoani, that provided the Nahua altepetl with its sense of distinction, along with the specific royal title that identified it, the altepetl's *teuhctocaitl*. This title was passed down from

ruler to ruler as he (or, occasionally, she) carried out the duties and roles associated with the institution (Schroeder 1991, 209; Lockhart 1992, 16). As one
of the most significant aspects of tlatocayotl, the teuhctocaitl had, Schroeder
(1991, 212) observes, "an aura, both sacred and ethnic, capable of lending legitimacy to any acceptable occupant. The title may go back to time immemorial
or it may have been granted by another group which already had it, but once
established it seems to have been a universally accepted or intrinsic possession of a given people." While the tlatocayotl was sometimes suspended, and
a substitute ruler put into place, she notes, the replacement never received
the legitimate ruler's full regalia or the ruler's title, and was referred to as a
cuauhtlatoque (literally, eagle-ruler) instead. In sum, she writes, the works
of Chimalpahin indicate that the altepetl was therefore never in its "fullest
glory" until its true rulership was in place, signified by the use of the teuhctocaitl and the symbolically charged regalia and accoutrements specific to each
tlatocayotl and associated with and tied to the ruler's power.

Significantly, this sense of the centrality of the tlatocayotl or the altepetl rulership to the identity, coherence and continuity of the altepetl did
not come to an immediate end with the conquest. Colonial period indigenous annals and histories reveal the tenacity with which indigenous groups
maintained their rulership in the face of high mortality rates (due to war and
disease), usurpations and confusions of old political boundaries, and other
challenges created and posed by the presence of new Spanish overlords—
encomenderos, corregidores, and religious officials.[12] For Chimalpahin and
Alva Ixtlilxochitl, Schroeder observes (1991, 202), the pre- and postconquest
history of the altepetl is a continuous entity, although Chimalpahin does not
"Christianize" his past like Alva Ixtlilxochitl. As she notes, rulerships of central Mexican polities continued to exist, though not always to flourish, far
into the sixteenth century and in some cases longer (185).

The emphasis on the longevity of the tlatocayotl or the institution of
rulership implies that the individual identity of the (properly selected and
installed) ruler mattered little in the historical and cultural scheme of things.
What was important was that the tlatoque fulfilled the duties and met the
expectations of the office. In the preconquest context, these duties and expectations were linked to the rulers' assumption of the ritual-cosmological functions of the position, as manifestations of the connection of the rulership to
the deities (in particular, the patron deity of the altepetl). An overview of the
scholarship on the Nahua vision of the tlatoani's role in the life of the altepetl
thus gives us an idea of the cultural elements that might have been in play

from a Nahua point of view when the Spanish outlawed traditional religious ceremonies and then gradually tried to impose a more purely bureaucratic vision of rulership on the pueblos, replacing the tlatocayotl with the office of gobernador or juez gobernador (a position that came to be known in Nahuatl as the gobernadoryotl) and instituting the cabildo. On the one hand, as Lockhart (1992, 32–33) notes, the transition to the cabildo system, which brought about the end of lifetime tenure for the gobernadores and the institution of a rotating post that shared governing responsibilities with other council members (who were also pipiltin), suited the pueblos in that it provided an escape valve for the tensions over rulership succession that commonly plagued preconquest altepeme. On the other hand, its deemphasis on the lifetime single ruler must have held sociocultural implications that the pueblos (as well as the privileged descendents of preconquest rulers and great rulers) had to come to terms with.[13] For Chimalpahin, Schroeder (2001) observes, the gobernador was a "counterpart" but not an "equivalent" (186) of the tlatoani, a title he withheld for Spaniards in positions of power and those rightful Nahuas actually invested in the traditional dynastic position during the colonial period (188).

TLATOQUE: THE NATURE AND FUNCTION OF THE PRE-HISPANIC TLATOANI IN THE NAHUA CONTEXT

As in the European context, with the notion of the divine right of kings,[14] the power and authority of pre-Hispanic Nahua tlatoque was ultimately rooted in and sustained by their connection with the sacred, with the "gods," or *teteo* [singular *teotl*]. Burkhart (1989, 37) has defined the Nahua conception of the divine implicit in the term *teotl* as a kind of "polytheistic monism": "A single divine principle . . . responsible for the nature of the cosmos. . . . [that] manifested itself in multiple forms." This connection was understood in part in a historical-genealogical sense, as well as in terms of the role and function of the ruler's position itself (López Austin 1973, 117–42). According to Alfredo López Austin (1976, 236–37), all pueblos established their identity and legitimacy through their tie to a particular patron deity whose power was at one time bestowed upon them at the top of a sacred mountain; its power was passed down through the heritage of an original leader who first made the connection with the god or through acts of piety carried out by certain members of the group. He writes that "La liga entre los hombres y las divinidades era a nivel de relación étnica y política. Según afirmaban, la proximidad étnica y lingüística no era sino consecuencia del parentesco de los dioses" (216; The connection between human beings and the gods was felt on the level of ethnic and political relationships. Ethnic and linguistic proximity, as they affirmed, was a direct result of kinship with the gods). The patron deity protected the pueblo but the pueblo also went to war in honor of their god and dedicated and enlarged their temple in the deity's honor (216–17). While all ethnic groups paid homage to the distinct gods of the pantheon, he writes, "Culto a los dioses generales y culto al dios tutelar eran dos relaciones distintas" (217; Worship of the general gods and worship of the patron deity implied two different relationships). When the rulership changed hands, it did so following long-standing patterns of genealogical succession, with a genealogy or lineage (the *tlatocatlacamecayotl*) traceable in most cases for centuries backward, to this founding ancestor (Schroeder 1991, 44, 211).[15]

Thus, while many things on the earthly plane of the cosmos contained or manifested the divine principle (often referred to as a divine fire), the Nahua ruler or tlatoani was considered to have entered into a particular pact with the tutelary divinity of the ethnic political body (López Austin 1973, 1976; Gruzinski 1989, 18–30). However, this does not mean that the ruler was thought of as a divine being per se, as Alfredo López Austin (1973, 111–21), Serge Gruzinski (1989, 18–30), and Michel Graulich (1998) all point out. In Nahuatl, the word tlatoani literally means "he who speaks," the implication being that the ruler speaks in the place of and as the gods or, more precisely, that the gods speak through or by means of the rulers. Rulers were considered to be the *ixiptla* of the gods, the literal definition of the word being "sheath" or "covering" and suggestive of the rulers' possession by the divine fire, of the power of the deity that they manifested in their careful participation in calendrical, seasonal rituals.[16] Michel Graulich (1998, 222) describes the ruler as a "receptacle" or "instrument" of the divine in the following manner:

> On ne peut définir plus clairement ce qu'on a appelé les « deux corps du roi »: l'homme n'est qu'un homme, la fonction est divine. Une parcelle de divinité entre en lui lors de son élection. Comment, sinon, pourrait-on le rendre responsable du maintien de l'ordre cosmique? Et c'est cette parcelle qu'on nourrit par des sacrifices.

> It is not possible to define more clearly what has been referred to as the "king's two bodies": the man is human, but his function is divine. A fragment of the divine enters into him after his enthronement. If it did not, then how could he be made responsible for maintaining the

cosmic order? And it is this fragment that is nourished by means of the sacrifices.

Indeed, as instruments or spokespersons of the gods in their communities, the tlatoque served as crucial intermediaries between the earthly plane and the realms of the gods and were responsible for ensuring that the power of the deity that they represented translated into benefits for the community. Rulers were not *necessarily* religious specialists, like the sages and soothsayers, the *tlamatinime* (singular tlamatini), or the shamans and shape-shifters, referred to as *nahualli* (Graulich 1998, 223).[17] However, in maintaining the regular observances of rituals and sacrifices, the tlatoque played vital roles in maintaining order, the cosmic balance and harmony with the gods, and thus in ensuring the timely arrival of the rains, successful harvests, victory in warfare, and other crucial aspects of an altepetl's immediate and long-term survival (López Austin 1984, 460).

In Nahua mythology, two deities in particular are closely associated with rulership and with each other: the rival creator deity pair, Tezcatlipoca and Quetzalcoatl. As Darlene Mysyk (2012) has put it, Quetzalcoatl was known as the "patron of royal lineages" while Tezcatlipoca "was the kingmaker and, that, on sheer whim." Together they signify the rulers' power and represent the vital spiritual and religious basis of their authority. This sponsorship of rulers cannot be separated from the large role that these deities play in many of the Nahua creation myths recorded by Franciscan friars in the early days of the colonial period, with one displacing the other as the new, ascendant "sun," a dynamic that lies (as we will see) at the heart of the stories of the Tolteca civilization's demise and of those of the Spanish conquest as well (Graulich 1981; Olivier [2003] 2008). Both figure heavily (as I shall show) in Alva Ixtlilxochitl's work, although it is only in his early writings that he explains the particular importance of Tezcatlipoca, as the patron deity of Tetzcoco, in Acolhua history. Quetzalcoatl, on the other hand—or a person by that name—comes to the forefront only in the later works.

RULERSHIP IN THE EARLY COLONIAL PERIOD: THE FRANCISCAN VISION

In the early years of Spanish colonization, the Crown upheld the authority of the tlatoque and thus many of the traditions surrounding their rulership as a means of efficiently ensuring the extraction of tribute payments (in goods and

labor) to the encomenderos or other officials in question. It was also an efficient means of diminishing the risk of uprisings against their authority (Baudot 1995, 42–57; Gibson 1964, especially 32–97, 155–93; Pérez-Rocha and Tena
2000b, 20–29). Gibson (1964, 32–97) and Lockhart (1992, 14–58) note that
although the Spanish system did entail a good amount of social and political continuity from the preconquest period, the former altepetl structure
could not be transferred wholesale into the encomienda without suffering
some disruption. The colonial period witnessed a great deal of maneuvering
for "cabecera" (a tribute-receiving regional "capital") status between towns
or settlements,[18] as well as lots of petitions and legislation regarding tribute
payments, especially as the population became smaller and there were fewer
hands to produce the goods and provide the ever-increasing amount of labor
demanded by the Spanish. Early ethnographic research by the Franciscans
(as well as lay persons) into the pre-Hispanic tribute system and the authority
and succession rites of rulers, therefore, as Baudot (1995, 49) reminds us, was
begun at least in part in response to requests by the Crown.

The Franciscan friars had their own reasons for engaging in ethnographic
research, of course: to understand indigenous society well enough to be able
to detect and eradicate all manifestations of "idolatry" while preserving those
aspects of the Nahua world that, in their view, conformed in an exemplary
way with the ideals of early Christianity and that therefore boded well for
their missionary and doctrinal efforts. These efforts were rooted in the Franciscan tradition, and at least in the early days, evidence suggests, more specifically in a strain of Franciscan millennialist theology aimed at establishing the
terrestrial paradise or the millennial reign of the saints on earth that would
precede the final judgment and the end of time (Baudot 1995, 187–89; Phelan
1970, 5–16; Gruzinski 1991, 74–75; Serna and Castany 2014, 70–79). The dialogue that the Franciscans began with the sons of Nahua nobility, as primary
targets in early evangelical and educational campaigns, cannot be separated
from the friars' theologically motivated vision of the "New World" (with its
humble and unselfish inhabitants) as a *locus amoenus* and site for the renewal
of Christianity.

These friars not only supported the upholding of the rights and privileges of the old indigenous nobility, they envisioned a time when ceremonies
of rulership succession could be reinstituted in a Christian-Indian context
overseen by friars, both indigenous and Spanish (Baudot 1995, 187–89). As
Baudot has noted, friar Andrés de Olmos was heavily implicated in Viceroy Mendoza's attempt to revive the title of teuhctli and institute an order of
"Tecle Knights" as a means of rewarding sincere Christian conversion and

leadership among indigenous officials. As far as the Franciscans were concerned, he writes,

> The Indians, because of their radical novelty, and also because of their intrinsic qualities, seemed to be the providential ideal foundation upon which to construct the new Church and the new community. Therefore it was important to preserve their originality by using the barrier of their language and customs. To do so, it was imperative to find out which particulars of their pre-Columbian social organization should be retained after they had been cleansed of any religious connection. Olmos devoted the second half of his work to that task. One relatively short part, in comparison with others, involved two topics: that of the ceremonies and customs that regulated access to political power and to the ruling class, and that of the education of children. Olmos, aware of the inadequate time at his disposal to investigate these topics, concentrated on the most important aspects. . . . A knowledge of the rules for succession to the throne in the three capitals of the triple alliance . . . and a description of the accession ceremonies to the supreme power, could later be very useful if one day a future Mexican monarch were to be installed by a ritual ceremony (a ceremony that had been cleansed and corrected, of course). Such a ceremony would assure a certain continuity by virtue of its links to the traditions recognized as authentic by the native population. The very suspicious attitude of the Spanish Crown toward the descendents of the Mexica emperor who met Cortés, the tlatoani Motecuhzoma Xocoyotzin, showed that the Council of the Indies had never completely discarded the possibility of such an event. (189)

This attitude, however, very quickly became suspect in many sectors of Spanish society, which increasingly saw the threat that the empowered religious orders, with their authority over and work with the indigenous communities, represented: first, to the power of the secular church and its authority; second, to the interests of Spanish colonists vying for "freer" or unhindered labor; and, finally, to Spanish rule as a whole. The friars' work on indigenous languages and cultures, particularly the effort to understand indigenous religious traditions and use aspects of them to "translate" Christian doctrine, was associated with "messianic" resistance movements and feared for its potential to inspire other movements envisioning a return to indigenous sovereignty and the rights of the "natural lords." As Gruzinski (1991, 74) puts it,

Los franciscanos habían soñado con una Nueva España en que sólo los indios y ellos pusieran las bases de una nueva cristiandad, se habían esforzado por servir de pantalla protectora entre las poblaciones sometidas y los conquistadores, habían tratado de difundir las técnicas de Occidente al mismo tiempo que conservaban lo que podía recibirse de las antiguas culturas. Como hemos visto, inspiraron muchas de las actividades, de las tentativas, de los compromisos que rodearon la definición de una cultura indocristiana.

The Franciscans had dreamed of a New Spain in which only they and the Indians would lay the foundations of a new Christianity. They had made every effort to serve as a protective screen between the subjected populations and the conquistadores, and they had tried to spread Western ways at the same time that they preserved what could be received from the ancient cultures. As we have seen, they inspired many of the activities, efforts, and compromises associated with the definition of an Indo-Christian culture.

Nevertheless, he writes, the early alliance with the indigenous elite became complicated by the very proliferation of "principales que no debían nada ni a la 'sangre' ni a la 'antigüedad'" (ibid.; nobility that owed nothing to either "blood" or "antiquity"). For Gruzinski, it was an alliance that was made impossible, in the final analysis, due to the great population losses of the sixteenth and early seventeenth centuries. It was this devastation, he notes, and the resulting changes in power relationships in the colonial system that "contribuyeron pues a detener el pleno desarrollo de una cultura original que lograba integrar la aportación cristiana y europea a un acervo y una tradición autóctonos. Pues era una cultura que moría a medida que surgía" (75; helped to stop in midstream the full development of an original culture that attempted to integrate Christian and European contributions and an autochthonous tradition. For it was a culture that was dying as fast as it emerged).

GOBERNADORES AND THE GOBERNADORYOTL

In the mid-sixteenth century, when the Crown changed the system of governance in indigenous pueblos, instituting the office of gobernador, or the gobernadoryotl, and imposed the Spanish-style cabildo, it often resulted in the alienation of the ruling line from official community governance and therefore also from the larger pueblo or community it used to serve. Unsurprisingly, the Nahuas resisted much of the potential shock of the new form by transferring, as Lockhart (1992, 31) puts it, the "aura, powers, and characteristics of the preconquest rulership," including the characteristic of lifetime tenure, to the gobernadoryotl. The traditional tlatoani (or cacique) now became gobernador as well; in filling the position, this person acted as the "fulcrum," to use Lockhart's term, joining the old system to the new one, as happened in the case of San Juan Teotihuacan under don Fernando Verdugo Quetzalmamalitzin Huetzin. However, as Schroeder (1991, 186) points out, "The first governor of an altepetl was almost always its tlatoani, but when the governorship began to rotate, others might come to hold it, and the two offices diverged, the governorship gradually gaining power and the dynastic tlatocayotl losing it."

As the altepetl suffered fracture and indigenous pueblos eventually gained new (or new-old) leadership from other local lords and nobles, the fate of the highly significant traditional institution of the tlatocayotl—in its sense of a titled lineage with specific relationship to local social organization, and to the larger community and its rites and customs—becomes difficult to trace. Schroeder (1991, 186) points out, for example, that while Chimalpahin respected the work of the cabildos and gobernadores as a "serious parallel" or "substitute" for the tlatocayotl, he expressed displeasure when persons outside of the principal dynastic line, "lesser nobility" or commoners (no matter how highly educated), were placed in positions of power. The Nahua pueblos clearly tried to preserve their tlatocayotl, in its sense of rulership as a dynastic lineage or tlatocatlacamecayotl, for as long as possible. It seems, however, that in time, as Lockhart (1992, 32) states, "dynastic rulership would inevitably lose some of its meaning."[19]

By the period of independence, the power of the remaining caciques seems largely to have been rooted in wealth, with no evidence that their relationship to the pueblos differed in any respect from the typical labor relations of the haciendas, or that the title of cacique and the institution of the cacicazgo in any way embodied or carried on concepts and roles associated with pre-Hispanic rulership. As Pérez-Rocha and Tena (2000b, 72) put it, the noble class as a whole lost their distinction in one of two ways: either through Hispanization—hanging onto prestige through imitation of Spanish cultural models—or "macehualicization," losing prestige altogether and blending into the fabric of common(er) life:

Como se ha visto, la desintegración de la sociedad prehispánica rompió, primero, la estructura político-territorial de sus señoríos, e, internamente, alteró la relación entre linaje, tierra, macehual de las casas señoriales o teccalli, en el caso de que éstas existieran en todos los señoríos de la Cuenca, hecho que se dio sobre todo cuando perdieron uno de sus elementos básicos, la tierra, al cual ya no tuvieron fácil acceso, para posteriormente perder el derecho al servicio y tributo de sus macehuales. . . . Puede decirse que, en su afán por preservar sus derechos y privilegios provenientes de la época prehispánica, los nobles indígenas se mantuvieron en una constante lucha; no obstante, poco a poco perdieron toda fuerza política y económica. A su vez, el proceso de aculturación efectuó cambios notables en la nobleza indígena, en su educación, vestido, hábitos, costumbres y demás. Su deseo de asimilarse a la sociedad novohispana hizo que cada día se desligaran más de sus comunidades; unos lograron su propósito, e incluso rebasaron la meta fijada y se establecieron en España; otros perecieron en el intento, y se borró su rastro como nobles indígenas, en un doloroso proceso de macehualización.

As has been seen, the disintegration of pre-Hispanic society ruptured, first, the political-territorial structure of their estates, and, internally, changed the relationship between lineage, land, macehual [commoner] of the noble houses or teccalli (if these [latter institutions] existed in all of the regions of the Basin), a fact which occurred above all when they lost one of their basic elements, the land, to which they no longer had easy access, only to later lose the right to service and tribute from their macehuales. . . . It is possible to say that, in their quest to preserve their rights and privileges deriving from the pre-Hispanic period, the indigenous nobles were engaged in a constant struggle; nevertheless, little by little they lost all political and economic power. At the same time, the process of acculturation created notable changes in the indigenous nobility, in their education, dress, habits, traditions, and everything else. Their desire to assimilate to the society of New Spain made it so that day by day they detached themselves more and more from their communities; some achieved their purpose, and even surpassed the goal by settling in Spain; other perished in the intent, and their trace as indigenous nobles was lost in a painful process of "macehualicization."

Despite the debilitation and apparent disappearance of the institution of the tlatocayotl, however, its importance in the pre-Hispanic altepetl and its implication in the doctrinal and ethnographic work of the Franciscans in the early years of the colony ensured that its loss did not happen quickly.

FRANCISCANS IN ACOLHUACAN: EARLY ETHNOGRAPHY AND NAHUA HISTORIOGRAPHY

From the very beginning of Spanish presence in the New World, strong ties were developed between the first Franciscan missionaries and the Acolhua region (Baudot 1995; Lesbre 1995; Ramírez López 2014, especially 20–34). In 1523 at the invitation of Fernando Cortés Ixtlilxochitl, three Flemish Franciscans, the friars Juan de Tecto, Juan de Agora, and Pedro de Gante, established the order's first monastery and missionary educational institution for children in the former palace of Nezahualpilli. Eventually, after the arrival of the famous twelve a year later, the Franciscan order founded a school for young men, mostly the sons of Acolhua nobility, in the San Antonio monastery of Tetzcoco, where generations were trained in Christian doctrine and European forms of literacy (Lesbre 1995, 167–69).

As Lesbre (1995, 169) makes clear, the response to this colonial agenda in Tetzcoco was complex. On the one hand, he cites clear evidence in the work of Torquemada and other documents that the students were also trained as *tlacuiloque* (singular tlacuilo; scribes or painters), and that at least some of the nobles sent proxies to the schools in place of their own children (including the tlatoani of Tetzcoco mentioned in the introduction, don Carlos Ometochtzin, who was burned at the stake in 1539 for practicing idolatry).[20] On the other hand, he specifies the decidedly regional pride with which Alva Ixtlilxochitl claims Tetzcoco as the place where Christianity took root in New Spain. As he puts it, "les affirmations d'Alva Ixtlilxochitl en matière de catholicité sont empreintes d'un régionalisme exacerbé, cherchant à tout prix à faire de Tezcoco le champion mexicain de la conversion et de l'évangélisation: premiers baptêmes, première église, premier synode, premier mariage chrétien, etc." (168; Alva Ixtlilxochitl's claims regarding Catholicism have a distinctly regionalist bent, and are aimed above all at making Tetzcoco the Mexican champion of the conversion and evangelization process: the place of the first baptisms, the first church, the first synod, the first Christian marriage, etc.).

Most significant for Lesbre (1995), however, is the fact that these first students educated in the European system took their knowledge back to their communities and taught their elders to write in the European forms and genres, an act that laid the foundation for the first alphabetic narratives and histories of the pre-Hispanic and conquest periods of Acolhuacan. Thus, while the Franciscan efforts resulted in Christian indoctrination, they also provided the Tetzcoco nobility with the ability to write books "destinés avant tout à préserver leur passé et leur culture" (170; destined, above all else, to preserve their past and their culture).[21] Although this new learning was primarily based in the Franciscan-run local school, a small segment of especially talented students were sent to the elite school for indigenous scholars, the College of Santa Cruz de Tlatelolco, in Mexico City. Students from Acolhuacan, writes Lesbre, played instrumental roles in the early cultural and literary ethnographic projects of the Franciscans, as key participants, for example, in Olmos's research in Nahua communities (1533–1539), in the work of the *Primeros memoriales* overseen by Sahagún in Tepepulco (1559–1561), in the construction of Molina's dictionary, and as producers of many works of cultural and literary translation from Latin and Castilian into Nahuatl. As he puts it,

> Ainsi se constitua une nouvelle élite d'indiens lettrés à l'occidentale, succédant aux tlacuilos. Ils jouèrent un rôle considérable dans la compilation de documents et traditions préhispaniques, mais aussi dans l'accès des chroniqueurs religieux espagnols à la culture indigène. La plupart d'entre eux furent en effet les collaborateurs zélés d'Olmos, Sahagun, Molina, contribuant ainsi à la préservation de l'historiographie préhispanique. (171)

> In this way a new group of indigenous elite, educated in the Western tradition, successors to the tlacuilos, was formed. They played a considerable role in the compilation of pre-Hispanic documents and traditions, but also in the Spanish friars' access to indigenous culture. The majority of them were in effect the zealous collaborators of Olmos, Sahagún, [and] Molina, contributing in this way to the preservation of pre-Hispanic historiography.

As Baudot (1995, 121–245) has argued, Olmos was responsible for collecting and recording some of the earliest material related to pre-Hispanic religious life, including some of the major cosmogonic texts and information on principal deities and religious practices. The *Historia de los mexicanos por sus pinturas* and the *Histoyre du Mechique*, he postulates, were copied from

Olmos's now-lost *Tratado de antigüedades mexicanas* (193–208). This suggests that the cosmogonies and Tolteca histories as Alva Ixtlilxochitl tells and retells them in the course of his career are the product of the long dialogue between Nahua historians (some of them from the Acolhua region) and Franciscan missionaries.

Certainly the works of these early friars, those associated with Olmos in particular, which were inherited and recapitulated by Torquemada, provide essential reference points against which both Alva Ixtlilxochitl's and Torquemada's historical vision, their manner of translating the history of Anahuac into the form of the European universal history, can be seen to part ways.[22] As mentioned earlier, Quetzalcoatl and Tezcatlipoca, the two rival creator gods and protagonists of the Nahua cosmogonies, were patrons of rulers and rulership, and Tezcatlipoca himself was the patron deity of Tetzcoco and an "ancestor" of the Acolhua. It is a historical figure (or set of figures) often called Quetzalcoatl, not the deity Tezcatlipoca, however, that eventually receives most of the attention of the friars and later historians who record the activities of a Tolteca ruler, also referred to as Huemac, Ce Acatl (One Reed) or (in some non-Acolhua accounts) as Topiltzin, who embodied Christian-like values and characteristics, such as resistance to human sacrifice, acts of penitence, and the establishment of laws (Lafaye [1977] 1995).

In *The Aztec Kings*, Susan Gillespie (1989, 173–230) argues for the retrospective construction of certain aspects of Tolteca history after—and in light of—the Spanish conquest. In her structuralist interpretation of the accounts, she makes the case that the story of the defeat, exile, disappearance, deification, and promised return of a great Tolteca ruler, eventually named Ce Acatl Topiltzin Quetzalcoatl, evolved gradually from both Spanish and Nahua sources in response to both cultures' needs for a "satisfactory" explanation or justification of the conquest. Camilla Townsend (2003) has used this point to argue against the commonplace notion that the Nahuas on the eve of the Spanish arrival were actually captivated with a sense of "fatalism" engendered by portents of doom and a mistaken identification of Cortés with this "Quetzalcoatl" figure. As Townsend emphasizes, scholars have overwhelmingly bought into that narrative, almost ubiquitously reading the "fully developed" (Ce Acatl Topiltzin) Quetzalcoatl figure back into the early narratives where he doesn't exist, or where he exists only in part. The *Historia de la nación chichimeca*, as we will see, certainly plays its part in cementing the notion that the Nahuas took Cortés to be a returning ruler/deity.

Before telling *that* story, however, it is imperative to finish the one at hand, to explore the fate of Teotihuacan's tlatocayotl—and the possible traces of an ancient connection between rulers and deities—in the life and documents of Francisco Verdugo Quetzalmamalitzin Huetzin. This is a story in which only hints and faint clues are visible, however, and whose backbone— the family ties and material, social, and economic alliances and disputes between the cacique-gobernador (and his heirs) and the San Juan Teotihuacan principales or governing elite—remains to be fully examined. Of these clues and relations, I limit myself to an overview of what the testamento of Alva Ixtlilxochitl's noble progenitor can reveal.

Here, in the legacy of rulership left by Alva Ixtlilxochitl's great-grandfather, I argue, the roots of the diglossic expression of the ruler's power in the *Historia de la nación chichimeca* can be found.

Part Two. The Life and Documents of Francisco Verdugo Quetzalmamalitzin Huetzin: A Nahua-Christian Tlatocayotl?

A NAHUA-CHRISTIAN LIFE

As a member of a Nahua ruling line, and the appointed successor to be installed as ruler at Teotihuacan, it would seem that Francisco Verdugo Quetzalmamalitzin Huetzin's education would have been carefully attended to by the San Juan Teotihuacan pueblo as well as its Franciscan priests. He does not appear to have received a formal Spanish education (outside of religious instruction), however, given the fact that at the conclusion of his testamento he asks the guardian of the monastery (Alonso de Vera) to sign the document on his behalf, "porque yo no sé escribir" (Pérez-Rocha and Tena 2000a, 269– 71; O'Gorman 1975–1977, 2:285–86; because I do not know how to write). The ties between Franciscans and San Juan Teotihuacan were strong, moreover, as evidenced by the rebellion from 1557 to 1559, led by Francisco Verdugo Quetzalmamalitzin Huetzin, against the Church's attempt to place Augustinian instead of Franciscan friars in charge of the local ministry (O'Gorman [1975–1977] 1985, 1:13).[23] On the surface, his life suggests an early and intentional Hispanization of the role of ruler alongside an equally intentional and successful effort to ally his pueblo with Spanish officials and the colonial endeavor as a whole. Careful consideration of the larger context of his upbringing, however, indicates a more complicated picture, and the ultimate inadequacy of the false "rupture vs. continuity" opposition, discussed by Lockhart (1991, 159–82), in assessing his life and work.

As stated above, according to Pérez-Rocha and Tena (2000, 45), the San Juan Teotihuacan nobility or pipiltin, in keeping with long-standing tradition, went to Tetzcoco to ask the ruler of Acolhuacan to appoint Francisco Verdugo Quetzalmamalitzin Huetzin to the position. Later that year, the Real Audiencia confirmed the appointment and the cacicazgo itself, "en todo su señorío, con sus tierras, tributarios y gobierno" (Münch 1976, 10; with its complete estate, with its lands, tribute-payers, and government). Some years thereafter, he married Ana Cortés Ixtlilxochitl (the daughter of Fernando Cortés Ixtlilxochitl), a marriage ordered by Archbishop Zumárraga (Pérez-Rocha and Tena 2000, 45, 61–63).[24] He went on to provide military service to the Crown in its ever-expanding conquest of New Spain, furnishing the Spanish with troops and supplies and participating alongside Viceroy Mendoza in the quelling of indigenous revolts in the region of Nueva Galicia, as testimony from a probanza (legal questionnaire or inquiry) in his favor evidences (203–10).

A paragraph from one of the witnesses sums up the gist of the information provided by all three witnesses, "indyanos vezinos" of Mexico City (Pérez-Rocha and Tena 2000, 206; Indian residents). According to Bernardino de Castañeda, don Francisco Verdugo Quetzalmamalitzin Huetzin, along with his father and other relatives, are loyal vassals of the king. He further testifies that

> Dicho don Francisco es muy amigo de españoles e sienpre les favoresçe e ayuda en todo lo que puede, dándoles dineros y de comer y ospedándoles muy bien, e haze muchos serviçios a frailes religiosos, y es muy honrado y buen christiano y muy devoto de Dios, y castiga los yndios que no son buenos christianos, y se trata como cavallero y tiene armas y cavallos continuamente para servir a su Magestad quando se ofresçe, e por tal es avido y tenido y comúnmente reputado entre todos los que le conosçen como este testigo. (207)

> Said don Francisco is a good friend of the Spanish and always favors and helps them in every way he can, giving them money and things to eat and hosting them very well; he performs many services for the religious friars, and he is very honorable and a good Christian and very devoted to God; he punishes the Indians who are not good Christians; he is regarded as a gentleman, and he always has arms and horses to serve your Majesty when possible and he is considered, understood

and commonly reputed as such among everyone who knows him, like this witness.

At the same time, however, the traditional petition to the Tetzcoca Chichimeca teuhctli for accession to the rulership, his marriage to the daughter of don Fernando Cortés Ixtlilxochitl, and the particular nature of his service (military) to the Spanish (who were, in a sense, the new overlords of Tetzcoco) suggest that his alliance (and excellent relations) with the Spanish was not regarded so much in terms of siding with an outsider but as a continuation of an official duty that reached back to preconquest times, in fact to the early days of rulership of Teotihuacan, and to after Nezahualcoyotl's restoration of Tetzcoca rule in the wake of the defeat of the Tepaneca. According to Alva Ixtlilxochitl, Quetzalmamalitzin, don Francisco Verdugo Quetzalmamalitzin's Huetzin's great-grandfather, was "uno de los catorce grandes y capitán general del reino de Tetzcuco" (1975–1977, 2:145; one of the fourteen greats [i.e., lords of the Tetzcoco altepetl] and captain general of the realm of Tetzcoco).[25] At one point, as the story goes, he even rescued Axayacatl, the Mexica ruler, wounded seriously in the leg and nearly captured by the ruler of Xiquipilco. For his valiant rescue, writes Alva Ixtlilxochitl, the rulers of the Triple Alliance granted him a coat of arms bearing the leg of a ruler with flames emanating from the thigh. Moreover, according to both O'Gorman ([1975–1977] 1985, 1:9) and Münch (1976, 9–10), Xiuhtototzin, don Francisco Verdugo Quetzalmamalitzin Huetzin's father, died fighting alongside Fernando Cortés Ixtlilxochitl and the Spanish while fleeing Tenochtitlan in 1520. Münch (1976, 9), in addition, relates that during the wars against the Tepaneca, the first independent ruler of Teotihuacan, Huetzin, fought bravely defending Tetzcoco for Nezahualcoyotl. When the war was over and the rulership restored to Tetzcoco, Nezahualcoyotl gave him one of his daughters to marry—beginning the long-standing tradition of intermarriage between the daughters of Tetzcoco's rulers and the Teotihuacan lords, which ended with the marriage of Francisco Verdugo Quetzalmamalitzin Huetzin to Fernando Cortés Ixtlilxochitl's daughter, doña Ana Cortés Ixtlilxochitl (Carrasco 1974).[26]

The testamento (Münch 1976, 44–46; Pérez-Rocha and Tena 2000a, 261–77; Alva Ixtlilxochitl 1975–1977, 2:281–86) provided by don Francisco Verdugo Quetzalmamalitzin Huetzin in 1563, shortly before his death, also suggests that cultural convergence and adaptation were a matter of deliberate strategy for this early colonial ruler of San Juan Teotihuacan. The most legally and economically significant aspect of the testamento is that it established a solid foundation under Spanish jurisprudence (under the laws of primogeniture) for his heir to inherit as (entailed) family property lands formerly held by and worked for the rulers and those associated with the temples of the altepetl. It accomplished this in large part through a careful and detailed denotation of these land types (including a separate addendum to the testamento that specifically lists them according to type and location [Pérez-Rocha and Tena 2000a, 279]).

Through this document, and its careful specification of the land types of the former altepetl, Francisco Verdugo Quetzalmamalitzin Huetzin prevented the lands from being broken up, keeping them in the possession of his direct descendents and out of the hands of those who eventually laid claim to them—Spaniards, members of the San Juan Teotihuacan pueblo, as well as its encomenderos. His testamento, moreover, in particular its opening section providing for his funerary rites, when read in light of the importance attributed to these rites as signs of cultural identification and transition in Alva Ixtlilxochitl's histories (and colonial ethnohistorical accounts more generally), provides a point of reference for thinking about the fate of the traditional nonterrestrial, or religious, aspects of Nahua rulership under the tenure of don Francisco Verdugo Quetzalmamalitzin Huetzin, to consider how he may have regarded and managed the connection of the tlatocayotl to the ancestor-deities and the Nahua cosmogonic tradition as those concepts and stories were being reworked in the encounter with Catholicism.

A NAHUA-CHRISTIAN DEATH: A COLONIAL CACIQUE'S FUNERARY RITES

The testamento begins in typical fashion for a wealthy early modern Catholic subject, with a brief introduction in which the cacique and gobernador commends his soul to God and the Virgin Mary, and asks that his body be returned in a Christian burial to the "madre tierra pues a ella pertenece" (mother earth because to her it belongs).[27] He then requests (and dedicates funds for) a number of masses and prayers to be said on his behalf (the first one, notably, by the priest of the "casa de nuestra señora Santa María de Guadalupe" [the home of our Lady St. Mary of Guadalupe]). Finally, right before stating his bequests, he asks to be buried in a habit donated by the Franciscans:

Item, ruego encarecidamente a los padres que están en este pueblo y
a mi padre fray Alonso [Vera] que me den por caridad un hábito con
que mi cuerpo sea enterrado, y confío en que me harán este favor como
hijos de señor San Francisco. (265)

Item, I beg that the fathers who are in this town, and my father friar
Alonso [Vera], donate a habit with which to bury my body, and I trust
that they will do me this favor as sons of lord Saint Francis.

Although an ordinary request, especially of a faithful devotee of the Franciscan order, it is illuminating to contemplate it in the context of the attention
given to funerary rites and to attire (both Tolteca and Chichimeca) in Alva
Ixtlilxochitl's texts, where, differently to their representation in the *Monarquía
indiana*, descriptions of rulers' obsequies play a predominant role in marking the Chichimeca acceptance and adoption of Tolteca traditions, including
their symbolization of the ruler's connection to the (Tolteca-associated) gods
(Tezcatlipoca, Quetzalcoatl, and Huitzilopochtli).[28]

In the *Sumaria relación de todas las cosas de la Nueva España*, Alva Ixtlilxochitl ([1975–1977] 1985, 1:341) is careful to mention that the hasty funerary
rites celebrated after the elder Ixtlilxochitl's assassination by the Tepaneca
were the *first*, albeit abridged, rites celebrated by the Chichimeca rulers in the
Tolteca style.[29] Instead of receiving a burial with his proper insignia or attire
in his palace, as did Xolotl, Ixtlilxochitl's body was cremated on a pyre.[30] (It
was recovered by Chichíquil, a Tolteca gentleman from the barrio of the Tlailotlaque, an altepetl subgroup whose people, according to Alva Ixtlilxochitl,
brought many Tolteca traditions to Acolhuacan, including artisanry and Tezcatlipoca's sacred bundle.) A few chapters later in the text, Alva Ixtlilxochitl
undertakes a thorough description of the first *full* set of Tolteca rites to be
provided for a Chichimeca ruler, in this case, Tezozomoc, the great Tepaneca tyrant himself. Here, Alva Ixtlilxochitl explicitly notes that the rites, first
established by Topiltzin, were performed in honor of Tezcatlipoca. Referring
to Tezozomoc, he writes,

Los señores sus vasallos y los sacerdotes, pusieron un velo a Tezcatlipoca, ídolo principal o señor de todos los ídolos de la tierra, como entre
los gentiles romanos a Júpiter, que era señal de gran sentimiento. Y esta
ceremonia fue ordenada de Topiltzin, que cuando el rey enfermaba le

ponían si era el monarca, a Tezcatlipuca un velo, y no se lo quitaban hasta que moría o sanaba. (350–51)

The lords his vassals and the priests established a vigil to Tezcatlipoca, the principal idol or lord of all of the idols of the land, like Jupiter among the Roman gentiles, which was a sign of great sentiment. And this ceremony was ordered by Topiltzin, so that when a ruler got sick, if he was the monarch they held a vigil to Tezcatlipoca and did not end it until he died or was cured.

The funeral rite celebrated after Tezozomoc's death involved wrapping the body in layers of cloth, placing a turquoise mask over the face, cremation with *ocote* wood and *copal* in the patio of the *templo mayor* (great temple) dedicated to Tezcatlipoca, and the sacrifice of slaves. At its conclusion, the body's ashes were thrown by priests into a carefully constructed and carved chest, which was then placed beside an altar dedicated to Tezcatlipoca.[31]

Although at the close of the chapter Alva Ixtlilxochitl promises to describe the increase in the practice of human sacrifice as evidenced in the funerary rites of Nezahualcoyotl and Nezahualpilli, he never follows through with the promise, as the narrative ends without depicting Nezahualcoyotl's death ([1975–1977] 1985, 1:353).[32] In the *Historia de la nación chichimeca*, moreover, Alva Ixtlilxochitl glosses over the practice with a simple "Otro día después de haber fallecido Nezahualcoyotzin se le hicieron sus honras y exequias con grande pompa y majestad, conforme a los ritos de los mexicanos, que por hallarse escritos en los autores modernos, no se hace particular mención" (1975–1977, 2:138; The day after Nezahualcoyotzin had died, they performed his honors and obsequies with great pomp and majesty, in conformity with the Mexica rites, of which, because they can be found in the modern authors, no particular mention is made). A brief description of Nezahualpilli's rites, including the specific number of slaves sacrificed in the event, however, is included in the *Historia de la nación chichimeca* (1975–1977, 2:188)[33] and is also among the documents appended to the *Sumaria relación de las cosas de la Nueva España* ([1975–1977] 1985, 1:386).[34] Following this latter appended document, moreover, appears the slightly longer descriptive summary of the rites of Topiltzin, who, as Alva Ixtlilxochitl reiterates in the fifth relación ([1975–1977] 1985, 1:282), established the practices in the first place.

Given the title "La orden y ceremonia para hacer a uno señor, las cuales constituyó Topiltzin, señor de Tula es lo que se sigue" (The rite and ceremony to make someone a lord, which were instituted by Topiltzin, lord of Tula, is what follows), the summary begins by describing the rites of inauguration of rulers but quickly jumps into a brief narration of the story of Topiltzin's departure and promise to return ([1975–1977] 1985, 1:387). The story coincides with the much longer version that Alva Ixtlilxochitl tells in the opening accounts of the *Sumaria relación de todas las cosas* dedicated to Tolteca history, except in two important areas: it states that he was worshipped as an idol in many towns or places where he left followers behind, and that people took the newly arrived Spaniards to be the returning Topiltzin because they arrived in the same year in which the latter had promised to return from the east. After this interlude, however, the document abruptly turns to a discussion of his obsequies, returning, in a sense, to the theme with which it began: the description of the Tolteca ceremonies whereby Chichimeca rulers confirmed and validated their rulership. While the inaugural rites associated with the taking of office open the selection, the funerary rites associated with its leave-taking conclude it, perhaps, as Townsend (2014, 9) suggests, as a means of emphasizing that Topiltzin did, indeed, die.

In the longer version of Topiltzin's story in the fifth relación of the Tolteca accounts within the *Sumaria relación de todas las cosas*, as Townsend (2014) and Lesbre (2000) have pointed out, Alva Ixtlilxochitl ([1975–1977] 1985, 1:283) expresses his consternation at the "popular" belief, similar to that of the Portuguese regarding King Sebastian, that Topiltzin (along with Nezahualcoyotl and Nezahualpilli) remained in Xicco (a cave where he had taken refuge in flight from his enemies), and would, at any moment, emerge to rescue his people. For Townsend, the insistence on Topiltzin's death and the display of his funeral rites signals Alva Ixtlilxochitl's early adherence to the "ancient" histories over the popular "superstitions" that developed in the colonial period. In her view, the idea of a still-alive Topiltzin who would someday return and "avenge" his usurped rulership is a distortion of pre-Hispanic beliefs similar to his eventual association with the god Quetzalcoatl, and then with Cortés and the Spanish, in a story that sought to explain the conquest in part as a case of fatalism, providentialism, and mistaken identity (9–13). Lesbre (2000, par. 91–97), however, emphasizes that Alva Ixtlilxochitl's revelation of the "popular" belief suggests the existence of a Nahua version of the Andean Inkarrí narrative, in which a previously defeated king would return to reconstitute Inca sovereignty.

In fact, Alva Ixtlilxochitl's insistence on Topiltzin's death would not necessarily indicate a supposedly non-"superstitious" approach to historiography (or a European "rationality") or suggest a departure from the structure implied in an Inkarrí-type narrative. Yet, even taking into account Alva Ixtlilxochitl's usual tendency to suppress or rationalize (for a European readership) the more "fantastical" and/or unorthodox aspects of his source texts (Lesbre 1999a), at this point he simply does not seem to be aware of the fact that a funerary cremation at Tlapalan might, in its own way, represent (or have been constructed to represent) similar (and perhaps related) "superstitions" (and/or "idolatry") on the part of the Tolteca parent culture he is describing. In other words, he does not as yet appear to have contemplated the relationship between the burials he describes and the more profound nature of timekeeping and temporality as represented in the Tolteca cosmogonies and in the Nahua calendar—something of which, as I argue, can be attested to in the *Historia de la nación chichimeca*—despite the fact that he presents an important version of the Tolteca story of the four ages of creation in the first relación ([1975–1977] 1985, 1:263–65) of the *Sumaria relación de todas las cosas*.

In any case, we should not lose sight of the fact that the initial story of Topiltzin that Alva Ixtlilxochitl ([1975–1977] 1985, 1:282–83) tells (in the *Sumaria relación de todas las cosas*) does speak of a prophecy of leave-taking and return on the date ce acatl, even if this early narrative of the destruction of the Tolteca makes a distinction between Topiltzin's pronouncement of a leave-taking and prophecy to return (made to the Culhuas at Tlapalan) and his death and cremation (also at Tlapalan) many years later. Moreover, the description of Topiltzin's funeral rites in the appended document accomplishes more than a mere emphasis on his death. In fact, it constitutes an important venue in which the identity of the great Tolteca ruler is assimilated to that of the figure of Quetzalcoatl as twin and opposed double of the trickster Tezcatlipoca. In the appended document, the function of Topiltzin as boundary figure and ennobler of rulers pointed out by Susan Gillespie in *The Aztec Kings* (1989, 53, 123–85) is clearly visible in his role as the founder of both the rites of ascension to rulership and the ruler's obsequies. It is not without significance, moreover, that it is the latter ceremony in which Tezcatlipoca—however obliquely—comes into the picture.

In the appended document, Alva Ixtlilxochitl explains how Topiltzin, said to return sometime in the future on the date ce acatl, was cremated, after which time the people "cogieron la ceniza que se hizo de su cuerpo, y echáronla en una bolsa hecha de cuero de tigre, y por esta causa todos los señores que aquel tiempo morían los quemaban" ([1975–1977] 1985, 1:387; took the ash that came from his body and threw it into a bag made from the hide of a tiger, and for that reason they cremated all of the lords who died in that time). If we assume that the "cuero de tigre" referred to in the text is a jaguar skin, as seems logical in this context,[35] its presence would symbolize and invoke the notion of rulership, conjuring the image of Tezcatlipoca and his avatar Tepeyollotl, or "the Heart of the Mountain," (a lord of the night in Nahua calendrics and associated with the jaguar), along with their connection to rulership and sorcery that Guilhem Olivier (2008, 92–97) sets out in his study on Tezcatlipoca. The description's similarities to the longer portrayal of the funeral rites given to Tezozomoc also provides evidence linking it to the image of Tezcatlipoca; although Tezozomoc's ashes are placed in a box in this latter description, Alva Ixtlilxochitl explicitly states numerous times that the rites are dedicated to Tezcatlipoca and that the box is later placed on the altar in the templo mayor dedicated in his honor ([1975–1977] 1985, 1:351). The smoke and incense burned along with the body are, like the jaguar, characteristic symbols of Tezcatlipoca, the Smoking Mirror.[36] The formation of the pyre and the act of cremation in general, moreover, evoke the early cosmogonic stories, collected by the Franciscans, of the gods throwing themselves into the fire to become the sun and moon. In the Tolteca-inspired cosmogonies of the four ages of creation, as in the Tolteca funerary rites practiced by the Acolhua described in Alva Ixtlilxochitl's work, endings and beginnings bear a close relationship: to speak of one is to speak of the other.

Yet, as we have seen, Alva Ixtlilxochitl's histories do not just speak of Tolteca funerary rites, but of the original acceptance of those rites among the Chichimeca descendents of Xolotl. In his analysis of a representation of the funerary bundle of Quinatzin (Xolotl's great-grandson who founded the dynasty in Tetzcoco) in the Mapa Quinatzin, Douglas (2010, 144) writes that it symbolized the rulers' connections with the gods and, in that context, "the shift from the simple nature worship of the Chichimeca nomads to the complex rituals associated with the deities whose avatar he is and the urban polities that they create and sustain through sacrifice." Indeed, the rulers' funerary bundles (Tezozomoc's like that of Topiltzin) resemble in structure the sacred bundles associated with the patron deity of the altepetl as a whole (Douglas 2003, 294). From Xolotl's burial with his royal insignia in a cave (Alva Ixtlilxochitl 1975–1977, 2:23) to Ixtlilxochitl's cremation by the Tlailotlaque at the site of his assassination, rulers' obsequies represent the cultural merger and transition that (most of) the Chichimeca under Xolotl underwent in their encounter with the Tolteca. As such, the rites are an important, but overlooked, signpost of the major narrative thematic—that of cultural encounter—that motivates and undergirds Alva Ixtlilxochitl's representation of the history of Mexico during the late Postclassic period in the *Historia de la nación chichimeca*.

Without any need to speculate on the "sincerity" of the Christianity of Alva Ixtlilxochitl's great-grandfather, then, we can see how his request to be buried in coarse, Christian cloth appears to be entirely in keeping with the kind of diglossia that characterized his actions described above: an outward sense of complete change and total adoption of Spanish ways, combined with an underlying structural consistency and continuity with respect to traditional Nahua ways, indicated precisely by an acceptance of new burial rites. In broad terms, the Franciscan symbols of humility and poverty can be considered in terms of their function as symbols of connection to the sacred. If the new garb indicated in the Catholic tradition humility and poverty of person, its bequeathal also would have implied in that context his sanction by the new priestly class—a tacit acknowledgment, therefore, of the ruler's ongoing, inherent, and religiously derived authority. Indeed, as a means of reaffirming the traditional ruler's power and legitimacy within (and according to the criteria established by) the political and religious ethos of the colonizers, the request is similar to his use of the accoutrement of the Spanish caballero in his military expeditions to Nueva Galicia, mentioned in the probanza (Pérez-Rocha and Tena 2000a, 207), and his successful petition to be granted a coat of arms by the Crown (66, 201–2).

In addition to continuing to signify a connection to the divine in the most general terms, however, there are other faint, but tantalizing, indications that the Christian rites or perceptions of death provided a space for coexistence with indigenous precedents, and that they did not have to be understood in purely European terms; there are hints that some of the old (or new-old) symbols associated with the divine in the (Tolteca-Chichimeca) Nahua tradition could have found a place within the Christian burial rites. For example, Francisco Verdugo Quetzalmamalitzin Huetzin's manner of requesting that his body be returned to the "seno de la madre tierra pues a ella pertenece" (to the heart of mother earth because to her it belongs), of asking for twisted candles to be purchased for a particular mass, and the burning of incense all have possible symbolic resonance in Nahua cultural-religious tradition.[37] Also suggestive is the significance that a habit-like tunic had come or was coming to bear in the colonial Mexican historiographical tradition as the typical attire asso-

ciated with the early Tolteca in general and with the Topiltzin/Quetzalcoatl
figure in particular as the latter was constructed and became swept up in a
providentialist and proto-Christian narrative of the conquest.

Indeed, there is a long history, from Hernán Cortés's *Segunda carta de
relación* to colonial Andean histories (Mazzotti 1996, 252), of implicit and
explicit comparison of Catholic monks and indigenous priests, including
descriptions of rites and practices as well as of their cloaks. In Mexico, however, as many scholars (Gillespie 1989, 173–230; LaFaye [1977] 1995, 211–300;
Lee 2008, 63–67) have pointed out, the image of the Tolteca underwent significant Christianization at the hands of friars searching for signs of the New
World and its people in biblical history. Given this context, it does not seem
unreasonable to think that Francisco Verdugo Quetzalmamalitzin Huetzin's
burial habit—and his pueblo's zealous attachment to the Franciscan friars in
general—served as a symbol or an artifact that expressed or connected him
(and his pueblo) to an ancient, noble Tolteca heritage and identity, even if it
was now a decidedly Christian-influenced vision of such a heritage. While it
is, of course, impossible to prove such an idea, an examination of descriptions
of Tolteca appearance and garb across Alva Ixtlilxochitl's writings, with an eye
to their particular associations (implicit or explicit) with Christian/European
figures, provides a sense of the evolution of Alva Ixtlilxochitl's vision of the
Tolteca accounts and of the relationship of those stories to the (Nahua or
Nahua-Christian) history and religious tradition that came after.

In the *Sumaria relación de todas las cosas*, Alva Ixtlilxochitl describes the
significant cultural attributes of the Tolteca as great artisans and legislators
and emphasizes their status as a people guided by an astrologer/soothsayer
and sage named Huema (or Hueman) whose prophecies and many cultural
contributions to the altepetl were recorded in a great Teoamoxtli ("god-book,"
or holy book, also the Nahuatl term used to refer to the Christian Bible)
handed down by the rulers/priests after his death (and consulted by Topiltzin
as he sought to confirm the signs of the imminent demise of his empire). He
also explicitly establishes their physical commonalities with the Spanish and
links this to their mistaken identity in the conquest:[38]

> Estos reyes eran altos de cuerpo y blancos, barbados como los
> españoles, y por esto los indios, cuando vino el Marqués, entendieron
> que era Topiltzin, como les había dicho que había de volver a cierto
> tiempo con sus vasallos antiguos de sus pasados, y con esta esperanza
> incierta estuvieron hasta la venida de los españoles, digo los simples, y

los que eran tultecas de nación, porque bien sabían los señores de esta tierra, que fue a morir en la provincia de Tlapalan y mandó guardar ciertas leyes, que después los reyes de estas tierras concedieron y guardaron sus vasallos. ([1975–1977] 1985, 1:271)

These kings were tall in body and white, bearded like the Spanish, and for this reason the Indians, when the marquis arrived, thought that it was Topiltzin, as he had told them he would return at a certain time with the ancient followers of his elders, and they remained with this tenuous hope until the arrival of the Spanish; I should say the ignorant ones did, and those who were from the Tolteca nations, because the lords of this land knew very well that he went to die in the province of Tlapalan and ordered certain laws to be obeyed, that later on the kings of these lands accepted, and which their vassals followed.

In addition, in a quote that will be examined in greater detail in chapters 2 and 3, he makes it clear that while the Tolteca were "grandes idólatros" [great idolaters], they did not engage in extensive human sacrifice like the later "mexicanos," by which he meant primarily the Mexica or Mexica-affiliated groups, but also all of the other groups in central Mexico (with the Tetzcoca under Nezahualcoyotl, of course, being a restraining influence). After describing the principal Tolteca deities (in line with the account of Juan Bautista Pomar), including the rites to Tlaloc, Alva Ixtlilxochitl concludes that,

Estos falsos dioses fueron los más principales y antiguos de más de dos mil años de los tultecas, y Tezcatlipuca y Huitzilopuchtli, y otros dioses, fueron después acá ciertos caballeros muy valerosos que los colocaron asimismo por dioses, y aun se halla que Tezcatlipuca fue un gran nigromántico, y fue causa de las grandes persecuciones de los tultecas, aunque es verdad que esta gente fueron grandiosos idólatras, no sacrificaban hombres ni hacían los supersticiosos sacrificios que los mexicanos después usaron. (273)

These false gods were the most important and ancient, from more than two-thousand years ago, of the Tolteca, and Tezcatlipoca and Huitzilopochtli, and other gods, were certain very valiant gentlemen over here, who were later for that reason considered to be gods, and one still finds that Tezcatlipoca was a great enchanter, and caused great travails for

the Tolteca, even though it is true that these people were great idolaters, they didn't sacrifice people or perform the superstitious sacrifices
that the Mexica used afterward.

Finally, the Tolteca and their priests in particular are described in terms that
indicate various similarities to the Catholic friars, an important aspect of
which were their garments:

> Los sacerdotes traían unas túnicas y otras negras que las llevaban hasta
> el suelo con sus capillas con que se tapaban las cabezas; el cabello largo
> entrenzado que llegaba hasta las espaldas, y los ojos siempre los traían
> bajos y humildes; descalzos al tiempo de sus ayunos y cuando estaban
> en el templo, y pocas veces se calzaban sino era cuando iban fuera y jor-
> nada larga; eran castos, no conocían mujeres ningunas, hacían ciertas
> penitencias cada veinte días cuando entraba el mes y el año; hablaban
> poco, enseñaban a los niños y mancebos a buenas costumbres y modo
> de vivir, artes buenas y malas a las que más se inclinaban. (274)

> The priests wore tunics, and other black ones that reached the ground,
> with hoods with which they covered their heads; long braided hair that
> reached their backs, and they focused their eyes always humbly down-
> ward; they were barefoot at the time of their fasts and when they were
> in the temple, and very few times did they put on shoes except when
> they went out and on a long journey; they were chaste, and didn't know
> any women, they performed certain penances every twenty days when
> the month and year began; they spoke little, taught children and young
> men good habits and ways of living, good and bad arts, whichever ones
> they were more inclined to.

Still referring to these rulers, he then comments that they were monog-
amous and, a few pages later, returns to a discussion of Tolteca attire, this
time explicitly making a connection with (and distinction from) the people's
clothing and the robes worn by Catholic friars:

> Asimismo se ponían los tultecas, demás de los vestidos que tengo
> dichos arriba, túnicas como las de los sacerdotes blancas, aunque
> diferentes ni más ni menos, que las túnicas que traen debajo nuestros
> religiosos, porque los sacerdotes, demás de ser como éstas, tienen las

mangas como las de los oidores y ciertas capillas como ya lo tengo declarado arriba. (283)

In the same way, the Tolteca, in addition to the attire I described above, wore white tunics like [those of] the[ir] priests, although different from the tunics that our friars wear beneath [their robes], because the priests' [tunics], in addition to being like these, have sleeves like [those of] judges and certain hoods, as I have stated above.

The resonance (and distinctions) listed in these passages between the Spanish Catholic monks and the Tolteca and their rulers takes an interesting turn in the *Historia de la nación chichimeca*, however, as Alva Ixtlilxochitl (1975–1977, 2:8) introduces a priest-like figure named Quetzalcoatl as a wise and saintly precursor to the Tolteca—an early apostle figure admonishing the inhabitants of the cities of the third age, those of the "ulmecas y xicalancas, y en especial en . . . Cholula, en donde asistió más" (Olmecas and Xicalancas, and especially in . . . Cholula, where he spent most of his time) to follow the "camino de la virtud" (the path of virtue) and avoid "los vicios y pecados" (vices and sins) by following the "leyes y buena doctrina" (laws and good doctrine) that he established. Here, it is a figure named Quetzalcoatl (or, he says, Huemac),[39] "de aspecto grave, blanco y barbado" (of solemn appearance, white and bearded) and whose "vestuario era una túnica larga" (attire was a long tunic), who promises to return on the date ce acatl, not Topiltzin, the last ruler of the Tolteca.[40] Instead of dying at Tlapalan, as in the previous stories, the Topiltzin of this last history simply disappears after the enemies of the starved Tolteca finally defeat them, a detail that indeed suggests his status as a "man-god," a status which, with respect to the popular imagination surrounding Topiltzin's descendents, Nezahualcoyotl and Nezahualpilli, became the subject of Alva Ixtlilxochitl's skepticism and justification in the *Sumaria relación de todas las cosas*. As Gruzinski puts it: "Did the man-god die? He left. He was not born; he returned" (1989, 23).

There is no acknowledgment of this implicit suggestion in the *Historia de la nación chichimeca*, however. Instead, without elaborating on the affair, Alva Ixtlilxochitl simply notes that "el rey Topiltzin se perdió, que nunca más se supo de él; y de dos hijos que tenía sólo el uno, que fue el príncipe Póchotl, lo escapó Tochcueie" (1975–1977, 2:13; the ruler Topiltzin disappeared, and nothing more was ever heard about him; and only one of the two sons that he had, prince Póchotl, was saved by Tochcueie). Of the Tolteca in general, moreover, the *Historia de la nación chichimeca* even changes the previous association of their attire with the Spaniards for a description of their robes as "unas túnicas largas a manera de los ropones que usan los japoneses" (ibid.; long tunics like the long robes the Japanese used). This latter distancing of Tolteca attire from any association with Spaniards or with Catholic monks combines with the new story of a figure named Quetzalcoatl to shift the weight of the history's Christian interpellation into the pre-Tolteca period, a shift whose significance (and sources) will be explored in depth in the next chapter.

For now, however, I point out the way in which Alva Ixtlilxochitl's descriptions of the Tolteca and their attire suggest that Francisco Verdugo Quetzalmamalitzin Huetzin's burial in Franciscan habit could have signified something more precise than the sanction of priests or a connection to (a new rendering of) the sacred. When regarded through the prism of Alva Ixtlilxo-chitl's histories and records of the Tolteca, the cacique and gobernador of San Juan Teotihuacan seems to embody the spirit of the storied Chichimeca from Xolotl's descendents onward—accepting new Tolteca-Christian rites without letting go of the best of the old Tolteca-Chichimeca heritage. In a reversal of Topiltzin's obsequies from the document discussed above, in fact, Francisco Verdugo Quetzalmamalitzin Huetzin is the waning and now dormant (but never eradicated) "Tezcatlipoca" wrapped in "Tolteca" (or "Tolteca-like") garb, as opposed to the Quetzalcoatl-associated Topiltzin enveloped in the jaguar hide associated with Tezcatlipoca. Mirroring the interment of his ancestor Xolotl, moreover, his burial in the (cave-like) sanctuary of the new mother church reverses the change in obsequies made by Alva Ixtlilxochitl's Chi-chimeca ancestors (according to his narrative) from Ixtlilxochitl onward. So viewed, Francisco Verdugo Quetzalmamalitzin Huetzin's burial takes on the quality of a return to an anterior Chichimeca rite. In that sense, it corresponds to the construal of prophecy as historical memory in Alva Ixtlilxochitl's (and his sources') constructions of Nezahualcoyotl's proto-monotheism, and their implication of both an early Chichimeca intuition of and exposure to a Christian (or Christian-like) sense of the sacred and a linear notion of time and history. At the same time, it can be regarded less as a rupture with tradition and a traditional sense of the sacred than as a symbolic rendering of the continuing revolution at the heart of the temporal dynamic of the universe and a manifestation of the specifically accretive, absorptive aftermath of warfare and conquest in the post-Tolteca Nahua world.

As I will show, this stubborn cyclical dynamic makes it way, vis-à-vis the figure of Quetzalcoatl (introduced as a stranger and apostle figure), into the *Historia de la nación chichimeca*, where it constitutes the marked (and therefore underlying) chronotope and historical cosmovision giving shape to and bestowing meaning upon the people, places, and events of the narrative. As stated above, and as Townsend (2003, 670; 2014, 10–11) has duly noted, it is only in his later works that Alva Ixtlilxochitl turns his full attention to the story of a person named Quetzalcoatl. He first appears, however, in the very opening clauses of the narrative's extremely long first sentence, where he identifies him as one of the esteemed "authors" of the region's history (1975–1977, 2:7; Townsend 2003, 670). A careful consideration of this phrase in juxtaposition with a very similar opening sentence in the prologue to Book I of the *Monarquía indiana* (1975, 1:n.p.) is highly instructive about the two historians' respective ways of confronting the literary heterogeneity that defines their task, that is, of negotiating the colonial and cultural divide between the world whose past they are representing and the histories (their source texts) in which that past was constructed on the one hand, and the language, form and audience of European humanist historiography on the other.

Part Three. Nahua Literacy and the *Historia general*: Alva Ixtlilxochitl and Friar Juan de Torquemada as Renaissance Historians

The first line of the *Historia de la nación chichimeca* (1975–1977, 2:7), echoing that of his closely related but shorter *Sumaria relación de la historia general*, begins by stating that

> Los más graves autores y históricos que hubo en la infidelidad de los más antiguos, se halla haber sido Quetzalcoatl el primero; y de los modernos Nezahualcoyotzin rey de Tetzcuco, y los dos infantes de México, Itzcoatzin y Xiuhcozcatzin, hijos del rey Huitzilhuitzin, sin otros muchos que hubo (que en donde fuere necesario los citaré)

> The most solemn authors and historians that lived in the faithless time of the ancients, are found to have been Quetzalcoatl, the first; and of the moderns, Nezahualcoyotzin king of Tetzcoco, and the two princes of Mexico, Itzcoatzin and Xiuhcozcatzin, sons of the king Huitzilhuitzin, without counting the many others that there were (whom I will cite when necessary)

Torquemada ([1723] 1975, 1:n.p.) begins his prologue to Book I of the *Monarquía indiana* in a similar fashion, with a reference to an "ancient and wise historian."[41] It is not a Tolteca or a Nahua historian he references, of course, but Plutarch: "Plutarco, historiador antiguo, y grave (en la Vida de Teseo) comenzando a escribir el curso de sus hazañas, y proezas, no con menos estilo grave, que elegante, dice estas formales palabras" (Plutarch, ancient and solemn historian, (in the Life of Theseus) as he begins to narrate the course of his feats and accomplishments, offers, with as much gravity as elegance, the following distinguished exposition"). With these contrasting formulaic openings, in which cited authors, both "ancient" and "modern," served as arbiters of truth and knowledge, key authorities and sources of wisdom about the world, Alva Ixtlilxochitl and Torquemada signal their immersion in the tradition of Renaissance humanism and assure their readers of the worth and reliability of their respective historical productions.

Under the influence of the humanist scholars, authorship had garnered a new importance within the changed landscape of the European universal history. As in the days of the medieval chronicle, histories had to be truthful narratives of actual past events. In the Renaissance, however, truth became more than ever a function of the work of the historian as a writer and scholar. Historiography, as Ernst Breisach ([1983] 2007, 126–30, 153–95) has pointed out, was no longer a matter of copying and adding onto an already established text, of a paratactical discourse intended only to reflect "the hidden hand of God" at work behind the events of the past. In the context of Renaissance humanist historiography, a truthful narrative, in the absence of the living eyewitness to events, depended upon a historian's firsthand access to a newly (re)discovered panoply of ancient texts that were to be read and translated in their original languages, both primary source texts and those of the classical world whose insights would lend a history legitimacy and perspective, a depth of learning derived from their influence. The new interest in human influence and mundane affairs—in the "secondary" causes and nature of events—thus turned historiography into a task for a new set of scholars whose expertise in languages and mastery of grammar and rhetoric vouchsafed the quality of their now properly *narrative* accounts of the past. As author, the Renaissance historian also had become responsible for establishing the proper order and context of events and the rightful means of relating the sacred and the mundane.

The European discovery of the "New" World, however, posed serious problems for traditional historiography and for this relationship between the sacred and the profane. As Breisach ([1983] 2007, 178) puts it, "In traditional universal histories the family of nations had had both a stable membership and a known ancestral home in the Middle East. But how did the strange inhabitants of the Americas or East Indies fit into that scheme? And fit they had to, because otherwise, universal history would in the past not have been universal and in the present and future would be impossible." The very *absence* of any clear trace of the land or the peoples of the "Americas," of a fourth part of the world, in the biblical and classical record challenged and stretched the previous faith in the age-old sources as founts of truth. The parameters within which fundamental (and ultimately religious) questions of a moral, cosmographical, and anthropological nature were contemplated had to be reworked (Hanke 1970; Pagden 1986). At the heart of these debates over the relative "barbarity" or "civility" of the newly discovered peoples, moreover, was the question of authorship, language, and writing (Mignolo 1995; Pagden 1986).

As Walter Mignolo (1995) has demonstrated, Europe's belief in the superiority of its own form of writing and literacy, rooted in the letter and the book, played an integral role in Spanish imperialism. In the writing of New World history, the historian (and especially the historian of indigenous ancestry) not only had to take a position on the major questions of the day regarding the origins and character or quality (and all the derivative questions) of the people they were writing about, they had to address the "problematic" nature of the nonalphabetic source texts (an indicator of relative barbarism) they relied on to write their own (alphabetic) histories. In order to legitimize their texts, historians of the New World needed to address the skepticism and suspicion that surrounded their sources of information.[42]

As we will see, Torquemada addresses these questions explicitly, and his head-on approach constitutes one of the most significant contrasts with Alva Ixtlilxochitl's writings. While Alva Ixtlilxochitl addresses *some* of these questions in a direct fashion, his approach differs from that of Torquemada. In general, with respect to the *Historia de la nación chichimeca*, Alva Ixtlilxochitl's answers (where he supplies them) are implicit, provided obliquely in the framing of the content of the narrative, specifically his means of representing (and translating) the material of his source texts in the framework of the universal history. Because it is not possible to discuss and compare their respective accounts of *all* of the key moral and philosophical questions that defined the thinking of the period (and which New World historians had to address), I focus here on the question of Nahua literacy. I do so because it receives explicit attention from *both* Alva Ixtlilxochitl and Torquemada. It is the issue that stands at the heart of the difference in the opening phrases of the *Historia de la nación chichimeca* and the *Monarquía indiana* and, most importantly, it is indicative of the way in which the two historians relate fundamentally to the Nahua historical tradition, determining the nature of the latter's imprint on their work.

As is evident from the opening phrases, Alva Ixtlilxochitl's reference to *Tolteca* and *Nahua* rulers as "authors" of ancient and traditional histories does more than signal an immersion in the learned tradition of humanist historiography. It also highlights the worth and legitimacy of *Nahua history as writing*. By making an implicit comparison between these figures and the classical writers of Greece and Rome, Alva Ixtlilxochitl engages what Rolena Adorno (1989) has referred to as his agenda of erasing his ancestors' cultural "otherness," and thereby pithily assures his European readership of the *reliability* of his sources: they are the products of *authors*, people who *write books*. In this sense it offers a direct challenge to the notion of Nahuas as a not-quite-civilized society, whose nonalphabetic forms of recording the past—although extremely sophisticated—were still, in the last analysis, considered to be "preliterate" forms of historicizing.

The *Sumaria relación de la historia general*, likely written around the same time as the *Historia de la nación chichimeca*, begins in a similar fashion except that in this text Alva Ixtlilxochitl does indeed qualify the notion of authorship, specifically mentioning the kind of writing—i.e., painting and song—that the "authors" engaged in. He writes, "Los más graves autores que pintaron las historias de esta tierra y compusieron cantos, que fueron Nezahualcoyotzin, rey de Tescoco, y los dos infantes de México, Xiuhcozcatzin y Tzahuatzin, dicen y declaran por ellas que el mundo tuvo y tiene cuatro edades" (1975–1977, 2:529; The most illustrious authors that painted the histories of this land and composed songs, who were Nezahualcoyotzin, king of Tetzcoco, and the two princes of Mexico, Xiuhcozcatzin and Tzahuatzin, state and declare in them that the world had and has four ages). In the prologue to the *Historia de la nación chichimeca*,[43] moreover, Alva Ixtlilxochitl describes pre-Hispanic historiography in detail.

Prólogo al lector
Considerando la variedad y contrarios pareceres de los autores que han tratado las historias de esta Nueva España, no he querido seguir a ninguno de ellos; y así me aproveché de las pinturas y caracteres que son

con que están escritas y memorizadas sus historias, por haberse pintado al tiempo y cuando sucedieron las cosas acaecidas, y de los cantos con que las observaban, autores muy graves en su modo de ciencia y facultad; pues fueron los mismos reyes y de la gente más ilustre y entendida, que siempre observaron y adquirieron la verdad, y ésta con tanta cuenta y razón, cuanta pudieran tener los más graves y fidedignos autores y históricos del mundo; porque tenían para cada género sus escritores, unos que trataban de los anales poniendo por su orden las cosas que acaecían en cada un año, con día, mes y hora. Otros tenían a su cargo las genealogías y descendencias de los reyes y señores y personas de linaje, asentando por cuenta y razón los que nacían y borraban los que morían, con la misma cuenta. Unos tenían cuidado de las pinturas de los términos, límites y mojoneras de las ciudades, provincias, pueblos y lugares, y de las suertes y repartimientos de las tierras, cuyas eran y a quién pertenecían. Otros, de los libros de las leyes, ritos y ceremonias que usaban en su infidelidad; y los sacerdotes, de los templos, de sus idolatryas y modo de su doctrina idolátrica y de las fiestas de sus falsos dioses y calendarios. Y finalmente, los filósofos y sabios que tenían entre ellos, estaba a su cargo el pintar todos los cantos que observaban sus ciencias e historias; todo lo cual mudó el tiempo con la caída de los reyes y señores, y [con] los trabajos y persecuciones de sus descendientes y la calamidad de sus súbditos y vasallos. ([1975–1977] 1985, 1:527)

Prologue to the reader
In considering the variety and contrary opinions of the authors that have treated the histories of this New Spain, I have not wanted to follow any of them; instead, I took advantage of the paintings and characters with which their histories are written and memorized for having been painted at the time when the events occurred, and of the songs with which the authors, very serious about their mode of science and authority, observed them. It was the very kings and the most illustrious and cultivated people that always observed and acquired the truth, with as much account and reason as the most dignified and truthful authors and historians of the world. They had writers for each genre, some that treated the annals, putting in order the things that happened each year, with the day, month and hour; others were in charge of the genealogies and the descendents of the kings and rulers and persons of lineage, carefully denoting those who were born and removing those who died,

with the same account. Some were in charge of the paintings of the borders and limits and the boundary markers of the cities, provinces, pueblos and places and the types and distributions of the lands, [designating] whose they were and to whom they belonged. Others, [were in charge of] the books of the laws, rites and ceremonies that they used in their unfaithfulness, [those of] the priests, the temples and their idolatries and the mode of the idolatrous doctrine and the feasts of their false gods and calendars. And finally, the philosophers and wise men who they had among them were in charge of painting all the songs that their sciences and histories observed, all of which changed with the fall of the kings and rulers, and [with] the labor and persecutions of their descendents and the calamity of their subjects and vassals.

Here, Alva Ixtlilxochitl lists different types of pre-Hispanic histories, mentions the important role of the philosophers or wise men, and provides a more ample and specified view of the identity of authors to include "los mismos reyes y de la gente más ilustre y entendida, que siempre observaron y adquirieron la verdad" (the very kings and others among the most distinguished and knowledgeable people, who always observed and acquired the truth; emphasis mine). Examining the passage from the prologue carefully, moreover, we see that its description of the pre-Hispanic Nahua tradition of writing is given as justification for Alva Ixtlilxochitl's statement regarding his decision to rely upon Native sources written in the early years after the conquest rather than upon the "other" (i.e., European/alphabetic) "contradictory" texts composed in the intervening years.

In order for this justification to be effective and convincing, however, Alva Ixtlilxochitl has to gloss over the fact that these sources are not alphabetic histories. Even in this most detailed passage, his principal strategy for doing so is to assimilate them in every way possible to classical and early modern European scholarship, a task he undertakes in a number of ways. First, he emphasizes the importance of song alongside pictorial representation in the passage—and of kings as composers of them. Focusing on the oral component of Nahua writing, although clearly an inferior mode of record keeping in European eyes, at least helps Alva Ixtlilxochitl to bridge the divide between the Nahua and European traditions through its implicit parallel to the popular historical ballads or romances rooted in the great epic songs of medieval Castile (and at which he tried his hand [O'Gorman 1975–1977, 2:270–73]). Second, Alva Ixtlilxochitl inflects his description of the pre-Hispanic practice

of "ciencias e historias," (the sciences and histories) with European forms
and values that are deemed universal. There are "autores muy graves en su
modo de ciencia y facultad" (authors who are very distinguished in their sci-
entific methods and knowledge) drawn from among the "la gente más ilustre
y entendida" (the most distinguished and knowledgeable people). Of these
"autores," Alva Ixtlilxochitl explicitly remarks that "observaron y adquirieron
la verdad . . . con tanta cuenta y razón, cuanta pudieran tener los más graves
y fidedignos autores y históricos del mundo" (they observed and acquired
the truth . . . with as much knowledge and reason as any of the world's most
illustrious and reliable authors and historians). This latter description echoes
the language of standards of scholarly excellence in Renaissance Europe, with
its insistence on observation, knowledge, and reason as the ground sine qua
non upon which he must validate the pre-Hispanic tradition, his colonial
sources, and his own methods for interpreting them. It also points out that it
is a universal (not solely European) criteria and modus operandi—something
shared by all the world's "reliable" authors and historians.

These instances of cultural assimilation, in which Alva Ixtlilxochitl
smoothes out or glosses over any differences or potential differences between
the Nahua and the European tradition of history writing, are accompanied by
a third form of assimilation visible in the prologue and, of course, throughout
his writing. This form, translation, is perhaps the most efficient, ubiquitous
and effective—if unavoidable—means that Alva Ixtlilxochitl uses to identify
the two historical and cultural traditions. In the prologue (and elsewhere),
Nahua tlamatinime (singular tlamatini) become "filósofos" (philosophers)
and "sabios" (sages), the tlacuiloque (singular tlacuilo) become "escritores"
(writers), and the *cuicatl* become "cantos" (songs). All of these translations
imply a distortion of meaning, especially where they are unaccompanied by
extended narrative explanation of the Nahua terms. Rather than fight against
this distortion, however, Alva Ixtlilxochitl strategically embraces it, affirming
in this way the validity of his historical sources and the Nahua historical tradition in a European cultural context without thereby also surrendering all of
its specificity or uniqueness.

The opening lines of the *Sumaria relación de la historia general* and the
Historia de la nación chichimeca, although very similar, manifest two distinct
ways in which Alva Ixtlilxochitl attends to the semantic slippage inherent
in the translation process. While the former text calls its list of historians
"autores" [authors] but specifies that they painted and composed (rather than
wrote), the latter text completely skips over any distinction between writing

and painting, perhaps because it had already undertaken that explanation in the longer and more carefully elaborated discourse of the prologue. By identifying those it mentions simply as "autores y históricos" (authors and historians), moreover, it leaves no room for questioning the eminence and worthiness of those Alva Ixtlilxochitl calls "authors." By creating a distinction between older (or more ancient) and "modern" authors, moreover, the opening sentence intensifies their association with the European tradition, and Alva Ixtlilxochitl even makes sure to specify that, where necessary, *he will be sure to cite them.* The addition of the figure of Quetzalcoatl into the first, formerly nonexistent, category is not a random move, moreover, nor is it unrelated to the larger thematic and structural architecture that Alva Ixtlilxochitl creates, as will become clear. For now, however, I wish to emphasize that the elision of the descriptive qualifiers at this point allows Alva Ixtlilxochitl to more effectively foreclose upon that inevitable and inimical (for the Renaissance reader) distinction between alphabetic and nonalphabetic writing.

As we have seen, Torquemada, like Alva Ixtlilxochitl, begins the prologue to his history by invoking Plutarch, not Quetzalcoatl. This venerable historian's "Life of Theseus" provides him with a quote he uses to justify, by way of comparison, certain "gaps" in the flow of his narrative that he anticipates will concern his reader, specifically, a lack of smooth or coherent documentation of the earliest history of the new lands, of the causes for the passage from one population or stage of civilization to the next (1975, 1:n.p.). Referencing Plutarch, and not long thereafter the work of Cicero, he writes,

> Pero haciendo lo que Plutarco dice del geógrafo, cubrimos los vacíos . . . y será posible, que a los que son curiosos, y discretos, no les haga buen sonido, algo del orden con que va distribuido por naciones, y familias, por cuanto se pasa de unos a otros, sin dar las causas, que hubo para hacer estos tránsitos: y a esto digo lo que Cicerón: que en la Historia se guarda la puntualidad de la verdad, a diferencia de la Poesía; en la qual no se pretende, sino deleitación del ánimo, y gusto del lenguaje. . . . , de manera, que como la Historia pide verdad, es fuerza, que el historiador, no apartándose de ella, vaya diciendo lo que sabe, según lo que halla escrito, o recibido por tradición; y por esto no doy más razón en este primer Libro del origen de estas gentes indianas, porque ni por relación, que me han hecho gentes antiguas de ellos, ni por escritos, que los sabios pasados a sus descendientes dejaron, se sabe más, ni más se platica entre ellos, como en sus mismos lugares decimos.

But doing what Plutarch says of the Geographer, we cover up the gaps . . . and it is possible, for those who are curious and discrete, that something about the order with which the nations and families are distributed, the way in which they pass from one to the other, without giving the causes that made these transitions happen, will not go over well: and regarding this I say the same as Cicero: that in history, one keeps to the letter of the truth, contrary to poetry, which does not claim anything other than delight to the soul and the pleasure of language . . . ; such that, as history demands truth, it is necessary that the historian, not straying from it, goes about saying what he knows, according to what he finds written, or received from tradition; and for this reason I don't provide more information in this first book of the origin of these Indian peoples, because neither from accounts that their elders have given me, nor in the writings that their past sages left to their descendents, is there more to be known, nor is anything else discussed among them, as we will state in the proper contexts.

As this passage demonstrates, Torquemada begins not only by establishing the European classical tradition as his constant reference point, his model "authors"—his first act is to anticipate the weakness in his narrative for which his sources are responsible. Although oblique, his message here is unmistakable: his sources' failure to supply the needed coherence and uniform information, making a clear, linearly sequenced narrative (much less a properly dated one), rooted in a proper logic of cause and effect impossible. This, in turn, imperils the text's cohesion, its unity, and its truthfulness; in the case of the Christian humanist historical tradition, as Jiménez (2001, 181) points out with respect to Francisco López de Gómara's histories, it also impedes its transcendent meaning.

With this quote, then, the full extent of the contrast between his and Alva Ixtlilxochitl's discursive framing of their indigenous sources becomes apparent. Torquemada's "authors" in this prologue are all of "Old World" vintage, while his "sources" are indigenous. Not only are Alva Ixtlilxochitl's indigenous sources authors, his prologue emphasizes the reliability and truthfulness of preconquest historical methods and texts, including the songs. Moreover, although Torquemada does not discuss the issue of pictorial versus alphabetic writing in the above passage, he does bring up the issue a few chapters into the *Monarquía indiana*.

In chapter 10 of book 1, while trying to convince his readers that the

people of the New World were Gentiles who had arrived overland shortly
after the (biblical) flood, Torquemada ([1723] 1975, 1:28–30) discusses a theory
proposed by Alejo Venegas (per a story found in Theophrastes/Aristotle) that
the inhabitants were descendents of Carthaginians or Phoenicians that had
arrived by sea. Torquemada concedes the possibility, but says that the theory,
to be feasible, must be slightly refined by taking writing into consideration.
He says, "Aquí se ofrece una dificultad, y es, que como los Fenices, inventaron
las letras; parece, que los Indios, como descendientes de ellos, habían de tener
algún uso, o rastro de letras, en planchas, o en piedras, lo cual, no tienen, ni
noticia ninguna de haberlas tenido" (29; Here a difficulty presents itself, and
that is, that seeing how the Phoenicians invented letters; that the Indians, as
their descendents, would have had some use or trace of letters, on sheets or in
stone, which they don't have, nor any kind of news of ever having had them).
He then expands on this exclusion of the inhabitants of New Spain from the
world of alphabetic writing in next chapter, entitled "Donde se declara, como
por la falta de historias que estas gentes tenían, no se puede averiguar bien,
su origen, y principio, y lo que dicen los Indios de su Origen, y venida a esta
Nueva-España, o Tierra de México, y sus Provincias" (Where it is declared,
how because of the lack of histories that these people had, it is not possible
to thoroughly look into their origins and beginnings, and at what the Indians
say of their origins and arrival here in New Spain, or the land of Mexico and
its provinces). The chapter begins with the following discussion:

> Una de las cosas, que mayor confusión causan en una república, y que
> más desatinados trae a los hombres que quieren tratar sus causas, es la
> poca puntualidad que hay en considerar sus historias. Porque si historia
> es una narración de cosas acaecidas y verdaderas, y los que las vieron
> y supieron no las dejaron por memoria, será fuerza al que después de
> acaecidas quiere escribirlas, que vaya a ciegas en el tratarlas, o que en
> cotejar las varias que se dicen, gaste la vida, y quede al fin de ella, sin
> haber sacado la verdad, en limpio. Esto (o casi esto) es lo que pasa, en
> esta historia de la Nueva-España; porque como los moradores antiguos
> de ella, no tenían letras, ni las conocían, así tampoco, no las historiaban.
> Verdad es, que usaban un modo de escritura (que eran pinturas) con
> las cuales se entendían; porque cada una de ellas, significaba una cosa,
> y a veces sucedía, que una sola figura, contenía la mayor parte del caso
> sucedido, o todo; y como este modo de historia no era común a todos,
> solo eran los rabinos, y maestros de ella, los que lo eran, en el arte del

pintar; y a esta causa sucedía, que la manera de los carácteres, y figu-
ras no fuesen concordes, y de una misma hechura en todos: por lo cual
era fácil variar el modo de la historia, y muchas veces desarrimarla de
la verdad, y aun apartarla del todo. Y de aquí ha venido, que aunque al
principio de la conquista, se hallaron muchos libros, que trataban de la
venida de estas gentes, a estas partes, no todos concordaban, porque en
muchas cosas, variaban los unos de los otros: y este yerro, nació de no
ser fija, y estable, la manera de escribirlas. (30–31)

One of the things that causes the most confusion in a republic, and
that most bewilders people who want to discuss its causes, is the lack of
precision that there is in considering their histories. Because if history
is a narration of true and actual events that have taken place, and those
that saw them and found out about them did not leave a record of them,
then the person who wants to write them down after they happened
proceeds blindly, or exhausts himself comparing the various versions,
without in the end having extracted the clear truth. This (or something
like this) is what is happening, in this History of New Spain; because,
as the ancient inhabitants had no letters, and did not understand them,
they did not write them down in histories. It is true that they used a
mode of writing (which were paintings) with which they understood
each other; [but] because each one of these signified something, and
sometimes a sole figure contained everything or the major part of whatever happened; and because this method of history was not common to
everyone, it was only the rabbis and the teachers who were [knowledge-
able] in the art of painting, and for this reason the characters and figures were not common [to everyone or] made the same every time: for
which reason it was easy to vary the method of the history, and many
times to detach it from the truth, and even to separate it entirely [there-
from]. And here it happened that, while at the beginning of the conquest many books were found that spoke of the arrival of these peoples
to these parts, not all of them were in agreement, because they varied
in many things from one to the other. This error was born from the fact
that the manner of writing them was not fixed and stable.

In this passage, Torquemada makes it clear that his pictorial and oral
source texts exist, for him, outside the world of *letras* (letters). His primary
concern is that, due to the variation and inconsistencies of the pictorial method

of writing, they failed to provide a stable and fixed narrative that all could agree upon, which constitutes a burden for the historian-"author" working to extract the proper interpretation, that is, the single/singular "truth" of the past. While Torquemada defends the integrity of pictorial script as writing, he also insists on its limitations and considers it to be inferior to alphabetic writing.

Like Torquemada, Alva Ixtlilxochitl, in his prologue cited above, expresses a concern with the quality of his narrative, anticipating his reader's potential discontent and asking in advance for forbearance. His request comes, however, directly after his long, elegant, and abundantly positive description of Nahua pre-Hispanic learning and without a hint of criticism toward his sources, and after specifying that they were among the works from the famous Tetzcoco royal archives that escaped the bonfires of postconquest religious zealotry and that they were entrusted to his care. The quote reads:

> Y de lo que escapó de los incendios y calamidades referidas, que guardaron mis mayores, vino a mis manos, de donde he sacado y traducido la historia que prometo, aunque al presente en breve y sumaria relación, alcanzada con harto trabajo y diligencia en entender la interpretación y conocimiento de las pinturas y caracteres que eran sus letras, y la traducción de los cantos en alcanzar su verdadero sentido; la cual irá sucinta y llana, sin adorno ni ayuda de ejemplos; ni tampoco trataré de las fábulas y ficciones que parecen en algunas de sus historias, por ser cosas superfluas. Y así pido muy encarecidamente al discreto lector supla los muchos defectos que hubiere en mi modo de narrar, que lo que es la historia puede estar seguro que es muy fidedigna y verdadera, y aprobada por tal de toda la gente principal e ilustre de esta Nueva España. ([1975–1977] 1985, 1:527–28)

> And what escaped from the fires and calamities referred to, that their elders preserved, came into my hands, from whence I have taken and translated the history that I promised. Although at present in brief and summary relation, [it was] achieved with great difficulty and diligence in understanding the interpretation and knowledge of the paintings and characters that were their letters, and the translation of the songs in order to grasp their true meaning, which will be presented succinctly and plainly without adornment or help of examples. Nor will I discuss the fables and fictions that appear in some of their histories, as they are

superfluous things. And so I urgently ask the discrete reader to fill in for the many defects that there may be in my mode of narrating, who, with respect to the history, can be sure that it is very true and faithful, and approved as such by all of the noble and illustrious people of this New Spain.

Here, in true Renaissance fashion, Alva Ixtlilxochitl assures his reader that he has told a truthful ("fidedigna y verdadera") tale about real events, one that weeds out the fictive elements ("fábulas y ficciones") embedded in his sources in order to narrate the past as it happened. More to the point, however, in referencing the "pinturas y carácteres" that he translated with difficulty, Alva Ixtlilxochitl emphasizes the similarity of these forms with the alphabet: they were "sus letras," or their letters. The parallelism he draws stands above any formal but ultimately incidental difference between the two forms of writing. The focus of Alva Ixtlilxochitl's discussion, moreover, is firmly on his own diligence and effort (and expertise) in interpreting and understanding his range of sources. In addition, he chooses to attribute the potential defects in the narrative to his own (lack of) style, rather than refer to any weakness or deficiencies in his sources, asking for the reader's patience with whatever defects his mode of narrating might contain—the "defectos que hubiere." By placing blame for a weak narrative on his personal style, his appeal to the reader simply manifests the signs of humbleness and self-deprecation expected of the writers of the day. Thus, although both Torquemada and Alva Ixtlilxochitl emphasize the difficulties of interpretation presented by their source texts, Alva Ixtlilxochitl only does so in the context of exerting his cultural and linguistic authority, his unique qualifications to engage in such a task. By highlighting his expertise, he upholds the values of humanist historiography and implicitly associates his own work as a historian with that of the humanist European scholars of Greek and Roman antiquity, who, in the absence of eyewitness authorities, undertook the arduous work of deciphering in their original languages the most ancient (and therefore authoritative) sources about the past.

Indeed, as this example demonstrates, Alva Ixtlilxochitl's ([1975–1977] 1985, 1:527) stated preference for relying on his indigenous sources over European ones, and his absolute lack of explicit reference to classical and biblical texts (especially when compared to Torquemada), does not mean that these sources or that the European tradition do not have their place in his narrative. On the contrary, in the *Historia de la nación chichimeca*, the Christian

European (humanist) tradition presents itself as an internal, often rhetorical, influence and not—like in the *Monarquía indiana*—as a separate stream of literature to be cited alongside or contrasted with the Nahua tradition and the texts that he places front and center. In other words, the "Europeanization" of the *Historia de la nación chichimeca*, with its preponderant reliance on and nearly exclusive reference to indigenous source texts (those written by and for Nahuas) from beginning to end, happens from within, from the inside out. As such, it reflects a process of hybridization or transculturation that, to be sure, did not originate with Alva Ixtlilxochitl and was not exclusive to it. Although the *Monarquía indiana* reflects an internal rhetorical influence as well, having shared many of the same sources used by Alva Ixtlilxochitl, it is not vested in sanitizing a past (or present) whose status as a problematic addendum to the larger Catholic, European historiographical tradition (regarded as the sole stream of truthful historical, geographical, knowledge) also gave Catholic Spain its pretext for colonialism and its mendicant missionaries their sense of calling.

What is significant about Alva Ixtlilxochitl's approach, however, is that, by absorbing the European tradition into his discourse as an un-cited and un-commented presence, he legitimizes the past of his Tetzcoca ancestors (in European terms, for his European audience), while simultaneously side-stepping the questions and debates motivating the mendicants' ethnographic histories, without even entertaining a discussion of the philosophical (and Eurocentric) notions whereby Christian Europe defined itself as a "civilized" entity. Unlike Torquemada (and others before him), Alva Ixtlilxochitl's works do not pause to offer reasoned discussion of the day's theories of the origins of the lands and peoples of the New World. Of the early works, the Compendio engages the topic in the most detail, asserting matter-of-factly a common origin (from the "división de Babilonia," or the Babylonian diaspora), in the "Gran Tartaria" (Great Tartary) for all of the peoples of the Anahuac, even the giants ([1975–1977] 1985, 1:417). In the *Historia de la nación chichimeca* and the *Sumaria relación de la historia general*, however, he cuts directly to the story of creation, which, as we will see, is a Nahua story with (in Alva Ixtlilxochitl's version) outstanding biblical credentials. His answer to the question of origins, therefore, lies in the mention of a "dios universal" (universal god) who creates an ancestral couple that could be Adam and Eve, and, in the *Historia de la nación chichimeca*, in the arrival of a foreigner shortly after the time of Christ who preaches and teaches a very Christian-like doctrine (1975–1977, 2:7–8). Without specifying in these histories where the first inhabitants of the region of his ancestors came from (apart from general references to the direction), he simply assumes the common origins of all humanity, as well as, in these two works, a local contact with Christianity (or a suspiciously Christian-like doctrine around the time of Christ) before the arrival of the Spanish (a point discussed more fully in the next chapters). Through a combination of censorship of specific (and verboten) aspects of pre-Hispanic Nahua culture represented in source texts (Lesbre 1999a) and use of particular versions of internal influences in or interpretations of that history and culture absorbed from European tradition, Alva Ixtlilxochitl creates in the *Historia de la nación chichimeca* a vision of pre-Hispanic Anahuac that both accounts for European cultural, historical, and religious prejudices, arrogance, and blind spots and, as I demonstrate in the next chapter, retains an essential, underlying, and unspoken affiliation with traditional elements found Nahua historicity and historical tradition.

A return to the opening clause of the *Historia de la nación chichimeca* adds one more dimension to our discussion of the implications of Alva Ixtlilxochitl's naming of important pre-Hispanic authors, in particular his inclusion of a personage called Quetzalcoatl as an "ancient" author. The sentence is clearly rooted in and related to (his construction of) the idea of Nezahualcoyotl as a poet-king and the parallel he creates between his Acolhua ruler-hero and the Old Testament David that Velazco (2003) and Lee (2008) have discussed. However, it is not only Nezahualcoyotl who becomes an "author," and the question arises as to his motive for including Quetzalcoatl and the Mexica princes in the list he provides.

In *Stories in Red and Black* (2000, 25), Elizabeth Hill Boone takes note of Alva Ixtlilxochitl's striking phrase, stating that "These esteemed historians were tlacuiloque, to be sure, but they also were tlamatinime, learned persons." Directly preceding this point, she notes Alva Ixtlilxochitl's discussion of the arrival of the Tlailotlaque and their painted manuscripts from the Mixteca area (portrayed in his principal pictorial source text, the *Codex Xolotl*) and how they were a people he regarded as descendents of the Tolteca and (therefore) skilled in all of the arts and crafts. She emphasizes, moreover, that "we should keep in mind that writing was associated with the Tolteca, those highly civilized forerunners of the Aztecs to whom extraordinary achievements were attributed, and that the Mixtecs (who were said to excel in the luxury crafts) were also called Tolteca, sons of Quetzalcoatl" (252–53n24).

Boone's comments providing the Nahua source and context of Alva Ixtlilxochitl's initial statement place into high relief the uncompromising attitude with which Alva Ixtlilxochitl approached his project of translating the basic facts of his Acolhua ancestors' culture and history—in this case their very means of preserving and carrying it on—into the Castilian language and cultural conceptions. There is no tergiversation, no hint of semantic slippage between tlacuiloque and tlamatinime and "autores y históricos" (authors and historians). There is especially no mention, of course, of the possibly religious dimensions or significations of the book as a material artifact, nor of the undisputed religious, ritual, and divinatory nature of the work of the tlamatinime.

It impossible to know to what extent Alva Ixtlilxochitl maintained or was aware of the distinctions between the two groups of words and corresponding sociocultural practices and associated institutions, although his awareness and use of the vibrant song tradition of his day and his encounter with the manuscript of the *Romances de los señores de la Nueva España*, collected by Juan Bautista Pomar (Bierhorst 2009), and his own composing of historical poems make it likely that he at least considered the matter. Whatever the case may be, in defining Quetzalcoatl and the later Nahua rulers as authors, Alva Ixtlilxochitl establishes a crucial link between rulership and writing, a link that—if not completely accurate vis-à-vis the tradition of writing in the pre-Hispanic period—nevertheless faithfully communicates its association with the elite sector of Nahua society as well as the high value that was placed on it (and in particular the writing of history) as the means of constituting and transmitting the legacy of the rulership and thus the memory of the altepetl itself.[44] In his statement, therefore, Alva Ixtlilxochitl reaffirms his personal ties to Acolhua nobility by implicating himself more deeply in the text as their noble heir (Townsend 2003, 670). If rulers were authors, then Alva Ixtlilxochitl, himself an author, proves to be their true and faithful offspring. The sense of cultural inheritance, the continuity of a "spiritual" or "artistic" legacy, becomes palpable even if Alva Ixtlilxochitl did not hold the same ideas of the ritual or sacred qualities of the book operating in pre-Hispanic times. After all, when the tlatoque spoke, they did so as representatives of the gods. As the power and uniqueness of the caciques decline in the historico-political world of the late sixteenth and early seventeenth centuries, on the literary plane, at least, Alva Ixtlilxochitl ushered a full array of their powers into the future.

CHAPTER TWO

Constructing the Nahua-
Christian Universal History

Rulers, Emplotment, and Chronotope

◆ WE HAVE SEEN HOW ALVA IXTLILXOCHITL NOT ONLY CAREFULLY
established his credentials as a historian in the humanistic tradition, pointing out his access to the texts and his expertise in reading and interpreting
them, but also proved himself the true and rightful heir of his illustrious
Acolhua ancestors, authors and historians in their own right. Here and in
the next chapter I show how, for Alva Ixtlilxochitl, the legacy of rulership
was a historical legacy but also a legacy of history, that is, of the writing of
history, of a practice whereby the symbolism, if not the exercise, of the ruler's
power could continue to be purveyed. If the Nahua nobility had lost their
practical, real-world function and significance, they did not have to lose it in
history.

In the *Historia de la nación chichimeca*, carrying on the legacy of rulership is not a simple matter of commemoration, of the creation of a glowing
(Christianized) portrait of principal ruler-heroes. Here we see how, through
its organization and representation of the Acolhua noble lineage and inheritance, the history configures two narrative structures at once and thus two
distinct renderings (or possible readings) of the meaning of the Spanish

conquest in historical time, one according to a Nahua (or Mesoamerican) vision of time and the other in terms of a Spanish or European one. Hinging the emplotments of the two historicities is the much-discussed figure of Quetzalcoatl and his relationship to Nezahualcoyotl and to Cortés. As we will see, the habit-like garb already associated with a figure by this name (and similar to the one in which Francisco Verdugo Quetzalmamalitzin Huetzin asked to buried) would once again be associated with a character bearing that name in Alva Ixtlilxochitl's last, signature work. He is given a double existence, in fact, along with Nezahualcoyotl and Cortés, as Alva Ixtlilxochitl both emphasizes his Christian-like presence in early missionary texts and grants him his traditional role in the Nahua cosmogonies and Tolteca histories as Tezcatlipoca's rival and ennobler of ruling lineages.

Part One. Christian and Nahua Timekeeping and Cosmovision: Divinity, Providentialism, and the Role of the Ruler in the Historical Chronotope

PLOTTING THE PAST: HISTORICAL NARRATIVE IN COLONIAL CONTEXTS

According to Paul Ricoeur's *Time and Narrative* ([1984] 1990, 1:92), histories (which, unlike fictional works, purport to tell *true* tales), endow the past of specific communities with meaning through their configuration of its events (and other heterogeneous elements) within a plot. Genres, whether historical or fictional, moreover, as Heather Dubrow's (1982) work emphasizes, are social constructions responding to the expectations of a community or group of readers. Any examination of the *Historia de la nación chichimeca*'s emplotment of the past, and, more generally speaking, its instantiation of the European universal history, therefore, must take into account its creation in a colonial context in which two mutually implicated but still separate and autonomous systems of historical thought and writing coexisted (Cornejo Polar 1999a 1999b).

For Ricoeur ([1984] 1990, 1), narratives represent a response to what he calls the "aporetics of time," the essential disjuncture between human time, or time as lived (that which passes), and cosmic time (that which endures) (5–30). They do so, he writes, by creating an image of the world in which events and diachrony become, by means of emplotment, synthesized into a unified order in which "concordance" takes priority over "discordance"; a plot is thus an "integrating process" that "draws a configuration from a succession" (31–51). However, while fictional narratives highlight the gap or make it visible, historical narratives suture it by relying on already constituted institutions such as the calendar (which ties the human and the everyday to the cosmic in its religious, ritual nature), the coexistence of generations (where stories from the past get handed down and whose figure presents the eternality of time), and the trace (the use of the remnant whose present is no longer with us) (89–94).

Although Ricoeur fails to directly address either the cross-cultural or colonial politics of writing, it is at this deeper, subcutaneous level of the narrative that he describes—its manner of configuring the past—that the *Historia de la nación chichimeca*'s allegorization of temporal structures inherent to both Christian and Nahua cosmologies, what we could think of as their structuring chronotopes, occurs. If, as Rhiannon Goldthorpe (2004, 85) describes Ricoeur's theory of configuration, emplotment "acts as the crucial pivot between our pre-comprehension of the temporality of practical action and the transfigured understanding of re-ordered temporality which we achieve in our reading of the literary work," then a text written between two cultures has to negotiate both cultural contexts and their respective ways of resolving the disjunction between the temporality of practical actions and cosmic/universal time. Luís Fernando Restrepo (2002, 97), commenting on the possibilities of a postcolonial appropriation of Ricoeur's work, writes that

> An inquiry into colonialism past and present is ultimately a matter of the hegemony of the Western notion of time. Western temporality or its experience of time (in)forms the story of colonialism. But no hegemony is total nor uncontested. Opposed, juxtaposed, or intertwined to Western temporality we can find multiple temporalities arising at any given moment from the heterogeneity of lived experience. These different and competing notions of time are experienced and made meaningful through narrative forms. The narrativization of time in contexts of colonization is thus a strategic site for a critical inquiry and for intervention. Opening and locating hegemonic time may prove useful to the postcolonial project of decolonization: to reveal the Othering of non-Western time narratives and to reinscribe the suppressed, marginalized time of the Other.

For Restrepo, Ricoeur's work has the potential of allowing us to uncover how narratives convey a *hegemonic* sense of collective time, literally *plotting* empire while at the same time manifesting alternative, resistant temporalities (97–98). Indeed, as Eduardo Natalino dos Santos (2007, 230–31) has argued, the implications of the Nahua calendar(s) as a structuring device and semiotic entity (as opposed to a subject of expository discourse) within many colonial Nahua histories—both pictorial and alphabetic—has been relatively underexamined in scholarship. Referring to the presence of two pairs of creator deities (Oxomoco and Cipactonal, and Quetzalcoatl and Tezcatlipoca) within a traditional fifty-two-year calendrical cycle presented in the *Códice Borbónico*, he writes,

> Todas esas deidades están engarzadas en una estructura calendárica que parece condicionar y organizar sus acciones e influencias. Dicho de otro modo, las acciones e influencias de las deidades que construyen al universo y al hombre—pero que también los destruyen—se consumen y se hacen inteligibles por medio de los ciclos del calendario, los cuales siempre aparecen como una de las primeras creaciones de las más antiguas deidades, hecho que parece indicar la necesidad de contar con los ciclos para el funcionamiento posterior del universo en sus diversas edades y, por ende, para su entendimiento por parte del hombre. (253)

> All of these deities are linked together in a calendrical structure that seems to condition and organize their actions and influences. In other words, the actions and influences of the gods that create the world and humanity—but that also destroy them—are managed and make themselves intelligible by means of the cycles of the calendar, which always appear as one of the first creations of the most ancient gods, a fact that seems to indicate the dependence on the cycles for the posterior functioning of the universe in its various ages, and as such, for its comprehension by man.

Before examining the way in which two of these creator deities—Tezcatlipoca and Quetzalcoatl—leave their mark on the *Historia de la nación chichimeca*'s narrative structure, however, a basic overview of Christian and Nahua temporality—a description of the general idea of human and cosmic time (or the human/terrestrial world and the world of the gods) in each tradition—is in order.

The most fundamental distinction between Nahua and European interpretations of time is, of course, so well known as to be almost a commonplace. Implicit in the structures of their calendars but also, most significantly, in the myth-historical traditions associated with them, the often-cited contrast between a European linear abstraction or conception of time (separated from an imagination of space and territory) and a Nahua (Mesoamerican) cyclical conception (which integrates space and time) holds true even as it represents an oversimplification of cultural conceptions and processes that entail complexity (both linear and cyclical senses in and of themselves) and local variation within the wider cultural schemes and contexts.

CHRISTIAN TEMPORALITY AND THE VISION OF THE EARLY FRANCISCANS

European Christian timekeeping is based on a linear temporal structure rooted in biblical eschatology. Relying on the Julian and then the Gregorian calendar (derived from the ancient Roman solar calendar), its year count succeeds progressively with its numbering based on the birth of Christ. It imagines a creation, a flood (as a new beginning), and all posterior events as unique moments leading to a variously conceptualized and theologically debated apocalypse or end point.[1] In this framework, all of "human time" comes to an end, subsumed in a vision of cosmic time as "eternity." A single divinity, generally seen as distinct and separate from the "natural world (and human life),"[2] and viewed in medieval Christian theology (with St. Thomas Aquinas) as the "prime mover," is attributed with the creation of the world (narrated in Old Testament cosmogony as a seven-day event) and is regarded as being responsible for its progression and culmination. Past, present, and future remain separate but linked in a (linear) chain of cause and effect (natural laws or "secondary" causes) and also ultimately dependent on the divine agency in charge of cosmic and terrestrial events. Human access to the divine in the (Catholic) Christian tradition takes place through religious ritual (such as prayer), which, for the most part, relies on the mediation of priests in deliverance of rites and sacraments and in the interpretation of the scriptures. Old Testament literature also, however, depicts a tradition of prophecy in which the Hebrew God directly spoke to specific individuals (usually leaders or rulers) and there was also a strong tradition of mysticism, in which direct and intimate knowledge of the divine was sought and experienced.

This basic linear scheme does not preclude cyclical aspects of marking the passage of time. Seasonal liturgical cycles, typological readings of sacred texts (which saw in past events foreshadowings or prototypes of present and future) as well as the idea of a *translatio imperii*, a rise and fall of empires, based on the "four empire" scheme found in the Book of Daniel had cyclical aspects or implications. The latter theory of history, which imagined Spain as "un pueblo destinado, cruzado—elegido" [a destined, crusader, people— chosen], "un gran imperio católico" [a great Catholic empire], was popularized in Spain beginning in fifteenth-century Castile and reached its apogee in the time of Ferdinand and Isabella and Charles V (Jiménez 2001, 185). And while these cyclical aspects of Christianity surely impacted processes of transculturation in central Mexico (and beyond) as "lines of confluence" (Olko 2007, 158) around which many aspects of indigenous tradition adapted and survived, in the Catholic tradition they were for the most part still associated with a notion of progress, a sense of culmination. Despite the repetition implied in these historical paradigms, they take place within an overall dynamic that emphasizes a singular, progressive temporal scheme.

NAHUA TEMPORALITY

As Elizabeth Hill Boone (2007, 13–18) points out in her work on the Nahua divinatory almanacs, *Cycles of Time and Meaning in the Mexican Books of Fate*, the Nahua timekeeping tradition, like other Mesoamerican systems, is based on a combination and confluence of two separate calendars. First, a 260-day ritual, divinatory calendar divided into a repeating sequence of 20 named days that are, in turn, accompanied by a sequential numerical count of thirteen. Then, a 365-day agricultural calendar that follows the solar cycle, marked (in pre-Hispanic times) with large festivals occurring at the end of each of the eighteen (20-day) "months," after which comes a period of 5 surfeit days, called *nemontemi*, that did not belong to any month and were considered unlucky. These two calendars converge (start their cycles on the same day—marked by the same combination of day sign and numerical coefficient) every fifty-two years, an event traditionally ushered in with New Fire ceremonies to celebrate the renewal of time. Each particular day in the 20-day cycle holds something in common with the other days marked by those same confluences of forces signaled by the day sign. While a particular day in one period or cycle (of 260 days) is not *identical* to the previous one, it is said to hold structural similarities. Time is thus cyclical and repetitive, best viewed, as Alfredo López Austin (1985, 78–79) describes it, as a series of ever-widening concentric circles. Theoretically, at least, at the very widest end of the spectrum, he writes, it would be possible for one day to exactly replicate another, for the confluence of forces to gain so much in common that the past would return (reexist) in its exact form or configuration.

In this structure, the mythical time of creation and the present moment are therefore in some sense not separable. Time is a force (a divine force) that makes itself present in and through a living landscape that replicates and manifests the eternal moment of creation and the forces responsible for it. In Katarzyna Mikulska's (2010, 337n24) paraphrasing of López Austin's work, it arrives at the earthly plane born from "the eternal struggle of opposing elements (or opposing divine essences)" such that time itself constitutes the very influence of the gods upon the terrestrial plane. Lakes, mountains, caves, springs, trees, and many other parts of the "sacred" landscape were conduits of the divine forces that shaped and influenced life on earth. The terrestrial plane, in other words, is part of—a product of—an "ever present time of creations and the gods" (Gruzinski 2007 [1991], 97–98).

This larger perception of life on the terrestrial plane as being imbued with or influenced by divine forces, with all of society—religion, architecture, household and political structures—oriented to replicating the act of foundation and maintaining order, went largely unperceived in the realm of the república de españoles. Gruzinski ([1991] 2007) writes how the friars were able to suppress (or transform) religious rites and books, but many less-overt aspects of Nahua religiosity remained unchanged.

> Fueran cuales fuesen las prácticas todavía en vigor en la época de las *Relaciones* [*geográficas*], no cabe duda que algunos indios siempre tenían presentes los ciclos diurnos y nocturnos, las secuencias de 13 y 20 días y las periodicidades anuales que estructuraban la temporalidad tradicional y le conferían una densidad, una sustancia, pues regían, como se recordará, la llegada y la combinación de los influjos que descendían de los cielos o subían de los mundos inferiores. . . . . Raros fueron los religiosos que se mostraron sensibles a la especificidad profunda del tiempo indígena y se escandalizaron por ella como Bernardino de Sahagún, quien hacia 1578–1580, por consiguiente en las mismas fechas, consignaba este refrán indígena: "Lo que se hacía hace mucho tiempo y ya no se hace, otra vez hará, otra vez así será,

como fue en lejanos tiempos; ellos los que ahora viven, otra vez vivirán,
serán . . . ," para agregar: "esta proposición es de Platón y el diablo la
enseñó acá porque es errónea, falsísima, es contra la fe." (97)

Whatever practices were taking place at the time of the *Relaciones*
[*geográficas*], there is no doubt that some Indians still had the cycles of
day and night, the sequences of 13 and 20 days and the annual period-
icities that structured traditional time and lent it a density, a substance,
because they governed, as will be recalled, the arrival and the combination of the forces that descended from the skies or ascended from the
underworlds [. . .] Few priests were sensitive to the profound specificity of indigenous time and were horrified by it, such as in the case of
Bernardino de Sahagún, who, around 1578–1580, about the same time,
recorded this indigenous proverb: "everything that used to be done a
long time ago but is not done now, it will be done again; once again
things will be as they were in ancient times; those who now live, will
live again, they will be . . . ," and he adds, "this proposition is Plato's and
the devil taught it here, for it is wrong, false, and against the faith."

Likewise, he describes how the Spanish were largely unaware of the importance of the sacred landscape in the *Relaciones geográficas* ordered by Viceroy
Velasco in the mid-sixteenth century:

Invisible para los españoles, otro tiempo se ocultaba en los ríos, dentro de las montañas, en lo más recóndito de las selvas. Allí adonde los
encuestadores sólo entendieron una interpretación anodina del paisaje,
algunos indios transmitieron informaciones fugitivas que rebasaron
considerablemente el terreno de la toponimia o de la geografía. . . .
[Ellos] consideraban que los lagos, las cuevas, las montañas eran puntos
de contacto privilegiados entre el mundo de los dioses y la superfi-
cie terrestre. Eran los conductos que comunicaban el tiempo siempre
presente de las creaciones y de los dioses con el de los humanos. . . .
Lugares de evolución de un tiempo a otro, objetos por naturaleza
indestructibles a diferencia de los templos, de las imágenes y de las
"pinturas," puntos de referencia secretos y guaridas de los dioses, estos
elementos del paisaje manifestaban y mantenían en su inmutabilidad
una antigua relación con los tiempos y con el entorno. (97–98)

Invisible to the Spaniards, another time was hiding in the rivers, inside the mountains, in the most remote parts of the jungles. There, where the researchers only perceived an anodyne interpretation of the landscape, some Indians transmitted fugitive information that considerably exceeded the terrain of geography or toponymy. . . . [They] considered lakes, caves, and mountains to be privileged sites of contact between the world of the gods and the terrestrial plane. They were the conduits that communicated the ever-present time of the creations and of the gods with that of humans. . . . Places of evolution from one time to another, objects indestructible by nature, contrary to the temples, the images and the "paintings," secret reference points and hide-outs of the gods, these elements of the landscape manifested and maintained in their immutability an ancient relationship with time and with their environment.

This sacred landscape, rooted in the interpenetration of the primordial past (the time of myth and creation, as López Austin [[1980] 1984, 68–71] calls it) and present time, carried with it specific implications for the way in which memories were recorded in the Nahua tradition. In his study of the maps of the *Relaciones geográficas* ([1991] 2007, 99) Gruzinski writes,

> Pues si la toponimia disimulaba por doquiera una cosmogonía, es que eran indisociables una de otra. . . . Será comprensible que, partiendo de enfoques distintos del medio y de la realidad, cada cual haya obedecido a su propósito y que el pasado según los españoles con frecuencia haya podido ser el presente de los indios, lo que se imponía por su propio peso, pues ese pasado era parte de la misma inmutable realidad. Por lo demás, sus testimonios no establecían diferencia alguna entre el "mito" y la historicidad. Cuando mucho había veces en que guardaban silencio sobre aspectos demasiado embarazosos. Sin embargo, aun edulcorado, el relato conservaba su coherencia, basando en un mismo registro lo "fabuloso" y lo político.

If the toponymy was disguising cosmogony, it is because they were impossible to separate. . . . It is feasible that, starting from different starting points regarding the medium and the reality, each would have been faithful to their own purposes and that the past according to the Spanish frequently could have been the present of the Indians, imposed by its own weight, because this past was part of the same immutable reality. Their testimonies didn't establish any difference between myth and historicality. At best, there were times in which they remained silent about particularly delicate phenomena. Nevertheless, even modified, the narration preserved its coherence, establishing both the "fantastic" and the political in the same record.

In the *Handbook of Middle American Indians*, Charles Gibson explains this correspondence or simultaneity of myth and history in the Nahua tradition by writing that "One of the most celebrated features of native Mesoamerican historical thought is its prophetic component, *the projection of historical sequences in a known future*" (1975, 15:319; emphasis mine). In the same volume, H. B. Nicholson discusses the difficult problem (for Western intellectuals) of distinguishing legendary "pattern histories" from "reliable chronicling of actual past events." He writes that "All the native histories represent a very selective and formalized image of the past, one which was obviously being constantly revised in response to various socio-political and religious changes within the groups in question. There has been too much naïve acceptance of the literal historicity of the earliest segments of these stylized histories" (491).

Corresponding with this notion of structured and parallel repetition, Michel Graulich (1981) has pointed out how the twenty-four hour day, with its alternating predominance of sun and moon (regarded as a "night sun"), forms the basis for understanding larger temporal cycles such as the agricultural and divinatory calendar rounds, as well as the rise and fall of empires. Nahua creation "myths" and Tolteca "history,"[3] he argues, are rooted in the same basic mythic story. They embody the same patterns of rise and fall centered on the twin gods Quetzalcoatl and Tezcatlipoca. The identities and relationship of these deities, as Graulich argues, ultimately assimilate and are parallel to the astral bodies, namely, the sun and moon. Nahua cosmogonies—stories that embody the cyclical dynamic of the twenty-four-hour day and the revolutions of the sun and moon—thus provide the template not just for Tolteca history, but for the composition of later Postclassic history (the rise and fall of the Triple Alliance) as well.

RULERSHIP AND TEMPORALITY

Quetzalcoatl and Tezcatlipoca, protagonists of the Nahua cosmogonies and Tolteca histories and regarded as "ennoblers" or "ancestors" of the rulers, are at the heart of the dynasties or the tlatocayotl because they represent the divine forces of the primordial time of creation: rulers (or rulership) and temporality are thus inseparable. Not only did rulers (in conjunction with priests) participate in sacrifices and religious ritual that followed the calendrical cycles, ensuring thereby cosmic balance and order—the stability (and re-creation) of the universe—the dynasties themselves underwent cycles of destruction and renewal such that dynastic lineage or the royal genealogy itself was, as Susan Gillespie (1989, 124) states, a "paramount" historical form. One could say that time (or the primordial time-space) is inherent in the ruler and that in the list of rulers the shape of history is encoded.

In *The Palace of Nezahualcoyotl* (2010, 97), Eduardo Douglas, describing the importance of dynastic genealogies in pre-Hispanic and colonial writing, states that "Like their colonial successors, Mesoamerica's pre-Hispanic rulers perceived ancestors as motive and sign of the right to rule. Dynastic genealogies endowed the individual ruler with the authority of his forebearers and permitted the dynasty to isolate the germ of the present in the past." He goes on to explain how "In order to transmute power into divine sanction, Mesoamerican rulers and their artists grafted dynastic births, marriages, and deaths onto the cycles of creation and destruction" (98). This transmutation can be seen, he writes, in late Postclassic burial rites, where some of the ashes of the rulers were placed in the great pyramid temple, which "anchored and oriented earth and cosmos, fusing them into a spatial continuum." The temple, he reminds us, was tied to the tlatoani who built or expanded it and who celebrated the rites of the rebirth of the gods therein. "Ce Acatl Topiltzin Quetzalcoatl's death or immolation brought about the Nahua world of the Late Postclassic Period, while, from one generation to the next," he writes, "the Acolhua and Mexica rulers, both as living men and as ashes, nourished and increased their cities' great temples, where gods and ruler, divine creator and human polity, became one" (ibid.).

As Gillespie (1989, 3–26) has shown for the rulers of Tenochtitlan and Douglas (2010) for those of Tetzcoco, structural analyses of dynastic lineages reveal patterned sequences of destruction and renewal, a process whereby the dynasty replicates the cosmic cycles of creation and destruction. Gillespie describes how this cyclical dynastic paradigm was built on "boundary figures" and their illicit, exogamous relationships with a "woman of discord"—a representation of the genetrix or earth-mother-goddess—responsible for the birth of the rulers. The boundary figures were structural equivalents, playing similar roles in each successive epoch, from the time of the gods through the

Tolteca and Mexica in the late Postclassic period. The arrival of the Spanish, along with the capture and defeat of Motecuhzoma, the Mexica tlatoani,
sparked a rapid and comprehensive revision of Mexica history according to
this paradigm, she argues, in which Motecuhzoma I (previously Ilhuicamina)
became the boundary figure equated with Topiltzin Quetzalcoatl (of Tolteca
fame). This backward revision (and creation of Tolteca history) explained the
defeat of Motecuhzoma in his rivalry with Cortés (another Topiltzin Quetzalcoatl) and coordinated it with previous defeats according to the regular
cyclical cadence of every fifth and ninth ruler.

Douglas (2010, 105–6) makes no connection between rulers' nobility and
a repeating genetrix figure for the Acolhua dynasties, although he does note
the marriages of Xolotl's sons to Tolteca wives and recurring cycles of imperial destruction and renewal every third generation (dividing the Tetzcoco
lineage of nine rulers by threes, instead of into two halves, as in the Mexica genealogy).[4] This begins, he notes (113–14), with Ome Tochtzin Ixtlilxochitl, or Ixtlilxochitl I, who as seen in the previous chapter, according to Alva
Ixtlilxochitl was the first Nahua, that is, the first Chichimeca ruler to be given
Tolteca funeral rites. As Douglas states, after this first Ixtlilxochitl lost the
empire to Tepaneca tyranny, his son, Nezahualcoyotl, replicates the founding
act of the Chichimeca Quinatzin (who established the Acolhua altepetl in
Tetzcoco as opposed to Tenayuca) three generations after Xolotl's arrival. Both
foundations take place in the year One Flint Knife, or ce tecpatl. Thus, differently than in the European historical tradition, these rulers acquire a position
within a cyclically structured temporality as representatives of the gods and
therefore crucial figures in maintaining cosmic order and equilibrium.

In sum, these historicities, both Mexica and Acolhua, seem to foreground
a certain type of stasis and harmony rooted in cyclical temporality—an equilibrium in which cyclically renewed or regenerated rulership (with rulers
having importance for their position rather than as individuals, or in addition
to their individual exploits) provided a sense of continuity through change
and upheaval. The Nahua cosmovision, with its sometimes mentioned fifth
and "final" sun or epoch of creation (usually in Mexica texts) and its preoccupation with ensuring the continuation of time (the astral cycles) through
sacrifice, also can be seen to imply a certain apocalyptic "finality." However,
this does not overcome or change the preoccupation in many colonial Nahua
myth-historical narratives with the various calendar-derived or associated
cycles and the image of the circle—of a universal, self-enclosed, chronotope.

In European historiography, as in the Nahua tradition(s), however, rulers and ruling lines also play a central role in the histories, which, as Pablo García Loaeza (2014) notes, often "told time by the passage of Kings." In his work on Alva Ixtlilxochitl, García lays out correspondences between Alva Ixtlilxochitl's historical narrative and the structure and discourse of the medieval European *nobiliarios*, texts meant to prove a family's antiquity, their connection to dynastic founders, and thus uphold and justify their power and privileges. While he argues that the *Historia de la nación chichimeca* functions as an extended nobiliario in the European tradition, he also cites in the work of Douglas, Boone, and others the overriding importance placed on genealogies of rulers in Mesoamerican historical tradition (discussed above). He thus leaves his reader with a sense of the overdetermination of the centrality of rulership, as a nexus of cultural convergence, in Alva Ixtlilxochitl's narrative. Indeed, this centrality is structural, but also symbolic and thematic and, given the overwhelming weight of the ruler and ruling lines in both Nahua and European histories, it could hardly be otherwise.

Although volume 1 of Torquemada's *Veintiun libros rituales y Monarquía indiana* (like most colonial histories of the Nahuas) proceeds with a concern for rulers and rulership, it is not centered on the Acolhuaque (singular Acolhua), as is the *Historia de la nación chichimeca*. Instead of glorifying a single ruling line, the *Monarquía indiana* consolidates and organizes in chronological fashion the political histories of most of the major groups or altepeme (singular altepetl), with the perspective(s) of the Mexica given rightful status and balanced prominence in the narrative. Its more expansive scope is not limited to its broader representation of political history, moreover. A second, more ethnographic, tome is dedicated to describing the beliefs, rites, social organization, and customs of the peoples whose histories are presented in volume 1, while a third volume concludes the history with an overview of the work of the Franciscan missionaries and missions.

The *Historia de la nación chichimeca* of course includes descriptive detail about other altepeme (singular altepetl) and their genealogies, religious, and social traditions and about the Spanish and Franciscan presence as well. Its more condensed and synthetic approach, however, is a result of its focus on the Acolhua dynastic lineage, which shapes and determines, on the historiographical axis of selection and combination, the nature of the content and detail (about other rulerships, events, and aspects of social and cultural practices) that Alva Ixtlilxochitl provides. Although they are based on some common sources and touch on similar themes and topics, the *Historia de la nación chichimeca* and the *Monarquía indiana* have very different centers of gravity.

RULES AND FRANCISCANS: NARRATIVE
"HEROES" OF THE *HISTORIA DE LA NACIÓN*
CHICHIMECA AND THE *MONARQUÍA INDIANA*

In addition to the humanist-inspired Renaissance history's new focus on establishing mundane and human causes and consequences of world history, the new form of the genre was also characterized by a narrower field of vision. Instead of aiming to tell the story of all Christendom (as a means of providing a tool to discern or uncover divine purpose in the world), Renaissance historians zeroed in on particular entities, such as the monastery or the newly derived concept of the patria (Breisach 1994 [1983], 179–80). Its focus on these specific (and more local) entities reflected the new world order of separate kingdoms vying for ascendancy rather than the medieval dream of a Christian world united under the authority of the pope in Rome. In practical terms, therefore, as Breisach indicates, many of the Renaissance histories were local histories whose primary purpose was to establish a local entity's affiliation with the larger scheme of Christian history, a scheme set out at the very beginning of the narrative with its representation of the biblical cosmogony. One of the major elements distinguishing Alva Ixtlilxochitl's history from that of Torquemada involves precisely this principle of the historical subject, narrowed from the medieval chronicle's focus on all of "Christendom." Indeed, their different interpretations or renditions of New Spain as a kind of "patria" or new space within the context of wider Christendom place into high relief their respective motives for writing their histories, motives arising from their positions in colonial society.

For Alva Ixtlilxochitl, belonging to (and working on behalf of) Nahua nobility, the humanist focus on the patria conveniently dovetails with the Nahua histories' own "micropatriotism," to use Schroeder's (1997, 6–7) term for the phenomenon. Juan de Torquemada, on the other hand, heir to the tradition of the Franciscan order of which he formed a part (and therefore to the long tradition of the monastic chronicle in Europe), creates a text that reflects the history of his order as well as his order's role in history. Notwithstanding the title of his work, Torquemada's concern with (and portrayal of) indigenous rulership takes a back seat to its *true protagonists*: the Franciscan friars who took it upon themselves to bring them (and their people) to the Christian religion. By "true protagonists," I refer to the moral or spiritual heroes of the narrative, those whose actions are regarded as central in the fulfillment of the Christian and providentialist understanding of time and human destiny undergirding these two texts' emplotments of Christian history, that is, at the center of their *configurations* of the relationship between human and cosmic time.

In contrast to the *Monarquía indiana*, the *Historia de la nación chichimeca*, as we have seen, uses the line of Acolhua rulers (as the representation of the "nación chichimeca" [Chichimeca nation]) to structure the narrative. To paraphrase García Loaeza (2014, 348), it is not *chronology* as such that constitutes the organizational backbone of the work, but *rulership itself*. The text's forward movement (in Christian time and according to the European reader's expectations of future events) derives from the narrative's focus on the Acolhua rulers, from their earliest links to the Tolteca (and Tolteca history) and the arrival of the Chichimeca leader Xolotl to the moment when the manuscript trails off in the middle of its description of the siege of Mexico. When dates are provided (and Alva Ixtlilxochitl dates events according to both Nahua and Christian calendars and prominent events associated with those dates in those worlds), they are almost always subordinated to the presentation or description of the event at hand (sometimes even interrupting the flow of the narrative) and the person or persons involved in them. Many chapters or groups of chapters begin and end by announcing the births, inaugurations, or deaths of rulers, and the actions are centered on explaining or highlighting their feats and the fate of the Acolhua rulership centered in Tetzcoco. If other rulers or ruling lines are described or other events are detailed, it is their connection to the events centered in Tetzcoco and involving the Acolhua ruling line that, for the most part, motivates the description.[5]

Although volume 1 of the *Monarquía indiana* represents the history of New Spain in terms of its sequences of civilizations and their rulers, its more balanced inclusion of Mexica and other lineages' histories creates a more expansive narrative that derives its coherence from its linear chronology and from its Christian teleology. In the *Monarquía indiana*, history remains exclusively a question of a larger *biblical* order, and its pages are dedicated to elucidating the meaning of the histories it recounts and of the discovery and conquest of the New World within that frame, a meaning that ultimately rests upon and is fulfilled in the work of the missionaries. This is clear from the very beginning of the text, in the framing and interpretation of the political history of the people of New Spain, in its framing and presentation of their religion and customs (in volume 2), and finally, of course, in the representation of the biographies of missionaries, with which the history culminates and concludes (in volume 3).

In the *Monarquía indiana*, the connections with "cosmic time" as imagined in Nahua texts, such as cyclical dynastic structures, are incidental,
rather than integrated into the fabric of the text. In the *Historia de la nación
chichimeca*, however, the focus on the Tetzcoca rulers as vital protagonists
in the realization of Christian history is the mechanism that enables Alva
Ixtlilxochitl's narrative to reflect two temporalities simultaneously: a linear
providentialism and the cyclical dynamic, described by Graulich (1981), consistent with patterns established in Nahua cosmogony and the histories of the
Tolteca. It is through his portrayal of rulers and their lineages that he creates
a text that reaches out in two directions simultaneously, toward both a Nahua
idea of the basis of the rulers' power and their role and place in the cosmological chronotope as well as a European conception. Enabling this feature of his
narrative, however, is an extremely significant difference between the *Historia de la nación chichimeca* and the *Monarquía indiana* as universal histories.
As he sets up the Acolhua rulers as key figures in the realization of Christian
history and provides his own answer to the question of the meaning of the
discovery and conquest of the New World, Alva Ixtlilxochitl adopts a quite
different strand of Christian providentialism from that of Torquemada: the
idea (more like an implication or a suggestion, in his text) that Anahuac had
perhaps heard of Christianity before the arrival of the Spanish.

ALVA IXTLILXOCHITL, TORQUEMADA AND THE
PRE-EVANGELIZATION OF THE NEW WORLD

In the *Historia de la nación chichimeca*, Alva Ixtlilxochitl blends into his narrative an insinuation of a previous evangelization of the region around the time
of Christ by an apostle-like figure named Quetzalcoatl. This theory of indigenous contact with Christianity before the arrival of Columbus, first and most
directly expressed, as Jacques LaFaye ([1998] 1995, 235–41, 254–59) has documented, in the work of Dominican friar Diego Durán, runs contrary to Torquemada's understanding of the peoples of the New World as wayward gentiles
and idolaters. In book 6, chapters 6–8 and 12–16, Torquemada describes how
people such as the Egyptians and later the Romans lost track of the true God
after the division of languages (and humanity) after the smiting of the Tower of
Babel, and then erringly (and with the help of the devil) created false substitutes
from known sources (usually those full of pleasure or goodness and worth)
such as the sun, certain human beings, and vile beasts. Although Torquemada
([1723] 1975, 2:48, 51, 52), citing Sahagún, indeed recounts an episode in which

a wealthy and revered priest (and sorcerer, later worshipped as a god) named Quetzalcoatl prophesies a future arrival of white men with white beards (his brothers and sons) who would become the rulers or lords of the land, he does not bring the story into the fold of (New Testament–era) Christian history. As H. B. Nicholson (2001, 113) has commented regarding Torquemada's writing on Quetzalcoatl: "the emphasis here, in contrast to the Durán account, is on cultural proselytization rather than moral or ritual."

Indeed, LaFaye's ([1977] 1995, 211–59, especially 229) analysis shows how Torquemada's perspective on the supposed prophesy of a returning Quetzalcoatl deity/cultural hero coincides with those of (some of) his sources, most importantly Sahagún and Las Casas. Although Torquemada mentions Quetzalcoatl's penitence and the gentleness of his rulership ([1723] 1975, 2:51), the overriding emphasis is on his status as a ruler and sorcerer in relationship to his counterpoint and rival, called Huemac, Tezcatlipoca ([1723] 1975, 1:254–56), or Titlacahuan ([1723] 1975, 2:20–21, 48–51). As León Portilla ([1969] 1975, xxvii–xxxi) notes in his introductory study to Torquemada's work, Torquemada did not regard the many similar practices, signs, and beliefs in New World religiosity and Christianity to be the result of actual previous contact with a Christian (or Christian-like) apostle but, on the contrary, the work of the devil taking advantage of humanity's dim memories of the Edenic, prelapsarian divine revelation (and innate need for God) as a means of leading them astray.

The political and ideological implications of these two approaches—an implicit preevangelization vs. a demonic appropriation of dim memories of the divine rooted in the book of nature and exploitation of human weakness and desire for God—are significant. The idea of a previous evangelization was untenable for the Franciscans, as LaFaye ([1977] 1995, 257–58, 263, 267) and Baudot (1995, 71–91) remark, as it would have undermined their millennialist faith in the final conversion of all the gentiles and their vision of the New World as a *locus amoenus* for the establishment of the primitive church. For others besides the Franciscans, the explanatory power of the idea of a preevangelization lay in its assertion that, despite the lack of a clear presence in biblical and classical texts, the New World and its peoples in fact had not been completely ignored or abandoned by God, who had surely created them, and that its ongoing suffering at the hands of greedy colonists was beyond the pale (LaFaye 1995, 235–50, 256, 260–72). This idea, says LaFaye, had the advantage of counteracting the cultural arrogance of the *peninsulares* (Spaniards from Spain), who often regarded the colonies and its castas ("castes" or groups of racial mixtures) with derision. Even more importantly, it opened a space for the inclusion of indigenous beliefs and practices within Christianity—the exact worry that Sahagún and the Franciscans, according to LaFaye, were so intent on combating (or, given the political circumstances, that they were at least intent on *saying* they were combating).⁶ For Sahagún, he notes, the work on ethnography in Nahuatl (and other indigenous languages) and on indigenous customs and beliefs was a means of maintaining a clear separation between Nahua religiosity and Catholicism, worlds that (as with the cult of the Virgin of Guadalupe) had altogether too much potential to meld together (217–19). It is noteworthy, therefore, that in spite of his scholarly affiliation with Torquemada, Alva Ixtlilxochitl, in presenting Quetzalcoatl as an apostle-like figure appearing around the time of Christ, implicitly embraces an idea first proposed by Durán (in the words of LaFaye, the first of the early missionary-historians of ancient Mexico to interpret that past "como la propia historia de su patria de adopción" [236; as the history of his own adopted homeland]) and then developed by "patriotic" criollo thinkers like Carlos de Sigüenza y Góngora, Mariano Veytia, and friar Servando Teresa de Mier (LaFaye [1977] 1995, 112–23, 273–300).

While Torquemada's providentialism centers on Cortés (regarded as another Moses), chosen by God to open "la puerta de esta gran tierra de Anahuac, y hacer camino a los predicadores de su evangelio, en este nuevo Mundo," Alva Ixtlilxochitl roots his version—which, in the *Historia de la nación chichimeca*, still gives Cortés a leading role—in early preconquest history, with the introduction of the figure of Quetzalcoatl ([1723] 1975, 1:340; the door to this great land of Anahuac and make a pathway for the preachers of its salvation in this New World). In the *Monarquía indiana*, the Spanish are the clear protagonists of the "discovery" and "conquest" of the inhabitants of the New World, with the missionaries, who sacrificed themselves in order to bring Christianity to the people, responsible for the realization of their providential nature and ultimate meaning. In the *Historia de la nación chichimeca*, on the contrary, the Acolhua themselves (under Nezahualcoyotl, Nezahualpilli, and Fernando Cortés Ixtlilxochitl) are focalized as agents of their own (historical) destiny, foreseeing and preparing for the advent of a destruction of their empire that would ironically also mean their salvation. In essence, these rulers are intentional and instrumental (if also extremely wistful) actors in the processes of conquest, colonization, and evangelization. The Spanish, on the other hand, fulfill *their* destiny only *because of* the vital aid provided by the indigenous "allies," namely, the Acolhua under Ixtlilxochitl and, secondarily, divine intervention in the form of miraculous apparitions through which the Tlaxcalteca are finally persuaded to fight in their favor as well (1975–1977, 2:237).

The full implications of this different rendering of Christian providentialism become apparent when we pay careful attention to the fact that the *Historia de la nación chichimeca* links Quetzalcoatl and Nezahualcoyotl, two rulers whose religious sagacity (and proto-Christian beliefs) distinguishes them from their contemporaries, to Cortés. By means of this association, the text roots itself in (and provides an image of) the linear and salvific narrative of biblical eschatology. At the same time, however, with the prophesied arrival of Cortés (its portrayal as a long awaited event) and the structural and discursive identification of all three protagonists, the text inscribes an element of repetition more proper to a cyclical temporality, and indeed the spiritual affinities (or legacy) of the three personae (Quetzalcoatl, Nezahualcoyotl, and Cortés) cannot be separated from the temporal scheme of the Nahua cosmogony with which Alva Ixtlilxochitl inaugurates his narrative.

It is here, once again at the very opening of the two histories, where the basic differences in the emplotment of Torquemada's and Alva Ixtlilxochitl's works are established. While Torquemada eventually *describes* the Nahua/Tolteca creation story in chapter 11 of his text, Alva Ixtlilxochitl inscribes—or, more accurately, *reinscribes*—it as the founding cosmogony of his universal history. Indeed, as we saw with respect to a discussion of their description and treatment of their sources in the last chapter, it should be no surprise that Torquemada commences his history not with the Nahua cosmogony, nor solely with the biblical stories, but by situating his biblical referents within a discussion of the thinking of the ancients.

Part Two. Rulers, Lineage, and the Articulation of Nahua Temporality in the *Historia de la nación chichimeca*

ESTABLISHING ORIGINS: ALVA IXTLILXOCHITL'S NAHUA-CHRISTIAN CREATION STORY

Chapter 1 of the first Book of the *Monarquía indiana*, entitled "De como crió Dios al mundo, para mostrar su poder, y grandeza, en su creación" (How God created the world, to demonstrate his power and greatness through his creation), begins by affirming Aristotle's definition of the world as a single entity made up of the heavens and the earth and everything in it: "un orden,

y concierto de todas las cosas . . . una disposición muy agradable, la cual de
los dioses, y por los dioses, se conserva, y guarda" ([1723] 1975, 1:1–2; an order
and unity of everything . . . a very pleasing order, that, by the gods and for the
gods, is maintained and preserved). In the next several chapters (2–6), in line
with many other humanist-influenced *cronistas de indias* (chroniclers of the
Indies), he turns to discussing the cosmography of the ancients and providing an up-to-date account of world cosmography and the place of the newly
discovered lands and their inhabitants within it.

Although the text thus begins neither with the Nahua cosmogony nor
with the story from Genesis, Torquemada's subsequent discussion of the
origins of the people of New Spain, which he arrives at in chapter 8 after
a presentation of the physical geography of the New World (16–20) and a
discussion of the name "Indias" [Indies] given to the region by Columbus
(although its original name, he notes, is Anahuac) (21–22), clearly takes the
biblical account as the point of reference through which to make sense of
the lands and peoples whose histories he is recounting. Of the many vex-
ing problems that the discovery of the Americas presented for the European
understanding of the world—for example, was there not supposed to be only
one world, an island, surrounded by a great ocean sea? Was all of the earth
inhabitable and inhabited, even the torrid zone? Was the world spherical with
opposing poles?[7]—the one that received the most sustained attention was the
question of the origins of the inhabitants of the New World. Rejecting the
notion that the ancient arrivals were descendents of tribes of Israel, Torquemada discusses various other theories but finally refuses to provide any definitive answer to the question, stating only his opinion that the inhabitants were
very ancient, descended from Noah's children from shortly after the flood
(likely the sons or grandsons of Ham, given their "color" [30]), and that they
likely arrived in the New World via land and not sea.

This ancient origin is suggested, he notes, by the very fact that there is no
documentation of it from either European or indigenous sources:

> No habiendo noticia de los antiguos moradores, y naturales de esta
> tierra, de qué gente sea, ni de qué familia haya venido, ni en nuestra
> España, haya tal noticia de ninguno de los escritores, que andemos, a
> ojos cerrados, dando vueltas, y rodeando la verdad, y por ventura, no
> llamando a su puerta en mucho tiempo; y así me parece, que debi-
> eron de ser de alguna gente antiquísima, de aquella, que se repartió,
> y dividió, luego después del diluvio; porque a ser de tiempos más

modernos, pienso que fuera muy posible, que hubiera, quién tratara de
ella: que no es de creer, que si en los tiempos, que ellos pasaron, hubiera
historiadores, dejaran de echarlos menos en algun reino, o provincia,
y ellos supieran dar raçon de sí mismos: la cual, no hallamos, aunque la tenemos de los más modernos (como en sus lugares, e historias
se dirá). (22)

There is a lack of information about the ancient inhabitants and natives
of this land, of what people they may be, or from which lineage they
came from. Nor is there such information in our Spain among the
writers, and so we go around and around forever, blindly and without
direction skirting the truth, never arriving at its door. It seems to me
that they must have been from a very ancient people, from those that
were dispersed and divided after the flood; because if [they arrived
from] more present times I think it would be very possible that someone would have mentioned them. Moreover, it is not credible that if
there had been historians during the time that they came over, that they
would have failed to mention their departure and absence, and they also
would have had their own accounts, which we don't find to be the case,
although we have them from the more modern ones (as in their places
and histories it will be noted.)

Only in chapter 11 does he begin to present the stories that the Nahuas
told about their own origins, although even here the *biblical* flood becomes
a major point of reference as he engages in a long discussion of whether the
very first inhabitants (the giants) could possibly have occupied the area *before*
the great cataclysm.

Instead of beginning his presentation of indigenous origin stories with a
version of the tale of the four suns (or ages) of creation, as does Alva Ixtlilxochitl, moreover, Torquemada opens with *another* origin story, one that Alva
Ixtlilxochitl brushes over, despite its (varied) presence in many recountings
of Nahua and Acolhua origins. A general discussion of the topic is followed
by a more specific presentation of the story itself:

Una cosa se ha de tener por infalible; y es, que todos concuerdan, en
que son advenedizos, y que su origen, es de hacia aquellas partes de
Jalixco, que es al poniente, respecto de Mexico: y para mayor claridad
de lo que vamos tratando, es fuerza decir, la variedad de pareceres, y

dichos, que se han podido colegir: unos dicen, que salieron de aquella gran cueva, que ellos llaman Chicomoztoc (que quiere decir, Siete Cuevas) y que vinieron sus pasados poco a poco poblando. . . . Los de Tetchcuco, dicen, ser primeros moradores, y ser Chichimecas (como es verdad, como se verá adelante, en la prosecucion desta Historia). (31)

One thing is certain, and that is that everyone agrees that they hail from, or that their place of origin is from around Jalisco, which is to the west with respect to Mexico. For more clarity about what we are saying, it is necessary to discuss the variety of opinions and ideas that have been gathered. Some say that they left from a great cave that they called Chicomoztoc (which means Seven Caves) and that their ancestors arrived little by little, settling in the area. . . . The people from Tetzcoco say they were the first inhabitants, and were Chichimeca (which is true, as will be seen further on in the unraveling of this History).

After recounting a general migration history given to friar Andrés de Olmos (whose lost work Torquemada cites often) by an elder member of the Tetzcoca nobility (who describes a series of migrations over time from a common area by different branches of a cave- or hut-dwelling hunter-gatherer people), Torquemada begins his next chapter by spelling out the story of the original, founding, ancestors of the migrants he referred to earlier: "Un viejo, y venerable anciano, llamado Iztac Mixcuatl, que residía en aquel lugar, llamado Siete-Cuevas . . . el cual siendo casado con Ilancueitl, hubo de ella seis Hijos" (32; An old man, a venerable elder, called Iztac Mixcoatl, who lived in that place, called Seven-Caves. . . . who, being married to Ilancueitl, had six children with her). What follows in his text is a very long discussion of the validity of the story as a historical reference, since the children of this ancestral couple bear the names of ethnic groups of differing linguistic heritage populating the region: Xelhua, Tenuch, Ulmecatl, Xicalancatl, Mixtecatl, Otomitl. In the end, Torquemada concludes that while the myth could indicate similar remote origins for the peoples it names, the six children in reality could not have spoken different languages and therefore must not have actually been descended from the same parents (33). He says, however, that they all certainly must have arrived after the reign and demise of the great Tolteca civilization.

In his discussion, Torquemada notably skips over the resonance of this ancestral couple (and/or their parallels) in other Nahua (cosmogonic) myths.

Alva Ixtlilxochitl, however, decides not to mention them at all, and thus both of them in this case evade the specter of their connection to "idolatry" and the gods.[8] In Alva Ixtlilxochitl's text, Chicomoztoc is indeed a place of origins, but it is only this: the place from which Xolotl began his journey, via Tula, into the heart of Mexico to take possession of the former Tolteca lands. There is no mention of it being a cave, although Alva Ixtlilxochitl does point out that the first place Xolotl stayed when he arrived in the region, in Tenayuca, was in caves (1975–1977, 2:14). For Alva Ixtlilxochitl, moreover, the Olmeca and the Xicalanca are peoples distinct from the Chichimeca who arrived later under the leadership of Xolotl; the former do not migrate with the other groups after the Tolteca demise but are civilizations that precede the Tolteca, arriving in the region after the *quinametin*, (or, as Alva Ixtlilxochitl calls them in the *Historia de la nación chichimeca* and the *Relación sumaria de la historia general*, the *quinametintzocuilhicxime*), that is, the (in)famous group of "giants" who both authors agree were the very first settlers of the region (7).

Whatever the reason may be that Alva Ixtlilxochitl skips entirely over the genealogical tale of Iztac Mixcoatl and Ilancueitl, the result is a much smoother narrative of the ancient history of the region, uninterrupted, in this case and as a whole, by confusing contradictions (or "gaps" in the narrative) and the extensive explanation, contextualization, and discussion they necessitate. As a general rule, Torquemada remains more faithful to the multiplicity of his source texts and treats them as separate entities as he attempts to place them for his readers in their rightful order within the scheme of what for him was necessarily a single, truthful narrative of universal history. While Alva Ixtlilxochitl presents a highly synthetic and focused account of early history in the *Historia de la nación chichimeca*, often choosing specific versions to present or combining information from different sources with very little explanation (except the most general) about his authorial decisions and editorial processes, Torquemada offers extended editorial commentary on the various problems that arise as he attempts to reconcile their differences and contradictions. It is thus unsurprising, and in keeping with this tendency to respect the boundaries of his sources, that Torquemada mentions the story of the four ages of creation only when he arrives at his discussion of the Tolteca. Although it is a cosmogony, for Torquemada its Tolteca provenance implies that it should be discussed only in that context.

The story, moreover, like Alva Ixtlilxochitl's reference to Chicomoztoc, is selective and incomplete. Assuming it to be a distorted version of biblical eschatology, Torquemada notes only the first and fourth creations, which end with a flood and with fire, respectively. As he puts it, the Tolteca were informed about "la creación del mundo, y como fue destruida la gente, de él, por el diluvio, y otras muchas cosas, que ellos tenían, en pintura, y historia. Y dicen también, que tuvieron noticia de como otra vez se ha de acabar el mundo, por consumación de fuego" (33; the creation of the world, and how its people were destroyed by the flood, and many other things that they had in their paintings and history. And they say also that they knew how the world once again must end, destroyed by fire). The wording—the use of the definite article in "el diluvio" and the implicit certainty underlying the phrase "se ha de acabar" makes clear the assumption of the biblical tradition as the truthful historical narrative or standard against which the Tolteca tradition was measured: the flood and fire alluded to by the Tolteca were the same ones discussed in Genesis and Revelation. In not replicating these biblical stories exactly, however, the writers of the creation story deviated from the norm and proved the inferiority of the ancient Tolteca culture to the European. For Torquemada, there can be only one master narrative of history that speaks a singular and unambiguous truth. After recounting the political history of the Tolteca (all within the same chapter), he jumps without transition into his discussion of the Chichimeca migrations, noting that their leader, Xolotl, came from a place called Amaqueme (another term used for Chicomoztoc).

Like Torquemada, Alva Ixtlilxochitl organizes his representation of the cosmogony of the four separate creations according to the biblical scheme, with the flood the means of the destruction of the first age and fire responsible for that of the last (yet to come). Even more than Torquemada, in fact, Alva Ixtlilxochitl looks for and presents parallels between his source texts and biblical tradition. As stated above, he makes a concerted effort to integrate his sources into the flow of the Christian temporal trajectory, but in doing so he is less concerned about presenting the entire gamut of possible and possibly conflicting variants of the story and of locating the stories in their respective contexts of origin. In this sense, the *Historia de la nación chichimeca* obeys an overall historical trajectory that favors Nahua representations of those "universal" events over an organization, like that found in the *Monarquía indiana*, that places Nahua narratives under the (chronologically ordered) domain of their place of origin. Alva Ixtlilxochitl's general organization of the early political history of central Mexico, however, is also—with the important exception of the place of the Olmeca and Xicalanca—consistent with the order presented by Torquemada: he regards the giants as the first settlers, after which come the Olmeca and Xicalanca, then the Tolteca, and finally the

Chichimeca (beginning with Xolotl), whose arrivals occur in small groups over time.[9] Unlike his fellow historian, however, Alva Ixtlilxochitl presents all four suns or ages of creation, and he places the story at the beginning of his narrative in the *Historia de la nación chichimeca*, integrating the arrivals and endings of the various civilizations into its fabric.

In sum, the *Historia de la nación chichimeca* grants the cosmogony of the four suns or ages of creation quite a different status than that found in Torquemada's text, where it remains a "Tolteca" story (discussed in its proper context). Appearing as it does at the beginning of Alva Ixtlilxochitl's narrative, its biblical parallels imbue it with the power of truth, such that it can stand on its own and stand in for the biblical story even as it remains in its intact form, with all four ages represented. It is regarded not as a reflection of a dim remembrance or awareness of ancient truth, as a distortion of a standard, but instead as an alternate version or expression of that truth. In other words, biblical (truthful) history is no longer a singular, univocal, monological entity.

Despite all of the Catholic Church's insistence on orthodoxy and fear of idolatry, it could not insulate the biblical texts and teachings from the operative historicities—Nahua and others—through which they were read or understood (Burkhart 1989; Gruzinski 2002). In its encounter with Nahua (and other indigenous) cosmogonies, biblical stories of the world's creation (and endings) gained new cultural dimensions and significations. A close look at Alva Ixtlilxochitl's cosmogony reveals some of these new dimensions, most notably its envelopment within a Nahua dynamic of cyclical dualism. Key to the cosmogony's allegorization and integration into the narrative as an additional means of connecting human and cosmic time is the *Historia de la nación chichimeca*'s innovative use of the idea of a previous evangelization of the region and the Quetzalcoatl-as-apostle figure.

After its presentation of "los más graves autores y históricos" (the most illustrious authors and historians), discussed in the previous chapter, the *Historia de la nación chichimeca* begins its historical narrative by relating these writers' tales:

> Declaran por sus historias que el dios Teotloquenahuaque Tlachiual-cípal Nemoani Ilhuicahua Tlalticpaque, que quiere decir conforme al verdadero sentido, el dios universal de todas las cosas, creador de ellas y a cuya voluntad viven todas las criaturas, señor del cielo y de la tierra, etcétera el cual después de haber creado todas las cosas visibles e

invisibles, creó a los primeros padres de los hombres, de donde procedieron todos los demás; y la morada y habitación que les dio fue el mundo, el cual dicen tener cuatro edades. La primera que fue desde su origen, llamada por ellos Atonatiuh, que significa sol de agua; que con sentido alegórico significan con este vocablo, aquella primera edad del mundo haber sido acabada con el diluvio e inundación de las aguas, con que se ahogaron todos los hombres y perecieron todas las cosas creadas.

They declare in their histories that the god Teotloquenahuaque Tlachiualcípal Nemoani Ilhuicahua Tlalticpaque (which, according to its true sense, means the universal god and creator of all things, by whose will all creatures live, lord of the sky and the earth, etcetera) after having created all the visible and invisible things, created the first forebearers of men, from whom proceeded everyone else; and the dwelling and home that he gave them was the world, which they say has four ages. The first was from its beginning called [by them] Atonatiuh, meaning water sun; allegorically what they mean by this name is that the first age of the world ended with the flooding and inundation of the waters, whereby everyone drowned and everything created perished.

In these sentences, it is quite clear that the Tolteca history (and other origin stories among his sources) has been recounted in such a way as to fit smoothly into the biblical mold. First, they present a single deity, not multiple gods, as responsible for the creation of the world. Second, the reference to a *single* world, "el mundo," reflecting Torquemada's preoccupation with the question of one world or many rooted in classical European texts, neutralizes any sense of essential difference (or otherness) of the Nahua cosmogony in the face of the biblical creation story. Third, instead of referring to four separate "creations" (and destructions), Alva Ixtlilxochitl talks about a world that is said to have had four "edades" or "ages"—a commonplace European term in discussing and defining historical trajectories. Fourth, he notes that this single deity created not only the world itself but the first couple, original ancestors from whom all people descend. Finally, the attribution of a Nahuatl name to a divinity described (in Spanish) in clearly biblical language is akin to its identification of the destruction of the first age of the Nahua cosmogony with the biblical flood.

However, these instances of setting up a parallelism with the biblical tradition do not replace or overtake the autonomy of the Nahuatl signifiers and the stories behind them, and of course, as the friars were aware, there was no failsafe means of ensuring readers' interpretation or understanding of them, of putting limits on the nature and value of the signified. For example, because Alva Ixtlilxochitl does not *name* his ancestral pair, we are free to assume that he is referencing either Adam and Eve *or* the ancestral couple of Chicomoztoc (or other ancestral pairs from other Nahua places and/or narratives), or both at once. Moreover, while the long and complex history of the origins and evolution of the colonial Nahuatl term often used in reference to the Christian God, "Tloque Nahuaque Ipal Nemoani," requires a longer discussion than what is possible to undertake in this context, linked, as it is, to Alva Ixtlilxochitl's larger vision of a pre-Hispanic monotheism (Lee 2008, 193–228; León Portilla 1999), a wholesale eradication of the epithets' original associations with Nahua deities (such as Tezcatlipoca) and concepts of the divine is doubtful. Alva Ixtlilxochitl's inclusion of the *entire* cosmogony, moreover, as stated above, preserves its integrity and also its essential *difference* from the cosmogony (or cosmogonies) found in Genesis.

In contrast to Torquemada, who *describes* them, Alva Ixtlilxochitl treats the Nahua stories and terms (those he decides to include) as integral parts of his linear narrative sequence or historical thread, putting them to work for his own (dual) purposes and leaving them on their own, without external editorial annotations. While Torquemada's text works to *differentiate* Nahua names and modes from Christian thinking (though he grants them their dim light of revelation) in order to highlight the accomplishments and context in which the missionaries worked, Alva Ixtlilxochitl's text creates a Nahua-Christian world in which many aspects of Nahua thought—the realm of the Nahua signified—can potentially remain active cocontributors to the shape and meaning of the narrative. In his refusal to disambiguate historical actors or events through a use of specific Nahuatl (or Christian) terms or editorial explanations, he allows them to bring along with them all of their potential for opening up multiple possibilities of signification. He also organizes the information at his disposal in a way that is consistent with his sense of history as told in both cultural frameworks, displacing episodes from the temporal or cultural landscape from which they originated.

Unlike Torquemada, he takes the (presumably originally) *Tolteca* history as an account of the world's beginnings (both merged with and standing in for biblical tradition) and presents it out of context, that is, *before* his discussion of the Tolteca themselves as originators of the story. In so doing, and like those who first recounted it, he accepts the creation story of the Tolteca as his own. At the same time, however, this Tolteca creation story's bare referencing of an "original couple" is quite pointedly divorced from that which, in the *Monarquía indiana*, includes a very significant and elaborate connection to the story of the creation of humanity at Chicomoztoc, of the sun (presumably at Teotihuacan), and of the sacred deity bundles of the Chichimeca (Torquemada [1723] 1975, 2:76–79).[10]

In Alva Ixtlilxochitl's text, the language that echoes Genesis and implies a Christian viewpoint works to create a reading that accepts a Nahua history of the past as a parallel to and/or a reflection of the hegemonic Christian narrative. The cyclical time of creations and destructions seemingly flattens out and/or is overcome by the linear perspective implied in the biblical language: Nahua historicity melds into Christian, helped along by the relentless censorship of stories that too obviously transgress the precepts of Catholic orthodoxy. Yet does this overlay of Christian history onto the hollowed-out Nahua stories reflect a solely assimilative purpose, or does it also comply with and respond to a properly Nahua historiographical agenda?

Despite its encasement in Christian, European genres and discursive paradigms, the uniqueness of the Nahua cosmogony remains. As we will see, by establishing the historicality of (its rendition of) Christian universal history through parallelism (a kind of superimposition), Alva Ixtlilxochitl allows the Nahua *chronotope* to (continue to) speak for itself, and hence for the text as a whole to speak doubly. The "single," "true" God retains a Nahuatl name, and the cycles of four ages (along with the dates themselves) continue to suggest a cyclical or repetitive iteration of time. A basic principle of Nahua historicity, established in and through the presentation of the cosmogony of the four suns or ages of creation, roots itself, entwined with the Christian perspective, in Alva Ixtlilxochitl's text.

EPOCHAL CREATIONS: COSMOGONIC AND POLITICAL AGES IN THE *HISTORIA DE LA NACIÓN CHICHIMECA*

The synthetic and hybrid vision of history described above with respect to Alva Ixtlilxochitl's overall representation of the cosmogony continues in his account of the second and third "edades" or ages of creation (which Torquemada leaves unmentioned):

> La segunda edad llamaron Tlalchitonatiuh, que significa sol de tierra, por haberse acabado con terremotos, abriéndose la tierra por muchas

partes, sumiéndose y derrocándose sierras y peñascos, de tal manera
que perecieron casi todos los hombres, con cuya edad y tiempo fueron
los gigantes que llamaron quinametintzocuilhicxime.

La tercera edad llamaron Ecatonatiuh, que quiere decir sol de aire,
porque feneció esta edad con aire, que fue tanto y tan recio el viento que
hizo entonces, que derrocó todos los edificios y árboles y aun deshizo
las peñas, y pereció la mayor parte de los hombres. (1975–1977, 2:7)

They called the second age Tlalchitonatiuh, which means earth sun, for
having come to an end with earthquakes, with the earth opening up in
many places and the mountains and cliffs crumbling and falling, such
that almost all of the people perished, in whose age and time lived the
giants that they called quinametintzocuilhicxime.

The third age they called Ecatonatiuh, which means wind sun,
because this age was destroyed by wind, which was so abundant and so
strong that it knocked over buildings and trees and even destroyed the
rocks, and the majority of the people perished.

What is significant about his representation of these ages is that, in addition to including them and their requisite means of destruction in his narrative, Alva Ixtlilxochitl merges them with the political history of the region by
introducing the "giants" as inhabitants of the *second* age (presenting his own
version of an answer to Torquemada's question of whether they had lived in
the region before or after the flood). He then continues in this vein in the
next few paragraphs by telling the story of a hostile encounter in the third age
between the surviving giants (of the second age) and its population, made up
of the "ulmecas" and the "xicalancas." Although the "giants" tried to make
the Olmeca and Xicalanca their vassals, the latter (very much like Odysseus's
adventure with Polyphemus) used their wits and military prowess to free
themselves from tyranny and exploitation (7). It is at the end of the third
age, when, as Alva Ixtlilxochitl relates, at the height of its prosperity, "llegó a
esta tierra un hombre a quien llamaron Quetzalcóatl y otros Huémac por sus
grandes virtudes" (8; a man they called Quetzalcoatl and others Huemac for
his great virtues, arrived in the land).

By blending the migration histories with the Tolteca cosmogony in his
own way—differently from Torquemada's truncated version of the four ages
of creation but expanded migration narratives relating to a primordial couple
(or couples)—Alva Ixtlilxochitl establishes a clear association in his history

between cosmic ages and political empires. As with his ambiguous reference to the ancestral couple, the division of political history according to ages lends the text the appearance of resignifying and rendering innocuous the possible Nahua religious and cultural significations of the cosmogony, retaining only a sense of the "rise and fall" of dynasties. However, Alva Ixtlilxochitl thereby not only introduces and embellishes the essential theme of cultural encounter—a defining feature of his narrative even in the early texts (and already a recognizable theme with familiar motifs in the New World from Columbus onward)[11]—his history also retains, or perhaps it is more accurate to say that it *recreates*, certain aspects of these meanings implicit in the story of the four "suns" of creation. This is accomplished in the introduction of the figure of Quetzalcoatl at the end, indeed, as the *means* of ending, the third age of creation.

While Alva Ixtlilxochitl's Quetzalcoatl is obviously a Christianized figure, his traditional significations in Nahua texts—his role in the cosmogonies and associations with rulership—also influence the shape and meaning of the narrative. Moreover, the new version of the story of the four ages that Alva Ixtlilxochitl tells here (and reflected also in the *Sumaria relación de la historia general*), wherein the Tolteca civilization arises in the *wake* of the destruction of the Olmeca and the Xicalanca centered in Cholula, bears certain similarities to the migration stories found in the myth-histories from the Tlaxcala region (such as that of Muñoz Camargo [(1892) 1972, 5–6]) and the works of the missionaries who spent significant time in the region (including Motolinía [1985, 99–101n5, 102–5, 107–13]), and a variation on this history and other elements of the story are also present in the *Monarquía indiana* itself ([1723] 1975, 1:256–64).[12] In any case, this shift in his rendering of the cosmogony and early political history of Anahuac evidences a rethinking on the part of Alva Ixtlilxochitl of the ancestral history of the region, and of his manner of representing it, perhaps in part under the influence of reading Torquemada's history and/or sources affiliated with it. For its contribution to the *Historia de la nación chichimeca*'s double emplotment of its historical narrative, a brief summary of the significant aspects of the ending of the third age and the beginning of the fourth age follows.

Although the new arrival and apostle-like Quetzalcoatl tried to teach the Olmeca and the Xicalanca to live virtuously, he ended up very disappointed in "el poco fruto que hacía con su doctrina" and eventually returned to the east from whence he had come (1975–1977, 2:8; the lack of fruit that his doctrine was bearing). Before departing off the coast of Coatzacoalco, he was careful to take leave of the people, telling them that "en los tiempos venideros, en un año que se llamaría ce ácatl, volvería" (in the future, in a year called ce acatl, he would return). His departure marked the end of the third age and inaugurated the beginning of the fourth age, which begins with the arrival of the "la nación tulteca" (10; the Toltec nation). These ages' modes of destruction (like those of the previous ages), are duly noted:

> Ido que fue [Quetzalcoatl], de allí a pocos días sucedió la destrucción y asolamiento referido de la tercera edad del mundo; y entonces se destruyó aquel edificio y torre tan memorable y suntuosa de la ciudad de Cholula, que era como otra segunda torre de Babel, que estas gentes edificaban casi con los mismos designios, deshaciéndola el viento. Y después los que escaparon de la consumición de la tercera edad, en las ruinas de ella edificaron un templo a Quetzalcóatl a quien colocaron por dios del aire, por haber sido causa de su destrucción el aire, entendiendo ellos que fue enviada de su mano esta calamidad; y le llamaron asimismo ce ácatl que fue el nombre del año de su venida. Y según parece por las historias referidas y por los anales, sucedió lo suso referido algunos años después de la encarnación de Cristo señor nuestro; y desde este tiempo acá entró la cuarta edad que dijeron llamarse Tletonátiuc, que significa sol de fuego, porque dijeron que esta cuarta y última edad del mundo se ha de acabar con fuego. Era Quetzalcóatl hombre bien dispuesto, de aspecto grave, blanco y barbado. Su vestuario era una túnica larga. (8–9)

A few days after Quetzalcoatl's departure, the destruction and devastation referred to of the third age of the world took place; and it was then that the very memorable and luxurious building and tower in the city of Cholula, which was like a second tower of Babel that these people built with almost the same intentions, was destroyed, with the wind breaking it apart. And afterward those who escaped the destruction of the third age built a temple to Quetzalcoatl, whom they installed as god of the wind, because the wind had caused its destruction, and they thought that the calamity had been sent by his hand; and they called him therefore ce acatl, which was the name of the year of his arrival. And it seems that according to the histories mentioned and to the annals, that the event took place some years after the incarnation of Christ our Lord; and from this time forward commenced the fourth age that they said

was called Tletonátiuc, which means fire sun, because they said that this
fourth and last age of the world must end with fire. Quetzalcoatl was a
well-disposed man of dignified stature, white, and bearded. His attire
was a long tunic.

Once again, the passage reveals Alva Ixtlilxochitl's penchant for parallels
between the Nahua and the biblical pasts, the comparison of the great temple
to Quetzalcoatl in Cholula with the tower of Babel being a case in point.
This is a common comparison in works from Motolinía to Torquemada, and,
although there is also a similar tower ("un zacuali . . . que quiere decir, 'la
torre altísima'") in the *Sumaria relación de todas las cosas*, there it is taken to
be the *actual* tower of Babel and associated with the myth of the creation of
languages in a projection of the account's cosmogony—and the origins of the
Tolteca—directly into the history and geography of biblical tradition ([1975–
1977] 1985, 1:263; a *zacuali* . . . which means "the very tall tower").

The key aspects of this passage with respect to its representation of Quetzalcoatl, however, are (1) his identification as a stranger from the east who
ultimately disappears in the direction from whence he came, (2) his portrayal
as an apostle-like figure teaching a clearly Christian-like doctrine (and associated temporally with the birth of Christ), (3) his association with the Nahua
date ce acatl, and (4) his announcement that he would *return* on that date.
These characteristics are by no means unique to Alva Ixtlilxochitl's Quetzalcoatl figure, and the third and fourth, of course, are embodied in the *Sumaria
relación de todas las cosas* in the roughly homologous figure of Topiltzin.
Other elements seem to be derived from sources such as the *Monarquía indiana*, for example, wherein Quetzalcoatl is also a stranger (a non-Native) who
arrives peacefully to the region bringing (among other gifts) fine artisanry
and architecture. In Torquemada's history, however, after arriving with his
people at Pánuco in the north, Quetzalcoatl first settles in Tula ([1723] 1975,
1:254–56). In the *Historia de la nación chichimeca*, on the contrary, Quetzalcoatl's *only* association with Tula and the Tolteca is the fact that the cataclysm
brought about by his departure from Cholula ushered in the fourth age, when
the Tolteca arrive on the scene. In Alva Ixtlilxochitl's histories, in fact, there
is not even a proper *Tolteca* culture hero to speak of, with Topiltzin's *fate*,
rather than his moral or ethical and religious character, consistently emphasized in the events that surround his epochal role.

Thus, although the story reflects Gillespie's (1989) sense of the Topiltzin
persona as a boundary figure in Nahua stories, the founding culture hero of

the narrative of the *Historia de la nación chichimeca*—the key to Alva Ixtlilxo-chitl's double emplotment of his history—is not Topiltzin, but the *non-Tolteca* Quetzalcoatl he introduces in the third age. Consistent with the deity Quet-zalcoatl's usual association (as god of the wind, Ehecatl Quetzalcoatl) with the great temple at Cholula, this persona also incarnates many of the positive attributes of Topiltzin Quetzalcoatl as Tolteca culture hero (associated with Tula or Tollan) found in other texts, which later evolve into his conflation with the apostle St. Thomas.[13]

What, however, does this portrayal accomplish in terms of the narrative configuration or emplotment of the text? Although the Tolteca cataclysm is followed by the arrival of a people new to the region—the Chichimeca under the ruler Xolotl—the reader is left with only the implicit association between the cosmogonical ages of creation and the "political epoch" to make sense of the transition: there is no description of a "fifth" and final creation of the sun. The narrative itself, moreover, seems less interested in defining the Chi-chimeca *apart* from the Tolteca than in describing the foundation of the great civilization (nevertheless still in need of salvation) that resulted from the *com-bination* of the world of the Chichimeca with that of the Tolteca. Indeed, as Alva Ixtlilxochitl insists in his earlier works, especially in the *Compendio*, the Tolteca *are* Chichimeca ([1975–1977] 1985, 1:417). In this latter text, as in the *Sumaria relación de todas las cosas*, Alva Ixtlilxochitl makes it clear that just as the Chichimeca founded their rule at Anahuac through the marriage of Xolotl's son to Tolteca royalty (Topiltzin's granddaughter), the Tolteca had earlier founded their dynasty by installing a Chichimeca nobleman (Chal-chiuhtlanextzin) as their first ruler and marrying him to the daughter of one of their principal dynastic lords (419). In the *Historia de la nación chi-chimeca*, his priority continues to be the theme of cultural merger, and the establishment of Tolteca-Chichimeca ties, but this time without reference to the prehistory of the Tolteca-Chichimeca interrelationships. Here, Xolotl is regarded as a direct successor to the Tolteca demise, with his arrival, how-ever, construed less as a moment of cosmogonical shift than as an oppor-tunity for cultural convergence and continuity. In this sense, the age of the Tolteca and that of the Chichimeca are regarded as a single, unified age—the age of the Tolteca-Chichimeca, which reaches its apogee under the rule of Nezahualcoyotl.

Predictably, Nezahualcoyotl descends from the marriage of Nopal-tzin (Xolotl's son) and Azcaxochitl, the daughter of Pochotl (the son of Topiltzin). In this context, Alva Ixtlilxochitl's representation of a non-Tolteca

Quetzalcoatl as founding culture hero, therefore, becomes significant in that it represents a separation of the proto-Christian *spiritual and religious* heritage most often associated with the Tolteca Topiltzin Quetzalcoatl figure (e.g., resistance to human sacrifice, penitence, fasting, and prayer) from the *cultural* accomplishments (e.g., jurisprudence, artisanry, agriculture, and architecture) the great civilization bequeathed. In that his histories indeed mention the idolatry of the Tolteca and of the later "mexicanos" (the Mexica and their affiliates), as opposed to the Chichimeca under Xolotl or Nezahualcoyotl (who "sólo decía que reconocía al sol por padre y a la tierra por madre" [1975–1977, 2:137; said only that he acknowledged the sun as father and the earth as mother]), this separation solves a logical difficulty that presents itself with his refusal to credit the resonances of Christianity among the rites of the peoples of Anahuac to the deceptive work of the devil and an insufficient rationality to see through it, as does Torquemada. Thus, while Quetzalcoatl (also called Huemac, but not Topiltzin) serves as the spiritual ruler-hero of the "third age" of Alva Ixtlilxochitl's history, as a *precursor* to the Tolteca, there is no Tolteca hero to take up that spiritual mantle for the fourth age. Rather, it is Nezahualcoyotl who incarnates the Christian-like spiritual lessons of this Quetzalcoatl, as well as the still important but less *vital* cultural attributes inherited from the Tolteca line through Pochotl.

In sum, it is not Topiltzin or the Tolteca who are the spiritual or religious centers of the fourth age, but the Acolhua under Nezahualcoyotl who, as *ruler*, incarnates the spiritual essence first brought by the apostle-like Quetzalcoatl associated with the early inhabitants of Cholula and its great pyramid temple but, as such, also with the *beginning* of the Tolteca period. In Alva Ixtlilxochitl's narrative, therefore, Quetzalcoatl—as ancient god of the Americas, and the "patron of royal lineages" (Mysyk 2012, 122)—*continues* (amid his "Christianization") to signify the rulers' power, to represent the vital religious basis of their authority.[14] As the thread (or cord) of the Acolhua ruling line, or the tlatocatlacamecayotl, plods along from the descendents of Nopaltzin and Azcaxochitl, passing along the cultural and spiritual lessons of their Tolteca forebearers (including idolatry but also the *memory* of the non-Tolteca Quetzalcoatl), the narrative sets up a separate spiritual lineage beginning with the arrival of the nonidolatrous Chichimeca under Xolotl and reflected in the special connection with the sacred and particular powers of prophecy and prescient wisdom that, from Nezahualcoyotl onward, sets especially certain figures apart from the crowd. The most basic line of descent of this "spiritual" or "religious" lineage forms a fierce triptych (a doubly holy threesome) that begins with Quetzalcoatl (a visitor who arrives in the east), passes through Nezahualcoyotl, and ends up with Cortés (another visitor arriving to, and from, the east).

QUETZALCOATL, TEZCATLIPOCA, AND CORTÉS: CHRISTIAN AND NAHUA-CHRISTIAN PROVIDENTIALISM

In the *Historia de la nación chichimeca*, the Spanish are associated with Quetzalcoatl in terms of the religion they bring, the date ce acatl, and their appearance from the east.[15] The history thus creates a symmetrical *and circular* structure by placing the ruler of the Acolhua, Nezahualcoyotl (whose life story is told from chapter 15 to chapter 49), between the precursor Quetzalcoatl (outsider/prophet of the third age) and the arrival of the Spanish under Cortés (outsider/conquerors of the fourth whose appearance is firmly considered by Alva Ixtlilxochitl to have been prophesied by Nezahualcoyotl). Only Motecuhzoma is seen contemplating a *direct* identification of the Spaniards as emissaries for the ancient, departed Quetzalcoatl; however, *all* of the Nahua rulers—especially those of Acolhua extraction, Nezahualpilli and then (Fernando Cortés) Ixtlilxochitl—regard the (impending) arrival of the Spanish as the fulfillment of Quetzalcoatl's promise, a promise that is first rearticulated and passed along in Nezahualcoyotl's prophetic discourses (discussed below).

Directly preceding the fulfillment of Quetzalcoatl's promise are ominous portents witnessed by Nezahualpilli and Motecuhzoma. The narrative at the beginning of chapter 72 reads:

> En el año de 1510 que llamaron macuili toxtli, fue cuando apareció en muchas noches un gran resplandor que nacía de la parte de oriente, subía en alto y parecía de forma piramidal, y con algunas llamas de fuego, el cual causó tan grande admiración y temor en toda la tierra que aun los muy entendidos en la astrología y conocimientos de sus adivinanzas y profecías, se hallaban confusos; aunque de muy atrás tenían noticias, y hallaban en sus historias, que ya se acercaban los tiempos en que se habían de cumplir las cosas que dijo y pronosticó Quetzalcóatl y otros filósofos y sabios antiguos; y a quienes más cuidado les daba era a los reyes Nezahualpiltzintli y Motecuhzoma, como personas que en ellos se había de ejecutar el rigor de las mudanzas del imperio; y como el rey de Tetzcuco era tan consumado en todas las ciencias que ellos

alcanzaban y sabían, en especial la astrología confirmada con las profecías de sus pasados, demás de la aflicción en que se veía, menospreció
su reino y señorío. (181)

In the year 1510, which they called macuili toxtli, a bright light that
originated in the east appeared and rose in the sky, looking like a pyramid with some licks of fire [around it]. It caused such great awe and
fear across the land that even those who were very versed in astrology
and the knowledge of their prophecies and auguries found themselves
confused, even though from way back they had information, and found
in their histories, that the time was approaching when the things that
Quetzalcoatl and other philosophers and ancient sages said and predicted were to be fulfilled. Those who were most worried were the kings
Nezahualpiltzintli and Motecuhzoma, as the ones on whom the rigor
of the changes of empire were to be carried out. And because the king
of Tetzcoco was so educated in all of the sciences that they had attained
and learned (especially in astrology complemented by the prophecies of
their forbearers), in addition to the affliction in which he found himself,
he scorned his dominion and his realm.

Two elements stand out in this passage. First, it presents a direct association between the portents announcing the imminent destruction of the
empire under the watch of Nezahualpiltzintli and Motecuhzoma and the
early predictions of Quetzalcoatl and other "philosophers and sages," which
the passage states were a part of the oral and written historical tradition,
and also now links to the Tolteca astrological "sciences." Second, the passage emphasizes the great learning and intelligence of Nezahualpilli, and
thus foreshadows the very different reception that the Mexica and the Acolhua rulers will lend to the Spanish when they arrive. In the idea of the
former group as less masterful (and committed to following the signs) in
religious arts than the latter already coming into focus here, the narrative
lays the foundation of the vision (and logic) around which its rendition of
conquest history will revolve.

This difference is first demonstrated when, after a meeting between
Cortés and Teotlili, one of Motecuhzoma's trusted ambassadors, the great
Mexica ruler calls together his advisors to decide on a course of action:

Llegados que fueron los mensajeros de Teotlili a la ciudad de México, fue grande la confusión y temor que causó al rey Motecuhzoma,

viendo que ya se empezaban a cumplir las profecías de sus pasados: citó a consejo a todos los señores del imperio para tratar lo que se debía hacer, y juntos les propuso todo lo que en el corazón le daba, y que si aquellos hombres orientales que habían llegado por ventura era el dios Quetzalcóatl y sus hijos que de tantos siglos esperaban, siendo así era fuerza que se habían de señorear de toda la tierra, y a ellos desposeerlos de ella, y que así sería bien atajarles los pasos, y no consentir que en su corte entrasen; o si como ellos decían, que eran embajadores de un gran señor del mundo en donde sale el sol, sería bien recibirlos y oírles su embajada. (200)

The messengers of Teotlili having arrived in the city of Mexico, there was great confusion and fear on the part of Motecuhzoma, seeing that the prophecies of his forebearers were beginning to come to pass. He called to council all of the lords of the empire to discuss what should be done, and when they were gathered he told them everything that he had in his heart: that if it were the case that these men from the east that had arrived were by chance the god Quetzalcoatl and his sons that for so many centuries they had been waiting for, then would it be a good idea to stop them in their tracks, and not to allow them to enter into the court, as it was inevitable that they would rule over and dispossess them of all the land; or if, as they said, they were ambassadors of a great lord of the world from where the sun rises, would it be a good idea to welcome them and hear their embassy.

Motecuhzoma's query—contingent on the interpretation of whether or not the new "hombres orientales" (men from the east) were perhaps "Quetzalcóatl y sus hijos que de tantos siglos esperaban"—hews very closely to the exact statements given by Quetzalcoatl at the beginning of the history. The association between Cortés and Quetzalcoatl is mentioned again (with less uncertainty) on the day when Cortés enters Tenochtitlan for the first time, "a ocho días del mes de noviembre del mismo año de mil quinientos diez y nueve," notes Alva Ixtlilxochitl in parentheses (218; on the eighth day of November in the same year, 1519):

Y dio muchas disculpas de lo que había porfiado por estorbar la entrada en México; y a cabo le vino a decir cómo sus pasados tenían pronosticado, que un gran señor que en tiempos antiguos había estado en esta tierra, había de volver a ella con los suyos a dar leyes con nueva doctrina, y que la poseerían y serían señores de ella; y que así creía que el rey de España había de ser aquel señor que esperaban.

And he begged pardon for having tried so hard to stop the entry into Mexico; and finally he told them how his ancestors had predicted that a great lord who in times past had been in this land would return to it with his people to provide laws and a new doctrine, and that they would possess the lands and be their natural lords; and thus he believed that the King of Spain must be this lord that they were waiting for.

Finally, when Motecuhzoma has been taken prisoner and Cortés asks him to call a meeting to discuss his arrival and to "dar principio a la conversión y fundación de nuestra santa fe católica" (225; begin the conversions and the founding of the Holy Catholic faith), his response is described in the following manner:

Motecuhzoma comenzó una larga plática y entre muchas razones que trajo para fundar y sustentar su determinación, vino a decir que daba muchas gracias a Dios por haberle hecho tanta merced, que haya alcanzado a ver a los cristianos, y tener noticia de aquel gran rey que sus pasados de años muy atrás deseaban que viniese, y que no podía creer que fuese otro, sino este que había enviado a aquellos españoles que estaban en su corte; y que si estaba determinado de lo alto que tuviese fin el imperio de las tres cabezas, culhuas, aculhuas y tepanecas, no quería resistir la voluntad de Dios, sino de muy buena gana y con gran voluntad dar la obediencia al rey de Castilla, y tenerlo por su cabeza y supremo señor, bajo de cuyo amparo y protección quería vivir y reconocerle por tal, y que les rogaba muy encarecidamente a ellos que hiciesen lo mismo.

Motecuhzoma began a long speech, and, among many points that he made to found and support his decision, he said that he was very grateful to God for having given him such great favor that he was able to see the Christians and hear news of that great king whom his ancestors from many years back were hoping would arrive. [He said] that he could not believe that it was anyone else but him who had sent these Spaniards that were in his court and that if it was determined from above that the empire of the triple alliance—Colhuas, Acolhuas and

Tepanecas—would come to an end, he did not want to resist the will of God, but rather with good will and great desire pledge obedience to the King of Castile, and have him for his superior and supreme lord, under whose refuge and protection he wanted to live and to recognize him as such, and he begged them very ardently that they do the same.

In these instances, Motecuhzoma moves from a query and intended resistance at the arrival of a *possible* returning Quetzalcoatl, to a confirmed identification of the Spanish with the Quetzalcoatl story, to an encouragement of his people to accept submission. In all circumstances, however, at first in a speculative fashion and then under duress, Motecuhzoma reiterates the language of the story of Quetzalcoatl from the beginning of the history (eventually associating this departed ancestral ruler with the King of Spain, however, not directly with Cortés). While Motecuhzoma and his allies initially resist the takeover of their empire, however, and strive to prevent Cortés from entering Tenochtitlan, the Tetzcoca Acolhua rulers who are the true "spiritual" heirs of Nezahualcoyotl (i.e., Fernando Cortés Ixtlilxochitl and not the Mexica-affiliated Cacama and his successors and allies) never deliberate or present any attempt to resist the intrusion of the Spaniards.

In chapter 69, Alva Ixtlilxochitl describes a series of portents that accompany the birth of (Fernando Cortés) Ixtlilxochitl. According to the signs, this rebellious and slighted heir to Acolhua rulership would

Recibir nueva ley y nuevas costumbres, y ser amigo de naciones extrañas y enemigo de su patria y nación, y que sería contra su propia sangre . . . y sería total enemigo de sus dioses y de su religión, ritos y ceremonias; con lo cual persuadía al rey su padre, que con tiempo le quitasen la vida; y él les respondió que era por demás ir contra lo determinado por el Dios criador de todas las cosas, pues no sin misterio y secreto juicio suyo le daba tal hijo al tiempo y cuando se acercaban las profecías de sus antepasados, que habían de venir nuevas gentes a poseer la tierra, como eran los hijos de Quetzalcóatl que aguardaban su venida de la parte oriental. (174)

Receive a new law and new traditions, and be a friend to foreign peoples and an enemy of his homeland and nation, and that he would go against his own kin . . . and that he would be a total enemy of his gods and his religion, rites, and ceremonies. For this, they tried to

persuade the king his father that in due time they should kill him but
he responded that it was useless to go against what God the creator of
everything had determined, as it was not without God's mystery and
secret judgment that he had been given such a son at the moment when
the time of the prophecies of his ancestors was approaching, when new
people were to come to possess the land, as they were the sons of Quetzalcoatl awaiting his coming from the east.

Nezahualpilli and (Fernando Cortés) Ixtlilxochitl, more preoccupied with
the religious or spiritual dimensions of the prophecy, *do not resist* what they
see as an inevitable defeat. While Nezahualpilli simply *resigns* himself to this
destiny, encouraging Motecuhzoma to do the same through an appropriately
symbolic victory on the ball court ([1975–1977] 1985, 1:181–82),[16] Fernando
Cortés Ixtlilxochitl, his son and heir, provides active and vital support to the
newcomers, enabling the conquest of Tenochtitlan and the defeat of the Triple
Alliance. In addition to his own military aid, moreover, he persuades other
groups not to fight Cortés and to accept the new rule and religion peacefully.

After the humiliating and deadly flight from Tenochtitlan in the Noche
Triste, Cortés is seen giving speeches of encouragement in an apparent
attempt to prevent defections from his ranks. Following a Tlaxcalteca source
(Tadeo de Niza),[17] Alva Ixtlilxochitl (1975–1977, 2:231) relates how, after the
stinging losses of the Noche Triste, Cortés seeks to encourage the lords of
Tlaxcala, Mexico, and Tetzcoco (those from the latter two groups had been
taken as hostages), telling them not to be sad, or lack courage, by saying that

> Él no tenía temor a los culhuas, ni estimaba en nada su vida, porque
> cuando a él le matasen y a todos los que con él iban, no faltarían otros
> cristianos que los sojuzgasen, porque la ley evangélica se había de plan-
> tar en esta tierra, aunque más impedimentos y resistencia hiciesen;
> y que les daba su fe y palabra a todos los señores que le eran leales y
> amigos, que si salía con victoria y conquistaba la tierra, no tan sola-
> mente los conservaría en sus estados y señoríos, sino que también en
> nombre del rey de España su señor, se los aumentaría y los haría partici-
> pantes de lo que así sojuzgase y conquistase.

> He was not afraid of the Culhuas, and valued his own life very little,
> because when they killed him and everyone else along with him, there
> would be no shortage of other Christians to subjugate them, because

Christian rule was going to be established in the land, even though they put up more impediments and resistance; and that he gave them his word of honor that if he was granted victory and conquered the land not only would all of the lords that were loyal to him and his friends preserve their realms and dominions, but, in the name of the King of Spain his lord, he would expand them and make them party to [the spoils of] whatever he would subjugate and conquer.

The sense of an unavoidable destiny expressed by Cortés in this passage— that Christianity would be imposed sooner or later, even if his own attempt at conquest would fail—reinforces the narrative's emphasis on the Tetzcoca rulers as prescient actors in a predetermined (but not universally interpreted) landscape. The wisdom of Cortés in making these promises (or bribes), more- over, becomes clear awhile later when Alva Ixtlilxochitl narrates a fascinating scene that represents a Mexica *response* to Cortés's offer to "liberate" its sub- jects (now Cortés's allies) from the "tyranny" (and eternal damnation) posed by their rule. It is significant in that it provides an alternate point of view from which the momentous events of the conquest are regarded, a point of view, as we will see, that ties into the double emplotment of the narrative.

The scene recounts the last-minute attempt of the Mexica to convince the groups that had allied with Cortés and the Spanish to renounce their alle- giance and unite to expel the "foreign invaders." To enact their mission, they sent ambassadors to the leaders of the groups in question, with Alva Ixtlilxo- chitl summarizing the content of their speech to the Tlaxcalteca:

> Entre los embajadores que despacharon, fueron seis a la Señoría de Tlaxcalan, personas de autoridad y respeto, los cuales dieron su emba- jada con muy grande elocuencia a la Señoría, persuadiéndola a que matasen o echasen de sus tierras a Cortés y a los suyos, pues era gente extraña, que venía con gran codicia de usurpar y quitar los señoríos; y otras cosas que a su propósito alegaban, trayéndoles a la memoria ser todos deudos y de su linaje, por cuya causa, dejando aparte pasiones y contiendas pasadas, tenían más obligación de favorecer a los suyos, que no a aquellos pocos extranjeros que venían a embaucar la tierra; dándoles la fe y palabra de sus reyes, que entre ellos desde aquel tiempo en adelante tendrían perpetua paz y concordia inviolablemente, y que entrarían en parte de todas las rentas de las provincias sujetas por el imperio. Tanto supieron decir a la Señoría estos embajadores, que casi

toda ella después de tratado y altercado muy bien el negocio, la redu-
jeron a su voluntad y deseo, y comenzaron entre sí a decir que tenían
razón los culhuas y sus consortes, y quedando la cosa establecida de la
manera que sus reyes se obligaban, les estaba más bien el favorecer y
amparar su causa, que no la de los españoles, gente extraña y que aún
no sabían en que vendrían a parar sus designios. (236)

Among the ambassadors that they sent, six went to Tlaxcala, people
of great authority and respect who delivered their embassy with great
eloquence to the other nobility, persuading them to kill or expel Cortés
and his allies from their lands because they were a strange people who
came with great avarice to usurp and take away the rulerships. They
also asserted other things in their favor, [including] a reminder that
they were all relatives and from the same lineage, for which cause, leaving aside the disputes and quarrels of the past, they were obligated to
privilege their own over those few strangers who came to deceive the
land; [and] he gave them the word and honor of his rulers, that between
them and from that time forward they would have perpetual peace
and inviolable harmony, and that they would share in part of all of the
profits from the provinces subjected by the empire. So well did these
ambassadors know how to talk to the nobles, that almost all of them
changed their minds after the matter was discussed and argued, and
began among themselves to say that the Colhuas and their allies were
right, and that, with the manner in which their rulers were obligated to
each other established, it was better for them to favor and protect their
cause rather than that of the Spanish, [who were] strange people, and
that they still did not know where their schemes would end.

Here, the persuasive power of the Mexica ambassadors lies in the reply's
emphasis on the newcomers as strangers, although there is no mention of
Quetzalcoatl or identification of them as departed ancestors, and their relatively small numbers. This group not only arrived with a great desire to take
over land and rulerships, argue the Mexica, they came to deceive, and just
how far or in what direction their intentions would take them no one could
predict. The use of the word "embaucar"—meaning to con, trick, and deceive
another—associates the Spanish with the rhetorical power of the trickster
(discussed at more length in the conclusion) and conjures an association with
Tezcatlipoca (and the devil). Although the association is purely a matter of

semantics, the word and its implications are not gratuitous, nor do they appear out of the blue, if we consider the dynamic of the Quetzalcoatl/Tezcatlipoca relationship in the Nahua myth-historical narratives. Indeed, Cortés may have been bringing at last the light of the gospel, long awaited by the Acolhua, to the shores of Anahuac, but his status as enemy, his military menace, in addition to his methods and his actions, full of trickery and deceit, indeed provide important context and grounds for an affiliation with Tezcatlipoca. From the point of view of Alva Ixtlilxochitl's Motecuhzoma, who would have considered himself heir to the Tolteca, and thus likewise connected to Quetzalcoatl, any threat to his rulership would have come in such a form. In this profound and profoundly rhetorical scene, the voice of Motecuhzoma's ambassadors—if ever so subtly—thus provides a subtle supplement to the overall scenario in which Cortés is viewed as a returning Quetzalcoatl. In the history, it serves as brief but nevertheless significant counternarrative that regards the conquest through the prism of Tezcatlipoca's well-known powers to upset the cosmic order, to deceive, but also, as we shall see in the next chapter, to reverse in a heartbeat the fortunes of rulers and anyone else.

In providing this new angle, or point of view, in the history, Alva Ixtlilxochitl also places the famous conquest story of the assimilation of Cortés to Quetzalcoatl (back) in a more properly Nahua frame, that of the rivalry between the two creator gods, outlined in the colonial cosmogonies of the four suns of creation and structurally present in the accounts of Tolteca history that he so diligently interpreted. In so doing, he reterritorializes the figure of Quetzalcoatl, hitching him once again to his ancient rival, and bringing Christianity as a whole, and the Spanish enterprise, into the fold of the cyclicality and duality implicit in their relation.[18] In this sense, the advent of the Spanish—unlike that of Xolotl—is viewed in the narrative as a cosmogonic sea change, a moment of destruction in an unending epic struggle between rival (but complementary) deities, of temporal reversal. The sense of inevitability, of an unarrestable fate or destiny, implicit in both the Christian providentialist framework and the cyclical duality of Tezcatlipoca and Quetzalcoatl—night sun and day sun—thus allows the Quetzalcoatl figure of the *Historia de la nación chichimeca* to operate in a double fashion: to signify in a Nahua semiotic context his ancient roots and ties to Tezcatlipoca (who has gone unnamed but not unreferenced in the text) and in the Christian to become an apostle-like persona suggestive of St. Thomas.

Although significant, this fleeting glimpse at a discrepant interpretation of Cortés (and the Spanish) as a deceptive and dangerous rival to established order is quickly brushed over with scenes that deepen and extend the earlier predominant and verbalized associations of him with a Christian-like Quetzalcoatl. Not only is Cortés associated with the date 1519 (and ce acatl), his actions in Tenochtitlan before the Noche Triste also directly echo and parallel those of Quetzalcoatl in the narrative. For example, after successfully taking Motecuhzoma prisoner, he manages to put a stop to the practice of human sacrifice and begins to destroy the "idols" of the temples. However, when Motecuhzoma insisted that he could not destroy the idols without risk to both of their lives, he resigns himself to simply preaching to people and telling them about the "blindness" in which they lived. The narrative description of Cortés's actions and rhetoric repeat almost exactly those of Quetzalcoatl in the "third" age of creation.

> Contentóse con decirles en la ceguedad en que vivían, y desengañarlos y meterlos en el camino verdadero de la virtud y ley evangélica, que había sido la causa principal de su venida; que no había sido tanto por sus riquezas, pues de ellas no habían tomado más de tan solamente lo que ellos les habían dado, ni habían llegado a sus mujeres y hijas ni hecho otros agravios, porque su principal intento no era más de salvar sus almas; que no había otro Dios, más tan solamente el que los cristianos adoraban, trino y uno, eterno, sin fin, criador y conservador de todas las cosas, que rige y gobierna los cielos y la tierra; y otras muchas razones, persuadiéndoles a nuestra santa fe católica, y abominando su idolatría y errores: con que se aseguraron un poco. (221)

> He contented himself with telling them about the blindness in which they lived, and enlightening them and placing them on the road to true virtue and the rule of Christ, which had been the primary cause of his arrival; that it had not been so much for their wealth, because he hadn't taken more than only that which they had given him, nor had he touched their women and daughters or committed other offenses, because his primary intent was nothing more than to save their souls. [He told them] that there was no other God, only the one that Christians adored, three in one, eternal, without end, creator and conserver of all things, that rules and governs the skies and the earth and [he made] many other points, persuading them to [accept] our Catholic faith, and to abandon their idolatry and errors. With this they became a little more reassured.

Cortés's preaching of the "camino . . . de la virtud" through word and by example, attempting to enlighten[19] the people, echoes the work of Quetzalcoatl, who went about "enseñándoles por obras y palabras el camino de la virtud y evitándoles los vicios y pecados, dando leyes y buena doctrina; y para refrenarles de sus deleites y deshonestidades les constituyó el ayuno" (8; teaching the path of virtue with deeds and words and preventing them from vice and sins, providing laws and good doctrine; and he instituted the fast to put some restraint on their pleasures and indecencies). Indeed, where Quetzalcoatl places a cross, Cortés (who had previously placed a cross in the templo mayor, along with an image of the Virgin Mary) speaks of the Holy Trinity. (His description of "Dios," the "creator and conserver of all things," also of course echoes language used by Alva Ixtlilxochitl at the beginning of the history to introduce the cosmogony of the four ages.) The two are thus nearly melded personalities, structurally the same, repeating the same actions in the same year (ce acatl).

Although (Fernando Cortés) Ixtlilxochitl is portrayed as a crucial figure in the (incomplete) conquest narrative, his role in the *Historia de la nación chichimeca* is secondary to that of Cortés, upon whom the narrative maintains a constant focus as the protagonist and agent of the events.[20] As Brian (2010, 135) has pointed out, one of the differences between the treatment of the conquest in the *Historia de la nación chichimeca* and the fuller picture of the event and its aftermath provided in the *Compendio* is the former's emphasis on the figure of Cortés over that of Ixtlilxochitl, Nezahualpilli's heir and ally to Cortés. While the *Compendio* served and reads as a relación de méritos y servicios, the *Historia de la nación chichimeca* represents a synthetic and polished official history, meant to take its place in the annals of European historiography as an official record of Acolhua past, in all its rhetorical luster. The emphasis on Cortés in this text ensures the approval of a Spanish readership interested in self-promotion, but it also must be viewed in light of Alva Ixtlilxochitl's investment in the role that he plays in the temporal and moral emplotment of the narrative. Cortés is Quetzalcoatl, the two figures that bookend this dually constructed, linear, and circular frame.

Confirming this association is the portrayal of the figure of his hero, Nezahualcoyotl, in the middle of the narrative. While the connection between Cortés and Quetzalcoatl is clear enough, the prophecies of Nezahualcoyotl make it concrete. In the *Historia de la nación chichimeca*, Nezahualcoyotl is Quetzalcoatl's spokesperson-equivalent—another proto-Christian or monotheistic[21] figure amid the masses of the lost—the inheritor of the latter's

beliefs and prophecies and another Old Testament King David. He foresees
the arrival of the Christians and lays the groundwork for his descendents and
heirs to ensure their victory over their rivals, the bloodthirsty and deeply misled Mexica. He represents both the Tolteca cultural inheritance handed down
through Pochotl and the religious/spiritual heritage of Quetzalcoatl.

Throughout the *Historia de la nación chichimeca*, Nezahualcoyotl is portrayed as a prescient and wise ruler who knows that the end of the empire is
imminent. In keeping with the evolving Tetzcoca tradition of his parallelism to the famous Old Testament King David (Velazco 2003; Lee 2008), Alva
Ixtlilxochitl portrays his "conversion" to a belief in a single, omnipotent god,
embellishing the story more than Bautista Pomar but not quite as intensely as
in his anonymous source text, the *Guerra de Chalco* (O'Gorman [1975–1977]
1985, 1:551–62), as Lesbre (2000) notes. One of his most important prophetic
moments (in which the "spiritual exceptionalism" of the Acolhua rulers is
made most clear) ironically occurs at the inauguration of the temple he built
in honor of Huitzilopochtli.

Here, in chapter 47, "Que trata de algunas profecías y dichos que dijo
el rey Nezahualcoyotzin" (Which discusses some of the prophecies and pronouncements made by King Nezahualcoyotzin), he is seen reciting various
"spring-time songs," or the "Xompancuicatl" which inform rulers of the
imminent calamities and suffering that their realms will soon experience.
When this happens, the songs recount, "serán deshechos y destrozados tus
vasallos . . . entonces de verdad, no estará en tu mano el señorío y mando
sino en la de Dios" (1975–1977, 2:132; your subjects will be undone and devastated . . . in truth, then, the realm and rule will be in God's hands, not yours).
The rulers' children and grandchildren, moreover,

> llorosos se acordarán de ti, viendo que los dejaste huérfanos en servi-
> cio de otros extraños en su misma patria Acolihuacan; porque en esto
> vienen a parar los mandos, imperios y señoríos, que duran poco y son
> de poca estabilidad. Lo de esta vida es prestado, que en un instante lo
> hemos de dejar como otros lo han dejado.

> will remember you weeping, seeing that you left them orphaned in the
> service of strangers in their own homeland Acolhuacan; because this is
> how the rulerships, empires, and dominions will end, which last only
> a short time and are very unstable. This life is fleeting, such that in an
> instant we must leave it, as others have already done.

The most important section of the scene, however, occurs when Alva Ixtlilxochitl describes a moment of individual contemplation on the part of Nezahualcoyotl:

> En el año de 1467 que llaman ce ácatl, se acabó y fue el estreno del templo mayor de la ciudad de Tetzcuco del ídolo Huitzilopochtli, y entonces dijo: "en tal año como éste se destruirá este templo, que ahora se estrena ¿quién se hallará presente?, ¿si será mi hijo o mi nieto?, entonces irá a disminución la tierra, y se acabarán los señores; de suerte que el maguey siendo pequeño y sin sazón, será talado. . . . etc. Sucederán cosas prodigiosas: las aves hablarán, y en este tiempo llegará el árbol de la luz, y de la salud y sustento. Para librar a vuestros hijos de estos vicios y calamidades, haced que desde niños se den a la virtud y trabajos." (132–33)

> In the year 1467, called ce acatl, the great temple of the city of Tetzcoco to the idol Huitzilopochtli was finished and inaugurated, and he said: "In a year just like this one [when] this temple that is now being inaugurated will be destroyed, Who will be present? Will it be my son or my nephew? At that time the earth will become depleted, and the nobility will no longer exist. The maguey plant, being small and without taste, will be cut down . . . etc. Prodigious things will happen: the birds will speak, and in this time the tree of light, health, and sustenance will arrive. To free your children from these vices and calamities, make sure that from childhood they lend themselves to work and virtue."

In analyzing this interlude of prophetic speech (born of a song text) on the part of Nezahualcoyotl, a number of points stand out. First, its characterization of the intrinsically ephemeral (and therefore in a sense cyclical and repetitive) nature of empires and rulerships: "porque en esto vienen a parar los mandos, imperios y señoríos, que duran poco y son de poca estabilidad" (because the dominions, empires, and estates, which last but a short time and are very unstable, come to such ends). Second, its reference to the people as being "orphaned" by a dead or disappeared ruler, which is a common means of address between rulers and ruled in Nahua societies. In Nahua speeches recorded in book 6 of the *Florentine Codex* (Anderson and Dibble, trans. [1969] 2012, 6:49, 54), for example, rulers are described and addressed (in part) as "father and mother" of the altepetl. And third, and most crucially, is its mention of the passage regarding the "tree of light, health, and sustenance."

First brought by Quetzalcoatl, the tree is certainly a double reference to the ubiquitous cosmic tree of Nahua mythology (López Austin 1997) and the cross of the crucifixion, and it thereby reinforces the significance of the date of the prophecy, ce acatl. Like the date, the tree refers both forward to the arrival of Christianity *and* backward to the third age of creation described by Alva Ixtlilxochitl at the beginning of the history, when the virtuous Quetzalcoatl tried to show its apathetic inhabitants (the Olmeca and Xicalanca) the "camino de la virtud" and was the first one to put in place and worship "la cruz que llamaron Quiahutzteotlchicahualiztéotl y otros Tonacaquáhuitl, que quiere decir: dios de las lluvias y de la salud y árbol del sustento o de la vida" (1975–1977, 2:8; the cross that they called Quiahutzteotlchicahualiztéotl and others Tonacaquáhuitl, which means: god of the rains and health and tree of sustenance or life).[22]

Thus, the passage sets forth the key nexus or hinge that enables Alva Ixtlilxochitl to construct his doubly emplotted historical narrative. The implied reference to Quetzalcoatl in the date ce acatl and the mention of the tree (or cross) endows the history with the linear, teleological timeline of the Christian *praeparatio evangelica*, as well as with the cyclical structure of Nahua time-reckoning. In the former instance, the arrival of Cortés fulfills and completes the failed mission of the earlier prophet Quetzalcoatl, enabling the salvation and eternal life of the descendents of Nezahualcoyotl—a progressive development as perceived in the framework of Christian history. In the latter, Alva Ixtlilxochitl uses the Christianized-Quetzalcoatl-as-returning-prophet motif as a means of associating the arrival of Cortés with the initiation of a new dynastic era, regarded not as a novelty but as a moment of *repetition* in the cosmic order.

In this overall-paradigm where one empire-age follows another, the arrival of the Spaniards becomes a foreseen event, and is regarded as the icing on a cake already made, the tragicomic arrival of Christian salvation. From this perspective, the logic behind Alva Ixtlilxochitl's synthetic account and his use of his sources—putting a (Christianized) Tolteca story of creation as *the* story of creation, and then blending the migration stories into it by placing Quetzalcoatl into association with the Olmeca and Xicalanca in Cholula in the *third age* as the fount of Christian influence and an influence on the region just *prior* to the arrival of the Tolteca—become clear. While Torquemada ([1723] 1975, 1:381), following Sahagún's 1585 version of book XII of his *Historia general de las cosas de la Nueva España*, affirms the story of Cortés's assimilation to Quetzalcoatl and also advances the idea of Tetzcoca exceptionalism—of Nezahualcoyotl and his descendents' doubt about their gods—as LaFaye has pointed out, the only divine providence he finds in the devil Quetzalcoatl's deceptive cloak of Christian-like belief and behavior rests in its usefulness for missionaries and in the divine wisdom and providence of God in allowing it. For Alva Ixtlilxochitl, on the contrary, not only is Quetzalcoatl a virtuous apostle who had "evangelized" the region around the time of the birth of Christ, he becomes a kind of *type* for Cortés, a precursor and forecast of an ineluctable future,[23] and also a means of incorporating Christianity into the ever-unfolding cycle of the cosmic ages of destruction and creation.

If Quetzalcoatl is the entry point into the architectural and semiotic subtext of Alva Ixtlilxochitl's narrative, to its ties to the cyclical dynamic of Nahua historicity and its world of signification, however, Nezahualcoyotl, as the terrestrial ruler-hero at the center of Alva Ixtlilxochitl's narrative, flanked between the religious torchbearer of one epoch and that of another, deepens and confirms the sense of Alva Ixtlilxochitl's creation of a double chronotope relating human and cosmic time according to the signposts of two different cultural contexts. Prescient, sagacious, prophetic, peace-loving civilizer and poet-king, Nezahualcoyotl is an ambivalent figure, caught between his alliance with the bloodthirsty, wayward Mexica and his representation of a new temporal dispensation to arrive in the form of Spanish conquerors as the "sons of Quetzalcoatl." In the next chapter I will show how the deployment of Nezahualcoyotl's religious prescience and his association with the figure of Quetzalcoatl in fact deepen the narrative's immersion in and connection to Nahua temporal structures and symbolism found in the Nahua tradition, particularly the cosmogonical and Tolteca stories. Through the figure of Nezahualcoyotl, the *Historia de la nación chichimeca* embraces and lives within the Christian order of history, but as a diglossic narrative with its own particular way of "transcending conquest" (Wood 2003).

CHAPTER THREE

Nezahualcoyotl as Tezcatlipoca

Alva Ixtlilxochitl's Colonial Mexican Trickster Tale

Tricksters have become anthropologists, but no anthropologist has ever understood a trickster. . . . The only way an anthropologist can understand a trickster is to know that tricksters are never possessed by understanding.

—GERALD VIZENOR, *Trickster Discourse: Comic and Tragic Themes in Native American Literature*

IN THE PREVIOUS CHAPTER, WE SAW HOW THE INTRODUCTION OF A Christianized Quetzalcoatl figure into the *Historia de la nación chichimeca* allowed for the creation of a doubly emplotted narrative that stakes out a place for the arrival of Cortés within both a cyclical frame (or chronotope) that emphasizes recurrence, prominent in Nahua calendrics, and a linear, eschatological structure, emphasized in Christian timekeeping. Despite Quetzalcoatl's clearly postconquest attributes and rise to significance, his deployment in the narrative serves to set up the structural parallelism between the ages of creation and the dynastic lineages of the great empires, or ruling altepetl, found in many Nahua histories. (In the Christian tradition, empires may rise and fall, but there is only one world, one creation, and one final destruction of the universe.) However, as I shall show, Quetzalcoatl's role in the narrative's manifestation of Nahua forms of temporality and historicity transcends his mere association with Cortés vis-à-vis the prophecy of a return and the date ce acatl. This becomes apparent when we examine the symbolic subtext of the narrative with Quetzalcoatl's relationship to his ever-present nemesis and complement, the great trickster god Tezcatlipoca, in mind.

Given the prominence of the duo in the political history of volume 1 ([1723] 1975, 1:254–56) and the religious and cultural focus of volume 2 ([1723] 1975, 2:20–21, 38–41, 48–52, 78–80; book 6, chapters 7, 20, 24, and 42–45) of the *Monarquía indiana*, Alva Ixtlilxochitl was almost certainly aware of their deeply rooted ties and likewise of Tezcatlipoca's mythological importance and the qualities, symbols, and associations attributed to him. Yet despite his late addition of a figure called Quetzalcoatl in the *Historia de la nación chichimeca* and the *Sumaria relación de la historia general*, there is no parallel addition of a named Tezcatlipoca character in these texts. The omission is no surprise, of course, in light of the entrenched Tetzcoca habit, followed assiduously by Alva Ixtlilxochitl, of censoring many of the religious or clearly mythical aspects of the Tetzcoca historical tradition to create a pre-Hispanic past recognizable and respectable within the Christian and classical European paradigms (Douglas 2010; Lesbre 1999a, 2001a). Although there is no space to discuss in detail here the multiple and extremely significant representations of Tezcatlipoca found in Torquemada's history, it is worth pointing out that he and his nemesis appear near the beginning of volume 2, in the context of the friar's long opening discussion of the causes and origins of idolatry in the world ([1723] 1975, 2:20–21). This short but important narrative discusses these rulers as man-gods, or "hombres encantadores": men who were (mis)taken for gods, "por embustes, que hacían," and whose falsified identities, as a scornful Torquemada remarks, were proclaimed by poets making use of their license to lie (20; for the tricks that they played). Specifically, it relates how the sorcerer "Titlacahuan" (another name for Tezcatlipoca) convinced Quetzalcoatl (considered to be a god by the Tolteca, Cholulteca, and almost everyone else, as Torquemada notes), to renounce his rule. As he puts it, "le hizo creer, que en el nacimiento de el Sol, estaba un varón viejo, que le llamaba, lo cual confirmó con una bebida, que le hizo beber . . . y quedó de allí adelante tan persuadido a que era verdad, que era llamado para gozar de nuevo, y mejor reino que él poseía" (20; he made him believe that where the Sun rises there was an old man who was calling him, which he confirmed with a beverage that he made him drink . . . and from that moment on he was persuaded that it was true that he was being called to enjoy a new, better kingdom than the one he possessed). Later stories (along with the one in the first volume) repeat with variations this basic tale (e.g., book 6, chapters 24 and 45), but Torquemada also describes the deity in and of himself: he is a major god on the order of Jupiter, another "ánima del mundo" (38; soul of the world). In addition, in chapters 41–45 of book 6, the friar provides glimpses of Tezcatlipoca in various related cosmogonic tales, where, for example, he orders devotees (bearers of his sacred bundle) to go to the house of the sun to bring back singers and instruments, or where he descends from the sky by hanging on a rope made of a spiderweb (76–80).

If Tezcatlipoca does not exist in name—as a singular and discrete entity—in Alva Ixtlilxochitl's later histories, however, his functions within their structurally coherent and persistent plot(s) perdure. In all of Alva Ixtlilxochitl's histories, in fact, the deity remains present and palpable—if renamed, multiple, divided, and diversified—in the roles he always inhabits and tied to the characteristic signs, symbols, and events that continue to point us in his direction. In the context of Alva Ixtlilxochitl's Tolteca histories in the *Sumaria relación de todas las cosas*, for example, Huemantzin covers certain aspects of his qualities and functions. More significantly for our purposes herein, however, is the way in which the figure of Nezahualcoyotl reflects his persona. Indeed, if at first glance Tezcatlipoca seems to be absent from the *Historia de la nación chichimeca*, upon closer examination it becomes clear that he continues to play a prominent, if surreptitious, role in the narrative's representation of Tetzcoca rulership and its significance within the history of the Spanish conquest and its aftermath. In the narrative, as I shall show, the explicit ethnographical discourse connecting Nezahualcoyotl with (the Christian-like) Quetzalcoatl coincides with an implicit, purely symbolic identification of his persona with Tezcatlipoca.

Guilhem Olivier ([2003] 2008) begins chapter 1 of his detailed study of Tezcatlipoca by citing his description in the *Florentine Codex* and with an invitation "to a protracted hunt for this elusive god—'whose abode was everywhere, in the land of the dead, on earth [and] in heaven' (noujian ynemjian: mictla, tlalticpac, ylhujcac) (CF 1:5)—for this shadow (ceoalli) that always slinks away." In an echo of Gerald Vizenor's statement in the epigraph to this chapter, he writes, "One must say that the Lord of the Smoking Mirror, as he appears under a variety of guises and names, seems to strive against any attempt at identifying or reducing him. Sorcerer god, master of transformations, he seems to amuse himself in ceaseless metamorphoses to the detriment of the Cartesian investigator" (11). Given this characterization of Tezcatlipoca as a sorcerer, and an omnipresent but elusive deity, perhaps it should not have been a surprise to find so many traces of him in the narrative and in particular to find them clustered around the figure of Nezahualcoyotl and his descendents. After all, according to both Acolhua and non-Acolhua sources, the Tetzcoca rulers were renowned sorcerers or "man-gods," beings able to represent or embody the voice or power of the gods as a means of bringing it to bear in the present (Gruzinski 1989, 23; López Austin 1973, 47–77).[1] As rulers and as sorcerers, they are thus doubly bound to Tezcatlipoca, "the omnipotent god of rulers, sorcerers and warriors," as Mary K. Miller and Karl Taube (1993, 164) describe him. They are also, therefore, true and faithful representatives of the patron deity of their altepetl, who was Tezcatlipoca himself.

As we saw in chapter 1, the tlatoque represented many gods in their capacity as rulers, but the ruler–patron deity relationship held particular importance within the religious framework of the altepetl (López Austin 1976, 216–17, 236–37). Therefore, while Tlaloc and Xiuhtecuhtli also take their place in Alva Ixtlilxochitl's portrayals of Nezahualcoyotl and the other Acolhua rulers,[2] the connection to Tezcatlipoca is of particular interest because of its centrality to the identity (and history) of the altepetl as a whole. It therefore also holds important implications for our understanding of the narrative and of Alva Ixtlilxochitl as a historiographer, in particular his place in and ties to the Nahua (and, more specifically, the Tetzcoca) historical tradition as it was being variously expressed and reconfigured in his generation.

Part One. Tezcatlipoca in Tetzcoco

According to both Alva Ixtlilxochitl ([1975–1977] 1985, 1:323–24; 1975–1977, 2:32) and Juan Bautista Pomar ([1891] 1975, 13), Tezcatlipoca's sacred bundle did not arrive at Tetzcoco until the Tlailotlaque, the Huitznahuaque or other groups of Tolteca brought it under the rule of Quinatzin and/or Techotlalatzin, his heir.[3] It is clear from comments made by Alva Ixtlilxochitl in the *Sumaria relación de todas las cosas de la Nueva España*, however, that the connection between Nezahualcoyotl and Tezcatlipoca was an established part of the Acolhua historical tradition. For example, while describing Nezahualcoyotl's amazing ability to thwart all of the Tepaneca emperor Maxtla's attempts to assassinate him, Alva Ixtlilxochitl writes,

> Muchas veces lo había querido matar y nunca había podido con él, porque era muy animoso y atrevido, y lo tenía por hombre invincible o

encantado, y por eso muchos naturales viejos decían que Nezahualcoyotzin descendía de los mayores dioses del mundo, y que así lo tenían
por inmortal, y no se engañaban en lo que era decir que descendía de
sus dioses, porque Tezcatlipuca y Huitzilopuchtli, que eran los mayores
de esta tierra, fueron sus antepasados, señores que por sus hazañas los
colocaron por tales, como entre los gentiles romanos y griegos, y otras
naciones han hecho otro tanto. ([1975–1977] 1985, 1:359)

Many times he wanted to kill him and had never been able to, because
he was very spirited and daring, and they took him to be invincible
or enchanted, and for this reason many of the native elders used to
say that Nezahualcoyotzin descended from the most powerful gods
in the world, and that he was therefore immortal. And they were not
fooling themselves when they said that he descended from their gods,
because Tezcatlipoca and Huitzilopochtli, who were the greatest of this
land, were their ancestors, lords for whose deeds they venerated them
as such, as [done] among the Roman and Greek gentiles; and other
nations have done so as well.

The *Historia de la nación chichimeca* makes no reference to a genealogical
connection between Nezahualcoyotl and Tezcatlipoca (or Huitzilopochtli),
nor does it explicitly associate their deeds with those of the great heroes of
the Roman and Greek epics as a means of explaining and legitimating them
for a European audience, as done here.[4] Its portrayal of Nezahualcoyotl's feats
(and those of his descendents), however, reflects the strong imprint of those
heroes and heroic acts, as well as those from the Old Testament (Velazco
2003), medieval histories (García Loaeza 2014b), and, as I discuss in the next
chapter, the anti-Machiavellian Christian prince. Alva Ixtlilxochitl's familiarity with European letters and tradition, his practice of early modern historiography (in particular his determination to separate *fábula* (fable) from
"fact" or "truth" in the Nahua context), however, does not lead to the complete
abandonment—to the erasure, or rather the total erasure (cf. Lesbre 1999a,
2010)—of specific and regionally significant aspects of Nahua signification,
most prominently that of the symbolic construction of the Acolhua ruler.[5]
Though displaced and allegorized, the footprints of Tezcatlipoca continue
to shadow the ruler and therefore, in that regard, to constitute properly (in
the form of an alphabetic narrative) the history of the Acolhua altepetl as an
entity whose identity was shaped around its ruler and his connection to gods

and the land. Thus, under (and undermining) what we might be tempted to call the "universal" or "archetypal" qualities of the mythical-literary-historical hero is a culturally and regionally specific means of encoding his actions and identity. While they have been disconnected from their explicitly religious and ritual frame of reference, "sanitized" (to use Patrick Lesbre's [1999] term) or "historicized" (as Olivier [2003] (2008) puts it), the reader familiar with sacred landscape in Nahua thought and with the rituals and signs of the ruler's power associated with it will not fail to recognize their ongoing presence in the narrative. Once again, Eduardo de J. Douglas's (2010, 14, 129–30, 132, 144–49, 159) observations about Alva Ixtlilxochitl's pictorial source texts (the *Codex Xolotl*, the Mapa Tlotzin, and the Mapa Quinatzin), in this case a distinction between their explicitly historiated mimetic narrative of events, accessible to all readers, and the texts' implicit metaphorical meanings, which require knowledge of Nahua rhetoric and semiosis in order to perceive them, apply to the *Historia de la nación chichimeca* as well.

The latter type of signification, notes Douglas (2010, 130, 134, 154), often suggests themes or ideas that, at the early postconquest era of their composition, had become dangerously suspect—for example, the relationship of rulers and gods, or cyclical notions of time encoded in dates of events. The significant time lapse between the creation of the pictorial histories during the 1530s–1550s and the composition of the *Historia de la nación chichimeca* anywhere from the mid-1620s to the 1640s prevents us from concluding with any certainty that Alva Ixtlilxochitl was aware of the specific details of the Nahua origins of his protagonist and pseudo culture hero's traits or that he consciously carried forward certain aspects of the footprint of the omniscient and omnipresent trickster god in his characterization of his ancestor.[6] Lesbre has demonstrated (1999a, 2000, 2001a), however, that Alva Ixtlilxochitl consciously worked to eliminate, downplay, and contextualize many of the overt fantastical or magical aspects of Nezahualcoyotl's persona, and thus it seems that the significance of the remaining less controversial characteristics would not have gone undetected.[7] A literary reading of the text, aware of Nahua tradition and open to accepting various (nonliteral or figurative) methods of signifying, indeed reveals not only a symbolic field in which specific ties between Nezahualcoyotl and the patron deity of his altepetl, the signs of royal power in the Nahua tradition, are put forth (and carried forward) in the narrative, but the way in which this domain relates to the text's expression of Nahua historicity in its cyclical rendering of time, as discussed in the last chapter. By linking Nezahualcoyotl to the mythical dynamic of the Quetzalcoatl/Tezcatlipoca duo,[8] the *Historia de la nación chichimeca* deepens both the concrete and symbolic significance that he and his descendents (the Acolhua rulership with whom Alva Ixtlilxochitl identifies) held for the Christian era. This mapping does not occur in the *Monarquía indiana*, whose trajectory of events regarding the life of Nezahualcoyotl is less detailed and concentrated, as it is interspersed with narrative focused on especially Mexica history and its relationship to events such as the conflicts with the Chalca. Although it resembles Alva Ixtlilxochitl's story in many respects, these major differences show the latter's dedication to preserving the full narrative and semiotic depth of Nezahualcoyotl's story and his more careful cultivation and propagation of the symbolic legacy that traditionally wrapped up his hero in a closely knit weave of attributes that signify an association (in the Nahua tradition) with the great Tezcatlipoca and his powers.

Although many anecdotes throughout the *Historia de la nación chichimeca* hint at Tezcatlipoca's presence, the focus here is on those scenes in which the connection between Nezahualcoyotl and the great trickster deity is most prominent and which play a major role in the narrative construction of Nezahualcoyotl's persona. In these episodes, the Tetzcoca ruler is identified with four of the deity's most important attributes. These interrelated attributes include (1) sorcery and shape-shifting, (2) transgression, (3) divination, and (4) the revelation of individual and collective destiny. The order of the characteristics presented roughly (but not exclusively) follows the chronological flow of Nezahualcoyotl's life story, and the discussion below also follows that arrangement. Not insignificantly, the scenes relating to points three and four are the same ones in which Nezahualcoyotl's explicit ties to Quetzalcoatl are also present. Uncovering in them the unspoken role of Tezcatlipoca and pointing out, where relevant, significant discrepancies (and commonalities) with Torquemada's version provide new vantage points from which to analyze Alva Ixtlilxochitl's narrative structure and assess its significance, as we shall see.

Part Two. Signifying Power: Nezahualcoyotl as "Tezcatlipoca" in the *Historia de la nación chichimeca*

THE RULER AS SORCERER: METONYM AND METAPHOR IN THE SACRED LANDSCAPE

The first indication that Nezahualcoyotl's life might have epochal or mythical implications comes in the description of his birth, which was, writes Alva Ixtlilxochitl, "muy notado . . . de los astrólogos y adivinos de aquel tiempo,

y fue por la mañana al salir el sol, con gran gusto de su padre . . ." (1975–
1977, 2:9; noted with interest . . . by the astrologers and diviners of the time,
and it was in the morning as the sun rose, to the enormous pleasure of his
father).[9] While Alva Ixtlilxochitl observes that the emperor Ixtlilxochitl was
very happy about the good fortune augured by the birth of his son at dawn,
he does not explain the traditional association of rulers with the sun in pre-
Hispanic Nahua society. In fact, it is possible to see in Nezahualcoyotl's identification with the rising sun his future as a great warrior and ruler. From this
perspective, Nezahualcoyotl's birth at dawn could also imply an association
with a new epoch and a new empire: the recovery of the Chichimeca rulership lost by his father, or even the arrival of the Spanish (which in postconquest days, as we have seen in the previous chapter and which Susan Gillespie
[1989, 123–24, 199–201] has argued in general, came to be regarded as the
advent of a new cycle or era). The epochal considerations of Nezahualcoyotl's
characterization and his *dual* affiliation with Quetzalcoatl *and* Tezcatlipoca,
instrumental deities in the creation and destruction of ages and empires
according to the interpretations of Graulich (1981) and Olivier ([2003] 2008,
2015), will be discussed in detail below. First, however, two subsequent scenes
also indicate metonymically—through physical contiguity to important symbolic aspects of the landscape—Nezahualcoyotl's supernatural potential, his
inherent connection to the gods, and testify to the significance and perdurance of Nahua landscape motifs in Alva Ixtlilxochitl's work.

In the first, Nezahualcoyotl and his father flee from Tepaneca persecutors
into a ravine. They camp beside the roots of a huge fallen tree, and the next
morning, as their assailants catch up with them, Nezahualcoyotl climbs into
another tree to save himself (1975–1977, 2:48). These trees evoke the cosmic
trees found in Nahua descriptions of the universe, which connect the celestial
upper world and the underworld at each of four corners of the universe, with
a great central tree as axis mundi at the center. At the very bottom layer, where
the roots of the tree end, is Mictlan, the land of the dead (López Austin 1984,
58–67; Burkhart 1989, 47). In the *Historia de los mexicanos por sus pinturas*,
Quetzalcoatl and Tezcatlipoca themselves turn into trees and become sky-
bearers. According to López Austin, they also unite as "opposites" in the form
of a helix, called a *malinalli* in Nahuatl, to create the great tree of Tamoan-
chan. Through its helices, the forces of the gods of the upper world and the
underworld travel to create the flow of time and animate life on the terrestrial
plane (1997, 92–97). Shamans and shape-shifters, called *nahuales*, used these
and other conduits (such as lakes, springs, and caves) to access the realms

of the gods and thus reestablish order on the terrestrial plane (López Austin 1984, 74). When examined from this point of view, the emperor Ixtlilxochitl's decision to journey downward into the ravine and to camp out under the roots of a fallen tree can be said to foreshadow his imminent death. Nezahualcoyotl's ascension into the treetops would thus indicate his future rise to the heights of power from which his father had just fallen. In addition, his proximity to the tree evokes his connection to sorcery and ability to travel the sacred conduits of the gods.[10]

In the second scene, Nezahualcoyotl, from a hiding place on the summit of a hill, watches a captain, an envoy of Tezozomoc, who is standing on top of a temple between Tetzcoco and Tepetlaoztoc, pronounce a death sentence against him (1975–1977, 2:51). Here, the contrast between the hill and the temple seems to imply a distinction between the fabricated power of the illegitimate usurper of the Acolhua ruler's true Tolteca-derived authority and Nezahualcoyotl's authentic rulership of the altepetl (the Nahua city-state). In addition, the perspective of Nezahualcoyotl on the hill (named Cuauhyacac), as an omniscient witness to his own fate and thus transcendent over that of Tezozomoc as well, aligns him with the powers associated with Tezcatlipoca.[11] As Olivier ([2003] 2008, 165) puts it, "The Lord of the Smoking Mirror was everywhere, in the streets of the city, around the bend of a road, or in the frightening obscurity of a forest." He was, moreover, a deity that inspired widespread fear for his ability to determine (and reveal) people's fate, to ensure their destiny—and his arrival usually implied a sudden change of course or reversal of fortune (15–20). Rulers, as the instruments through which the gods spoke, were also regarded as the "mirrors" of the people, and showed them their destinies (255–56).

It is at this point in the narrative that Nezahualcoyotl begins to take matters into his own hands, to pursue the recuperation of his rulership as he runs from the Tepaneca. Similar to his invisible presence on the hilltop, his actions begin to mimic Tezcatlipoca's powers of sorcery. In the first scene, Nezahualcoyotl spends time in Chalco disguised as a warrior after witnessing the pronouncement of his death sentence. He blows his own cover, however, revealing his penchant for justice, and hence his nobility, when he murders his hostess for running a clandestine pulque-selling business and getting people drunk. His identity revealed, he is imprisoned by the local ruler and ordered not to be given food or drink for eight days.[12] However, the ruler's brother, Quetzalmacatzin, slips him meals and helps him to escape by donning his clothing and taking his place inside the cage. As a consequence, he is condemned to suffer the death intended for Nezahualcoyotl (51–52). In its play of doubles (which we will see more of below), the story reminds us of Nezahualcoyotl's supposed immortality, the common tales that Alva Ixtlilxochitl contextualizes by comparing them to those told about the Portuguese King Sebastian, as mentioned in the discussion of funeral rites in chapter 1 (1975–1977, 2:283; Lesbre 2000). His actions also recall, however, Tezcatlipoca's fame for appearing in disguise, his status as a shape-shifter, his role as justice-maker or master of confessions, and his association with the revelation and reversal of fortunes (Olivier [2003] 2008, 15–20, 24–25, 250–59). The mythical context (or subtext) of the scene emerges most clearly with the reference to pulque, however, and the strength of Nezahualcoyotl's reaction to its illicit consumption and selling.

In Tolteca histories, pulque plays a major role in spelling the end of the empire, drunkenness and excess being linked also to sexual transgressions that initiate its demise (Olivier [2003] 2008, 121–22). In the *Annals of Cuauhtitlan*, for example, Tezcatlipoca, through his mediators, convinces Quetzalcoatl to drink five portions of pulque, instead of just four, after which he is forced into exile (Bierhorst 1992, 34–35). Examined with this context in mind, the scene becomes a rich prism in which the old lesson of Tezcatlipoca's role in the change of eras and empires is reflected. Nezahualcoyotl's indignation at the illicit selling of pulque, the substance so important to the exercise of power and the maintenance or demise of social order, should thus come as no surprise. While Tezozomoc's lack of control over the substance reveals the illicit nature of his government and signals its impending doom, Nezahulcoyotl's assassination of the vendor establishes the authenticity of his rule and the moral compass (or mirror) at its heart.

After his narrow escape, Nezahualcoyotl spends time under the protection of relatives in Tlaxcala and Mexico but is eventually allowed to return to live in Tetzcoco. Once there, of course, he begins to think about how to reclaim his position and restore his father's empire. As he does so, the emperor Tezozomoc, on his deathbed, has a dream, or rather a nightmare:

> El tirano Tezozómoc soñó una madrugada, cuando por el oriente salía
> la estrella del alba, que al príncipe Nezahualcoyotzin veía transformarse
> en figura de águila real y que le desgarraba y comía a pedazos el cora-
> zón; y otra vez se transformaba en tigre, que con unas uñas y dientes
> le despedazaba los pies; se metía dentro de las aguas, y lo mismo hacía
> dentro de las montañas y sierras convirtiéndose en corazón de ellas;

con lo cual despertó espantado, despavorido, y con cuidado, y así hizo
llamar luego a sus adivinos para que le declarasen este sueño. (1975–
1977, 2:54)

The tyrant Tezozomoc dreamed one morning at dawn, when the morning star was rising in the east, that he saw prince Nezahualcoyotzin
transformed into the figure of a golden eagle and that he was tearing
apart and eating his heart in bits and pieces. Another time he was transformed into a jaguar, and with his nails and teeth he was tearing apart
his feet, and [then] he entered into the waters and likewise into the
mountains and the hills, changing himself into their heart, with which
scene he awoke, frightened, terrified, and anxious, and so he later had
his soothsayers called to come and interpret the dream.

In their interpretation of the dream, the soothsayers get straight to the
point when they tell Tezozomoc that Nezahualcoyotl will take back his empire
unless he is killed. What they fail to reveal in Alva Ixtlilxochitl's rendition of
the event—was it perhaps too obvious to mention?—is the reason for their
conclusion. Representing the two major schools of warriors in late Postclassic
central Mexico, the eagles and jaguars symbolize Nezahualcoyotl's prowess as
a warrior and his impending military victory over the Tepaneca. Most significantly, however, the dream clearly evokes his religious power in the form of
Tezcatlipoca the shape-shifter, and he appears in the form of his jaguar avatar
Tepeyollotl, the "heart of the mountain." This all-but-explicit identification of
Nezahualcoyotl with Tepeyollotl also provides an important window into his
character and his power.[13]

Tezozomoc's dream indeed comes true as Nezahualcoyotl escapes from
subsequent Tepaneca assassination plots ordered by Tezozomoc's successor,
Maxtla, and goes on to recover his empire and to create and expand the powers of the Triple Alliance, which ruled over the region until the arrival of the
Spanish. The first escape scenes involve his uncle, the Mexica ruler Chimalpopoca, who has been imprisoned for plotting to help Maxtla's brother, Tayatzin,
the legitimate heir to Tezozomoc's rule, come to power. After hearing of
his uncle's plight, Nezahualcoyotl rather foolishly appears before Maxtla to
ask for leniency for his uncle. Maxtla considers assassinating him then and
there, but postpones the endeavor because an advisor, evidently unaware of
Nezahualcoyotl's extraordinary abilities, tells him that Nezahualcoyotl "no
se escaparía de sus manos, pues no se podía meter dentro de los árboles ni

Figure 2. Drawing of the scene depicting Tezozomoc's dream based on a segment from Plate VIII of the *Codex Xolotl*, located in the Bibliotèque nacional de France. Taken from the digital edition of *El héroe entre el mito y la historia*, first copublished in print by the Universidad Nacional Autónoma de México (IIH-UNAM) and the Centro de Estudios Mexicanos y Centroamericanos (CEMCA). Courtesy of CEMCA.

las peñas" (1975–1977, 2:59; that he wouldn't slip through his hands, because of course he couldn't hide himself inside the very trees or rocks).[14] Thus, with Maxtla's permission, Nezahualcoyotl visits his uncle in prison, where he receives important and life-saving advice encouraging him, metaphorically, to do exactly what Maxtla's gravely misled advisor claimed he could not.

After thanking him for his daring visit, Chimalpopoca warns Nezahual-coyotl to ensure that "vuestra silla y asiento esté trasminado, no en algún tiempo pronuncie sentencia de muerte el tirano Maxtla: andad siempre sobre aviso y con cuidado" (1975–1977, 2:59; your chair and seat be perforated, in case at some moment Maxtla pronounces a death sentence: always go about forewarned and with caution). Nezahualcoyotl's response to this advice, as narrated by Alva Ixtlilxochitl, hints at his own imminent change of fortune. It also speaks as much to his readers as to the situation at hand. He writes,

> Muy en el alma de Nezahualcoyotl quedaron escritas las palabras de su
> tío Chimalpopoca, por cuya causa no tan solamente guardó y cumplió

sus consejos, *que alegóricamente y por metáforas le había dicho sino que también ejecutó el sentido literal de ellas*, pues así como llegó a la ciudad de Tetzcuco, mandó luego de secreto trasminar las paredes por donde cabía su estrado y asiento, que después le valió para escaparse con la vida (como delante se dirá). (60; emphasis mine)

The words of his uncle Chimalpopoca were engraved deeply in Nezahualcoyotl's heart, because of which not only did he remember and follow the advice given *allegorically and through metaphor, he also executed it in its literal sense*, for as soon as he arrived at the city of Tetzcoco, he secretly ordered that the walls behind his throne and chair be perforated, which later allowed him to escape with his life (as will be told further along).

While Nezahualcoyotl understands the metaphorical significance of his uncle's words, he chooses to take them literally as well, says Alva Ixtlilxochitl.[15] (Just as his readers, of course, must examine Nezahualcoyotl's actions for their metaphorical, not just their "literal" significance, in order to understand them fully.) After his visit, Nezahualcoyotl returns to thank Maxtla for his generosity. He finds, however, that he must implement his uncle's advice right away in order to escape from Maxtla's palace and avoid immediate execution. With all of the exits blocked and Maxtla's troops amassed, Nezahualcoyotl slips through holes in the wall and roof of the palace (61).[16] Taken at face value, it is a feat of ingenuity; "metaphorically," it stands as a demonstration of the sorcerer's abilities to transgress the boundaries of the terrestrial world and access the realms of the gods.

Not long after this first flight through improvised escape hatches, moreover, Nezahualcoyotl foils an assassination attempt with the use of another double. This time, his faithful tutor Huitzilhuitzin (himself a known sorcerer) warns him about a plot to kill him at a party thrown by one of his half-brothers at Maxtla's behest.

Huitzilhuitzin, un caballero de la ciudad de Tetzcuco, dado a la ciencia de los astros y ayo suyo, supo esta traición y según su ciencia hallaba, que corría gran detrimento su persona si en este convite se hallaba, y para librarle de él dio orden que se trajesen un mancebo labrador, natural de Coatépec en la provincia de Otompan, que se parecía al príncipe y era de su misma edad, al cual tuvo algunos días, que no fueron muchos, en secreto, industriándole del modo de cortesía y usanza que tenían los príncipes. (63)

Huitzilhuitzin, a gentleman from the city of Tetzcoco, given to the science of the stars and a tutor of his, knew of this tradition and according to his science he found that he ran a great risk to his life if he were to be found at this gathering, and to get him out of it, he gave an order to bring him a young worker from Coatépec in the province of Otompan who looked like the prince and was his same age. They had him with them a few days (which was not much) in secret, training him in the modes of courtesy and the forms of address belonging to the nobility.

After knocking the young man unconscious, his assassins decapitate him in order to present to Maxtla what they think is Nezahualcoyotzin's head. When messengers arrive in Mexico to announce the news of his death, however, they discover Nezahualcoyotl alive and well, and conversing with the ruler Itzcoatzin. Alva Ixtlilxochitl's description of Nezahualcoyotl's response to their astonishment is significant. He writes that Nezahualcoyotl, "conociendo lo que en sus ánimos tenían, les dijo que no se cansasen en quererle matar, porque el alto y poderoso dios le había hecho inmortal" (64; knowing what they had in their hearts, told them not to wear themselves out wanting to kill him, because the great and powerful god had made him immortal). Blurring the line between the Christian sense of immortality and the continuous existence of the ruler as the Nahuas might have imagined it, Alva Ixtlilxochitl nevertheless continues to evoke his hero's supernatural ability to transcend the limits of everyday human existence, to signify an ancient connection to the god Tezcatlipoca.

In addition, Maxtla, usurper of Nezahualcoyotl's power and eternal victim of his trickery, discovers in the end that he can control neither his personal destiny nor that of his empire. According to Olivier ([2003] 2008, 17, 35–39), there is a clear connection between Tezcatlipoca and decapitation, visible in anecdotes that describe his nocturnal appearances (in the form of a decapitated body or a large skull, for example) and in the fact that one of his names was Ce Miquiztli (one death), a Nahua calendrical date represented in pictorial writing by means of a skull glyph. The skull, he writes, represents the moon, with all of its associations with fertility, water, and darkness; it is an association that can be seen, for example, in the representations of the decapitated Coyolxauhqui of the Mexica foundation myth and in scenes from various cosmogonies depicting the striking of the moon with a vase or other instrument (36–38). Most significantly, in *La historia de los mexicanos por sus pinturas*, as Olivier (94–95) relates, Quetzalcoatl strikes the down the sun Tezcatlipoca with a large stick, making him fall into the sea, from whence he emerges in the form of a jaguar (also a figure associated with darkness, water, fertility, and the moon) to devour the giants that had inhabited the first age. Alva Ixtlilxochitl's story cloaks itself in myth, then, not only by depicting the decapitation of his double, but also in the initial blow that rendered him unconscious. When read in light of Olivier's remarks about the alternation of powers in the cyclical change of epochs (the moon and the sun represented by Tezcatlipoca and Quetzalcoatl), the scene appears not only to link Neza-hualcoyotl to Tezcatlipoca, but to invoke Maxtla's demise and the impend-ing change of powers as well. Upon presenting Maxtla with Nezahualcoyotl's head, the assassins not only handed him supposedly irrefutable proof of his enemy's death, they also gave him an object charged with cosmogonic impli-cations. Maxtla, however, eternal victim of the trickster, only *thought* he had succeeded in knocking down the sun, and he only *thought* the skull he pos-sessed was that of the ruler of Acolhuacan.

At this point, Nezahualcoyotl's historicized shamanic mastery reaches its climax as he prepares to face the full brunt of Tepaneca wrath and undertake the reconquest of his rulership. To delay his capture by Tepaneca armies (by now well advised of his feats of escape), he invites four of the chief warriors to a ball game, itself a sure sign of a change of rule or impending conquest (Oliv-ier [2003] 2008, 141–42). First, however, Nezahualcoyotl enjoins his guests to have a meal, at which time he proves the wisdom of having taken his uncle Chimalpopoca's advice literally as well as metaphorically. While the Tepaneca visitors were eating, writes Alva Ixtlilxochitl, "Nezahualcoyotl se salió por el agujero y mina referida hasta otro que estaba hecho por un caño de agua, que entraba dentro de palacio, con que se pudo librar y le aprovechó el consejo de su tío Chimalpopoca" (1975–1977, 2:65; Nezahualcoyotl escaped through the hole and opening described into another that was made through a water channel that was inside the palace, through which he was able to free him-self, his uncle Chimalpopoca's advice benefiting him). Here, it is important to remember that in the Mesoamerican context, the rulers' mats or thrones (*petlatl* or *icpalli*) held great significance and were considered to be the places in which their powers inhered. Moreover, the escape hatches—through the throne (or the wall directly behind it) and the water channel—provide yet another example of the figurative connection to sorcery.[17]

Figure 3. Drawing of the scene depicting Nezahualcoyotl's escape from the palace based on a segment from Plate IX of the *Codex Xolotl*, located in the Bibliotèque nacional de France. Taken from the digital edition of *El héroe entre el mito y la historia*, edited by Federico Navarrete Linares and Guilhem Olivier, first copublished in print by the Universidad Nacional Autónoma de México (IIH-UNAM) and the Centro de Estudios Mexicanos y Centroamericanos (CEMCA). Courtesy of CEMCA.

Finally, as Nezahualcoyotl runs from his enemies, he finds hiding places that also serve to bolster his image as a powerful ruler: he hides under a platform covered with maguey hemp and a pile of recently harvested chia, as well as inside of a drum (67–69). These places provide singular images of what López Austin (1993, 114–16, 126) refers to as the "invisible" forces that animate and imbue the natural world with essential energy or life force. As tlatoani and therefore the representative or spokesperson of the patron deity, Nezahualcoyotl is in charge of agricultural rituals to ensure the altepetl's well-being (López Austin 1984, 83–97); he also transmits the voice and the breath of the god himself to his pueblo, just as Olivier describes with respect to the function of music in the preconquest context, noting that it came from Tezcatlipoca ([2003] 2008, 12–14, 214–18). Much more could be said about the positioning of Nezahualcoyotl on the landscape during the march in which he gathers his allies and initiates his campaign against the Tepaneca forces. For now, however, we shift from a discussion of Nezahualcoyotl the transformer and escape artist to a discussion of Nezahualcoyotl the soothsayer. If

Nezahualcoyotl's birth at sunrise provided a faint hint of the "epochal" implications of his life, his unerring vision of the fate of the empire in the hands of his descendents leaves no doubt.

THE RULER AS SOOTHSAYER AND REVEALER OF DESTINIES: NEZAHUALCOYOTL'S PROPHECIES AND TRANSGRESSION

With his eponymous Smoking Mirror, Tezcatlipoca is ineluctably tied to the art of divination and the revelation of destinies, both personal and collective (Olivier [2003] 2008, 248–59). Olivier writes, "Whether the end of eras disappearing in cyclical catastrophes, the periodical fall of the empires, or the unavoidable corruption of their lords, the mirror ineluctably reflected the fates of men as well as that of the universe" (257). It is here that Tezcatlipoca joins ranks with the better-known North American trickster figures as a comic persona. Discussing the way in which "the vagaries of life were linked to the ever-changing will of Tezcatlipoca" (who concedes and takes away wealth, honors, riches, good fortune, etc.), Olivier remarks that "These changes in status seem to have caused no end of hilarity in Tezcatlipoca" (16). Elaborating on this sense of mirth, he writes,

> The "malicious" acts used by Tezcatlipoca to mock men and ridicule them also undoubtedly illustrate the full power of the god and men's dependence on him. That being the case, these jokes constitute trials at the end of which individuals can discover the fate that is to be theirs. The change in status or the inversion of a given situation is translated into the laughter of Tezcatlipoca, who is both master of fates and models for transformations. (20)

In the following scenes, Nezahualcoyotl's affiliation with Tezcatlipoca becomes clear both in the general sense of his role as a forecaster of fates and also in terms of the very specific imagery in which this deity makes his appearance as such.

All of Nezahualcoyotl's overt predictions of the future in fact center on the impending arrival of newcomers who will put an end to the rulership of the Triple Alliance. In the most prominent of these scenes, Nezahualcoyotl's (mostly) explicit or "above-ground" association with Quetzalcoatl and his "underground" approximation to Tezcatlipoca come together. In them,

Nezahualcoyotl's soothsaying, as well as that of his heir, Nezahualpilli, centers on the coming destruction of the empire at the hands of the returning Quetzalcoatl.

The final section of chapter 36 (which describes Nezahualcoyotl's palace complex)[18] presents one of the first episodes in which Nezahualcoyotl directly exercises his ability as a soothsayer. Describing some workers who were building some of the more than three hundred rooms pertaining to Nezahualcoyotl's living quarters, Alva Ixtlilxochitl (1975–1977, 2:97) writes,

Y al tiempo que se cubrían algunas de las salas, queriendo cortar las maderas y planchas por los extremos, y quitar las maromas con que las habían arrastrado, que eran de increíble grandeza, les mandó el rey que las dejasen así, que tiempo vendría que sirviesen a otros, y no tendrían trabajo de hacerles nuevos huracos, ni ponerles nuevas maromas para arrastrarlas, y así se hizo; e yo los he visto dentro de los huecos de los pilares y portadas sobre que cargaba; y se cumplió su profecía, pues lo han desbaratado y aprovechándose de la madera.

And when they were covering some of the rooms, wanting to cut the wood and the planks off at the ends, and remove the ropes with which they had been carried, which were incredibly huge, the king ordered them to leave them as they were, that the time would come when they would be of use to others, and they wouldn't have the work of making new holes and putting new ropes in them to drag them with, and so they left them as they were; and I have seen them inside of the holes of the pillars and façades above which they lay; and his prophecy was fulfilled, because they have taken them down and made use of the wood.

This image of the ropes that remained in the palace beams, used later to tear down the newly built palace room, expresses what actually happened after the conquest, of course, when the Spanish razed preconquest edifices and used the stones to construct their own buildings. The presence of the author as eyewitness, providing evidence of the truth of his statement, moreover, adds an element of poignancy to the description, in which a direct descendent of the ruler who spoke those words sees them come to pass. The other important aspect of this scene, however, is its implied sense of time, what Kay Read has called the "logic of destructive transformation" (1998, 84). This sense of a destroyed era or epoch that nevertheless paves the way for the inevitable arrival of another recalls the cosmogony of the four suns (and Tezcatlipoca's role therein). Also suggestive is the passage's focus on the building's wooden beams and the ropes used to carry them. For the preconquest Nahuas both items had cosmological dimensions. Wooden beams were said to carry the force or power of their gods, to retain their ancient living powers, while the ropes twisted in the shape of the malinalli symbolize the important conduits of the forces of the gods (López Austin 1993, 116; Lesbre 1999b). In this context, Nezahualcoyotl's insistence that they remain in place makes him an advocate and a visionary of the enduring legacy of the past in the new cosmic dispensation he knows is coming. The Spanish may have started their buildings from scratch, but in using the ancient materials they surrounded themselves with—and gave new life to—the building blocks, the cosmic forces, of the ancient past.[19]

This story is followed shortly thereafter by the narrative of Nezahualcoyotl's decision, at the behest of his advisors, to build a temple to Huitzilopochtli and carry out sacrifices to him. At the moment, he had just been tricked into executing his only legitimate son and heir to the throne (1975–1977, 2:121–22) and was facing serious challenge to his rule by the Chalca, who had just killed two of his other sons (124). It is significant and perfectly in keeping with Tezcatlipoca's character that at this moment Nezahualcoyotl the trickster has become the victim of trickery. In many stories, his figure is linked directly to transgression, which *precipitates* not only a personal change of fortune but also that of an entire age or epoch. For example, various sources portray Tezcatlipoca kidnapping Xochiquetzal, the wife of Tlaloc (Olivier [2003] 2008, 31–34, 141, 148–49). In the chapters preceding Nezahualcoyotl's duping by his concubine, Alva Ixtlilxochitl tells the story of how he murdered the tlatoani of Tepechpan in order to marry his betrothed (1975–1977, 2:119–20). Although not strictly adultery, this crime, committed with all secrecy, indeed seems to have threatened the dynastic line of Tetzcoco rulership.[20] In due time, of course, the Acolhua dynasty will come to an end, as Nezahualcoyotl had already foreseen. For the moment, however, things get a bit better since, having decided that the temple construction and sacrifices were ineffective, Nezahualcoyotl goes to Tetzcotzinco to search for an answer to his dilemmas in his own way.

Once there, he fasts for forty days (his name means "fasting coyote")[21] and prays four times a day to the "Dios no conocido" (unknown god) in whose honor he composed over sixty songs, "que el día de hoy se guardan, de mucha moralidad y sentencias, y con muy sublimes nombres y renombres propios a él" (Alva Ixtlilxochitl 1975–1977, 2:125; that are preserved to this day, of great morality and pronouncements, and with very sublime names and titles that belonged to him).[22] At the end of forty days, Itztapalotzin, a nobleman who was accompanying Nezahualcoyotl, heard someone call his name in the middle of the night. Stepping outside to see who it was,

> Vido a un mancebo de agradable aspecto y el lugar en donde estaba claro y refulgente, que le dijo que no temiese, que entrase y dijese al rey su señor que el día siguiente antes del mediodía su hijo el infante Axoquentzin ganaría la batalla de los chalcas, y que la reina su mujer pariría un hijo que le sucedería en el reino, muy sabio y suficiente para el gobierno de él. (125)

> He saw a pleasant looking young man in a light and radiant place, who told him not to be afraid, to go inside and tell the king his lord that the next day before noontime his son the prince Axoquentzin would win the battle of the Chalcas, and that the queen his wife would give birth to a son that would succeed him in the realm, [and would be] very wise and able to govern it.

When he then goes to tell Nezahualcoyotl about his vision, he finds the ruler in the middle of "oración y sacrificio de incienso y perfumes, mirando hacia donde nace el sol" (prayer and sacrifice with incense and perfumes, looking toward where the sun rises). In this episode, Nezahualcoyotl is ostensibly seen making a clean break from the gods and religious practices of the Mexica. The clear Old Testament borrowings and references to the "Dios no conocido" make it one of the most clearly "contrived" and "Christianizing" passages of Alva Ixtlilxochitl's "truthful" history. However, the mention of the god's many epithets also recalls the many names or titles that the missionaries borrowed from Tezcatlipoca in the early colonial years as a way of describing the Christian God (Burkhart 1989, 39–42; Lee 2003; Lesbre 2012, 20–23), and the moral character of the songs or poems also evokes Tezcatlipoca's role as judge and confessor of penitents. In addition, Tezcatlipoca's rites, during the festival of Toxcatl, as Bautista Pomar (1975, 10) makes clear, involved great quantities of incense-burning.

The most interesting aspect of the scene, however, is the "mancebo de agradable aspecto," who closely resembles Tezcatlipoca's aspect as Telpochtli. As Olivier ([2003] 2008, 26–27) points out, in his pre-Hispanic (or less

Christianized) form, Telpochtli was an important part of the education of the young warriors in the *telpochcalli*, a school for young men who were not members of the elite. It thus makes perfect sense that he should appear in the narrative just before the story that tells how Axoquentzin, Nezahualcoyotl's young and inexperienced son, defies his brothers and enters the battlefield with the Chalca only to capture their chief military commander. Telpochtli was also said to represent eternal and vigorous youth, which the ruler maintained through sacrificing the captives of warfare (273). It should also be noted that the appearance of this figure at midnight coincides with Tezcatlipoca's nocturnal character, and his dreaded nocturnal manifestations (17).[23] In addition, his appearance in the midst of Nezahualcoyotl's immersion in his prayers suggests that the two phenomena are closely related. Thus, this ever-so-"Christianized" scene continues to reflect Nezahualcoyotl's ties to the ancient Tezcatlipoca as well as the sacrifices that it claims Nezahualcoyotl eschewed upon going to Tetzcotzinco.[24]

The next significant moment when Nezahualcoyotl's ability to predict the future manifests itself, as we have already seen in the last chapter, occurs a short time after the defeat of the Chalca and the birth of Nezahualpilli. Alva Ixtlilxochitl dedicates all of chapter 47, "Que trata de algunas profecías y dichos que dijo el rey Nezahualcoyotzin" (Which treats some prophecies and sayings that Nezahualcoyotzin pronounced) to the subject. It begins with descriptions of songs (the *xompancuicatl*) that he composed, whose prophetic pronouncements or sayings, notes Alva Ixtlilxochitl, "muy a la clara en nuestros tiempos se han cumplido y visto" (1975–1977, 2:132; have very clearly in our times been fulfilled and seen). Although they are "springtime songs," they are all laments about the coming destruction of the "reinos y señoríos" in which the rulers would be stripped of their power and the people (the subjects, or "vasallos") would be devastated and ruined. In addition to these laments, however, Alva Ixtlilxochitl narrates Nezahualcoyotl's reaction, in the year ce acatl, to the inauguration ceremony of the great temple to Huitzilopochtli that he had begun to build years earlier. We have already discussed the significance of the date in its connection to the circular structure of the narrative, being the same year in which Cortés arrives on the Gulf coast, and in which Quetzalcoatl promised that he would return (8). With respect to the series of prophecies contained in the pronouncement made by Nezahualcoyotl in the inauguration of the temple, however, it is important to point out their unhappy nature; that is, they are prognostications of doom and misfortune, of the onset of chaos after conquest. They focus on the *end* of the reinos and the señoríos—the destruction of the altepetl dynasty in which rulers and rulerships took responsibility for the well-being of the people through maintaining their purity and continuing the proper practice of religious rituals and fiestas. At the apex of his empire's power, symbolized in the completed expansion of the temple to Huitzilopochtli, Nezahualcoyotl foresees its demise, pointing out (as we saw in the previous chapter) the cyclical and repetitive historical inevitability of the end of a rulership: "porque en esto vienen a parar los mandos, imperios y señoríos, que duran poco y son de poca estabilidad. Lo de esta vida es prestado" (132; because in this the dominions, empires, and estates, which last but a short time and are very unstable, will come to a halt. Everything in this life is borrowed).[25]

The structural diglossia encoded in the passage (its simultaneously linear and cyclical emplotment) is matched by its ambivalent attitude toward the conquest: there are tones of resignation and thankfulness, but also of deep sadness and lament. The core of the passage's ambivalence, however, lies in the figure of Nezahualcoyotl, who *knows* the "truth"—the impending arrival of the "sons of Quetzalcoatl" as his heir Nezahualpilli will call them (1975–1977, 2:175)—but knows it because of an extraordinary faculty of prescience with which he is endowed. Alva Ixtlilxochitl implicitly relates this wisdom to that of Quetzalcoatl in the beginning of the narrative, and to the ancients of the European classical tradition whose study of the "book of nature" brought them close to an understanding of the divine truth as defined by Christianity (136–37). As I have shown, however, this prescience, a capacity for divination and the revelation of the fates of individuals and empires, also relates his figure (back) to Tezcatlipoca.

One of the features of Tezcatlipoca that most significantly distinguishes him from the deity Quetzalcoatl as portrayed in early colonial Nahua myths (and with whom he nevertheless shares a great many characteristics) was the particular nature of his soothsaying (Olivier [2003] 2008, 275–76). In his role as a diviner, one of his primary functions "was the forecasting of the ends of the eras, the announcement of the rise of future lords, and the emergence of new suns" (274). Olivier concludes his book on Tezcatlipoca by saying that

> Quetzalcoatl and Tezcatlipoca seem to diverge in that the former
> has a more creative function, while the latter works toward the com-
> pletion and the destruction of the cycles. In that sense, Quetzal-
> coatl and Tezcatlipoca are the alpha and omega of ancient Mexican
> mythology. (277)

In the *Historia de la nación chichimeca*, Nezahualcoyotl is nothing if not the announcer of the end of the polytheistic and bloodthirsty rule of the Triple Alliance. He also embodies, however, the spiritual essence of the new (and ancient, pre-Tolteca) dispensation about to arrive on the shores of the Gulf coast. Following Graulich's (1981) notion that the rise and fall of the sun represents the rise and fall of the ages of creation, which are assimilated to epochs of imperial rule, Tezcatlipoca and Quetzalcoatl alternate as predominating "suns" or astral "overseers" of an age, or an empire. In Alva Ixtlilxochitl's history, Nezahualcoyotl embodies both figures simultaneously. Not only do the Acolhua rulers successfully divine their own downfall at the hands of the explicitly Quetzalcoatl-assimilated Spanish conquerors, they also ally themselves with these forces and aid in the destruction of their own people, just like the jaguar that emerges from the water at the end of the first sun of creation in the *Historia de los mexicanos por sus pinturas* (Olivier [2003] 2008, 94).²⁶

Part Three. Alva Ixtlilxochitl's Colonial Mexican Trickster Tale

The overt association of Nezahualcoyotl's Christian-like qualities with the figure of Quetzalcóatl, present only in the *Historia de la nación chichimeca*,²⁷ therefore, must also be considered in light of his implicit, more traditional, and more ancient alliance with the figure of Tezcatlipoca, with the Nahua semiotic context that—despite or amid Alva Ixtlilxochitl's careful censorship— continues to be perceptible in his work. By introducing the apostle-like Quetzalcoatl into his narrative, Alva Ixtlilxochitl seems to—indeed he *does*—take a step in the direction of the progressive "Europeanization" of the Acolhua Nahua past, engaging in an act of transcultural resemanticization that abets the process of cultural colonization (Lienhard 1991, 95–129). With this same act, however, he also, as I have shown, brings his narrative into deeper (or perhaps more obvious) alignment with the cyclical patterns present in Nahua histories. In his narrative, the past of Acolhuacan and greater Mexico as he tells it takes its place in the parallel and repetitive schema in which the cosmic ages of creation, and the rise and fall of empires, play themselves out in the actions and under the auspices of a predictable cast of characters, most significantly in those of the twin gods Quetzalcoatl and Tezcatlipoca. Not only does Tezcatlipoca continue to be an absent presence shadowing Tetzcoco's ruler-hero in the *Historia de la nación chichimeca*, Alva Ixtlilxochitl has superimposed the name Quetzalcoatl, and thus its historical and cosmic weight, *onto* this ancient identification. Although both the explicit rendering of Quetzalcoatl and the implicit figuration of Tezcatlipoca have been construed in the colonial context to reflect Catholic sensibilities, their continued association as the alpha and the omega, creator and destroyer, within Alva Ixtlilxochitl's text marks its difference from the European Christianity and culture of the colonizer, or, in Walter Mignolo's terminology, its *discontinuity* with the European classical tradition.

Most importantly, however, by adding the identification of Nezahualcoyotl with Quetzalcoatl to his protagonist's more ancient association with Tezcatlipoca, Alva Ixtlilxochitl creates his emblem of the conquest. In his history, Nezahualcoyotl and the entire line of Acolhuacan rulers bear the weight of beginnings and endings, incarnating the forces of their own destruction but also the means of their survival. As the embodiment of this great mythical dyad of conflictive but also generative duality, Nezahualcoyotl becomes the figure of time as it is lived in both worlds, the great cultural mediator for whom rupture and continuity were never mutually exclusive terms.

Part Four. Postscript: More Evidence and an Anecdotal Segue

A curious scene drawn by Alva Ixtlilxochitl at the end of the thirteenth relación of the *Compendio* seems to confirm—allegorically, of course—this resemanticized, but still very Nahua, construal of the Quetzalcoatl/Tezcatlipoca pair and its placement at the roots of Catholicism in New Spain. In the scene, (Fernando Cortés) Ixtlilxochitl (one of Nezahualcoyotl's grandsons, who aided Cortés in the conquest) and other Acolhua rulers return from the Hibueras expedition to discover that "fake" nobles had taken over the señorío (estate) and, once in control, had "acted like Spaniards." In other words, they had been greedy and spent all of the tribute payments ([1975–1977] 1985, 1:515). Ixtlilxochitl and the other "true" nobles were then left to carry out the tribute labor—the building of the Church of San Francisco of Mexico City—assigned to their usurpers. The nobles are, of course, upset. Ixtlilxochitl, however, responds by calling all of the lords together and orders that each of them:

> Tomase un huácatl, que son unos como espuertas, ya de madera, ya de cueros de animales y llevase cargados en ellos materiales a México para edificar los templos de San Francisco [e] iglesia mayor; y Ixtlilxúchitl,

como capitán, siendo el primero en esto cargó un gran huácatl de cuero
de tigre lleno de piedra; se partió a México delante de la gente ilustre
que iban cargados de piedras, cal y arena, y otros atrás, tirando madera,
el cual les fue animando, y entre otras razones les dijo, que tuviesen
paciencia y mostrasen ánimo porque viesen los villanos traidores que,
aunque a ellos no pertenecía aquel oficio, lo sabían bien hacer sin ayuda
de los rebeldes, y que sus vasallos, la gente plebeya, tomasen ejemplo
para que con más ánimo los que quisiesen seguirles fuesen a hacer este
servicio a Dios en edificarle su iglesia, pues ellos, como cabezas, fuesen
los primeros que pusieron por obra el edificar templos a Dios, pues él
había sido el primero en el bautismo y en las batallas en servicio de
Dios y del emperador. (516)

Take a *huacatl*, which are things like baskets, sometimes made of wood,
or animal hide, and carry them full of materials to Mexico to build
the temples of San Francisco and the main church; and Ixtlilxochitl, as
captain, was the first to carry a large huacatl made of jaguar skin full of
rocks; he left for México leading the group of distinguished people that
were going loaded with rocks, lime and sand, with others behind, haul-
ing wood. He was encouraging them, telling them, among other things,
to have patience and show courage so that the treacherous commoners
would see that even though the job did not belong to them, they knew
how to do it without the help of the rebels, and so that their vassals,
the plebeians, would see their example. [And he said that] those who
wanted to follow them would do this service to God in building him
his church, because as leaders they should be the first to undertake the
work of building the churches to God, just as he and been the first baptized and in battle in service to God and the emperor.

Here, the image of the jaguar-skin huacatl full of stones for the construction of the Church of San Francisco in Mexico bears a significant symbolic
relationship to the description of Topiltzin's obsequies provided by Alva
Ixtlilxochitl in the fifth addendum of the *Sumaria relación de todas las cosas
de la Nueva España*. In this latter passage, as we have seen, Alva Ixtlilxochitl describes how the Acolhua enthronement and burial rites, adopted from
the death of Ixtlilxochitl onward, were based on Tolteca rites that had been
initiated with Topiltzin ([1975–1977] 1985, 1:387). This ruler, said to return
sometime in the future on the date ce acatl, was cremated, after which time

the people "cogieron la ceniza que se hizo de su cuerpo, y echáronla en una bolsa hecha de cuero de tigre, y por esta causa todos los señores que aquel tiempo morían los quemaban" (collected the ashes made from his body, and threw them in a bag made of jaguar skin, and for this reason all of the lords who died in those times were cremated). This brief description compares favorably to the longer portrayal of the funeral rites given to Tezozomoc, as we have seen, about which Alva Ixtlilxochitl writes in great detail in the text of the *Sumaria relación de todas las cosas de la Nueva España*, declaring it to have been ordered by Topiltzin and to have been the model for all of the rest of the burials of rulers from that time forward ([1975–1977] 1985, 1:349–53). This funerary bundle—Topiltzin/Quetzalcoatl's ashes stored in a jaguar skin symbolic of rulership and associated with Tezcatlipoca/Tepeyollotl—seems, in turn, to be a kind of still life or snapshot representation of the stories in which Tezcatlipoca tricks Quetzalcoatl into looking into his mirror or into drinking pulque, bringing about the end of his rule, or of those of the creation of the sun and the moon, for example, when Nanahuatzin jumps into the pyre at Teotihuacan to become the sun, while Tecuciztecatl, according to Olivier (who associates him with the lunar Tezcatlipoca [Olivier (2003) 2008, 132–34]) jumps into the ashes to become the moon. Yet, how does the description of Topiltzin's funerary bundle inform Alva Ixtlilxochitl's story of Ixtlilxochitl's rock-filled huacatl?

Given the Tetzcoco rulers' relationship to the cyclical Tezcatlipoca/Quetzalcoatl dynamic, described above, it is possible to interpret this scene as an allegorical incorporation of Christianity into the folds of the Nahua (or the Nahua-Christian) cosmovision. While the first jaguar skin contains the ashes of Topiltzin, the second bears the materials bound for the edification of the churches of Mexico. In this scenario, Ixtlilxochitl-Tezcatlipoca provides the raw materials—stones standing in for Topiltzin's ashes—with which the religious institutions of the new era, the sun of Quetzalcoatl, will be built, literally, on top of the destruction of the old ones. As he concludes his story, Alva Ixtlilxochitl remarks upon the sacrifices and commitment to Christianity made by his namesake Ixtlilxochitl, whose reversal of fortune was severe and whose recompense for *aiding* the Spanish in the destruction of his own empire was not forthcoming. His glorious ancestor, however, ruler in more than just name, decided to provide the example of good conduct for his people and lead the brigade to Mexico, where he stayed a few days, "de gran capitán y señor de toda la tierra, hecho albañil" ([1975–1977] 1985, 1:516; a great captain and lord of all the land, turned into a construction worker).[28] Like his grandfather Nezahualcoyotl, Ixtlilxochitl retains the qualities of ruler amid his hard luck. His deeds, like those of Nezahualcoyotl in Chalco, revealed his true identity despite the "disguise." Indeed, after narrating his return to Tetzcoco after the grueling campaign to conquer Hibueras, during which Cortés hangs Cuauhtemoc, Tetlapanquezatzin, and various other rulers, including Cohuanacochtzin (Fernando Cortés Ixtlilxochitl's brother) (502–3), Alva Ixtlilxochitl takes a moment to reflect on the heroism of his great ancestor, and to compare him to those who went before.

> Fue uno de los mayores trabajos que ha padecido príncipe en este nuevo mundo, al que padeció Ixtlilxúchitl, y así parece que fue en suma mayor que ninguno de los que padecieron sus antepasados, fuera de Topiltzin último rey y monarca de los tultecas, que casi fue igual el trabajo y por el mismo camino según las historias. Xólotl peregrinó mucho, pero no padeció lo que este príncipe. Su abuelo Nezahualcoyotzin, como se ha visto, también padeció mucho y peregrinó hartos años, pero con todo esto fue dentro de su patria y reino, y así me parece, que casi en todo fue otro segundo Topiltzin en lo que es peregrinación, trabajos y última destrucción de imperio que en él se acabó el imperio tulteca, que duró quinientos setenta y dos años, y lo mismo ha sido en Ixtlilxúchitl, que se acabó en su muerte el imperio chichimeca meridional que duró otro tanto tiempo. (514)

> It was one of the greatest travails ever suffered by any prince in this New World, what Ixtlilxochitl went through, and in total even greater, it appears, than those suffered by his predecessors, except for Topiltzin, the last ruler and king of the Tolteca, whose suffering was almost equal or along the same lines, according to the histories. Xolotl wandered far, but he didn't suffer what this prince did; his grandfather Nezahualcoyotzin, as we have seen, also suffered a lot and wandered many years, but even for all of that, it was still within his homeland and kingdom, and so it seems to me, that, all in all, he was a second Topiltzin with respect to his wandering, travails, and the final destruction of the empire. In him the Tolteca empire, which lasted 572 years, came to an end, and the same has occurred in Ixtlilxochitl: in his death the meridional Chichimeca empire ended, which also lasted about that much time.

Thus, in both Nezahualcoyotl's and Ixtlilxochitl's influence on the construction and the creation of the Mexican church, perhaps we can divine the invisible presence, ultimately indivisible from that of Quetzalcoatl, of the hand of Tezcatlipoca. If it has taken us this long to fully "see" Tezcatlipoca hiding in plain sight, running alongside Nezahualcoyotl—and the entire Tetzcoco ruling line—perhaps, now, we can also begin to hear him laughing.

CHAPTER FOUR

Nezahualcoyotl as Christian Prince

Crisis, Tribute, and the Rhetoric of Exemplarity

Y la causa de ser unos de político vivir, y otros muy toscos y de bajos pensamientos, o soberbios altivos, y amigos de mandar, ha sido el tener virtuosos o malos príncipes.

And the reason why some lived a cultivated life and others were very base and of lowly or proud and haughty thoughts, with a love for power, was their having had virtuous or immoral princes.

—ALVA IXTLILXOCHITL, *Primera relación of the Compendio histórico*

⚘ IN HIS PORTRAIT OF IXTLILXOCHITL AS THE EMPEROR-TURNED-*albañil* (construction worker), Alva Ixtlilxochitl (re)creates a pithy and rhetorically potent emblem expressive of the reversal of fortunes experienced by the ever more irrelevant and (in Alva Ixtlilxochitl's day) endangered status of the indigenous nobility, especially that of Acolhuacan. As discussed in chapter 1, by the early decades of the seventeenth century, as Alva Ixtlilxochitl was in his prime, the privileges and benefits (even the very identity) of the indigenous nobility had become almost nonexistent. The fact that the Teotihuacan cacicazgo was one of the longest enduring entities of its kind witnesses the tenacity of the Alva Ixtlilxochitl family and their legal prowess as they maintained it against many obstacles and throughout a changing economic context and political milieu. Yet the early seventeenth-century cacicazgo differed little from the other forms of land tenure that surrounded it, as discussed in chapter 1. The preconquest altepetl, which implied a combination of people, land, and rulership (Schroeder 1991, 209), had all but disappeared, with the third element of the triad suffering the greatest negative impact. While the discursive strategy used by Alva Ixtlilxochitl in his histories (in part to defend his family's rights to their cacicazgo) harkens back to the long tradition of appeals to the Crown on the part of indigenous polities (or other entities) for compensation for alliance and services rendered to the Spanish during and after the conquest (Villella 2014), the *Historia de la nación chichimeca*, as a work written in the form of the European universal history, nevertheless remains rooted in particular aspects of Nahua historiography, with its focus on rulership constituting a fertile venue for the creation of a diglossic and double-voiced representation of a Nahua historical-temporal structure and of the ruler-hero himself. One final and very significant aspect of Alva Ixtlilxochitl's aesthetic engagement with the idea and image of the ruler remains to be addressed. Here, the specular nature of the ruler's relationship to his subjects (and of his projection of power and authority), already seen in his ties to Tezcatlipoca described in the previous chapter, finds a complement in the European tradition of the mirror for princes.

In her work on Alva Ixtlilxochitl, Brian (2007, 112–13; 2016, 96–99, 106) notes that his rendition of Nezahualcoyotl as the ideal Christian prince fits neatly into this tradition, a genre of writing with a long history and varied manifestations in Europe. Indeed, in all of Alva Ixtlilxochitl's writing, but most prominently in the *Compendio* and the *Historia de la nación chichimeca* (with their aggrandizement of the Acolhua rulership's character and record of service to the Spanish), the pronounced influence of the thought and discourse of the Counter-Reformation *de regimine principis* should not be overlooked. The debates over the proper nature of a good ruler and the duties of the prince after the publication of Machiavelli's appeal to political pragmatism and expediency in *The Prince* and *The Discourses* provide a significant historical and literary context in which the construction of the image of Nezahualcoyotl in the colonial period took place, and in which it must be understood.

From the beginning, moreover, the Europeanization (and glorification) of Nezahualcoyotl served purposes beyond that of shoring up his descendents' rights, in Spanish jurisprudence, to royal privileges as the señores naturales (natural lords) of the land. It also abetted the effort of the mendicant orders to maintain their sole religious authority over a (theoretically) segregated república de indios. In the hands of Bartolomé de las Casas, moreover, the Europeanized grandeur of Nezahualcoyotl and his legacy became an instrument of colonial critique, used in the *Apologética historia* as evidence to prove the full humanity of Mexico's "Indians" and to incriminate the Spanish conquistadores for their violation of natural law in refusing to respect the rights of kings and therefore to carry out the Crown's responsibilities to Christianize the newly acquired territories (Brading 1991, 281–82). As someone whose income came at least in part from his positions within the colonial bureaucracy and institutions, Alva Ixtlilxochitl could not have engaged in such polemics, or have written with such an exclusive, dedicated agenda of colonial critique and reform. This does not mean, however, that his rendition of Nezahualcoyotl was limited to the need to aggrandize his ancestors or keep claim to privileges.

In general, scholars of Alva Ixtlilxochitl, emphasizing his commitment to and praise of the Spanish colonial enterprise, as well as his immersion in the dominant world of European letters, have been duly reluctant to consider the possibility that he might be using his representation of the pre-Hispanic past (and its "princes") as an implicit critique of colonial rulership (Brian 2007, 112–13). However, to say that Alva Ixtlilxochitl's work embodies such a critique is not to argue that he held an anti-Spanish or anticolonial attitude. Like any other writer and member of a social elite, Alva Ixtlilxochitl would not have been immune to or isolated from the debates of his time, especially those surrounding the nature of indigenous culture and the status and fate of indigenous languages and communities (Townsend 2014, 4). On one level, moreover, his intentions as an author are irrelevant: whatever his aim in writing the *Historia de la nación chichimeca* may have been, it cannot escape its status as a universal history and the expectations of didacticism and exemplarity pertaining to the genre. As I point out below, in the humanist tradition, both the explicitly denominated mirror for princes and a history filled with the exemplary tales of notable rulers (good and bad), was considered to be a "mirror," that is, a book written for the edification of its readers—princely or otherwise.

In this context, even the garbs of the Old Testament (or classical) hero, the persistent development of Nezahualcoyotl's religious exceptionalism with respect to the rest of the pre-Hispanic indigenous rulership (Lesbre 2000)—from the arrival of the Franciscans onward, he lacked only the knowledge of Christ for his enlightenment to have been complete—cannot overcome the perils involved in presenting a previously (and not so anciently) idolatrous ruler of a conquered, now colonized, people, as the site of an ideal prince in the colonizer's scheme of things. The text thus becomes a space of contradiction, caught in the crosshairs of the demands of the relación de méritos y servicios and the didactic history when, inadvertently, it finds itself reflecting, and hence reflecting upon, the even more recent past and present of the colonial milieu of its composition.

Part One. The Exempla in Early Modern Historiography and the Anti-Machiavellian Mirror for Princes

The literary-rhetorical genre known as the "mirror for princes" evolves in the Middle Ages from both Islamic and Christian sources, reaching its apogee (as in other areas) during the Renaissance as monarchical power consolidated (Tang 1996, 188–89; Ricquoi and Bizzarri 2005). At this time, the genre shows the heavy influence of the classical Greek and Roman writers, especially Aristotle, Cicero, and Xenophon, whose portrait of the Persian king Cyrus was regarded as its own kind of "mirror for princes." Although varied, the genre at its core provided advice and instruction to the ruler regarding the character traits, abilities, and education necessary for successful governance. David Nogales Rincón (2006, 9–10), in his overview of the tradition in "Los espejos de príncipes en Castilla (siglos XIII–XV)," defines them in this way:

> Los espejos o tratados de educación de príncipes son obras de carácter político-moral que recogen un conjunto de directrices morales y de gobierno básicas que han de inspirar la actuación del buen soberano cristiano. Por ello, estos tratados se convertirán, en un sentido figurado, en espejos, en los cuales todo príncipe cristiano debería mirarse para guiar su actuación. . . .
>
>   Estas guías partían de la base de que sólo la conciencia del rey adecuadamente encauzada podía asegurar la buena marcha del reino, partiendo de dos hechos. Por un lado, la idea de que sólo el rey que sabía gobernarse a sí mismo podría gobernar adecuadamente a su pueblo.

Por otro, la concepción del rey como espejo, es decir, como modelo, para sus súbditos.

The mirrors or educational treatises of the princes are discourses of a political-moral type that gather together a group of basic moral and governmental directives aimed at influencing the behavior of the good Christian ruler. As such, these treatises become, in a figurative sense, mirrors, in which every Christian prince must examine himself as a guide for his actions. . . .

These guides started from the idea that only the king's conscience, properly directed, could assure the well-being of the realm, starting with two points. On the one hand, the idea that only the king who knew how to govern himself could adequately govern his people. On the other, the idea of the king as a mirror, that is, as a model, for his subjects.

The European tradition, then, just like the expectations for the Nahua ruler described in the previous chapter, emphasizes the necessity of moral and ethical comportment on behalf of the ruler, his duty to model and to be a "mirror" for his people. Unlike the tlatoani, the Christian prince is not, of course, endowed with supernatural power to see the future and look into the souls of his subjects. In both cases, however, the importance of this ethical behavior for the smooth operation and the perdurance of the state stand out.

In "La tradición del *exemplum* en el discurso historiográfico y político de la España imperial," Victoria Pineda (2005, 32) writes that, although some "mirrors" presented their advice in more strictly didactic terms, or as precepts, the use of the exemplum was a common feature of the Renaissance history and discourse in general. "La preponderancia concedida al ejemplo sobre el precepto," she writes, "resultará clave en el discurso histórico y político del Renacimiento, que hace de los *exempla* su principal instrumento persuasivo y, a la vez, asegura con ellos la pervivencia de los valores morales de la Antigüedad" (the preponderance conceded to the example over the precept will be key in the historical and political discourse of the Renaissance, which makes the *exempla* its principal persuasive instrument, and, at the same time, assures along with them the survival of the moral values of Antiquity). For Pineda, the exempla provide the principal means by which historians and rulers' advisors would transmit and effectively persuade their readers (often, their royal readers) of the political expediency and urgency of their message; it was the means through which they made the past relevant in the present and proposed "modelos de conducta útiles y válidos—otro objetivo primordial" (models of useful and valid conduct—another fundamental objective).

José Antonio Maravall (1944) also expresses this sentiment, differentiating the practical and political aims of the later seventeenth-century Counter-Reformation history from the earlier humanist approach to the genre. "La historia, en el siglo XVII," he writes, "no tiene la finalidad panegírica y elocuente que buscó en ella el Humanismo, sino un valor pragmático y ejemplar" (64–65; The history, in the seventeenth century . . . does not aim for the panegyrics and eloquence that Humanism expected of histories; it rather held pragmatic and exemplary value). More than theology or jurisprudence, he points out, history was the prime medium used by those who wrote on the new art of politics, whose aim was to teach the prince how to govern well by providing both positive and negative examples from the past (66–67). "Estudiar el pasado, disponer el presente y prevenir el futuro," he writes, "son tres partes íntimamente ligadas del arte político por excelencia, y de ellas, las dos últimas dependen en gran medida de la primera, de la noticia y ejemplo de lo pasado. Para penetrar en el porvenir solo se nos ha dado un camino, que da la vuelta por el pretérito." (66; The study of the past, the preparation of the present and the anticipation of the future are three intimately related parts of the political art par excellence, and of these, the latter two depend in great measure on the first, that of the lesson and the example of the past. To penetrate into the future we only have one road, which takes a turn through the preterite.) As Maravall, and, much later, Timothy Hampton (1990) emphasize, exemplary figures were meant to inspire the positive, imitative action of the prince (and others). For Renaissance writers of history, says Hampton, "Heroism is a rhetoric—a deliberative rhetoric intended to provoke action. The image of the exemplary figure exhorts the reader, recalling in the most direct way Cicero's definition of rhetoric as 'speech designed to persuade' . . . or Augustine's characterization of the aim of rhetoric as 'inducement to action'" (4).

As Rolena Adorno (2007, 143–44) has pointed out, Alva Ixtlilxochitl wrote against the grain and in the language of the colonizer in order to convince a Spanish audience in Spanish terms of the bona fide valor and value of his Acolhua ancestors. Just as his rulers were valiant warriors, they were also model Christian princes. Moreover, if, as Thomas Ward (2011) noted, the preconquest rulers become the ancient Romans, then they *also* serve as exempla for the translatio imperii that the Spanish Crown imagined. A brief look at the values associated with the Counter-Reformation prince (in comparison with the prince of the early humanists) enables us to examine Alva Ixtlilxochitl's construction of Nezahualcoyotl in light of this discourse.

Part Two. The Counter-Reformation Christian Prince

Frank Tang (1996) provides an excellent summary of the essential qualities of the ideal prince as elaborated by the humanist Christian writers. He notes that

> Though the humanists discussed the purpose of princely authority and the personal motives of a ruler in more secular terms, they retained the idea that virtue was the best means of achieving political stability and personal glory. In this respect they followed the medieval Christian tradition, as well as the classical moralists. Cicero, the classical author who was esteemed most by the humanists, maintained that a political leader should have virtus. According to the humanists, virtus comprised not only the cardinal virtues iustitia, temperantia, fortitudo and prudentia, but also Christian virtues such as faith and piety. A monarch was moreover expected to display such typically princely virtues as generosity, magnificence and clemency, and always to keep his word.

In the fifteenth century, when the question of how a ruler could best service his subjects was gradually supplanted by the question of how he could remain in power, demands for moral integrity and faith continued to be made. According to authors such as Giovanni Pontano, Diomede Carafa, and Francesco Patrizi, these virtues provided the best protection against fortuna's fickleness (194).

Writing with respect to Renaissance Spain, Maravall (1944) pithily differentiates the Counter-Reformation version of virtue from that of Machiavelli, describing how the anti-Machiavellian writers, such as Pedro de Rivadeneyra, Diego de Saavedra Fajardo, and many others, construed those qualities bound up in it. He notes that while they accepted (and strove to address) the need for a new "art" of politics and governance as displayed by Machiavelli, they vehemently rejected his exclusion of religion (and ethics) from the rank of highest priority in the duties of the prince. Without adherence to the true faith (Catholicism), he writes, the anti-Machiavellians argued that the prince would be capable of only a poor copy or imitation of true virtue, and without true virtue, it would be impossible to preserve and expand the kingdom (270). As men of their time, however, concerned with the sovereignty of the state and the power of the monarch, the Spanish writers created templates of princely behavior that accepted and allowed for the mistrustful and pessimistic vision of human action in the world. They did not, however, accept a division between the public and private persona of the prince. Any goal or action that lay outside Christian morals, and that (therefore) contradicted the ultimate goal of preserving the truth of Christianity as expressed in the Catholic Church, was illegitimate and would necessarily be ineffective (270–72).

Just how important was the creation of an "alternative program for state building" that would not depart from notions central to Christian morality in early modern Spain is made clear in Robert Bireley's *The Counter-Reformation Prince* (1990, 25, 24–44). According to Bireley, the anti-Machiavellian "tradition" was intent on proving that politics was not incompatible with the Christian life, that it did *not* necessitate a "pragmatic" infringement of Christian morality and ethics on the part of the prince, a separation of the "good" from the "useful" (27). Rather, the anti-Machiavellians argued that "the good and the useful belonged together," that if a prince followed Christian principles he would surely have success, especially if "he possessed intelligence and skill" (30). In more technical terms, they argued (with the neo-Thomists of the Salamanca school) that a strong state that maintained the stability and "political well-being" of the people was necessary so that the Church could effectively operate to ensure their "spiritual well-being," but that this state could *best* and *only* be maintained through the application of Christian principles and ethics (including honesty).

To prove their point, writes Bireley (1990, 30–31), the anti-Machiavellians did not engage in Scholastic argumentation, but rather relied on two principal lines of reasoning: providentialist pragmatism and immanent or intrinsic pragmatism. The first assumed that "God bestowed victory and success in this world, at least in most cases, on rulers and peoples that served him faithfully and uprightly. This he did either through a direct, miraculous intervention in the course of events or, much more likely, through his skillful guidance of secondary causes. Such an argument presupposed the capacity to discern God's hand in history and led in the direction of a theology of history." The second assumed that "Moral action by its very nature was useful; immoral action was counterproductive . . . [and that] violation of the natural law, which was based on reason, inevitably brought its own retribution on states as well as individuals." In the end, he notes, "Both types of pragmatism . . . called for the use of history" (31).

As will become clear, Alva Ixtlilxochitl's Nezahualcoyotl incarnates the vision of these anti-Machiavellian prescriptions. He fulfills his duties, regaining his father's lost dominion and maintaining and expanding it with an insistence on justice, and with a *prudent* and *ethical* use of cunning and patience. He does so, in other words, without ever crossing the line into displays of aggressive and offensive outright lies and deceit. He is patient and keeps his focus on the *razón de estado* [reason of state], regarded as the ultimate motive or higher purpose of his rule, which—in the Christian moral framework of the plot—lay in preparing the ground for the providential arrival of Christianity (and miraculous acts in favor of its eventual victory). This was an event that he, in his princely (and holy) wisdom, foresaw. Before demonstrating in detail the Acolhua ruler's alignment with the discourse of the anti-Machiavellians, however, a brief examination of the existence and arrival of the tradition in the Americas is in order. It is impossible to say which, if any, of their works Alva Ixtlilxochitl read or was familiar with; however, as Leonard Irving's ([1949] 1992) lists of imported books attest, many books perceived as guides for princes arrived in Mexico throughout the latter half of the sixteenth century.

Part Three. The Mirror for Princes in New Spain and Alva Ixtlilxochitl's Histories

According to Irving ([1949] 1992, 334–403), the work of Juan Luis Vives, along with other Renaissance promoters of the exemplum and the mirror for princes tradition, were present in Mexico as early as 1576. The *Marco Aurelio* by Antonio de Guevara is listed twice in the *Protocolos* of Antonio Alonso (338; 346) and another mirror for princes, Francisco de Monzón's *Espejos del príncipe christiano* (339),[1] is also on the list. In addition, the *Cancionero* by Jorge de Montemayor (343, 382) is part of the same *Protocolo* and is also on the list of the shipment of Luis de Padilla, from the Archivo General de Indias, Contratación.[2] Of direct significance to Alva Ixtlilxochitl's writing, however, is the attested presence of the collected works of Xenophon, an author to whom Alva Ixtlilxochitl explicitly refers, as I will point out below. Finally, although it does not appear in any of the shipments Irving lists as going to

New Spain, Pedro de Rivadeneyra's *Obras* traveled to Lima in 1606 (398) as did his *Tratado de la religion y virtudes que deue tener el Príncipe Christiano para gouernar y conseruar sus Estados* (402), and Juan de Mariana's *Historia general de España* (394, 400).[3] Given the prevalence of the tradition and the presence of its major sources in New Spain, as well as Alva Ixtlilxochitl's contact with Torquemada and potential access to the library at San Francisco (Townsend 2014, 6), it is possible to assume a general familiarity with the tradition, at least in its broadest outlines.[4] There are a few moments in Alva Ixtlilxochitl's writing, moreover, in which his direct familiarity with the tradition is attested.

The statement cited in the epithet at the beginning of this chapter, from the first relación of the *Compendio*, signals his awareness of the discourse and his belief in its validity ([1975–1977] 1985, 1:417). The remark is made as an authorial aside or commentary on the history of the earliest Chichimeca migrations (from the Great Tartary, he says), wherein he describes how the settlers of the region were very different peoples, despite the fact that they were all Chichimeca. Directly and without equivocation, it places the responsibility of the conduct of the people, their loyalty as well as the quality of their behavior, squarely on the shoulders of their rulers. In this sense, it provides a remarkably succinct summation of the philosophy (and the purpose) of rulership in the mirror for princes tradition, as described above: the ruler, uninterested in perpetuating his personal power (becoming a tyrant), promotes the stability and economic well-being of the kingdom by exhibiting ethical behavior that conforms to Christian morals. In this capacity, he serves as a mirror or example for his subjects, who remain peaceful and loyal to the extent that the common good prevails. The "political well-being" of the people then enables the Church to promote and foster the cultivation of the higher, spiritual life of the subjects.

In addition, one prominent exception to the observation I made in chapter 1 that Torquemada's *Monarquía indiana* is rife with citations of classical and humanist authors of history while Alva Ixtlilxochitl cites and emphasizes the authorship of his indigenous sources involves a reference to the ancient Greek historian Xenophon. At the beginning of the eleventh relación of the *Compendio*, dedicated to narrating the life of Nezahualcoyotl, Alva Ixtlilxochitl writes that:

No fue menos las excelentes virtudes del que ahora se nos ofrece que la de cada uno de sus pasados, y cierto, muchas veces me ha parecido, que

los historiadores antiguos que pintaron la vida de este singular príncipe hacen lo que se cuenta de Xenofonte, que todos dicen de él, que en
la vida que escribió de Ciro, rey de los persas, no fue tanto su intento
escribir vida de un hombre en particular, cuanto pintar un buen rey en
las partes que conviene que tenga, y así parece que quien quisiera pintar y hacer relación de un buen monarca, aunque bárbaro, de cuantos
hubo en este Nuevo mundo, no tenía que hacer más de poner delante
la vida del rey Nezahualcoyotzin, porque fue un dechado de Buenos
y excelentes príncipes, como en el discurso de su historia se podrá
ver. ([1975–1977] 1985, 1:439)

These excellent virtues before us now are not less than those of each of
his ancestors, and, certainly, many times it has seemed to me that the
ancient historians that painted the life of this singular prince do what
is talked about with respect to Xenophon, where everyone says of him,
regarding the biography that he wrote of Cyrus king of the Persians,
that it wasn't so much his intention to write the biography of a particular man, but to portray the life of a good king, with respect to the
qualities he should have; and so it seems that whoever wants to portray
and tell the story of a good king, though he may be barbarous, of all the
ones in this New World, a person would have to do nothing other than
to put in front of him the life of King Nezahualcoyotl, because he was
the exemplar of good and excellent princes, as will be seen in the course
of his history.

As with the above citation, this quote points to a direct familiarity with
the mirror for princes tradition (as well as the discourse of barbarism [Pag-
den 1986, 15–26]). In its comments on Xenophon, moreover, it communicates awareness that writers could (and did) manipulate their narratives to
serve a "higher" moral purpose. While Alva Ixtlilxochitl admits here that
it often *seemed* to him that Nezahualcoyotl's image could have been ideal-
ized, like that of Xenophon's Cyrus, he stops just short of admitting that the
tlatoani's image was anything less than "truthful," emphasizing instead that
Nezahualcoyotl was (in *fact*) "un dechado de Buenos y excelentes príncipes"
(an exemplar of good and excellent princes). These two concrete, if tangential,
mentions of the mirror for princes tradition would mean little, perhaps, if it
were not for the extent to which his protagonists, the Acolhua rulers (Nezahualcoyotl in particular), reflect and embody the principal characteristics

that, according to Maravall, Bireley, and others, define the ideal Christian prince and his actions in this prescriptive and example-laden discourse.

Part Four. Nezahualcoyotl as Christian Prince

At distinct moments throughout his histories, usually after concluding his narrative of the life of Nezahualcoyotl, Alva Ixtlilxochitl steps back to summarize, in eulogistic fashion, his hero's most important virtues. The summaries vary in scope and duration, but not in the basic outlines of their content. In them, Nezahualcoyotl's rulership was characterized by (1) his military prowess and large number of conquests, (2) his wisdom and prudence, (3) his impartial and complete justice, (4) his good government and laws, (5) his charity and generosity, and (6) his fair compensation and rewards for services rendered. At a glance, one sees how closely these explicit characteristics, reiterated across Alva Ixtlilxochitl's works, hew to the classical notion of *virtus* with its four cardinal components of *iustitia, temperantia, fortitudo*, and *prudentia*. The summaries, however, are only the most punctual representations of these qualities exhibited by Nezahualcoyotl, which are actually ubiquitous in Alva Ixtlilxochitl's tale of his exemplary life.

The most prominent aspect of Nezahualcoyotl's embodiment of the ideals of the Christian prince is his unusual wisdom, or *prudentia*. In the Renaissance, in the wake of Machiavelli, this quality took on greater importance than the other virtues, as the "virtud de gobierno, tanto de sí mismo, como de la sociedad . . . necesaria para el arreglo de la vida moral entera," as Maravall (1944; virtue of government, as much of oneself as of society . . . necessary for the establishment of the complete moral life) describes it. While it was always considered difficult to govern, as Maravall goes on to say, "en la situación que tienen ante sí los escritores del siglo XVII les parece a éstos que esa dificultad ha llegado al extremo. Para el Rey ya no es suficiente ser, lisa y llanamente, bueno; necesita saber serlo" (244; in the situation faced by the writers of the seventeenth century, it seems to them that this difficulty had reached its limit. For the King it no longer suffices to be, plainly and simply, good; he needs to know how to be good). Of course, wisdom had its component parts, summarized by Maravall as: "memoria, inteligencia, previsión, precaución, docilidad y otras cualidades análogas, y sus partes potenciales: buen consejo, buen sentido, sagacidad" (245; memory, intelligence, foresight, precaution, docility and other analogous qualities, and their potential aspects: good advice, good sense, and wisdom). For Saavedra, in fact, as Maravall points out, these qualities boil down to only three basic principles, all of which Nezahualcoyotl abundantly manifests: "memoria de lo pasado, inteligencia de lo presente y providencia de lo futuro" (246; memory of the past, knowledge of the present, and prescience of the future).

In the figure of Nezahualcoyotl this wisdom is principally and most significantly manifested in his adherence to a Christian-like monotheism rooted in tales of a returning ancestor and spiritual reformer (Quetzalcoatl in the two later works, as we have seen). In correspondence with the role and importance of history in the decisions and actions of the prince, the Acolhua rulers paid heed to these tales, their keen awareness of the past orienting their successful navigation of their present and ensuring them a strong position for a successful future under Spanish rule. Their wisdom is confirmed with the completion of the providentialist plot of the narrative, as described in chapter 2, when this iconoclastic but tenacious belief system led the Acolhua rulers to side with the Spanish newcomers when they arrived on the scene. In so doing, it is important to note, both Nezahualcoyotl and Nezahualpilli bear out the anti-Machiavellian principle that the razón de estado is never an *end* in itself, but an instrument to be used in the service of religion (Maravall 1944, 270–73).

This idea of the subservience of the state to religion is visible in Nezahualcoyotl's mournful prophecy of the downfall of his own empire and the arrival of the "strangers," as well as in the fact that Nezahualpilli, upon seeing the astrological portents of the imminent destruction of the empire, stops the practice of flower wars, "para que el poco de tiempo que le restaba de señorío y mando, le gozasen con toda paz y tranquilidad" (1975–1977, 2:181; in order to enjoy in peace and tranquility what little time remained of his realm and rule). For these rulers, truth, or the inevitable victory of the *true* religion—Christianity (or the faith in the "unknown god")—took precedence at all times over the lust for power and guided their actions (or inactions).

Amid their sagacious religiosity sanctioned by divine favor, the Acolhua rulers—Nezahualcoyotl in particular—also exhibited a great deal of fortitudio, iustitia, and temperantia. Fortitudio or *fortaleza* principally refers to bravery and skill in warfare, a bravery which the anti-Machiavellians pointed out was not debilitated but rather *strengthened* by religious faith (Maravall 1944, 267–70). For Rivadeneyra, as Maravall points out, fortaleza/fortitudio has much more to do with internal morality, adherence to the interior life, and renunciation of worldly goods and effects. It consisted of

Una capacidad y manera de obrar del hombre en desprecio de las cosas exteriores . . . [y] una realización de cosas grandes, heroicas, árduas, llenas de trabajos y de peligros para la vida, que se aceptan y sufren por el bien público. Pero esto es posible por aquel ánimo interior que mueve al hombre a abandonar los goces para procurar la virtud, manifestada aquí en el sacrificio por la Patria. Con esto está clara la refutación de Maquiavelo; sin aquella disposición interior, que es una virtud cristiana, no cabe la Fortaleza en su Segundo aspecto. (267)

A capacity and manner of working disdainful of external things . . . [and] the doing of great, heroic, arduous things, full of difficulties and dangers for living, that they accept and suffer for the common good. But this is possible because of the internal spirit that moves man to abandon pleasures to procure virtue, manifested here in the sacrifice for the Patria. With this Machiavelli's refutation is clear; without that internal disposition, which is a Christian virtue, there is no place for Fortitude in its Second characteristic.

Thus, the Christian soldier (and prince) are more brave and motivated—not less—than those who operate under a secular banner, as witnessed in the examples of the martyrs, of Christian soldiers past and present, and the miraculous victories that God granted on the battlefield for those fighting on his behalf (267–68).

The clearest example of this sense of a religious backing to military victory in the *Historia de la nación chichimeca* comes when Nezahualcoyotl was fighting the losing battle against the Chalca, described in chapter 3, and his Old Testament-like solitary fasting and penance, his "piety," was rewarded with the miraculous vision of the angelic young man who informed his assistant that Nezahualcoyotl's young son would soon be successful on the battlefield, turning the tables on the losing war (1975–1977, 2:125–26). Just as the anti-Machiavellians claimed, the success of the campaign, and hence of the ruler, came about due to a faithful adherence to the true (Catholic, or Catholic-like) faith. His unparalleled military prowess is demonstrated, moreover, by the long lists of conquests and campaigns he undertook both as he regained his throne and later, as part of the Triple Alliance, in conjunction with Mexico and Tlacopan. Most detail about his military guidance and actions, however, is found in the stories that recount the years of his exile and efforts to reinstate Acolhua rule (usurped by the Tepaneca) in Tetzcoco.

In these scenes, prudentia also comes into the picture, this time as the key virtue, according to the anti-Machiavellians, needed to ascertain the ruler's room for maneuver in the face of a dishonest, deceptive, and cunning enemy. In Machiavellian thinking, Nezahualcoyotl's trickery and deception would have been regarded as a strategic or tactical sacrifice of complete honesty and integrity in the name of the public, higher calling of the prince on behalf of the state. For the anti-Machiavellians, however, outright lying, an affront to Christian ethics, was never permissible. However, as Maravall (1944, 246–48; 255–58) notes, the anti-Machiavellians made a clear distinction between lying and deception on the one hand and dissimulation on the other, as well as between an offensive struggle for control and a defensive attitude of caution and reserve. In the latter case, it was considered necessary for the prince to "simulate" and "dissimulate" in order to be able apprehend and be one step ahead of the enemy's plans. Under these circumstances, the trickery and cunning Nezahualcoyotl used to escape from the clutches of the Tepaneca warriors would be justified. Maravall cites the words of Gracián, who notes that "a falta de fuerza, destreza; por un camino o por otro, o por el real del valor o por el atajo del artificio" (246–47; in the absence of force, skill; by one path or the other, the genuine one of courage or the short cut of artifice), as well as those of Rivadeneyra's *El Príncipe cristiano* (1595), which says that "Esta prudencia debe ser verdadera prudencia y no aparente; cristiana y no política; virtud sólida y no astucia engañosa" (quoted in Maravall 1944, 246–47; This prudence should be true prudence and not apparent; Christian and not for show; pure virtue and not deceptive cunning).

For the Catholic political writers, a prince also manifested prudentia (and a certain amount of cunning), moreover, by being able to bide his time and wait, if necessary, in order to successfully respond to an affront or undertake a risky endeavor (Maravall 1944, 248–49). As a young man, Nezahualcoyotl was in no rush to gain back his empire. Rather, he spends his time in exile patiently cultivating his alliances and waiting for the right moment to begin his campaign to reconquer his kingdom. Even when he has regained his power, moreover, he still instinctively knows his limits. He knows, for example, that he cannot directly oppose the other rulers' plans to begin the mass sacrifice of human beings as a response to the huge drought and famine that swept the area. Instead, he proposes a compromise (the sacrifice of prisoners of war) (1975–1977, 2:112). Interpreted and justified in an anti-Machiavellian sense, it was not a matter of complicity in immorality for the convenience of maintaining one's status or power, but of biding time until action can be effectively (and morally) undertaken. While for the Machia-vellians there was no moral (neither good nor evil) attributed to pragmatic actions aimed at a higher cause (power), for the anti-Machiavellians, these actions (whose ethical standing is never neutral) are nevertheless ultimately judged precisely according to their end—the higher cause (Catholicism as the razón de estado) that they are aimed at serving.

Other examples of Nezahualcoyotl's manifestation of wise rulership or prudentia as defined by the anti-Machiavellians include his proper recom-pense of those who render service to him, his great sense of justice, and his generosity and mercy toward others. These attitudes also fall under the cat-egory of prudentia, as they aim at ensuring the image and the reputation of the ruler among his people, seeding the will to proper service and behavior (Maravall 1944, 262–63). Concrete demonstrations of this kind of prudent statecraft include the scene where Nezahualcoyotl, after defeating the Mexica, restores the rulers of the pre-Tepaneca pueblos to their old positions, without any punishment for their having allied with Tezozomoc against his father (Alva Ixtlilxochitl 1975–1977, 2:88–91), as well as in his acts of charity to the poor but loyal subjects (128–29) and in the elegy Alva Ixtlilxochitl writes as he narrates his passing (135–37).

Although oft-repeated with variations and different permutations throughout his works, this narrative of Nezahualcoyotl's selflessness and gen-erosity is extremely revealing as a moment in which the text seems to reflect its image upon the colonial present of narration. In it, Alva Ixtlilxochitl notes how Nezahualcoyotl, who always did penance for his moral weaknesses or shortcomings, cared more about "el bien común que el suyo particular" (136; the common good rather than his own well-being) and how he was

> tan misericordioso con los pobres, que no se había de sentar a comer hasta haberlo remediado, como de ordinario usaba con los de la plaza y mercado, comprándoles a doblado precio de lo que podía valer, la miseria de lo que traían a vender, para darlo a otros; teniendo muy par-ticular cuidado de la viuda, del huérfano y del viejo y demás imposibil-itados; y en los años estériles abría sus trojes para dar y repartir a sus súbditos y vasallos el sustento necesario, que para el efecto siempre se guardaba; y alzaba los pechos y derechos que tenían obligación de trib-utarle en tales tiempos sus vasallos.

> so compassionate with the poor, that he wouldn't sit down to eat until he had remedied it, as he ordinarily did with those in the plaza and the

market, buying whatever trifle they could manage to bring to sell at double the price that it was worth, in order to give it to others; taking particular care of the widow, the orphan, the old man, and other vulnerable people; and in the years of famine, he opened the granaries to give and disburse to his subjects and vassals the necessary sustenance, which was always stored; and in such times he lifted the tributes and taxes that his vassals were obliged to pay.

Here, the biblical/Christian discourse of the passage, its *reversal* of the idols-behind-altars discourse (Nezahualcoyotl finds a single god behind the false idols), and its references to the poor, the widows, the orphans, the elderly, and the disabled, reaffirms and authenticates the "Christian" status of Alva Ixtlilxochitl's "prince." The specific colonial context in which these (and other) acts of generosity—buying goods at double the price that they were worth (rather than forcing sales at low prices), for example—will be discussed in more detail below.

First, however, one final quality of the Christian prince that Nezahualcoyotl exhibited in abundance that remains to be mentioned is his concern for iustitia. A few examples of his sense of justice can be seen in the long descriptions of the laws he instituted and courts he set up (Alva Ixtlilxochitl 1975–1977, 2:101–5), as well as in the fact that he had his own son put to death in the belief that he had committed wrongdoing (121–23). In sum, these are but a few of the concrete examples that demonstrate the conformity of the portrayals of Nezahualcoyotl with the ideal of the Christian prince as set out in the mirror for princes tradition. With the notable exception of the scene in which Nezahualcoyotl, in keeping with the Old Testament story of David and Uriah, orders the assassination of Quaquauhtzin (ruler of Tepechpan) in order to marry his betrothed (117–20), it is difficult to encounter a scene or an event in which the Tetzcoca rulers *fail* to embody the virtus expected and hoped for in the great—and powerful—Catholic princes of the age. Whether the aim was to gain compensation for the assistance provided by his ancestors in the conquest, or to create an enduring vision of Tetzcoca history for posterity, or both at once, the *Historia de la nación chichimeca*, by virtue of its relationship to the mirror for princes tradition and the didacticism associated with the general history of the time, cannot escape its status as an extended exemplum of great rulership. It becomes, in effect, a mirror in which the events, and rulership, of the Spanish colonial period—construed as the predestined inheritor of that previous age of praeparatio evangelica—cannot help but be reflected.

In the tradition of the didactic history that values the exempla over the precept, Alva Ixtlilxochitl creates in his preconquest Acolhua rulers, especially Nezahualcoyotl, a de facto mirror whose reflection looks outward into the moment of the narrative, where they contrast with the Mexica (and other Nahua) rulers. The reflection also, however, projects itself into the narrative's colonial future and Alva Ixtlilxochitl's present, into the unrealized potential, the failed promise, of the arrival of Christianity under the rulership of the Spanish. It becomes acutely operational and most tangible in specific contexts, however, especially those that relate stories about the perennial culprits behind humanitarian crises and the upending of social order in central Mexico from pre-Hispanic times onward. In the *Historia de la nación chichimeca*, problems of drought and flooding, famine and tribute, turn into simple but dramatic exposés of the incompetence and inefficiency with which the Spanish bureaucracy reacted to those events.

It is true that in other colonial Mexican histories, some of the actions attributed to Nezahualcoyotl, such as the lifting of tributes in times of famine, are also attributed to other pre-Hispanic rulers (such as Motecuhzoma), and that they therefore function on some level as stock phrases probably reflecting widespread pre-Hispanic cultural patterns of response to crisis and their discursive historicization. However, I am interested here in their use and deployment in the overall context of Nezahualcoyotl's construal in the text as an exceptional and indeed exemplary (and Christian-like) ruler. In general, Motecuhzoma's image in colonial literature, despite these moments where his good rulership stands out, is much less Christianized than that of Nezahualcoyotl. Indeed, in some ways he becomes the latter's foil, hardly rising above his treatment as a hesitant ruler with a decided lack of religious prescience.

Part Five. History as Mirror and Example: Alva Ixtlilxochitl on the Past and the Present

True to Cicero's idea of history as life's teacher, Alva Ixtlilxochitl in fact did not shy away from pointing out the failures of the current regime in which he lived, extracting lessons from the past for the present. For example, when Nezahualcoyotl foresees the impending conquest of the Triple Alliance by newcomers, he also makes dire predictions about the iniquity and moral vices into which his people would fall—*despite* and *amid* the possibility of eternal salvation offered by the new religion. Putting the finishing touch on Nezahualcoyotl's moralizing in this scene, Alva Ixtlilxochitl cannot help noting that "Todas estas mudanzas aquí contenidas y aumentos de vicios, se han cumplido a la letra" (1975–1977, 2:132–33; all of these changes and increase in vice here contained, have been completely fulfilled). He then goes on to lament the sorry level to which social mores had sunk in his day compared to the times before the conquest (drunkenness and young marriages, for example). Seen from within the context of the early modern exempla and the mirror for princes tradition, this statement implies a certain failure of colonial rulership, either (or both) Nahua and Spanish. Despite its "idolatrous" or "un-enlightened" state, the moral standards and uprightness of the people's lives and habits, the behavior of the pre-Hispanic Acolhua and hence their governance were, by far, more *exemplary* than those of the present-day New Spain that Alva Ixtlilxochitl inhabited.

In a few passages, moreover, Alva Ixtlilxochitl directly condemns the abuses and cruelties of the Spanish toward the indigenous populations during and after the conquest. In the thirteenth relación of the *Compendio*, he launches unselfconscious attacks on the abuses and injustices committed by Cortés and his allies in the execution of the conquest. He sums up his sentiments in the following passage that occurs near the end of the document:

Gran cosa por cierto que hizo Cortés y los demás conquistadores en plantar la ley evangélica en este Nuevo mundo, si no hubieran hecho las crueldades y las cosas referidas en esta historia y las demás que están escritas y en lo que se sigue, y así Dios ha permitido que hay muy poca memoria de ellos, y los más de ellos han acabado en mal, y entiendo que Quauhtémoc y los demás que murieron con él, pues ya eran cristianos y conocían a Dios, ya que perdieron sus reinos y señoríos que son perecederos les daría Dios el del cielo que es eterno, y que a nosotros importa más que cuantas honras y riquezas y las demás cosas que tiene el mundo; *y plegua a Dios que muchas sillas de las que debían ser de los primeros españoles que vinieron a estas partes, no las posean en la vida eternal los desventurados naturales, y aun algunos de los que hoy viven,* porque es tanta su miseria que he leído a muchos autores que tratan de tiranías y crueldades de otras naciones y ninguna de ellas y todas juntas tienen que ver con los trabajos y esclavonía grande de los naturales, los cuales, como ellos lo dicen, más querían ser esclavos herrados y no de la manera que hoy viven, porque de esta manera los españoles que los tratan mal todavía tuvieran alguna lástima de ellos por no perder sus dineros, y es tanta su desventura que si uno tropieza y cae y se lastima, es tanto el gusto que de ello reciben que no se puede encarecer, y no obstante esto, sino que cuantas maldiciones les viene a la imaginación, le echan, y si se mueren dicen que ya el diablo se los había de haber llevado a todos; digo esto porque cada instante sucede y lo oigo decir, y pues Dios lo consiente, su majestad sabe por qué y démosle mil gracias por ello. ([1975–1977] 1985, 1:505–6)

A great thing it was that Cortés and the other conquistadors accomplished in planting Christian rule in this New World, if [only] they had not committed the cruelties and other things mentioned in this history and the others that are written and in that which follows; and thus God has permitted that there is very little remembrance of them, and the majority of them have come to a bad end; and I understand that Cuauhtemoc and the others that died with him, that they were already Christians and knew God, and since they had already lost their dominions and estates, which are transitory, God gave them heaven instead which is eternal, and which is more important to us than the number of honors or riches and other things of this world; *and pray to God that many thrones that were supposed to have been those of the first Spaniards that came to these parts, are not possessed by the unfortunate natives in the hereafter, and even some of those that are living today,* because their misery is so great that I have read many authors that treat of the tyrannies and cruelties of other nations and none of them individually or together compare to the suffering and great enslavement of the native people, who, as they say, would rather have been branded slaves than live as they do today, because in this way the Spanish that treat them badly would still have to have some pity for them in order not to lose their money; and such is their misfortune that if one trips and falls and gets hurt, the pleasure that they receive from it cannot be exaggerated, and if this was not enough, whatever curses come to their minds, they express them, and if people die they say that now the devil should have taken them all; I say this because it happens all the time, and I hear it discussed, and if God allows it, his Holiness knows why, and let us give a thousand thanks for it.

Here, the conquistadors' behavior leads to both terrestrial oblivion and even perhaps (he speculates) eternal damnation. On the contrary, Cuauhtemoc and the other rulers unjustly executed by Cortés might have lost their lands and peoples, or their rulerships, but their baptism had assured them of eternal life, something that he can't help noting that "to us" (to the Nahuas, presumably, with whom Alva Ixtlilxochitl identifies at this moment) was worth more than all honors and riches that the world could offer. What is more, Alva Ixtlilxochitl asserts that the people were treated worse than slaves, and that they continued to suffer such abuse.

This latter sentiment is also expressed by Alva Ixtlilxochitl in the *Sumaria relación de todas las cosas*, as he describes how Tezozomoc, the Tepaneca tyrant, divided up the rulership of the provinces that had formerly been under Acolhua dominance and ordered the tributes that they would have to pay. As in the above example, he states that the losers would have been better off as slaves:

> Fue esta carga que les dio Tezozómoc tan gravada, que ellos lo tuvieron por mejor ser más aínas esclavos si pudiera ser, que no acudir a tantas y tan grandes cosas, que comparan los viejos esta sujeción y esclavonía que les dio Tezozómoc, a la que hoy en día tienen sobre sí, que no puede ser mayor en el mundo, lo cual acudieron siete años con el mayor trabajo que se puede decir, hasta que su legítimo señor los libertó, que les parecieron siete mil años de penas, pues con sus bienes, hijos y mujeres acudieron a todo lo referido. . . . y con esto todos se fueron a sus tierras muy tristes y desconsolados con tantas persecuciones y tra-bajos. ([1975–1977] 1985, 1:347)

> This burden that Tezozomoc gave them was so heavy, that they con-sidered it better to be slaves if possible than to try to comply with so many and such great tasks, such that the elders compare this subjec-tion and enslavement by Tezozomoc to the one that they are faced with now, which could not be greater, and they served for seven years with the heaviest labor imaginable, until their legitimate ruler freed them, which seemed like seven thousand years of suffering, as they met their demands with their goods, their wives, and their children . . . and so everyone went to their lands very sad and disconsolate with so much work and persecution.

Alva Ixtlilxochitl's extension of his criticism of the conquistadors' behavior to include the suffering and mistreatment of people in his own times illus-trates concretely his historiographical modus operandi, in which he shuffles between ancient and colonial past, connecting Nahua rulership before and after the conquest (and by implication laying bare the negative consequences of the marginalization of that rulership in colonial times).

As Alva Ixtlilxochitl reconstructs the pre-Hispanic past, he enshrines in it the model of a Christian governance that, upon its actual (and expected/ prophesied) arrival, found itself in many respects out of touch with its own razón de estado (i.e., the well-being and conversion of the people and implantation of the Catholic Church) and burdened with ineffective and inadequate management of its subjects and resources. This is demonstrated in the scenes discussed below, in which Alva Ixtlilxochitl presents a pre-Hispanic past in which major crises also faced by the colonial period government (especially regarding indigenous populations)—both before and during Alva Ixtlilxochitl's day—are handled by the Acolhua rulership as they should have been in the era of the "ley evangélica" (law of Christ): unstintingly and unequivocally in favor of the well-being of the people they were charged with protecting and bringing into the folds of the Catholic faith.

In the historical records for fifteenth-century Mexico, recurring periods of famine caused by drought and/or frost leave a strong imprint, and Alva Ixtlilxochitl's histories are no exception. Also prominent in the historical record for that time are episodes relating floods, with particular importance lent to the story of the overflow of the Acuecuexatl, a spring in Coyoacán, recorded in historical documents from various regions of the central valley. If problems of flooding were serious in the pre-Hispanic world, however, they took on grandiose (and disastrous) proportions in the colonial context. Food shortages and grain prices were also important issues throughout the colonial period and when Alva Ixtlilxochitl was writing. A close look at Alva Ixtlilxochitl's representations of famine and flooding, specifically the great famine of the 1450s and the flooding of the Acuecuexatl, reveals the way in which his representations (can) never leave behind the close interfacing of pre-Hispanic and colonial pasts. In them, as I will show, recurring demonstrations of rulers' spiritual and technological prowess and motifs of their unfettered mercy and generosity in times of need confront a colonial period record of blunders, corruption, and exploitation—despite the Crown's constant legislation to correct and amend matters.

Part Six. Rulership in (Times of) Crisis: The Colonial Pre-Hispanic Event of the *Historia de la nación chichimeca*

Chapter 41 of the *Historia de la nación chichimeca* begins with the following observation:

Estando las cosas del imperio en grande prosperidad por la abundancia de mantenimientos y máquina grande de gentes (que era de tal
manera que hasta los montes y sierras fragosas las tenían ocupadas con
sembrados y otros aprovechamientos, y el menor pueblo de aquellos
tiempos tenía más gente que la mejor ciudad que el día de hoy hay
en la Nueva España, según parece por los padrones reales de aquellos
tiempos), como las cosas de esta vida tienen mil mudanzas y nunca
faltan calamidades (como las que en esta sazón acontecieron y fueron
las primeras), en el año de 1450 que llaman matlactli tochtli fue tan
excesiva la nieve que cayó en toda la tierra que subió en las más partes
estado y medio, con que se arruinaron y cayeron muchas casas y se
destruyeron todas las arboledas y plantas, y resfrió de tal manera la
tierra que hubo un catarro pestilencial con que murieron muchas gentes, y en especial la gente mayor; y los tres años siguientes se perdieron
todas las sementeras y frutos de la tierra, en tal conformidad que pereció la mayor parte de la gente, en el siguiente de 1454 a los principios
de él hubo un eclipse muy grande de sol, y luego se aumentó más la
enfermedad, y moría tanta gente que parecía que no había de quedar
persona alguna, según era la calamidad que sobre esta tierra había
venido. (1975–1977, 2:111)

With the things of the empire in such great prosperity due to the abundance of upkeep and of people (which was such that even the hills and
dense mountains were planted and used for other beneficial things, and
the smallest pueblo of those times had more people than the best city
that there is today in New Spain, as it appears from the royal census
of those days), as the things of this life are always in flux and they are
never without catastrophes (like the ones that happened in that sea-
son and were the first), in the year 1450, that they call *matlactli tochtli*,
so much snow fell that it reached an *estado* and a half in most places,
and the crops were ruined and many houses fell and all of the groves
and plants were destroyed, and it got so cold that a pestilential cough
took hold that killed many people, especially the elderly; and the three
following years they lost all of the plantings and fruits of the land, so
that the majority of the people perished, and in the next year, 1454, at
the beginning, there was a huge eclipse of the sun. Later the disease got
worse, and so many people died that it seemed like there would be no
one left. Such was the calamity that had come to this land.

Here, in parenthetical asides, Alva Ixtlilxochitl again places the pre-Hispanic past of his narrative in direct dialogue with the colonial context from which he writes. First, he compares the population of the time with that of New Spain: "y el menor pueblo de aquellos tiempos tenía más gente que la mejor ciudad que el día de hoy hay en la Nueva España" (the smallest town of those times had more people than the largest city that there is today in New Spain). Then, he refers to the "catastrophes"—the frost, pestilence, and famine—as "the first ones" to affect the region, thus indirectly referencing *subsequent* disasters. This reinforces the preceding implicit comparison of the teeming population (and productive land use) of the pre-Hispanic times to the drastically reduced population of his time—significant due to the increasing usurpation of indigenous lands in this period and the importance that Spanish rule placed on the *productivity* (or vacancy) of land in the colonial period (Gibson 1964, 272–99, 406–9).

Although the passage does not go into detail, it is important to understand the colonial context that Alva Ixtlilxochitl references within it. In the early seventeenth century, the indigenous population had reached its nadir in the aftermath of the conquest and following the waves of successive epidemics that swept through central Mexico after the arrival of the Spanish. Although the population numbers vary among scholars, Robert McCaa (1995, under "Conclusions") notes that "experts point to overall levels of demographic destruction over the sixteenth century for central Mexico exceeding 50%, probably ranging beyond 75%, and even topping 90% in some large regions such as the tropical lowlands." For the Valley of Mexico, McCaa cites Gibson's estimates at 1.5 million in 1519 declining to 0.2 million by 1595, an 87% decline in a span of seventy-six years, a decline that continues into the seventeenth century before the population begins to rebound. As the population declined, indigenous lands became vacated and ripe for usurpation by Spaniards and others (Blanco and Romero Sotelo 2004, 39–43). Moreover, the loss of tribute labor (and goods) from the agricultural sector due to epidemics and the siphoning of agricultural workers into the silver mines and public works projects (Blanco and Romero Sotelo 2004, 32; Gibson 1964), threatened food and other shortages in Mexico City and beyond, occasionally exacerbated by natural disasters such as flooding, freezing, and drought (Gibson 1964, 202–4; R. Lee 1947, 657). In the above passage, Alva Ixtlilxochitl's juxtaposition and comparison of past and present places Spanish and pre-Hispanic rulership on a par, with the text standing as a kind of passing philosophical commentary on the vulnerability of human society and its rulers to the forces of nature. Although the comparison between the precolonial past and Alva Ixtlilxochitl's present is not directly carried over into the ensuing segment of Nezahualcoyotl's *response* to the crisis, it continues to reverberate in the narrative, raising the specter, as we will see, of the large gap between colonial *rhetoric* and colonial *reality*.

After describing the drought, Alva Ixtlilxochitl presents the rulers' immediate "political" solution to the problem, and then their final, desperate, "religious" response. First, they open stores of grain that they had been accumulating for many years, feeding the people until there is nothing left and lifting tribute payments for six years.

> Y aunque Nezahualcoyotzin en su tierra y reino, Motecuhzomatzin y Totoquihuatzin en los suyos, hicieron todo lo posible por socorrer a sus súbditos y vasallos (porque demás de haberles alzado los tributos por seis años que fue el tiempo que duraron estas calamidades, les dieron y repartieron todas las rentas de maíz que tenían en las trojes guardadas y reservadas de a diez, doce años y más tiempo), viendo que no cesaba la calamidad se juntaron todos tres. (111–12)

> And even though Nezahualcoyotzin in his land and dominion, and Motecuhzomatzin and Totoquihuatzin in theirs, did everything possible to help their subjects and vassals (because in addition to having lifted their tributes for six years, which was the time that these catastrophes lasted, they gave out and distributed all of the excess corn that they had stored in the reserves for ten, twelve years and more), upon realizing that the catastrophe didn't end, they all got together.

The text goes on to narrate how, with people eating roots, begging, and selling their children and themselves into slavery in Totonacapan, the rulers are urged by their priests to placate the anger of the gods through the sacrifice of their sons and daughters (112). Nezahualcoyotl, according to Alva Ixtlilxochitl a staunch opponent of human sacrifice, finally proposes the institution of the "flower wars"—the sacrifice of captive warriors—as a compromise solution. Here, the unified "political" response to the disaster on the part of all three rulers contrasts with Nezahualcoyotl's attempt to distance himself from the proposed "religious" solution. With this unanimity, and its presentation in parentheses as an aside, the political solution takes on the quality of the obvious, the sense that it is a response so common that it is almost unnecessary to spell it out.

Two more scenes from the *Historia de la nación chichimeca* add to the above picture of good rulership by illustrating the particularly important role that tribute policy plays in defining or characterizing good rulership within the narrative. In chapter 76, right before the introduction of the arrival of Cortés, as Alva Ixtlilxochitl is explaining the political divisions within the Triple Alliance that preceded and aided his conquest, he mentions Motecuhzoma's tyrannical tribute demands as a source of rebellion:

> Asimismo en este atrevimiento y discordia que hubo con sus hermanos y tíos, se alteraron muchas provincias que querían negar la obediencia a Motecuhzoma por las demasiadas imposiciones de tributos que cada día les ponía, usando más de crueldad y tiranía que de piedad, como había sido costumbre entre los reyes sus pasados; y los que esto más frecuentaban fueron los de las provincias de Tonacapan que llegaban hasta las costas del Mar del Norte, que parece que su Divina Majestad iba disponiendo las cosas como veía que convenía para la entrada de su santa fe católica en este Nuevo mundo. (192)

> Amid this daring and discord among the sons and brothers, many provinces tried to deny obedience to Motecuhzoma for the high tribute payments that he increasingly burdened them with, making more use of cruelty and tyranny than pity, as had been the custom among the kings his forbearers; and those that did this most often were the provinces of Tonacapan that reached the coasts of the North Sea, such that it appears that his Divine Majesty was arranging things as he saw fit for the easy entrance of the Holy Catholic faith into this New World.

Here, we learn that Motecuhzoma's tribute ethics are not always as ideal as they were in times of famine. In line with Renaissance political and moral terminology, Alva Ixtlilxochitl directly associates the imposing of excessive tribute demands with "cruelty" and "tyranny." The good ruler, he implies, is the one that practices "mercy," or "compassion." This scene's use of Motecuhzoma as an example of bad rulership, moreover, provides an important counterpoint to an earlier scene from chapter 46, in which Nezahualcoyotl acts to relieve the undue suffering of the defeated Chalca who, although "legitimately" put to work building palaces for the empire's rulers as punishment for their rebellion against the Triple Alliance, were being treated inhumanely.

Nezahualcoyotl observed the Chalca, writes Alva Ixtlilxochitl, as they transported from their own territories all of the raw materials for new buildings, "con tan grave y excesivo trabajo suyo que más no podía ser en el mundo" (128; with such excess burden that nothing in the world could have been worse). He also noted, we are told, how even women were compelled to work, since the majority of the men had died in the years of warfare that preceded their defeat. Finally, Alva Ixtlilxochitl points out Nezahualcoyotl's acuity and wisdom in observing this state of affairs, by writing that

> El rey Nezahualcoyotzin acertó a ver esta calamidad que padecían los chalcas y lo peor de todo que perecían de hambre, el cual confundido y lastimado de ver esto mandó que hiciesen unas muy grandes casas pajizas que llaman jacales, y que en ellas sus mayordomos tuviesen grandísima máquina de comida para los chalcas que andaba ocupados en los edificios referidos. Demás de que ellos recibieron este gran refugio, fue parte para poder sobrellevar la hambre que corría en aquellos tiempos en su provincia; con que de su voluntad venían bandadas de ellos a la obra que hacían, viendo que con esto mitigaban la hambre que tenían; habiéndose ocupado los chalcas casi en estos cuatro años sucesivos. (ibid.)

> King Nezahualcoyotl did well to observe this calamity that the Chalca were experiencing, and, worst of all, that they suffered from hunger. Confused and pained to see this, he ordered great straw houses called jacales to be made in which their overseers would provide huge quantities of food for the Chalca who were busy working on the buildings mentioned. In addition to receiving this great refuge, it enabled them in part to survive the famine that was happening at the time in their province, so that many groups came voluntarily to work on the projects, seeing that they mitigated their hunger in this way, the Chalca having worked on this almost four years straight.

In addition to solidifying the distinction between Motecuhzoma's tyranny and Nezahualcoyotl's "princely" rulership in the *Historia de la nación chichimeca*, this scene serves as a contrasting example to the claims of Spanish lack of recognition and compensation of the Tetzcoca nobility for their services, found, for example, in the seventh addendum to the *Sumaria relación de todas las cosas de la Nueva España* ([1975–1977] 1985, 1:392–93). As a depiction of the services rendered to the defeated enemies of warfare, moreover, Nezahualcoyotl's insistence on compensating the Chalca through provision of food and housing coincides with the ideals expressed in Spanish governance as it appropriated (and exploited) indigenous labor (first through the encomienda and later in the system of rotary draft labor called the *repartimiento*), just as the *reality* of the Chalcas' initial exploitation more closely reflects the *reality* of those institutions as they were carried out. Of course, as allies of the Spanish, the Acolhua under (Fernando Cortés) Ixtlilxochitl were not even *technically* defeated, and of course, he and the other Tetzcoca nobles should not have been obligated to work as laborers in the first place.

Indeed, the scene from the *Compendio* constitutes one of the glaring moments in which the gap between theory and practice in the relationship between the Crown and the indigenous pueblos, and Alva Ixtlilxochitl's consciousness of it, seeps into his narratives, making a crack in the divide between past and present. When the officials of Otumba give the *Compendio* their seal of approval, they note ([1975–1977] 1985, 1:520):

> Le damos esta nuestra aprobación para que conste al rey nuestro señor cómo es cierto y verdadero lo que tiene escrito, así en las cosas de su historia como en la relación que hace de nuestros trabajos y calamidades, especialmente el servicio personal que es lo que ahora nos va consumiendo; y los pastores y señores de ganado nos destruyen nuestras sementeras con sus ganados, y se los roban nuestros hijos y hijas y mujeres, y muchas de nuestras tierras nos las quitan, y se van alzando con ellas algunas personas, sin otros mil agravios que se nos hacen como se verá especificadamente en la dicha historia.

> We give our approval so that the King our lord knows that what is written is correct and truthful, in the things of the history as well in the narrative that he writes of our suffering and calamities, especially with respect to personal service, which is what is consuming us now; and the shepherds and owners of the livestock are destroying our plantings with their herds, and they rob us of our sons and daughters and women, and take away many of our lands, and some people go about stealing them from us, not to mention the other thousand injuries that they do to us as will be seen in detail in said history.

A significant aspect of these "political" responses on the part of the pre-Hispanic rulership (lifting tributes and opening grain stores) to times of crisis, in fact, is its repetition in a number of contexts in the narrative, *as well as in* Mexica and other non-Acolhua-based sources *and* in colonial documents that refer to the *colonial* period epidemics and the Spanish response to them. The solutions have the quality of a refrain or motif, of being an established part of the *discourse* of response to historical catastrophe, even if it was not part of the actual governmental response itself across both pre-Hispanic and colonial eras. Reflecting the fusion between the Nahua and Spanish historical traditions, at least on the level of narrative (if not practice), the common discourse itself (above and beyond Alva Ixtlilxochitl's explicit juxtaposition) brings together the pre-Hispanic and colonial experience of famine and epidemic into a shared (moral and political) frame of reference and opens up the possibility of examining the narrative of the pre-Hispanic event in light of the recent colonial *experience*. In other words, it sets up an inevitable comparison (or contrast) between the *discourse* of Nezahualcoyotl's response (as the pre-Hispanic ruler)—a response that is in line with ideals, aims, and intentions of the colonial government—and the *actual* response (its success or failure) of the colonial viceroyalty to the situation. While the possible failures and realities of a pre-Hispanic reaction to crisis are distant and thus hidden in the historical record, those of the colonial period were on display for all to see.

In general, the Crown responded to the ongoing demographic catastrophe in New Spain in part by constantly attempting to set manageable tribute levels and to control abuse and exploitation of the tribute system it developed after the conquest, a combination of pre-Hispanic and Iberian models (Blanco and Romero Sotelo 2004; Gibson 1964, 58–97; Miranda 1980 [1952]). In times of crisis, it did indeed stipulate the temporary lifting of tribute requirements (Gibson 1964, 206), although this action, along with its attempts to curb abuse (and even the constant revision to tribute guidelines in general) had the effect of reactive gestures, doing little to alleviate or make manageable the burden that tribute payments represented for indigenous communities throughout the sixteenth and early seventeenth centuries (62–63). As Gibson notes, communities as a whole were held responsible for accumulating sums:

> The largest single expenditure of the Indian communities . . . was the Spanish tribute. . . . This was a burden that no community was able to bear consistently over a long period, and it was the one that brought the greatest stress to community finance. The 1560's, the period of major

changes from Indian to Spanish systems of tribute exaction, mark the beginnings of large-scale tribute deficit in the towns. Arrears developed gradually, through delays in payment and modest accumulations of debts, to become a standard condition of community financial life. In the 1570's and 1580's many towns fell seriously into debt for back tributes. Even in 1570 Tenochtitlan and Tlatelolco owed ten thousand pesos and Texcoco owed nine thousand pesos. (217)

In the colonial period, the already difficult demands of the tribute system were compounded by its abuses, and in all the burden was simply too much for the communities to be able to meet. As José Miranda (1980 [1852], 224) puts it,

> A lo exagerado o abusivo, del tributo fijado por concierto o tasación, uniéronse los excesos y atropellos de los encomenderos en el terreno tributario, los verdaderos abusos, consistentes, generalmente, en exigir más de lo concertado o tasado y en engañar, coaccionar y maltratar a los indios para que cumpliesen lo exigido. Estos abusos provocaron también infinidad de quejas de los indios.

> To the exaggerated and abusive nature of the tribute fixed by agreement or taxation were added the excesses and abuses of the encomenderos in the tributary realm, the true abuses, all being consistent, in general, in demanding more than what was agreed upon or taxed and in deceiving, coercing, and mistreating the Indians so that they would comply with the demands. These abuses provoked endless complaints from the Indians.

In addition to the abuses by the Spanish authorities and citizens, Gibson (1964, 206) discusses the huge number of complaints about *derramas*, or excesses of tribute collected (and pocketed) by Spanish officials and caciques, which the Crown tried to control. Significantly, in the *Historia de la nación chichimeca* (1975–1977, 2:143–44) Alva Ixtlilxochitl makes it quite clear that under Nezahualcoyotl's rule such abuses were never tolerated:

> En el cuarto y último consejo, que era el de hacienda, se guardaban las leyes convenientes a ella acerca de la cobranza de tributos y distribución

de ellos y de los padrones reales. Tenían pena de muerte los cobradores que cobraban más de lo que debían pagar los súbditos y vasallos. Los jueces de estos tribunales no podían recibir ningún cohecho, ni ser parciales a ninguna de las partes, pena de la vida; a todos los cuales el rey sustentaba, cada ochenta días hacía mercedes.

The fourth and final governing council was that of finance, which kept the laws appropriate to that area about the charging of tribute and its distribution and the royal censuses. The tax collectors that charged more than the subjects and vassals should pay were put to death. The judges of these tribunals could not receive any bribe, or be partial to any of the parties, under penalty of death; all of which the king maintained, giving rewards every eighty days.

On top of his just implementation of tribute policies, Nezahualcoyotl had one major attribute that the Spanish officials lacked: he was an expert in hydraulic engineering. Throughout the sixteenth and seventeenth centuries, constant flooding in the central valley caused (among other disasters) severe shortages of grains and speculations in grain prices. In a work entitled *El desagüe del valle de México durante la época novohispana*, Jorge Gurría Lacroix (1978) writes that despite numerous problems with flooding in the years 1555, 1580, and 1604, only after a major inundation in 1607 did the Spanish government finally get serious about building the desagüe and solving the problem.[5] The work did not go so well, however, and in 1621 the new viceroy, don Diego Carrillo de Mendoza y Pimentel, the Marquis of Gelves, put an end to the plan.

The marquis, with a long history of military service to the Spanish Crown, had been sent by Philip IV to crack down on crime and corruption and ensure that remittances (taxes and tributes) were duly paid and sent to Spain (Israel 1976, 40–41; 1980). At the time, Spain was reigniting its war with Holland, and the Crown was in dire need of funds to finance it; under the leadership of the Count-Duke of Olivares, it entered a period of reform and austerity (Martínez Vega 1990; Israel 1976). Gelves's decision to put an end to the construction of the drainage system, however, resulted in what Gurría calls the "mayor desastre que ha padecido la ciudad, pues estuvo anegada seis años, destruyéndose buena parte de sus construcciones, despoblándose por muerte o abandono de sus vecinos" (1978, 104; the worst disaster that has happened in the city, for it was under water for six years, with a large part of its buildings destroyed, losing its population through the death or abandonment of its inhabitants).

Against these shortsighted policies and the woefully incompetent (and inadequate) water management on the part of the viceroyalty stands the fame of Nezahualcoyotl as the principal engineer in charge of the great pre-Hispanic central Mexican aqueducts, and the storied success of Nezahualpilli at controlling the rushing waters of the Acuecuexatl as they flowed unimpeded into Tenochtitlan.[6] Only with this context in mind is it possible to appreciate the full significance of the superior wisdom of the Acolhua rulers (especially vis-à-vis the Mexica) in their ancient connection to the aquatic, telluric world of caves and mountains and to Tepeyollotl in/and his relationship to Tlaloc (Contel 2015; Olivier [2003] 2008) in Alva Ixtlilxochitl's narrative.[7]

The final, great flood to which Gurría refers did not take place until 1629. The Marquis of Gelves, however, made himself unpopular as a viceroy long before that, beginning, in fact, in his journey from Veracruz to Mexico City, when he declined as an unnecessary and wasteful expense the usual pomp and circumstance with which new viceroys were welcomed to the city (Bancroft 1883, 34). In 1623 his stoppage of work on drainage projects for similar reasons—particularly ongoing work on a channel to divert the flow of the Cuauhtitlan River away from the lakes—caused water levels in Mexico City rise. And they rose concomitantly, as Richard Boyer (1977, 478) put it, with his steep descent in public opinion.[8] The very next year, in 1624, a general uprising resulted in his overthrow, the particulars of which lead down a path that takes us to Alva Ixtlilxochitl's doorstep, both in terms of his personal connection to the event's major protagonists as well as with respect to his writing, specifically, to his vision of Nezahualcoyotl's unfailing provisioning of stored grain to the people in times of need.

Part Seven. Viceroy Gelves, Archbishop Pérez de la Serna, and the Dedicatory "Princes" of Alva Ixtlilxochitl and Torquemada

According to Boyer (1977) and Zárate Toscano (1996), the Marquis of Gelves took his job as viceroy so seriously that he alienated all of the established parties of New Spain's political landscape, already divided between criollos and peninsulares, and between the secular priesthood and the monastic orders. Behind these conflicts lay the priority and control given to Spanish officials (corregidores) and the regular orders over the labor, tributes, and affairs of the república de indios. The creole population resented the institution of the repartimiento and wanted more access to labor (free contract, which they finally got in 1632, due to the flooding itself). The secular clergy (led by Archbishop Pérez de la Serna) for its part wanted the end of the power of the regular orders (predominantly governed by peninsulares) over the jobs, tithes, and other benefits accruing from the servicing of the Indian parishes.

In addition to refusing gifts (and bribes) and clamping down on corruption and conflicts of interest in judicial matters (involving *oidores* or judges of the Audiencia), the new viceroy raised taxes, enforced their collection, and cracked down on all kinds of corruption (Israel 1974, 41–42) in an effort to defend the interests of the poor against those who would exploit and take advantage of them (i.e., by cracking down on thieves and extortionists on road from Veracruz, and by preventing hoarding and price speculation on basic grains). In so doing, however, he also ensured that a greater share of the colony's dividends landed in the Crown's coffers rather than those of (or those controlled by) the traditional elite of New Spain—criollos and interested (allied) peninsulares. In his relentless pursuit of "justice," the Marquis of Gelves ended up with very few friends and allies. Even those with differing interests allied against his rule (Elliott 2006, 199; Simpson 1966, 151–56) and, due to the ingrained system of patronage, those whose interests he was (theoretically) trying to defend (working classes, servants, the indigenous pueblos) also joined in the popular revolt that deposed him. In the end, he was supported mostly by the Franciscans, one of the few groups backing him, because of his refusal to turn over to the secular church their authority over indigenous pueblos (Elliott 2006, 199).

As Lesley Byrd Simpson (1966, 151–56) has emphasized, two major actions taken by the viceroy, in which prominent officials were stopped from profiting from illegal activities, conspired to light the fuse that set the revolt in motion. First, he cracked down on grain hoarding and speculation, and second, he tried to interfere with the workings of the secular Church. In the first instance, the viceroy discovered that the government was doing nothing to control the prices of grain, which, due to the flooding and its impact on local agriculture, was in short supply. Instead of controlling the market through the system of public granaries as was supposed to happen, the granaries were allowed to remain empty, while the local grain market was largely cornered by corrupt officials who forced sales at cheap prices and then sold at famine prices, conspiring to control the prices established at the *alhóndiga* (or exchange) in Mexico City (Feijoo 1964; Boyer 1977). Not only were government officials turning a blind eye to the practice, they didn't even protest when Melchor Pérez de Varaez, an Audiencia member who was alcalde mayor [chief judge or official] of Metepec (a source of the supply) also became governor/alcalde mayor of Mexico City (the point of distribution) (Boyer 1977). Viceroy Gelves responded by prosecuting Pérez de Varaez, whose cronies in the Audiencia did everything in their power to protect him. At this point, the archbishop of Mexico, Juan Pérez de la Serna, became involved in the matter.

Although at first supportive of the viceroy's crackdown on the grain market rigging, Pérez de la Serna was not happy that he refused to support the secularization of the parishes (Israel 1974; Feijoo 1964). Then, he was himself placed under sanction for running an illegal butcher shop from his parish offices. In addition, the Marquis of Gelves wrote Pérez de Varaez a letter privately communicating various accusations of corruption in Church practices that he wanted the archbishop to amend—a direct affront, from the archbishop's viewpoint, to the autonomous authority and power of the Church.[9] In this way, the viceroy earned the bitter enmity of powerful forces in New Spain—the Audiencia and the most powerful authority figure of the Catholic Church in Mexico—who soon made common cause.

When the viceroy refused to let Pérez de Varaez off the hook, the archbishop reacted by excommunicating him, and he in turn ordered the archbishop sent to Spain. On his way to the port of Veracruz, however, Pérez de la Serna stopped in San Juan Teotihuacan and entered the church. When officials tried to remove him, he grabbed the host (making him untouchable) and refused to budge. He also declared a *cessatio a divinis*, the end of all Church masses and services across New Spain, a radical order that succeeded in garnering the attention of a wide public whose sentiments were exploited by the powerful interests already seething under the austerity and strictness of the viceroy's oversight. Thus scapegoated, the viceroy's days were numbered, and when Pérez de Varaez and his lawyers were denied access to the viceregal palaces, a large crowd pressed for the release of the archbishop. From there, with the archbishop on his way back to Mexico City, things did not calm down but rather escalated—including an order by the viceroy for his guards to open fire on the crowd—and ended in his donning of a disguise (the cape and hat of one of his servants) in order to escape to the streets, where he joined the crowd calling him a Lutheran and shouting "Death to the viceroy!"[10] Pérez de la Serna, on the other hand, rode back into the city in triumph and was celebrated as a hero. Despite this, the Crown eventually ordered his return to Spain where he served as bishop in Zamora.

It might have been purely due to the fact that San Juan Teotihuacan lay on the road to Veracruz that Pérez de la Serna made his protest there. However, Schwaller (1999) remarks that there was apparently a deep friendship between the Alva Ixtlilxochitl family and the archbishop. O'Gorman ([1975–1977] 1985, 1:232), moreover, assumes that he is the addressee of the "Dedicatoria" written by Alva Ixtlilxochitl and placed before the *Historia de la nación chichimeca* in the bound manuscripts (but which O'Gorman says pertains to the *Sumaria relación de la historia general*), making Pérez de la Serna a potential benefactor and patron of Alva Ixtlilxochitl's historical work. In addition, long before the revolt, Alva Ixtlilxochitl himself became caught up in the reforming viceroy's efforts. In 1621, while serving in his appointment as juez gobernador of Chalco province, Alva Ixtlilxochitl was ordered by the new viceroy (who did not appoint him) to investigate accusations of corruption (improper distribution of indigenous labor) by the alcalde mayor of the region, the elder Antonio de la Mota, and to make the results of his investigation public (O'Gorman [1975–1977] 1985, 1:26–28). Alva Ixtlilxochitl obliges, but the request might have placed him in something of an awkward situation, given what were likely strong family ties between the Alva y Cortés family and the La Mota clan: as is clear from Alva Ixtlilxochitl's mother's last will and testament (O'Gorman 1977, 348), she owned houses that were mortgaged in their favor (Schwaller 1999).

There is no reason, in fact, to think that Alva Ixtlilxochitl would not have been sympathetic to the colonizers' frustration with the repartimiento and their desire to have more access to indigenous labor. The cacicazgo lands belonging to the family were rented out to Spaniards who depended on a cheap labor supply in order to produce goods and pay their rent. The economic interests of the cacicazgo to some degree would have been tied to those of the estancias and the tenants that worked their extensive lands. The increases in market controls and taxes would also have negatively affected those interests. Alva Ixtlilxochitl needed Crown favor for his political appointments, but it seems that there was also plenty of reason for him to be exasperated with the viceregal administration and to be allied with or closely tied to the creole and/or mestizo elite.

In general, it seems that the people of Mexico City, rich and poor, creoles and castas, overwhelmingly supported Pérez de la Serna, even though the viceroy's many reforms in theory were destined to have brought more fairness (less exploitation) to those who did not hold the strings of power, and notwithstanding his support for the continued authority of the monasteries over the indigenous parishes (Boyer 1977; Zárate Toscano 1996). Bancroft

(1887, 3:58–79) and others (Feijoo 1964; Simpson 1966, 155–56) conclude that Pérez de la Serna played his cards very well and whipped up public sentiment and angry crowds in his favor; Viceroy Gelves, not Pérez de Varaez, was popularly blamed for high grain prices.[11] Moreover, his attack on the archbishop was considered to be an attack on the Church itself. As Verónica Zárate Toscano (1996, 40) puts it,

> Con la intervención del arzobispo, el conflicto adquirió el carácter de fricción entre autoridad civil y religiosa. Esta situación sirvió como detonante, generando con ello la participación y radicalización de otros sectores. . . . La labor de agitación por ciertos grupos religiosos, dio como resultado un enfrentamiento violento. "La plebe" participó en la defensa de los intereses del arzobispo. Adelantando conclusiones, podemos afirmar que la autoridad religiosa tenía en ese momento un mayor poder político que el propio virrey, que representaba a la máxima autoridad terrenal, mientras el arzobispo era el símbolo que encarnaba el poder divino.[12]

> With the intervention of the archbishop, the conflict acquired the character of a dispute between civil and religious authority. This situation served as a trigger, generating the participation and radicalization of the other sectors. . . . The work of agitation by certain religious groups resulted in a violent confrontation. "The masses" participated in the defense of the interests of the archbishop. In the end, we can affirm that the religious authority had more power in this moment than the viceroy himself, who represented the maximum earthly authority, while the archbishop was the symbol that incarnated divine power.

When the crowd forced the Marquis of Gelves to finally flee the viceregal palace, according to Zárate Toscano (44), they took the *estandarte del rey* [king's banner] that had been flying over the viceregal palace and flew it over the cathedral. She writes,

> Las reacciones ante el hecho consumado fueron tan diversas como se puede imaginar. En 1624, una vez conocida la proclama expedida por la Audiencia, se hizo sentir un beneplácito en prácticamente todos los sectores; incluso se popularizó el verso "Ahora vivamos en nuestra ley/ que ya no hay virrey." (48)

The reactions in the face of the finished deed were as diverse as it is possible to imagine. In 1624, once the proclamation expedited by the Audiencia was published, a general consent made itself felt in all sectors; even the poetic lines, "Now we may live by our law/because the viceroy is no more" became popular.

We don't know what Alva Ixtlilxochitl thought about the revolt. From his works, however, we know that that he had a clear (and clearly positive) vision of what that law—"nuestra ley" (our law)—*used to* look like before the conquest, according to its ever-evolving image in the colonial record, with a ruler and lawmaker (Nezahualcoyotl) who—but for the fact that he could not have been Christian—was an exemplary Christian prince in nearly every respect. We also know that, on the sidelines of a seemingly out-of-touch colonial viceroyalty, the descendents of the ruling classes of that old order looked on, witnessing the devastation of the indigenous pueblos and trying to preserve the memory of their great leaders for the generations to come. If those memories—his histories—could be put to good use, to serve as a general example for the present times, yet another aspect of his work as a historian would also be served.

These didactic aspirations of his writing find concrete expression and context in the "Dedicatoria," mentioned above, that Alva Ixtlilxochitl addresses to an "Ilustrísimo señor," and whom he calls, significantly, a "príncipe." O'Gorman ([1975–1977] 1985, 1:232), assuming the text referred to the *Sumaria relación de la historia general* and not to the *Historia de la nación chichimeca*, suggests that Alva Ixtlilxochitl could have entrusted his manuscript to Pérez de la Serna before he left to return to Spain as bishop of Zamora. As the case may be, in concluding his statement, Alva Ixtlilxochitl writes, "Sólo me resta ahora el amparo y protección de un príncipe tan grande como lo es V. S. I. debajo del cual saldrá a luz mi trabajo, a quien he querido ofrecer y dedicar esta relación sumaria de la historia general de esta Nueva España, como a quien le pertenece y viene de derecho" ([1975–1977] 1985, 1:525; The only thing I now lack is the refuge and protection of a prince as great Your Illustrious Majesty under which my work will see the light of day, [and] to whom I have wished to offer and dedicate this summary account of the general history of this New Spain, as to someone to whom it belongs and comes to by right). If O'Gorman's assumption of Pérez de Serna as addressee is correct, the standoff between this archbishop and the viceroy imbues the use of the term "príncipe" in this context with a weight that it would not have had otherwise, signaling in addition the power of the Church hierarchy in the civil and political affairs of the time. Yet, if Pérez de la Serna read or was affected by his charge (if indeed he was the addressee), he did not or could not fulfill the implied request. Perhaps he did not have the social and/or political will, once back in Spain, to publish or disseminate a work whose protagonists and author descended from a line of rulers whose existence, now that the early days of colonization were safely in the past, it was much more politically convenient to sweep under the rug. It was a work, after all, in which rulership was a key thematic motif and structuring principle, and whose specularity, therefore, it was difficult to avoid. Pérez de la Serna, moreover, would not have wanted to draw any kind of attention to his recent actions that led to the ouster of a standing viceroy, actions for which he had been returned to Spain, demoted to the post of bishop. In the mid-1620s, the once-burgeoning power

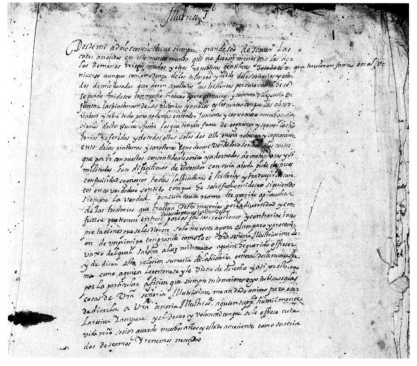

Figure 4. Alva Ixtlilxochitl's *Dedicatoria* taken from the digitalized *Códice Chimalpahin*, located in the Biblioteca Nacional de Antropología e Historia, Mexico City. Courtesy of INAH.

of the Spanish Crown and its revival of the medieval notion of a universal Christian empire had all but vanished (Maravall 1944); decided barriers, if not impossible roadblocks, placed into serious doubt its hegemony in Europe and even in the Americas itself. The overthrow of Viceroy Gelves showed the Spanish Crown that the elites of New Spain were focused internally, and Spain ignored them and meted out its justice to them at its peril (Boyer 1977).

Alva Ixtlilxochitl's great Acolhua rulers (revised and Christianized), as with all pre-Hispanic kings, became, in the lead-up to the struggle for independence, symbols of a unique identity. They served as an early point of pride for creole intellectuals such as Sigüenza y Góngora, who proudly placed the Mexica kings on the triumphal arch he created for the arrival of Viceroy Paredes (Brading 1991, 362–63), and they also bore with them a history of representing an inherent threat to the power of the Crown for their potential to coalesce discontent or spark rebellion in the república de indios (Bierhorst 2009, under "Introduction: 'Before the 1590s' and 'Revitalization'"; LaFaye [1977] 1995, 57–66, 225–30; Gruzinski 1989). If these rulers, however, were becoming useful to, and being appropriated by, the new creole elite, the latter did not necessarily appreciate (or care about) the nature and extent of the cultural memory and historical ties that Nahua historians such as Alva Ixtlilxochitl were recording, and claiming, as part of their heritage.

If the finer points of royal lineage were perhaps lost on Pérez de la Serna, however, they do not seem to have escaped the attention of fray Juan de Torquemada, who appears to have given a great deal of thought to the matter before publishing his *Veintiun libros rituales y Monarquía indiana*. A history whose title suggests the link between the divine and the dynastic, it was Torquemada's purpose therein to tell the stories of missionaries who first worked to sever and reformulate that link so that they could then also Christianize the masses. As he read Alva Ixtlilxochitl's early work, perhaps he realized the ever-contingent and potentially ambivalent nature of the results of that effort—and perhaps he reflected, too, on the Spanish rulers and their often less than ideal or "princely" stances regarding the república de indios and the work of the Church (in particular that of the regular clergy) therein— for he dedicates *his* dedication of his work—his Carta Nuncupatoria [Dedicatory letter]—to "la Sacratísima Magestad del Rei del cielo Dios Nuestro Señor" (the King of Heaven's most Holy Majesty God our Lord) ([1723] 1975, 1:n.p.). The tripled use of dynastic titles—King, Majesty, Lord—for the identification of the divine leaves no doubt about the topic of his discourse therein.

In his letter, Torquemada addresses the Catholic God directly, as a humble servant of a *sacred, divine* ruler to whom he entrusts his work. The indirect addressee of his missive, however, the human reader, is provided with an elegant justification for his choice of patron. In this discourse, Torquemada expounds on the uselessness and vanity of choosing wealthy and powerful human patrons for books: which patron, he asks, ever passed a book entrusted to them to their heirs for its continued safekeeping after his death? There is only one truly reliable sponsor, and only one true King of Kings, one being whose "hidalguía y limpieza es eternal, y sin principio, y tan inmenso vuestro nombre" (nobility and purity is eternal, and without beginning, and as immense [as] your name). Yet, he writes, authors nevertheless try to ingratiate themselves with powerful people to protect their work from attack, and in so doing—thinking that they are pleasing their patrons—they undertake lengthy investigations into these prospective patrons' past lineage until they arrive, he writes, "al tronco, y Cepa, donde comenzó su nobleza" (ibid.; at the trunk and vine where their nobility began). In a stinging reminder of the *humanity* of the nobility, Torquemada writes that these patron-seekers, at the end of their investigations,

> Al fin dan en laja, pues llegan a término, don se acaban las caballerías, y en el mismo se comienza a descubrir la hilaza de la masa de Adán, dónde toda nobleza e hidalguía, quedó por el suelo abatida, y el sambenito de la culpa primera puesto a los pechos, que aunque más se quiera cubrir con hábitos de San Juan de Calatrava, Alcántara, y Santiago, no es posible, por cuanto él campea sobre todos.

> They come up empty, because they arrive at the same point as the knightly romances, and they begin to discover the link to the multitude of Adam, where all aristocracy and nobility are finally defeated, with the stigma of the first sin placed on their chests, such that no matter how much one wants to cover it with habits of St. John of Calatrava, Alcántara, and James, it is not possible, because it looms over everyone.

And if we are looking for feats and marvelous deeds, he goes on to say, what can be more incredible than the creation of the world and of mankind? And, finally, he writes,

> Qué armas puede haber de tanta calificación, como las vuestras, donde ni hay Castillas, ni Leones, sino un mundo redondo, en vuestra mano,

que incluye a Castilla, y a León, y a Francia, y a Inglaterra, y todos los demás reinos del mundo? Siendo, pues, esto así, a Vos (mi Señor, y mi Dios) os ofrezco mis escritos, porque sois el Criador de las gentes, que en ellos se contienen: Vos los decubristéis; Vos los vencistéis; Vos los convertistéis; y Vos los conserváis en el numero, que sois servido, a los convertidos.

What arms, such as yours, have been so great, where there are no Castiles, or Leones, just one round world in your hands that includes Castile and León and France and England, and all the other Kingdoms of the World? With things being as they are, it is to You (my Lord and my God) that I offer my writings, because you are the Creator of the peoples that are described in them: You discovered them; You conquered them; You converted them; and You preserve the converted in the number by which you are served.

This passage emphasizes the worth of the Native peoples of New Spain by placing them in the context of the world's kingdoms alongside Castile, León, France, and England. They are not as well known, perhaps, he implies, but they are the subjects of his book, and were (also) created by God. Moreover, the valiant acts for which many Spaniards would claim nobility—the discovery, conquest, and conversion of the people about whom (and about whose kingdoms) he writes—were in fact the work of God.

As with his earlier admonishment to those seeking noble patrons, Torquemada leaves no doubt in his dedication as to the ultimate and original source of nobility and noble acts. The people themselves, therefore, as well as the entire colonial enterprise that brought them (back) into the fold of Christianity were the work of God. Such an emphasis seems to reveal a latent but potent exasperation with the pretensions and attitudes of the Spanish colonial settler class. Perhaps the versions of the ancient past of New Spain sketched out by early Franciscan and Dominican priests with close relationships and structural ties to the land and people, and later inherited by a new generation of indigenous elite, reminded Torquemada of the unfulfilled hopes for the creation of a truly apostolic New World, and how much it had been impacted by the corruption of the Old.

Whatever the object of its discourse or its intended audience, the emphasis of the Carta Nuncupatoria also represents a strong rejoinder to much of the narrative thrust and raison d'être of the early historical work of Alva

Ixtlilxochitl: its emphasis on proving the authenticity, nobility and worth of the Acolhua rulers according to notions of lineage in the European tradition and within the proper biblically sanctioned tradition (e.g., Alva Ixtlilxochitl [1975–1977] 1985, 1:417–18]). That Alva Ixtlilxochitl's deified ancestor-heroes underwent a redeification, and that this redeification nevertheless carried with it all of the inerasable and insuppressible traces of their links to the old gods of Anahuac, moreover, turns Torquemada's statement into something of a warning, a stark reminder that the work of conversion, even in the best of old Christian families, was never a finished affair or something to be taken for granted.

Conclusion

Rulers, Rhetors, Tricksters, and the Composition of History

❧ BEHIND THE FERVENT DISCOURSE OF TORQUEMADA'S CARTA NUN-
cupatoria lies a quintessentially Counter-Reformation appreciation—and
suspicion—of rhetoric itself. By casting his addressee, the Catholic God, in
dynastic language, as the King of Kings—the only noble entity with completely pure blood (true limpieza de sangre)—Torquemada attempts to keep
his readers from an overzealous reverence for those whose power rests on the
fact that they are not quite like the rest of humanity. Sometimes themselves
objects of deification, rulers derive their power by virtue of a close and ancient
connection to the sacred. Yet Torquemada insists on their sameness, on their
humanity, that is, on the original sin that in the Christian tradition forms a
barrier between creator and created human beings that, as he believed, can
only be crossed by virtue of the established sacred rites and holy offices of the
Catholic Church.

Defined by sin, the world of humans is a world of appearances and deception. The antiquity of a ruler's ties to the true religion, the greatness of the
deeds performed, the amount of adulation heaped upon the intended patron
of the historiographical or literary offering, are all in the last analysis mean-
ingless, empty, shallow, insincere, and doomed to failure: "De manera (Señor,
y Dios Poderoso) que todo lo de esta vida es engaño, y lo más firme, sin

firmeza; y lo que parece favor, es fingimiento, y mentira" ([1723] 1975, n.p.;
So that, (Lord and Omnipotent God) everything in this life is deception, and
that which is the most stable, is without stability; and what seems like favor
is trickery and lies). Over and over in his Carta Nuncupatoria, Torquemada
trains our focus away from the worldly ruler to place it on the ultimate source
of all the power of all the dynasties, nobles, kings, and lords: the Catholic God
conceived of as a monolithic, monological, stable, and transcendental signified. He is concerned to establish in the mind of the reader and against the
grain of the Renaissance emphasis on the world of appearances a metaphysics
of presence that transcends the world of deception, instability, and lies.

As Wayne A. Rebhorn (1992) points out, the theme of deception and
trickery ran deep in the literature of the Renaissance, which is full of various
kinds of tricksters, from *pícaros* (rogues) to buffoons, *burladores* (pranksters),
and cunning princes. Without fail, he writes, these characters are "masters of
language who use their skill with words to satisfy their desires through the
manipulation and control of others" (31). While the medieval period had its
tricksters as well, Renaissance tricksters take this structure to the extreme,
he notes, with the art of deception becoming an end in its own right, above
and beyond any other intended outcome. In this context, the field of rhetoric
begins to take on ideological dimensions, and the trickster-orator becomes
associated with mastery and rulership and identified in the literature as
"nothing less than 'the emperor of men's minds'" (42). In the Renaissance,
Rebhorn writes, "the rhetor was actually imagined as a real prince, just as
rhetoric was seen as an art to be used by rulers, offered to them as a means to
shape and control their subjects and ensure their thrones and titles" (57–58).
And it is here, in the in-between place where the life of the European and the
Nahua trickster meet in their claims to ultimate power, wherein the divide
between Torquemada's dedication and that of Alva Ixtlilxochitl, and between
the two closely connected historians' visions of rulership and of the rulers'
role in shaping the past of Anahuac, comes most sharply into focus.

If Torquemada, like the later Sahagún, warned against the threat of
idolatry and insisted on the continuing need for the work of the friars, Alva
Ixtlilxochitl, like the first generations of Franciscans missionaries, but certainly with less naiveté, in his later works seems to embrace the nodes of con-
gruency in which Nahua thought and belief and Christian rites lose their
distinction, dissolving into moments of undecidability and ambivalence. In
so doing, he enacts in writing that which his ancestral namesake, Fernando
Cortés Ixtlilxochitl, undertook on the battlefields of the Spanish conquest of

Mexico: alliance with and accommodation of the Spanish invaders. Complicity with Spanish aggression and violence, however, did not make Fernando Cortés Ixtlilxochitl Spanish or a conquistador in the Spanish sense of the term. Nor did it—if we take the thirteenth relación of the *Compendio* at its word—make him a completely silent and unresisting witness to its atrocities.

In the *Historia de la nación chichimeca*, the long-evolving merger of Tetzcoca historical memory with the Christian tradition continues to take shape, institutionalizing itself most profoundly through its discursive elaboration of the biblical portrait of its ruler-heroes, Quetzalcoatl and Nezahualcoyotl, and through censorship of any and all "idolatrous" or taboo elements (Lesbre 1999a, 2000, 2010; Lee 2008). As Rolena Adorno (2011) has keenly observed with respect to cultural production and creole consciousness in the *barroco de indias* (Baroque of the Indies)—which she describes as a kind of "taking possession" of Latin America from within (78)—"For those of European background, it meant celebrating the pre-Columbian past while holding themselves apart from its contemporary heirs; for those who identified with Amerindian civilizations and communicated with Western audiences, it meant either suppressing certain dimensions of their ancestral cultures or acknowledging and rejecting them" (79). While undeniably furthering colonial agenda through suppression of specific indigenous elements and a deepening of the discursive affiliation of Tetzcoco and its rulers with biblical and classical tradition, Alva Ixtlilxochitl's writing and its silences—his complicity—also ensured an illustrious posterity for his Tetzcoca ancestors in Catholic New Spain and beyond, eking out a space for their memory in a changing world. In his later works, moreover, as I have argued, his silence becomes more apparent, in a sense, than real; it is a *sly* silence undertaken with a wink and in the full knowledge that the play (and work) of destiny lies beyond all human ability to grasp and to control it.

To Torquemada's emphatic dedication of the fruit of his labor and orientation of his readers' awareness toward the Christian Divine as sole, true king, the *Historia de la nación chichimeca* poses the play of Tezcatlipoca's invisible presence and, in his relationship with Quetzalcoatl-Cortés as the new sun, the idea of the Spanish as the incarnation of a new—but never final—era. And to Torquemada's efforts to save within the bounds of his published, voluminous tomes the details of the past and its stories as accurately as they could be understood, and as closely as possible to the way in which they were related to his predecessors and to himself (leaving space for informed opining on the inevitable contradictions), Alva Ixtlilxochitl leaves behind a collection of copied histories of indigenous authorship, his own historical manuscripts that engage the past from a Tetzcoca point of view, and a history—the *Historia de la nación chichimeca*—that, in its structure and characterizations of its ruler-heroes, embraces the duality of its literary heritage and leaves behind a clear impression of the vast power of the princely author-rhetor-trickster and of its composer's personal identity as a true son of his Tetzcoca noble ancestors.

The *Historia de la nación chichimeca* is a history that, from the outset and at its heart, refuses the kind of singular order of truth behind the thinking of the *Monarquía indiana* and that, in its rendering of the (proto-)Christian past of Anahuac, leaves open the door for new and multiple understandings of that world, some of them in close harmony with the one that the missionaries had tried their best to displace. If for Torquemada the great work of the missionaries of his order remained incomplete, Alva Ixtlilxochitl—whatever his opinion of the actions of Pérez de la Serna in thwarting the power of the viceroy—seems to have found at least some grounds for embracing (and indeed fomenting) the appropriation and (apparent) creolization (or Catholicizing) of the indigenous past. With his ruler-writers and trickster-ruler-heroes, Alva Ixtlilxochitl plants himself firmly in the terrestrial world of the Renaissance trickster aesthetic that Torquemada warns against, an aesthetic that unmasks presence and certainty (and certainly metaphysical presence) at every turn. His ruler-heroes glorify and make (justified) use of deception for their power; they are known for their wit and their cunning used against the (less sagacious and idolatrous) enemy. Regarded in the context of Nahua (and Tolteca) narrative, this is a sure sign of their connection to the nonterrestrial realms of the sacred and to the age-old nemesis of the now Christianized, apostle-like Quetzalcoatl.

In the body of his "Dedicatoria," before addressing his intended patron, Alva Ixtlilxochitl describes his motivation for undertaking the research to write his history:

Desde mi adolescencia tuve siempre gran deseo de saber las cosas acaecidas en este Nuevo Mundo, que no fueron menos que las de los romanos, griegos, medos y otras repúblicas gentílicas que tuvieron fama en el universo aunque con la mudanza de los tiempos y caída de los señoríos y estados de mis pasados, quedaron sepultadas sus historias; por cuya causa he conseguido mi deseo con mucho trabajo, peregrinación y suma diligencia en juntar las pinturas de las historias y anales, y los cantos con que las observaban; y sobre todo para poderlas entender, juntando y convocando a muchos principales de esta Nueva España, los que tenían fama de conocer y saber las historias referidas. ([1975–1977] 1985, 1:525)

Ever since I was an adolescent, I have always had a strong desire to understand the things that happened in this New World, which were not less than those of the Romans, Greeks, Medes, and other gentile republics that were famous in the world, although with the changing times and the downfall of the estates and nations of my ancestors, their histories remained buried; for which cause I have fulfilled my wish with a lot of work, pilgrimage, and utmost diligence in gathering the paintings of the histories and the annals, and the songs with which they observed them, above all in order to understand them, bringing together and convening many of the notables of this New Spain who were famous for knowing and understanding these histories.

Likely written after he had completed his later works, this passage relates Alva Ixtlilxochitl in his capacity as historian to the great themes of his histories and to the legacy of the great Chichimeca teteuhctin (singular teuchtli) of Tetzcoco. Readers familiar with Alva Ixtlilxochitl's writings will perhaps recognize in it the echo of the moment of narrative digression from the thirteenth relación ([1975–1977] 1985, 1:514) (discussed at the end of the chapter 3), which compares the arduous pilgrimages of Topiltzin, Xolotl, Nezahualcoyotl, and Fernando Cortés Ixtlilxochitl and in which Alva Ixtlilxochitl declares that although all three rulers endured great sacrifice and suffering, there could have been no more arduous journeys than those undertaken by Fernando Cortés Ixtlilxochitl in the service of the Spanish. In the wording used to describe Alva Ixtlilxochitl's efforts as a historian, the "mucho trabajo, peregrinación, y suma diligencia" (extensive work, pilgrimage, and utmost diligence) required to gather the "pinturas de las historias y anales, y los cantos con que las observaban" (the paintings of the histories and the annals, and the songs with which they observed them), the "Dedicatoria" passage suggests a parallel between Alva Ixtlilxochitl's life endeavors and the migrations that his Chichimeca ancestors undertook in their own contexts as they left Chicomoztoc or Tetzcoco to undertake new lives in Anahuac. Perhaps Alva Ixtlilxochitl's historical research did indeed lead him (back) to

a new or deeper understanding of home and enable him to identify with—
and write himself into—one of the great themes of his histories (and those of
Anahuac in general), that of exile and migration to a new (but always recognizable) homeland. Even more significant than this glimpse of a metaphorical
identification of his journeys as a historian with the exile, migrations, and
various homecomings of his Tetzcoca ancestors, however, is the insight into
the *nature* and *stakes* of his literal, material act of preserving the histories, and
his role as author in (re)writing them, that the "Dedicatoria" offers us. It is
not only the lived process of researching and gathering the histories that ties
him to his Tetzcoca ancestors in this passage, but the work of memory that
constitutes its aim.

In the passage, Alva Ixtlilxochitl notes that the particular difficulty of
his efforts, the reason they required so much "work," "pilgrimage," and "diligence," in fact, was because the ancestral histories he strove to preserve had
almost disappeared with the "mudanza de los tiempos y caída de los señoríos
y estados de mis pasados" (the changing times and the downfall of the estates
and nations of my ancestors). In describing them as having remained "sepultadas" (buried), however, Alva Ixtlilxochitl joins them semantically with the
rulers—Xolotl, Topiltzin, Ixtlilxochitl, and Nezahualcoyotl—whose burials,
and whose *deaths* or *non-deaths* constitute, in his narratives, key signifiers
of cultural affiliation and the empire's change of fortune. And in his association of forgetting with death, the work of gathering and preservation—an
implicit disinterment—becomes an act of remembering regarded as a kind
of resurrection.

In its brief but pithy description of Alva Ixtlilxochitl's research *methodology*, moreover, the passage points to the deeper significance of this act
of remembering as a kind of resurrection. In the first place, it makes clear
his determination to obtain specifically *indigenous* source texts—paintings,
annals, and songs—and then to bring together those "principales" (nobles or
notables) who knew how to interpret them, so that he himself could understand them. We don't know if these were truly gatherings of educated notables, or if he meant that he interviewed various people separately. If the former
is the case, we don't know if those gatherings involved the singing and/or
recording of songs, or if Alva Ixtlilxochitl's connection to the Nahua song
tradition consisted solely of a reading (and possible copying) of the collec-
tions already found in the *Cantares* (Bierhorst 1985) and the *Romances de los
señores de la Nueva España* (Bierhorst 2009). As Lee (2008, 209–24) and Bierhorst (2009, under "Introduction" and "After 1590s") have made clear, Alva

Ixtlilxochitl seems to have followed in the footsteps of Juan Bautista Pomar (probable collector and original copyist of the *Romances*) and his sources in, as Lee (2008, 214) puts it, "willfully" misinterpreting the texts in order to create a Christianized version of Nezahualcoyotl. Certainly Alva Ixtlilxochitl's translations and recomposition of historical song texts (O'Gorman 1975–1977, 2: 267–73, especially 270) and the presence of many song fragments that he presents from time to time in his histories, usually as an expression of the renown and praiseworthiness of rulers, indicate his keen awareness of the significance of the songs as vital vehicles for the creation and transmission of cultural memory and historical knowledge in both Castilian and Nahua contexts. The first song fragment that Alva Ixtlilxochitl records in his own historical oeuvre, moreover, is not about Nezahualcoyotl, but Fernando Cortés Ixtlilxochitl (his grandson).

It appears in the very first relación of the Chichimeca portion of the *Sumaria relación de todas las cosas*, during his discussion of the diversity of the Chichimeca peoples and the greatness of the Tetzcoca among them, and right after the quote with which this book begins, where he declares that to call someone a Chichimeca was to address them with the highest possible praise ([1975–1977] 1985, 1:290). The song, writes Alva Ixtlilxochitl, is a merchant's song, "por ser de peregrinación" (because it is about pilgrimage). When well translated, he states, it goes like this: "'¡Oh aculhuas naciones! Yo soy aquel chichimeco que fui prosiguiendo con mi rodela triste y pensativo, adonde tengo de ir a perderme u volveré con bien, aunque con trabajos y guerras llegué hasta la provincia de Tlapalan.'" ('Oh Acolhua nations! I am that Chichimeca who continued onward with my shield, sad and pensive, [to] where I must go to lose myself or [from whence] will I return with good; although it was with struggle and wars, I arrived at the province of Tlapalan.') Clearly abstract and difficult to comprehend in its metaphorical phrasing, Alva Ixtlilxochitl goes on to explain that it is a song about the "trabajos, peregrinaciones y conquistas" (work, pilgrimages, and conquests) undertaken by the valiant Ixtlilxochitl, and informs his reader that this person was later called "don Fernando señor de Tezcuco," and that it was he who sided with the Spanish, serving God and king.

In the first-person voice of this song, translated by Alva Ixtlilxochitl, the ruler defines himself as a shield-bearing wanderer, and thus as a kind of warrior, but the sentiment of the excerpt is one of declared sadness and reflection, made palpable through its opening apostrophe, which both sets the speaker apart from his addressees (clearly but broadly defined as his physically and temporally removed compatriots) and supplies the weight and force of its exclamation. The poignant bravery of the speaker or singer derives not from a literal battlefield but from the song's mise-en-scène as an enactment or reenactment of the ruler's leave-taking of his people. It is not an expression of the fierce courage of the warrior in the heat of the fight but the bittersweet renunciation and acceptance of the ruler-sage on the verge of a final, inexorable parting of ways.

The excerpt contains no historical specifics or concrete details as to a precipitating cause of the ruler's exile, referencing the wandering, on the contrary, only in the broadest, *epic* terms as a journey, a departure from home and people.[1] Its two concrete identifiers, the departing ruler's name (Fernando Cortés Ixtlilxochitl) and his destination (Tlapalan), do little to lend the song text any sense of historical facticity or verisimilitude. The latter name, in fact, ensures that the particular circumstances and contingencies of the historical life of Fernando Cortés Ixtlilxochitl—only identified as the subject of the song in Alva Ixtlilxochitl's commentary following the excerpt—are wrapped up in the mantle of traditional tales or myths, in the continuity of Nahua tradition as embedded and expressed in its stories. The Tolteca history presented by Alva Ixtlilxochitl in the *Sumaria relación de todas las cosas*, moreover, leaves no doubt as to the parallel being drawn in the song, and ultimately of its (and Alva Ixtlilxochitl's) framing of his great-great-grandfather's life within the Nahua myth-historical context. As his earliest rendering of Tolteca history makes clear, Tlapalan is New World homeland of the Tolteca, where the sun was made to move once again and where the first great meeting of all the learned ones, astrologers, and other artists took place ([1975–1977] 1985, 1:266–67). It is the place where the last ruler of the Tolteca, Topiltzin, went to die and from whence he promised to return, on a certain date, asking that his people wait for him, which was the same year, according to the accounts of the history, in which the Spanish arrived in New Spain: "y desde que los vieron venir de donde sale el sol, tenían entendido que era Topiltzin" (271, 282–83, 387; and since they saw them arrive from the place [where] the sun rises, they understood that it was Topiltzin).

What, then, is the best way to understand Fernando Cortés Ixtlilxochitl's relationship to the figure of Topiltzin, whose similarly contested rulership placed him, like the latter figure, on the cusp of the sudden collapse of an empire seemingly at the height of its glory? And how should we interpret the parallelism between the destruction of the Tolteca and the (Mexica-dominated) Triple Alliance by warmongering outsider forces that ignored multiple entreaties to refrain from entering their territories ([1975–1977] 1985, 1:277–85; 451–52)? Is Fernando Cortés Ixtlilxochitl to be regarded as the incarnation of a new sun, and a new age?

In "The Solar Christ in Nahuatl Doctrinal Texts of Early Colonial Mexico," Louise Burkhart (1988) discusses representations of the European (specifically Franciscan) Solar Christ in early Mexican catechistic texts and its possible reception by the Nahua catechumens of the time. Describing the early Franciscan missionaries' transcendental vision of the sacred and typological conceptions of biblical history in contradistinction to the immanence of Nahua conceptions of the divine and history, she notes that Franciscan typology and images of the Solar Christ could have provided a "gateway" for Nahua ideas of the sun (and history) to inhabit Christian rites and religious belief after the conquest. She writes,

> If the Old Testament is a type for the New Testament, and the preconversion Indians are placed symbolically in an Old Testament world (which was, after all, a world of temples, sacrifices, prophets, wars of conquest, kings, and priests), then preconversion culture can act as a type for Indian Christianity. While Christianity must supersede what came before it, typological identifications establish links between present and past; the same mode of thinking that made the Old Testament relevant to Christianity could permit certain Nahua beliefs to slip across into Christianity in accordance with an accepted hermeneutical principle. For the Indians, the significance of history lay in the cyclical repetition of ancient patterns, by which the present was brought into line with the past. The temporal direction of typological thinking could easily be reversed: rather than their sun being a mere type for Christ, Christ could be assimilated to their sun as a new embodiment of a primordial being. (240)

She adds that while the friars would have assumed that their catechumens understood their typological figures in the same way that a European audience would have,

> to the Nahua audience, however, these tropes could have suggested a closer identification. Christ could be interpreted as a deity who has taken the place of the sun, thus becoming a new sun presiding over a new segment of history. The solar aspects of his character could be

interpreted as having a direct bearing on the conditions of earthly
life, rather than being removed onto a spiritual, metaphysical level of
reality. (240–41)

If we read typologically, then, Fernando Cortés Ixtlilxochitl, with his
acceptance of Christianity and alliance with the Spanish invaders, could be
(and could have been) regarded as the realization, under the law of Christ, of
the rulership of which Topiltzin was the type or which he prefigured, just as
the Tolteca collapse (and arrival of the Chichimeca under Xolotl) could be
seen as a prefiguration of the fall of the Triple Alliance to Spanish rule. As
such, Fernando Cortés Ixtlilxochitl would have ushered in the incarnation
of a new sun and new rites that, however regarded from a European point
of view, when examined from a vantage point informed by Nahua myth-
histories, could have looked in some respects very much like the old. For their
part, the Tetzcoca authors and historians reworking their narratives under
the auspices of the Franciscans in the early colonial period could have discovered fertile terrain upon which to relay in the colonizers' world of linear
temporality, Christian eschatology, and alphabetically rendered narratives, a
historical tradition grounded not in linear but cyclical conceptions of time,
and in which to maintain, therefore, a significant element of continuity with
traditional ways of regarding and transmitting the past.

The *Historia de la nación chichimeca* trails off before providing its readers with any kind of conclusion or insight into the role that Alva Ixtlilxochitl
might have assigned to his great-great-grandfather in the conquest period.
We have no way of assuming that the Fernando Cortés Ixtlilxochitl of the
early accounts is (or would have been) that of the later. If the early narratives
can serve as a guidepost, however, indicating that his sacrifices in war and his
example in life and death were still being remembered in song, or even just
identified with the song tradition by Alva Ixtlilxochitl himself, Tezcatlipoca
could not have been far away. In Nahua myths, as Olivier ([2003] 2008, 12–14,
214–18) reminds us and as Torquemada ([1723] 1975, 2:78) relates, it was after
the sacrifice of the gods and the creation of the sacred bundles, and when
the people were wandering about, sad and pensive, that Tezcatlipoca built
a bridge across the sea and sent one of his devotees to the house of sun to
fetch the singers and the musical instruments with which they could remember him.

Notes

INTRODUCTION

1. All translations are my own, unless otherwise noted.
2. The title of the *Historia de la nación chichimeca* in the manuscript from the Sigüenza y Góngora collection is simply *Sumaria relación* (BNAH CC 2, 7; Ruwet fol. 2r). On the whole, this study relies in all respects (including its use of titles) upon the two-volume O'Gorman edition of Alva Ixtlilxochitl's *Obras históricas*, although on a few occasions I refer to the newly digitalized Sigüenza manuscripts, now held at the archives of the Biblioteca Nacional de Antropología e Historia (National Library of Anthropology and History) in Mexico and named the *Códice Chimalpahin* (Chimalpahin codex). As in the above citation, when referencing the digitalized Sigüenza manuscripts, I use the initials BNAH CC with their corresponding volume number (1, 2, or 3) and references to the digital pagination on that website. Where possible, I also provide the folio numbers (or the range of numbers) set out by Wayne Ruwet (1997, 17–24) in his "Physical Description of the Manuscripts." (Note that Ruwet's description switches the references to volumes 1 and 2 as they were originally ordered, and that his foliation is not the original foliation written in the texts bound in the Sigüenza volumes, but an all-inclusive sequential numbering of each folio in the bindings.) These manuscripts contain the oldest versions of all of Alva Ixtlilxochitl's extant prose histories, and were rediscovered in the Bible Society Library of Cambridge, England, in 1983 by Ruwet. Before they had again come to light, however, Edmundo O'Gorman edited and published all of Alva Ixtlilxochitl's known prose histories. O'Gorman's edition includes a significant scholarly introduction (in volume 1) and an appendix of archival texts (in volume 2) with relevant contextual material. The edition was based on early eighteenth-century copies of the Sigüenza manuscripts made by Lorenzo Boturini (corresponding to the Alva Ixtlilxochitl histories in BNAH CC volume 1 of the Sigüenza manuscripts) and late eighteenth-century copies of Mariano Fernández de Echevarría y Veytia's *mid*-eighteenth-century copy of the Boturini manuscripts (corresponding to the Alva Ixtlilxochitl histories in volume 2 of the Sigüenza texts).

Many of Alva Ixtlilxochitl's original manuscripts were placed in the custody of the great Mexican savant and scholar, Carlos de Sigüenza y Góngora (1645–1700), by Alva Ixtlilxochitl's son, Juan de Alva y Cortés (1624?–1680–1682?) (O'Gorman [1975–1977] 1985, 1:29, 40; 1975–1977, 2:393, 396–97). The two were acquaintances, and Juan de Alva y Cortés entrusted Sigüenza y Góngora with the legal affairs of the cacicazgo (which he inherited after his uncle, Alva Ixtlilxochitl's older brother Francisco de Navas Huetzin, died without heirs) and named him executor of his estate (Brian 2014b, 91–93; Münch 1976, 27–32; O'Gorman [1975–1977] 1985, 1:40–42). It is assumed that Sigüenza himself bound the manuscripts together in their current form, although Schroeder notes that there is no way to be certain without further study (Martínez Baracs 2015, n. p.; Ruwet 1997, 17; Schroeder 1997, 3–5). After his death, the volumes became part of the library of the Colegio de San Pedro y San Pablo, where they were copied by Lorenzo Boturini and consulted by many prominent eighteenth-century historians, and eventually of the library of the associated Colegio de San Ildefonso, where they were also consulted by scholars until the late eighteenth century (Vásquez 2013, 143–44). In 1827, in the upheaval of the post-independence years, José María Luis Mora, political liberal and at one time the latter institution's librarian, gifted them to a member of the British and Foreign Bible Society in exchange for Protestant Bibles, and their trace was lost (Schroeder 1997, 3–5; Brian 2014b, 93). Although Alva Ixtlilxochitl's works were not published until the nineteenth century, first by Lord Kingsborough and then by Alfredo Chavero, their consultation in manuscript form and subsequent copying during the eighteenth century ensured their lasting influence on Mexican historiography (Brian 2014b; García 2006, 2007, 2009; Villella 2016). In May of 2014, one day before they were to be auctioned off to the public by Christie's of London, the Mexican government, through the Instituto Nacional de Antropología e Historia, or INAH, completed a private acquisition of the manuscripts, returning them to Mexico as an essential part of its cultural patrimony. Digitalized and placed online, they are now freely accessible. For a description of these latest proceedings, see Martínez Baracs (2015) and an announcement by INAH, "El Gobierno de México recupera el *Códice Chimalpahin*" (*Boletín* 2014). See also Vásquez (2013, 143–54) for a comprehensive narrative summary and diagram of the history and fate of Alva Ixtlilxochitl's writings and their copies. Future studies on the paleography, binding, and other aspects of the manuscripts will undoubtedly reveal a great deal about Alva Ixtlilxochitl and his work and influence on Mexican historiography, one important recent example of which can be found in Whittaker (2016).

3. Much of the literature on the work of Alva Ixtlilxochitl concentrates on his Acolhua "bias." This scholarly suspicion begins early, with Carlos de Sigüenza y Góngora's notation at the beginning of the manuscript of the *Compendio*: "El autor de este Compendio histórico de los reyes de Tetzcoco es D. Fernando de Alva Ixtlilxochitl, el qual se debe leer con grande cautela pues por engrandecer a su progenitor don Fernando Cortés Ixtlilxúchitl señor de Tetzcoco falta en muchas cosas a la verdad"

(The author of this historical compendium of the kings of Tetzcoco is D. Fernando de Alva Ixtlilxochitl, and it should be read with great caution, for in order to extol his ancestor, Fernando Cortés Ixtlilxúchitl, lord of Tetzcoco, in many respects he strays from the truth) (BNAH CC 2, 296–97; Ruwet fol. 147r; O'Gorman [1975–1977] 1985, 1:168). Among recent scholars, James Lockhart (1991, 143; 1992, 25) considers Alva Ixtlilxochitl to have held a generally "distorted" and inaccurate view the pre-Hispanic past, while for Enrique Florescano (1994, 100–183) Alva Ixtlilxochitl's work likewise represents a major effort to bring the pre-Hispanic past of his ancestors into the fold of Christian, European history. In *The Allure of Nezahualcoyotl* (2008), Jongsoo Lee, contrasting Alva Ixtlilxochitl's work with texts rooted in non-Acolhua historical traditions, such as those of the Mexica, deconstructs the false vision of Nezahualcoyotl (and pre-Hispanic central Mexico in general) that developed largely thanks to Alva Ixtlilxochitl's histories. Pablo García Loaeza (2010, 2014) likewise discusses how Alva Ixtlilxochitl was less interested in "accurate" portrayals of the past than in fabricating versions of the pre-Hispanic past that paralleled the great themes and currents of medieval European historiography as a means of legitimating his ancestry. Benton (2014) and Villella (2016) similarly regard Alva Ixtlilxochitl as a thoroughly European and Europeanizing writer of Acolhua history, with the latter describing how the strategic process of cacique reinvention in the tradition of European nobility provided the foundation for creole patriotism.

Other critics, less concerned with evaluating Alva Ixtlilxochitl's histories in terms of a notion of historical accuracy, focus on understanding Alva Ixtlilxochitl as a writer. Rolena Adorno (1989, 1994), Salvador Velazco (2003), Thomas Ward (2011), and Frederick Schwaller (2014) regard Alva Ixtlilxochitl as a castizo writer whose ties to Nahua nobility nevertheless shaped his Christianization of the Acolhua past. It is within this current that my own research situates itself and with which it most closely resonates. In addition to the perspectives of these scholars, the work of Amber Brian (2007, 2010, 2014a, 2014b, 2016) provides a strong basis for understanding Alva Ixtlilxochitl and his histories in their contexts, delineating most crucially their relationship to other Nahua writers and the Nahua elite of the time and presenting a concrete assessment of their work as bridges (2007, 2) between the Nahua and European worlds. The monumental work of Patrick Lesbre with Alva Ixtlilxochitl's corpus accomplishes the essential task of comparing his writing to a wide range of European and indigenous sources, pictorial and alphabetic, from the early Franciscan tradition and friar Juan de Torquemada to the Acolhua-based iconic script texts and other colonial writers working in the Nahua tradition, including Chimalpahin. For Lesbre (e.g., 1999a, 2001, 2010, 2012), Alva Ixtlilxochitl's personal stake in and connection to the Acolhua nobility meant that he sometimes exaggerated or left out stories or information provided in his sources that his contemporary, friar Juan de Torquemada, did not distort or shy away from. However, insofar as Lesbre's work reveals Alva Ixtlilxochitl to be a historian *aware* of those traditions and of the political context in which he wrote, it lays the foundation for my reading of the more subtle, subtextual presence and *negotiation* of a Nahua semiotic and discursive field present in the *Historia de la nación chichimeca*. (For more on this latter point, see Kauffmann [2014].) Jerome Offner (2014), moreover, whose scholarship concentrates on pre-Hispanic Tetzcoco and its environs, points out the significance of Alva Ixtlilxochitl's writing for an understanding of this region both before and after the arrival of the Spanish. Referencing the commonplace malignment of his historiography in scholarly circles, Offner comments,

> Alva Ixtlilxochitl knew far more than we do about Texcocan history, languages, and cultures; and we should not mistake the few documents left to us by history (largely thanks to him, in any event) for the totality of the cultural context of the time, much less the totality of what he knew and understood. To reiterate one point: How much of the *Códice Xolotl*, for example, would we understand—accurately—without Alva Ixtlilxochitl? (44)

4. For more information on "indios ladinos," their place in colonial Spanish America, and common characteristics of their historiography, see Adorno (1994). See also Brian's (2007, 47–53) early discussion of Alva Ixtlilxochitl as a translator of Nahua language and culture, as well as Schwaller's (2014) discussion of the work of Alva Ixtlilxochitl and his brother, Bartolomé, as important mediators, both literary and nonliterary.

5. Indeed, it is not insignificant that in the early days of the colony the Spanish regarded the "Indians" as "Gentiles" and therefore considered them to be free from the "taint" said to accompany Muslim or Jewish ancestry (Martínez 2004, 483–85). However, as Martínez's work (2008) makes clear, *limpieza de sangre* was soon understood less in religious and cultural terms, becoming increasingly "biological," "racial," and "essentialist" in conception. Mörner (1967, 60–68) astutely points out the huge gap between the legal and social status of the *castas*: while "Indians" ranked highly with regards to their legal rights, their social-economic condition and status placed them at the bottom of the colonial hierarchy (61). Many critics have discussed Alva Ixtlilxochitl's ethnic affiliation, regarding him (with various degrees of nuance and complexity) as *criollo* (a person born in the New World but of Spanish descent), a mestizo (a person with one Spanish and one Indian parent), Indian-identified, or in terms of his official status in New Spain: as a castizo (someone of mostly Spanish descent but with some non-Spanish ancestry) (Whittaker 2016, 34–40). In his highly significant study of Alva Ixtlilxochitl's earliest, holograph manuscripts, "The Identities of Fernando de Alva Ixtlilxochitl," Gordon Whittaker (2016) observes a primary rootedness in the Spanish language, with an early exposure to but imperfect knowledge of Nahuatl and the Nahua religious tradition (39–53) and of pictorial script (53–56) that becomes increasingly proficient

over time. His training in both Spanish and Nahuatl was not formal or elite as was that of his university-educated younger brother Bartolomé (52–53), who was trained in Latin and, as Schwaller (1994b) notes, worked with Nahuatl grammarians in the circle of the Jesuit linguist Horacio Carochi. Although, as Schwaller (2014, 55) points out, Alva Ixtlilxochitl does not perfectly fit into the category of "native nobility" (or that of "creole"), in my view he is necessarily regarded with respect to his status as a member of the variously constituted and rapidly disappearing class of colonial indigenous elite. There is a great deal we don't know about his connections to the Nahua historico-literary tradition(s) and his family's concrete social and economic relationships in Teotihuacan and in the Spanish world in which they moved, but it is clear that his works owe their existence to his ancestral connection to the Tetzcoca rulership and to his eventual engagement with that history.

6. Tetzcoco was the urban religious and political center of the Acolhua *altepetl* (ethnic polity or city-state), from whence his most famous ancestors held sway over a vast swath of Mesoamerica, along with the *tlatoque* (rulers; singular *tlatoani*) (or, more precisely, the *huey tlatoque* [great rulers]) centered in the urban nuclei of Tenochtitlan and Tlacopan. (The famous "Triple Alliance" of the Acolhua, Mexica, and Tepaneca *altepeme* [singular altepetl] dominated the peoples of territories stretching from central Mexico down into today's El Salvador.) Note that multiple spellings of Tetzcoco (i.e., Tezcuco, Texcoco) exist in the literature. With respect to the orthography used here for Nahuatl words, I have decided for the sake of consistency to stick to common spellings that unfortunately often omit important Nahuatl phonemes such as the glottal stop and vowel length. Thus, I have opted for "tlatoani," for example, because it is often spelled as such, although a more accurate orthography would be "tlahtoani" (with the "h" representing the glottal stop). I do, however, use Nahuatl markers to indicate adjective forms (Tetzcoca rather than Tetzcocan) and plurals, albeit without the required glottal stops in the Nahuatl. Therefore I refer to "tlatoque" rather than "tlatoanis," for example, and to the "Tetzcoca," the "Chichimeca" and the "Tolteca" rather than to the "Tetzcocans" "Chichimecs" and "Toltecs."

7. O'Gorman's "Apéndice documental" (1975–1977, 2:265–402, appendix of documents) includes the entire document (334–35). His "Estudio introductorio" is in volume 1 of the edition ([1975–1977] 1985, 1:1–257, introduction).

8. Things did not go so well for Alva Ixtlilxochitl, however, and it seems that the townspeople soon retracted their initial support, if indeed it ever truly existed, as the document claims. His appointment, according to Benton (2014, 45–47), lasted only slightly over a month, and he was asked to leave by the Spanish *alcalde mayor* and the members of the indigenous *cabildo*, or town council, for his inexperience in government and his incompetence in collecting tributes, which they claimed, as Benton writes, "would soon lead the city and the cabildo members themselves into financial ruin" (46).

9. For the full document see O'Gorman's "Apéndice documental" (1975–1977, 2:343).

10. Frederick Schwaller (2014) discounts any direct political influence behind this shared profession in the courts. Commenting on Alva Ixtlilxochitl's appointment in the Juzgado General de Indios, he writes, "Coincidentally, his grandfather, Juan Grande, had held a similar position in the Real Audiencia more than half a century earlier. Alva Ixtlilxochitl and his grandfather served in two distinct courts. In all likelihood it was a coincidence that they were both interpreters, but significant because of the role of cultural intermediary played over several generations in the family" (44; General Indian Court).

11. For an informative discussion of the role of interpreters and interpretation in colonial New Spain, see Araguás (2015), who reminds us of the key social and political function played by bilinguals in a context in which Spanish as a lingua franca was very slow to take hold.

12. An encomendero was a Spaniard granted access to the tribute and tribute labor of specific indigenous populations in return for service to the Spanish Crown (usually dating from the conquest period) and in accordance with certain regulations and responsibilities, such as religious instruction, that they were to fulfill with respect to those populations. For a more detailed discussion of the concept and its implementation in central Mexico, see Gibson (1964, 58–81).

13. Note that the descriptions and significance of these cases in Brian, Lee, Münch, and O'Gorman differ slightly. Relevant archival documents are published in the "Apéndice documental" of the O'Gorman edition (1975–1977, 2:294–333, 349–69). Münch (1976, 27) erroneously reports the death of Alva Ixtlilxochitl's older brother and inheritor of the cacicazgo in 1645. In reality, Alva Ixtlilxochitl dies in 1650, around ten years before his older brother Francisco de Navas Huetzin, who did not have children (O'Gorman 1985, 37).

14. From context I infer that this title refers to the office of a surveyor specifically assigned to issue rulings and adjudicate on matters of boundaries and territorial extension.

15. A full summary of Alva Ixtlilxochitl's named sources can be found in O'Gorman's "Estudio introductorio" ([1975–1977] 1985, 1:47–85). The testamento (last will and testament), of Francisco Verdugo Quetzalmamalitzin Huetzin, Alva Ixtlilxochitl's grandfather, so crucial to the preservation of the cacicazgo privileges for Alva Ixtlilxochitl's family, is printed in Münch (1976, 44–46), O'Gorman (1975–1977, 2:281–86), and Pérez-Rocha and Tena (2000a, 261–77). There is also a Nahuatl language history of the Teotihuacan rulers, referred to as the *Ytlahtollo yn Teotihuacan tlahtocaiotl* (*Relación del señorío de Teotihuacan* or account of the royal estate of Teotihuacan) transcribed or put together in 1621 from "antiguos documentos" by a copyist named Juan Tecante (Pérez-Rocha and Tena 2000a, 379–97; ancient documents). It is unclear if Alva Ixtlilxochitl used this or its underlying documents for his history. The early history of the Tolteca destruction and Chichimeca arrival under Xolotl that it recounts mirrors in broad strokes Alva Ixtlilxochitl's renditions of the same, although the text branches off from its focus

on the Tetzcoco rulers to zero in on the Teotihuacan rulership after its foundation by Techotlalatzin (Pérez-Rocha and Tena 2000a, 381–82). The text follows the ruling line through 1621, when Alva Ixtlilxochitl's older brother, Francisco de Navas Pérez de Peraleda, became cacique. The arrival of the "castellanos" and the "santa fe," in ce acatl [1 Reed or 1519] merits only a brief mention, although it marks a clear turning point, with the sub-altepetl's greatness and close ties to Tetzcoco emphasized beforehand and the many unsuccessful legal challenges to its legitimacy taking center stage afterward.

16. For more detail on the Nahua altepetl and its constituent groups, see Gibson (1964, 9–31) and Lockhart (1991, 9–11; 1992, 14–58); regarding its relationship to the colonial encomienda system, see also Gibson (1964, 58–81).

17. The bibliography on this point is manifold. Some English-language works include the volumes of the *Handbook of Middle American Indians* (1964–1976) dedicated to Mesoamerican ethnohistory (vols. 12–15), which provide an unsurpassed general overview and discussions of the corpus of extant documents from the pre-Hispanic period on; Joyce Marcus, *Mesoamerican Writing Systems* (1992); H. B. Nicholson's "Pre-Hispanic Central Mexican Historiography" (1971); Mathew Restall's article "Heirs to the Hieroglyphs" (1997); and Justyna Olko's "Alphabetic Writing in the Hands of the Colonial Nahua Nobility" (2010). Particularly pertinent, however, is the work of Elizabeth Hill Boone, including (but not limited to) her two major book-length studies *Stories in Red and Black* (2000) and *Cycles of Time and Meaning in the Mexican Books of Fate* (2007). She also coedited *Writing without Words* (1994) with Walter Mignolo and has an excellent article, "Pictorial Documents and Visual Thinking in Postconquest Mexico," in a volume, *Native Traditions in the Post-conquest World* (1992), that she edited with Tom Cummins. For an important touchstone and entryway into work on the sacred aspects of Nahua writing and its relationship to speech see Katarzyna Mikulska's "'Secret Language in Oral and Graphic Forms': Religious-Magic Discourse in Aztec Speeches and Manuscripts" (2010). Other general discussions of writing exclusively focused on the Nahua context include James Lockhart's *The Nahuas after the Conquest* (1992) and the work of Susan Schroeder (e.g. 1991), on Chimalpahin, but in particular her indispensable article, "The Meaning of 'Amoxtli' (Book) in Nahua New Spain" (2006). In the introduction to *The Learned Ones: Nahua Intellectuals in Postconquest Mexico* (2014, 3–33), Kelly S. McDonough offers an incisive general discussion of the writing *and* reading of Nahua documents from colonial to contemporary times. For an overview of traditions and styles of pictorial analysis across the major research languages in the field, see Michel R. Oudijk's (2008) "De tradiciones y métodos: investigaciones pictográficas."

18. Boone (2000, 24–25) writes, however, that the tlacuiloque were not all necessarily members of the noble class.

19. See also McDonough (2014, 3–18) for a discussion of the concept of the tlamatini and of the Nahua intellectual in a historical and contemporary context.

20. In her testamento, Alva Ixtlilxochitl's grandmother (Alva Ixtlilxochitl 1975–1977, 2:288), as the daughter of Fernando Cortés Ixtlilxochitl, also makes a claim to lands of the Tetzcoca cacicazgo being disputed in the courts; his mother reasserts these claims and importunes her children to pursue them (348). See Lee (2016) for a discussion of the relevance of the family's interest in their Tetzcoca claims for Alva Ixtlilxochitl's writing, especially the way in which he creates (or participates in the construction of) an early hero of his great-great-grandfather, Fernando Cortés Ixtlilxochitl, who disputed legitimate succession for rule with Cohuana-cochtzin, a brother. This dispute spilled over into the colonial period and helped erode the Tetzcoca cacicazgo early on.

21. In addition to his five prose histories, Alva Ixtlilxochitl is said to be responsible for translations and versions of popular songs (including a paraphrase, a poem in the form of a *lira* and another as a *romance*) attributed to Nezahualcoyotl, and for a separate poem (also a romance) entitled, "Romance del rey don Sancho o El cerco de Zamora" (O'Gorman [1975–1977] 1985, 1:221–22; 1975–1977, 2:267–73). The romances are found in the same manuscript as Juan Bautista Pomar's *Relación de Texcoco*, both of which were likely copied by Alva Ixtlilxochitl (Brian 2016, 25, 78, 101). Also copied by Alva Ixtlilxochitl, according to O'Gorman, are parts of the third section of the (mistitled) *Códice Ixtlilxóchitl* and the *Códice Chimalpopoca* ([1975–1977] 1985, 1:223–24). Schwaller (1994a, 101–2) provides evidence suggesting that the latter possibly could have belonged to Alva Ixtlilxochitl's brother, Bartolomé de Alva, referred to in note 5, who was a beneficed priest and author of a *confesionario* (confessionary) in Nahuatl. For more on the two brothers and their literary endeavors, see Brian (2010) and Schwaller (2014).

22. The work of Gordon Whittaker (2016, 57–66) on the Sigüenza manuscripts (the *Códice Chimalpahin*) confirms O'Gorman's *overall* ordering, dividing the texts into two groups. First, three early holographic works, which include the *Sumaria relación de todas las cosas que han sucedido en esta Nueva España* (whose section on Tolteca history was begun not earlier than 1601, and last revised in 1607) as well as the *Relación sucinta en forma de memorial* and the *Compendio histórico del reino de Texcoco* (which are dated around 1608). Second, two later, non-holographic works, which include the *Historia de la nación chichimeca* and the *Sumaria relación de la historia general*. Whittaker refrains from giving exact time frames for these latter texts, although he notes that they are written at least after 1615, the publication date of Torquemada's *Monarquía indiana*, which Alva Ixtlilxochitl mentions in the *Historia de la nación chichimeca*. He also mentions O'Gorman's suggestion of a composition date of shortly before 1625, if the unnamed addressee of the "Dedicatoria" (dedication) belonging to one of the later works was indeed Archbishop Pérez de la Serna. (Regarding this latter point, see note 25 below and chapter 4.)

23. The first work is divided into two segments, with a five-part representation of Tolteca history ([1975–1977] 1985, 1:261–88) that runs from the creation of the world

through the empire's demise followed by a thirteen-part history (289–381) of the
Chichimeca colonization of the region that runs from the arrival of Xolotl through
Nezahualcoyotl's reestablishment of Acolhua rule over the region after the defeat
of the Tepaneca. It concludes with a description of Nezahualcoyotl's installation of
a subordinate (tribute-paying) nobility or elite in conquered territories—including
in Teotihuacan with the installation (or reinstallation) of Alva Ixtlilxochitl's direct
ancestor (a great-great-great-great-grandfather) Mamalitzin (Münch [1976, 9]
calls him Quetzalmamalitzin), as ruler—along with an overview of the educational, religious, legal, military, and agricultural/labor order established by Nezahualcoyotl (378–81). The second text (395–413) is indeed very "succinct" and
comes with a dedication to a viceroy—most likely Luís de Velasco the younger,
Marquis of Salinas (204)—asking him to remember "los pobres descendientes
de estos señores" (the poor descendents of these lords). It is made up of twelve
relaciones (accounts) highlighting Tolteca (relaciones 1 and 2) and Chichimeca
(relaciones 3–12) royal lineages, picking up on Chichimeca history with Xolotl's
great-grandfather and providing a narrative of the lives of each ruler in succession,
following the Acolhua line through the reign of Nezahualpilli (Nezahualcoyotl's
son and heir). At the end of the text (408–12) there are three supplementary sections providing full recountings of Mexica and Xochimilca genealogy, the former
through the rule of Cuauhtemoc. The third text, the *Compendio histórico del reino
de Texcoco*, is made up of a total of thirteen relaciones, the last of which (450–517)
is longer than the first twelve (417–50) put together. Relaciones one through twelve
trace the identity and origins of the earliest inhabitants of the Central Mexican
region from the (legendary) giants and the Tolteca—including their Chichimeca
origins—through their descendents in the Acolhua ruling line up to the death of
Nezahualpilli. The famous thirteenth relación is dedicated exclusively to narrating
the Spanish wars of invasion and conquest, with a focus on the contributions of the
Acolhua, especially of (Fernando Cortés) Ixtlilxochitl, Alva Ixtlilxochitl's direct
ancestor, to the Spanish cause. In addition to relating the conquest of Tenochtitlan, it discusses Cortés's posterior, disastrous, expedition to Hibueras (now Hon-
duras), where Cortés killed Cuauhtemoc as well as the tlatoque of Tlacopan and
Tetzcoco (albeit indirectly in the latter case, due to Fernando Cortés Ixtlilxochitl's
intervention) (503). The reader should also note Schwaller's (2014, 45) description of Alva Ixtlilxochitl's historical works, based more closely on their appearance in Boturini's catalogue, and creating a distinction between the Tolteca and
Chichimeca accounts. Here, Schwaller reminds us of Alva Ixtlilxochitl's research
methods, as a "compiler and translator" (43) and "interpreter" of his sources who
strove to make Tetzcoca history legible to a Spanish audience and who "clearly
saw that he could occupy an important mediating position between the dominant
Spanish culture and the colonized Nahua culture of Texcoco" (48).

24. It is certainly the magnum opus of his known texts, and O'Gorman assumes that
it is his major historical endeavor. There remains the mystery, however, of Alva

Ixtlilxochitl's reference on several occasions to a text (or texts) that he is writing or plans to write (i.e., to a work divided into "libros" or based on the nine Chichimeca rulers in the *Relación sucinta en forma de memorial* ([1975–1977] 1985, 1:412) and to a history including the story of an original migration of the Chichimeca from "la Gran Tartaria . . . de los de la división de Babilonia" (417; the Great Tartary . . . of those from the division of Babylon) in the *Compendio*, but which do not specifically conform to anything in his known body of work. Whittaker (2016, e.g., 58, 63) assumes that the *Relación sucinta* refers to (or summarizes) the *Compendio*. O'Gorman ([1975–1977] 1985, 1:230–31), on the other hand, surmising a closer relationship between the *Relación sucinta* and the *Sumaria relación de todas las cosas*, suggests that Alva Ixtlilxochitl simply never followed through with that early plan and points to other indications of missing texts, including Alva Ixtlilxochitl's Spanish-language translations of speeches given to young girls who were being dedicated to temples, which Sigüenza included in his *Parayso occidental* (218–20). It is perhaps not *impossible* that Alva Ixtlilxochitl could have planned or begun to write other works or another history (or other histories), although nothing else seems to have reached the hands of Sigüenza y Góngora, nor has any trace of other works surfaced elsewhere in the intervening years.

25. In O'Gorman's ([1975–1977] 1985, 1:214, 216, 231–32) view, the *Sumaria relación de la historia general* was likely written shortly before the *Historia de la nación chichimeca*, serving as a guide or outline for the longer project. He bases his discussion on the content of the texts and a reference in the "Prólogo al lector" (prologue to the reader) in which Alva Ixtlilxochitl refers to the burning of the pre-Hispanic Tetzcoco archives and how he came to be in possession of (what he assumed were) the surviving texts, "de donde he sacado y traducido la historia que prometo, aunque al presente en breve y sumaria relación" (527; from which I have taken and translated the history that I promise [to write], although [it is] at present a brief and summary account). Brian (2014b, 99) seems certain that the "Prólogo" and the "Dedicatoria" or dedication (written on the same folio) belong to the *Historia de la nación chichimeca*, in front of which they are placed in the binding of the manuscripts (BNAH CC 2, 5–6; Ruwet fol. 1r and v) although she does not specify her reasons for thinking this. O'Gorman ([1975–1977] 1985, 1:212–13) was *aware* that the prefatory texts were likely *bound* with the *Historia de la nación chichimeca* in Sigüenza's original, but nevertheless continued to believe that they were *written* for the *Sumaria relación de la historia general*. It is true that, in the manuscripts, as Brian notes (2014b, 86), the *Historia de la nación chichimeca* (also) bears the title "*Sumaria relación*," thus confusing Alva Ixtlilxochitl's reference to the "current" text (as opposed to the one he was "promising") as a "breve y sumaria relación" (brief and summary account). Without clear evidence from a close study of the manuscripts and their binding, it is impossible to make any kind of judgment on this matter. However, if indeed the "Prologue" does belong with the *Historia de la nación chichimeca*, one wonders, once again (see note 24 above), what longer history he might have been promising to write.

The chronology established by O'Gorman ([1975–1977] 1985, 1:229–33) (with useful information also found in his analytical bibliography [197–225] of Alva Ixtlilxochitl's texts) is based on substantial evidence gleaned from the texts themselves, such as comparisons of content, their stylistic features, chronologies, and internal dates to contemporary events as well as his comparison of the extant copies made of the texts and the annotations of their copyists. There is no reason to believe that Sigüenza's ordering of the manuscripts in their current binding (if indeed it was Sigüenza who bound them together) conforms to or reflects their order of composition, since the manuscripts themselves are undated (except for the *Compendio*), and Sigüenza received them from Alva Ixtlilxochitl's son. Indeed, the binding arrangement seems to follow other criteria, namely, the placement of the *Historia de la nación chichimeca* and the *Compendio* together in a single volume as a "complete" history of the Acolhua reign through the conquest period; the placement of the rest of Alva Ixtlilxochitl's (known) texts alongside their addenda and other Spanish-language documents (collected by Alva Ixtlilxochitl) by indigenous nobility in another volume; and, in a third, the Nahuatl-language work of Chimalpahin along with various other (mostly Nahuatl language) texts and works of indigenous historiography. (See Ruwet (1997, 1:17–24) for a listing of the contents and their foliation, and Brian (2014b) and Whittaker (2016) for discussions of the manuscripts and their dates and order of composition.)

26. I agree wholeheartedly with the following assessment by O'Gorman ([1975–1977] 1985, 1:217–18) and seek to explicate especially his sense of the text's unity, its provision of a sense of "clasicismo propio" (its own classicism) to Mexican historiography, its indispensability for understanding Alva Ixtlilxochitl's historical vision of the pre-Hispanic past, and its status as a text of utmost importance in the formation of "la conciencia novohispana y . . . nacional" (the identity of New Spain and . . . the nation):

> Ciertamente, el propósito de exaltar sobre los demás el señorío texcocano y el valor, virtud y sabiduría de sus monarcas le ha atraído a la obra la condenación de la crítica objetivista, pero independientemente del elemento de ceguera que implica semejante criterio, lo que importa es subrayar la concepción unitaria que domina al relato y que pone en relieve una secuencia lógica de los sucesos como marcha hacia el cumplimiento del más alto destino. Se ofrece, así, un panorama congruente y significativo del antiguo acontecer histórico de México, que le concede al libro, pese a su transparente parcialidad e incluso gracias a ella, el privilegio de ser, si no el primero, uno de los primeros y mejor logrado intento de proporcionarle a la incipiente conciencia novohispana el indispensable apoyo de contar con un clasicismo propio que cuente como un valor en el marco de la historia universal.
>
> La historia no es solo, pues, la obra definitiva del autor a la que debe recurrirse preferentemente para captar su concepción del pasado indígena, sino una obra de la más subida importancia en el complejo proceso de la

formación de la conciencia novohispana y en último término, de la conciencia nacional.

Certainly, the purpose of exalting the Texcoca realm and the worth, virtue and wisdom of its rulers above all others has earned the work the condemnation of objectivist criticism, but apart from the element of blindness that this type of critique implies, what is important is to underscore the unitary conception that pervades the work and that emphasizes a logical sequence of events as a march toward the fulfillment of the highest destiny. In this way, a congruent and significant panorama of ancient historical occurrences in Mexico is offered that lends the book, despite its transparent bias and even thanks to it, the privilege of being, if not the first, one of the first and best attempts to lend to the incipient [self] consciousness of New Spain the indispensable support of relying on an autochthonous New Spanish classicism of recognizable value in the context of the universal history.

The history is not only, then, the definitive work of the author to which we must preferably recur in order to capture his conception of the indigenous past, but also a work of utmost importance in the complex process of the formation of the consciousness of New Spain, and, in the final analysis, of national consciousness.

27. For more on the relationship between the Alva Ixtlilxochitl family and Carlos de Sigüenza y Góngora, and Alva Ixtlilxochitl's work in the context of the creation of a Native archive, see Brian (2007, 2014b, 2016) as well as Inoue Okubo (2007, especially 78–85). Townsend (2014, 2016) argues that Alva Ixtlilxochitl gained access to some of his Franciscan materials, including the *Codex Chimalpopoca* (which contains two Nahuatl-language annals with versions of the legend of the suns), through fray Juan de Torquemada and the library of the Church of San Francisco in Mexico City. Regarding the connection of his writing to the now-lost work of don Alonso Axayaca, a historian of Tetzcoco with connections to both Acolhua and Mexica ancestry, see Lesbre (1995, 178–80), Villella (2016, 121), and Pérez-Rocha and Tena (2000b, 56–57). Lesbre's article traces the history of alphabeticization (and evangelization) in Acolhuacan, and provides a detailed summary of early and unpublished (or recently published) sources for Acolhua history whose traces are found in Alva Ixtlilxochitl's work and other texts.

28. These are but two important recent examples. For the *Codex Xolotl*, Charles E. Dibble's (1951) reproduction and study continues to be an indispensable starting point.

29. Schwaller (1994a, 95–96; 1999, 4) argues that it does not seem likely, as it is sometimes assumed given the clear familiarity with humanist tradition in his oeuvre, that Alva Ixtlilxochitl attended the famous Colegio de Tlatelolco, as presented in the full title (seen in O'Gorman [1975–1977] 1985, 1:214) of the Veytia copy of the

Boturini text. Based on a close examination of his handwriting, Whittaker (2016, 41) infers a less sophisticated level of education, suggesting that he possibly received his education from someone in the legal profession. Townsend (2014, 3) says that "he must have been educated in the city, and he was certainly an apt student, for his family expected for a number of years that he would become a priest." Brian (2016, 93–95) assumes a basic level of education with some knowledge of the humanistic tradition, perhaps gained through his reading of Torquemada and others.

30. Schwaller (1994a, 96) notes that his parents had their "principal residence and held the bulk of their land" in San Juan Teotihuacan. Discussing his arduous task as a historian, Alva Ixtlilxochitl comments, "y cierto que con tener las historias en mi poder, y saber la lengua como los mismos naturales, porque me crié con ellos [*sic*], y conocer a todos los viejos y principales de esta tierra para haber de sacar esto en limpio, me ha costado harto estudio y trabajo, procurando siempre la verdad de cada cosa de estas que tengo escrito, y escribiré en la historia de los chichimecos" ([1975–1977] 1985, 1:288; and truly even with the histories in my possession, and knowing the language like the Indians themselves, because I was raised with them [*sic*], and knowing all the elders and lords of this land, finishing this has cost me abundant study and work, always striving for the truth of everything that I have written, and will write in the history of the Chichimeca). See the discussion of this passage and its transcription in O'Gorman by Whittaker (2016, 50–51); instead of "me crié con ellos" Whittaker reads "it" (or "con él").

31. It is a positive assessment of him:

> On the same said day of Wednesday in the said [month], as night came, was when there passed away Juan Grande, a Spaniard, who interpreted for the lord viceroy; he died very old, and for many years he interpreted for other lords viceroys, all those who have come here to New Spain and ruled. The said Juan Grande was a very good person; he did not cheat poor commoners who come to bring suit before the viceroys, like another person who interpreted, who died earlier, whose name was Francisco de Leiva; he was evil and greatly mistreated the poor commoners. The said Juan Grande was governor here in Mexico Tenochtitlan; [the office] belonged to him, given to him by the lord viceroy don Luis de Velasco, Marqués de Salinas, and for five years he held the governorship. The mestizo whose name was mentioned above, named don Juan Pérez de Monterrey, is just his representative and helps him, is just hired by him, so that he himself is the appointed governor here in Mexico Tenochtitlan, and it is said that the two of them, [Pérez de Monterrey] and the said Juan Grande, share the salary. (Chimalpahin 2006, 305)

32. In his "Dedicatoria" to the *Historia de la nación chichimeca* (or to its related *Sumaria relación de la historia general*, as the case may be [see note 25]), he writes, "Desde mi adolescencia tuve siempre gran deseo de saber las cosas acaecidas en

este Nuevo Mundo, que no fueron menos que las de los romanos, griegos, medos y otras repúblicas gentílicas que tuvieron fama en el universo" ([1975–1977] 1985, 1:525; Ever since I was an adolescent I have had a great desire to know about the things that have happened in this New World, which were not less than those of the Romans, Greeks, Medes, and other gentile republics that were famous in the world). For further discussion of this important text, see chapter 4 and the conclusion.

33. In the *Historia de la nación chichimeca*, for example, Alva Ixtlilxochitl carefully explains that he follows the Tlaxcalteca sources in his description of the entrance of Cortés to the region, rather than the Spanish:

> Y todo lo más que he escrito y adelante escribiré, es según las relaciones y pinturas que escribieron los señores naturales recién ganada la tierra, que se hallaron en los lances acontecidos en aquellos tiempos; porque en cuanto a las cosas de nuestros españoles, y más notables en aquestos tiempos, Francisco de Gómara en su *Historia de Indias*, Antonio de Herrera en su *Crónica*, el reverendo padre fray Juan Torquemada en su *Monarquía indiana*, y como testigo de vista el invictísimo don Fernando Cortés, marqués del Valle, en las cartas y relaciones que envió a su majestad, todos tratan muy especificadamente, en donde los curiosos lectores hallarán a medida de sus deseos lo que quisieren. (1975–1977, 2:235)

> And everything else that I have written and will write in the future is according to the accounts and paintings that the rightful lords wrote soon after the land was conquered, [and] who found themselves in the predicaments that occurred during that time; because with respect to things about our Spaniards, the most noteworthy of those times are explained very carefully by Francisco de Gómara in his *Historia de Indias*, Antonio de Herrera in his *Crónica*, the revered father friar Juan de Torquemada in his *Monarquía indiana*, and as eye-witness the unconquerable sir Fernando Cortés, Marquis of the Valley, in the letters and accounts that he sent to his Majesty, wherein curious readers will find whatever they wish to know, in accordance with their desires.

He also notes his predilection for certain (especially elite) native sources over Spanish in his commentary succeeding the Tolteca histories of the *Sumaria relación de todas las cosas*: "Muchas historias he leído de españoles que han escrito las cosas de esta tierra, que todas ellas son tan fuera de lo que está en la original historia y las de todos éstos, y entre las falsas, la que en alguna cosa conforma es la de Francisco Gómara" ([1975–1977] 1985, 1:287; I have read many histories by Spaniards who have written of the things of this land, which all fall far outside of what is in the original history, and of all of these, and among the false ones, the one which in some respect conforms to it is that of Francisco Gómara).

34. In this sense, my work picks up on that of García Loaeza (2006, 2010, 2014), which tells the important story—rooted in postcolonial theory—of how Fernando de Alva Ixtlilxochitl created a version of the indigenous past that conformed in every way to the medieval heritage of the European tradition and yet retained enough of a particular, exotic veneer to serve the purposes of creole historians looking to root their claims of difference from the metropolis in a venerable autochthonous tradition. (For more on this latter point see also García Loaeza [2009] and Villella [2016].) While García Loaeza emphasizes the fabricated and European nature of Alva Ixtlilxochitl's version of the past, however, I focus on the presence and significance of aspects of the Nahua historiographical tradition that *remain* in his writing, arguing that his histories are not as "European" as they (are made to) appear. Like García Loaeza (2006, 27–37), I am interested in the ways that Alva Ixtlilxochitl and Torquemada use and frame the information they gleaned from their source texts (many of which they had in common) for their own ends.

35. As Elsa Cecilia Frost (1983, 71–72) points out, at the time of its publication in 1615, the *Monarquía indiana* was one of the only printed accounts written in the New World about its pre-Hispanic history and peoples. It was, moreover, the very first history of New Spain to be published by a Franciscan. This fact, along with the supplementary material it provides on Tetzcoco, missing in López de Gómara's history, could help explain—given the plethora of historical *manuscripts* in circulation—Alva Ixtlilxochitl's use of the term *primer* to describe Torquemada as a historian. Alva Ixtlilxochitl's respect for his contemporary is unequivocal, but his work, as León Portilla (1983b, 101) and Townsend (2014, 12) remark, clearly reflects *independent* scholarship and his own engagement with the past.

36. In particular, see León Portilla (1983c, 99–102); Lesbre (2001); O'Gorman ([1975–1977] 1985, 1:84) and Townsend (2014). In his critical edition of Torquemada's history, moreover, León Portilla (1983d, under "Volúmen 7. Tablas de análisis de las fuentes") provides an extensive table of *all* of Torquemada's probable source material. In this invaluable resource, the convergences and divergences with Alva Ixtlilxochitl's texts, as well as with Tetzcoca materials the two likely had in common, are identified. Lesbre's (2001) comments on the two historians' potential relationship occur in the context of a detailed study of their respective presentations of a particular story. Speaking of the two historians' works in general, however, he notes that,

> Leurs rapports contrastés justifieraient à eux seuls une étudie approfondie tant ils sont nombreux et changeants. (Ixtlilxochitl passant alternativement du statut d'informateur ou collaborateur à celui d'historien s'inspirant de l'oeuvre de son contemporain.) (13)

Their contrasting accounts deserve their own in-depth study, as they are so numerous and variable. (Ixtlilxochitl's status changes from that of informant or collaborator to historian taking inspiration from the work of his contemporary.)

   A truly detailed study of Alva Ixtlilxochitl's sources (as undertaken by León Portilla for Torquemada) is still waiting to be done. However, a few brief observations are in order. First, Lee (2008, 27–45) provides an excellent summary account of Alva Ixtlilxochitl's source material for his representation of Nezahualcoyotl, which I think holds true for his work in general. He notes the roots of Alva Ixtlilxochitl's depictions in the work of Motolinía and Olmos and points to the fact that every constituency had its particular use for the representation of the Tetzcoca ruler, writing that "the Franciscans tried to prove that the natives were capable of building a Christian kingdom in the New World, and the Dominican Las Casas presented it as clear evidence of rationality. The Texcoca chroniclers such as Alva Ixtlilxochitl, on the other hand, built on the Franciscan image of Nezahualcoyotl, adding a Christian dimension to their ancestors' achievements in order to obtain favor from the king" (37). Second, I will add that, for purposes of this book, it is important to note that certain elements of the early history of Anahuac (previous to the arrival of Xolotl) presented in the *Monarquía indiana* ([1723] 1975, 1:255–68), and also found (with variants) in the Tlaxcalteca writings of Muñoz Camargo that constituted Torquemada's source material (León Portilla 1983d, under "Volúmen 7. Tablas de análisis de las fuentes, libro III, cap. 7–12"), beginning with the notion of Quetzalcoatl as an outsider arrived from the east (or north, Pánuco) and eventually associated with Cholula, make a significant appearance only in the *Historia de la nación chichimeca* and the *Sumaria relación de la historia general*. Finally, note also that Douglas (2010) and Lesbre (e.g., 199b, 2012) treat points of convergence and divergence with Alva Ixtlilxochitl's *pictorial* source texts.

37. For more on this matter, see, for example, Baudot (1995, 71–120) and Phelan (1956). It is important to note that the early Tetzcoca sources themselves of course would have been influenced by the missionary context, and the later works by the same early Franciscan sources used by Torquemada.

38. For a history of the school at Santiago Tlatelolco and the early ethnohistorical work of the Franciscans, see José María Kobayashi (1974) and also Baudot (1995, 104–20), who roots the establishment of the school in the early ethnographic work of the Franciscans and the discovery of the *calmecac* and its patron, the god Quetzalcoatl (106–7).

39. The term is taken from Bakhtin (1981) who, in general terms, uses it to refer to the ways that time and space are related in literature. I rely here, however, on Michael Holquist's ([1990] 2002, chapters 5 and 6) in-depth discussion of the term in Bakhtin's oeuvre. See note 43, for a description.

40. When Walter Mignolo talks about how colonial literature (or colonial semiosis) represents the "discontinuity" of the classical tradition, he refers to the way in which it interrupts and appropriates for its own ends the European tradition of historical writing rooted in Christianity and based on the classical Greek and Roman models, historical writing that was forged in the universities of the European Renaissance (1992a, 185, 187–89, 191–92, 197, 199; 1992b, 303, 324–25; 1995, 204). For Mignolo, the spread of Western literacy undertaken by the Spanish friars in the early colonial years implied the colonization of indigenous languages, forms of expression, memories, and histories. However, he notes, the native speakers of indigenous languages educated by these friars used and adapted their training as Renaissance European men of letters "to sustain their own cultural traditions" and to write histories that "punctuate . . . the plurilingual and multicultural character of colonial situations" and that reveal "the fractured symbolic world of colonial situations" (1992b, 324–25).

41. Cornejo Polar ([1995] 2005a) uses the term to emphasize the multiple contexts in which literature—from different traditions—is produced within Latin American nation states. It strives to maintain its distance from notions of mestizaje and its theoretical corollary, transculturation, which he argues fail to take fully into account the contradictory and conflictive dynamics of colonial situations, especially in the Andes. Heterogeneity—the dynamic coexistence of multiple literary traditions—can be seen in a single text, as well as within a single national context, what he refers to as a "totalidad contradictoria" (1983). In contrast to homogenous literature ([1978] 2005b, 104)—"The mobilization of all instances of the literary process within the same sociocultural order" or a "society speaking to itself"—"the duplicity or plurality of the sociocultural signs of the productive process characterizes the heterogeneous literatures: in summary, it has to do with a process that has at least one element that does not coincide with the filiation of the others and thus necessarily creates a zone of ambiguity and conflict." They are "two distinct systems of literary production" (105). In a beautiful summation of his vision of Latin American literature, he writes that it is most incisively characterized by

> la copiosa red de conflictos y contradicciones sobre la que se teje un discurso excepcionalmente complejo, complejo porque es producido y produce formas de conciencia muy dispares, a veces entre si incompatibles; porque entrecruzan discursos de varia procedencia y contextura, donde el multilingüismo o las diglosias fuertes son frecuentes y decisivas, incluyendo los muchos niveles que tiene la confrontación entre oralidad y escritura; o porque, en fin, supone una historia hecha de muchos tiempos y ritmos, algo así como una multihistoria que tanto adelanta en el tiempo como se abisma, acumulativamente, en su solo momento. Como decía Enrique Lihn en un verso memorable, los latinoamericanos "somos contemporáneos de historias diferentes." (1999, 11)

the copious network of conflicts and contradictions over which an excep-
tionally complex discourse is woven, complex because it is produced by and
produces very disparate forms of consciousness, sometimes incompatible
within themselves; because discourses of various origins and make-up inter-
twine, where multilingualism or strong diglossias are frequent and decisive,
including the many levels of the confrontation between orality and writing;
or because, in the end, it supposes a history made from many times and
rhythms, something like a multihistory that progresses in time as much as it
sinks, little by little, into its sole moment. As Enrique Lihn wrote in a memorable line, we Latin Americans "are contemporaries of different histories."

42. This is not to say that Alva Ixtlilxochitl does not criticize, both explicitly and
implicitly, certain aspects of colonial violence. Indeed, his work as a whole can be
read as a lament of lost possibilities in the face of Spanish failures to maintain and
build on the (supposed) strengths of the world they encountered in carrying out
their providential mission. In this sense, it echoes the disappointments expressed
by the early Franciscans in New Spain.

43. In "Discourse and the Novel," Bakhtin (1981, see especially 324–29) refers to
double-voiced discourse in terms of the way in which the (socially stratified) languages of the novel belong to the characters but also to the author as the one who,
in constructing the work of art, orchestrates their interaction and also refracts,
through each of them (and in the larger scheme), his or her own intentions. The
discourse of the novel is thus "internally dialogized" in recreating (representing)
the speech of the characters and allowing them to speak for themselves (with their
own ideological positions or frameworks) and to each other, but also in carrying
forth, through those characters, the meanings or intentions of the author who
organizes the characters' speech and creates the dialogic world of the novel. In *Historia de la literatura nahuatl*, Ángel María Garibay (1953, 1:493), in his discussion
of the Nezahualcoyotl stories, refers to Alva Ixtlilxochitl's "novelistic" discourse;
indeed, although it is *not* a novel, I believe the *Historia de la nación chichimeca*
reflects what Holquist ([1990] 2002, 73) calls Bakhtin's concept of "novelness,"
which is, as Holquist puts it, "the name of his real hero." As the quality of the
novel that accounts for its artistry and power, but which is not *bound* to the genre,
Holquist writes that, "Novelness is a means for charting changes that have come
about as a result of increasing sensitivity to the problem of non-identity. Greater
or lesser degrees of novelness can serve as an index of greater or lesser awareness of otherness. The history of the novel has its place in literary history, but the
history of novelness is situated in the history of human consciousness." In other
words, novelness reflects an awareness of the nonunitary nature of language and
the world; it is opposed to world of the epic, which admits no gap between a word,
its meaning, and the world it represents. While Torquemada faithfully records the
history of the other, he appropriates it into his *epic*, into his monological version

of the European universal history. Alva Ixtlilxochitl, I contend, appropriates that "epic" historical consciousness and dialogizes it, imbuing it with an *other* sense of history, of time, place, and the events that (con)figure it. An incisive analysis of the relevance of Bakhtin for studying the literature of colonial Latin America (and of cultural encounter more generally) can be found in Michael Palencia-Roth's (1992) "Quarta Orbis Pars: Monologizing the New World."

44. For more on the encomienda (grants of "Indian" labor to Spanish conquistadores in reward for their service to the Crown), see the reference in note 12.

45. For discussion on the significant role of women in traditional Nahua genealogies, see, for example, Gillespie (1989). Brian (2016, 42–62) describes the importance of women in Alva Ixtlilxochitl's own lineage.

46. Holquist ([1990] 2002, 107–82) places Bakhtin's use of this term in the context of the distinction (originating in Shlovsky) between the actual chronology of events and their arrangement in the plot (the fábula or story), wherein the art of the narrative lies in its *deformation* (vis-à-vis the emplotment of events) of the story (or the events "as they happened"). As Holquist notes, however, Bakhtin, informed by Einstein's 1905 presentation of his theory of relativity, crucially does not assume a transparent, universal, chronology of events (in "real life") (114–16). The perspectival nature of time/space and its reflection of (or immersion in) events and the ways these are represented in written texts is key to my sense of Alva Ixtlilxochitl's figuration (or figures) of time and its/their relation to (his portrayal of) the events of the conquest and its significance. "In other words," writes Holquist, "the means by which any presumed plot deforms any particular story will depend not only on formal ('made') features in a given text, but also on generally held conceptions of how time and space relate to each other in a particular culture at a particular time ('given' features)" (116). I do not explicate herein the *many* chronotopes (140–45) that inhabit the *Historia de la nación chichimeca*, although there is a rich array of essays that could be written. Instead, I focus on those figures that play an important role in the structuration of "plot" or narrative in the text.

47. If Alva Ixtlilxochitl was not aware of Tezcatlipoca's importance or his place alongside Quetzalcoatl in myth as he wrote his early histories, he would certainly have been aware after reading the *Monarquía indiana*.

48. Although the *memoria testamentaria* (testamentary account) of his wife notes that he *did* at least leave a testamento legitimizing his children. Identifying her three children, the memoria declares that they are legitimate and a product of her marriage to Fernando de Alva Ixtlilxochitl, "el cual, en el testamento que otorgó en esta ciudad, ante Jacinto Curiel, escribano real, so cuya disposición falleció, deja asimismo nombrados por sus hijos legítimos a los susodichos, y otras cosas contenidas en dicho testamento, que hoy para en poder del dicho don Juan de Alba Cortés, su hijo" (1975–1977, 2:390; who, in the testament that he gave in this city before Jacinto Curiel, royal notary, under the authority of which he died, leaves the aforementioned identified as his legitimate offspring, as well as other things con-

tained in said testament, which is today held by Juan de Alba Cortés, his son). In the court case that Alva Ixtlilxochitl's younger brother (Luis) brings against Alva Ixtlilxochitl's eldest son (Juan) for possession of the cacicazgo, there is no mention of a testament by Alva Ixtlilxochitl, although there is a mention of a declaration that the cacique (Alva Ixtlilxochitl's older brother, Francisco, who died after Alva Ixtlilxochitl) made confirming Alva Ixtlilxochitl's son as "legítimo sucesor de dicho cacicazgo por ser hijo legítimo de su hermano inmediato don Fernando" and in favor of his right to possession of the cacicazgo (1975–1977, 2:381; legitimate heir of said cacicazgo as the legitimate son of his closest brother, don Fernando).

49. Among the many particular devotions expressed in the last wills and testaments of Alva Ixtlilxochitl's forebearers, such as the one to Saint Francis, there seems to have been a long-standing devotion to Saint Catharine, martyr, in the family, as Vásquez (2013, 140) points out. This is first seen with Alva Ixtlilxochitl's grandmother, who asks that priests from the parish of Santa Catarina Mártir accompany her body to its place of burial in the church at Santiago Tlatelolco in Mexico City (1975–1977, 2:287). The testamentos of Alva Ixtlilxochitl's great-grandfather and grandmother (Alva Ixtlilxochitl 1975–1977, 2:281–91), mother (338–42), and father (346–49) reveal many particular devotions and memberships in religious brotherhoods, or cofradías, and can be found in the invaluable "Apéndice documental" (O'Gorman 1975–1977, 2:265–402) in O'Gorman's edition of Alva Ixtlilxochitl's works.

CHAPTER ONE

1. Although Münch (1976) provides some interesting clues to the fate of the town of San Juan Teotihuacan under and also after don Francisco Verdugo Quetzalmamalitzin Huetzin's tenure, when the cabildo or town council took over, Lee (2016) provides a slightly contrasting account. The introduction to the Pérez-Rocha and Tena (2000b, 20–29) collection contains a concise and illuminating summary of the broader sociopolitical and legislative issues facing the nobility as a whole, from the time of Cortés onward, placing the Teotihuacan cacicazgo in this context. Manuel Gamio's *La población del Valle de Teotihuacan* (1922) also provides a comprehensive and region-specific picture of the social, economic, and geographical status of the town in the colonial period and of Alva Ixtlilxochitl's family within it. Not all of its assumptions on various matters are correct or can be corroborated, however.

2. See also Schwaller (1994b) on scholars (most notably Alva Ixtlilxochitl's younger brother, Bartolomé) and manuscripts affiliated with the work of the Jesuit priest (and Nahuatl scholar) Horacio Carochi and on the brothers' distinguished participation in an early seventeenth-century "flowering of a literary tradition that in many ways synthesized the pre-Columbian Nahua tradition of Texcoco with the new Spanish culture" (2014, 43).

3. This was an effort that was aimed at separating the "wheat" from the "chaff" of the

indigenous cultures, so to speak. The Franciscans were interested in preserving those aspects of indigenous cultures, including forms of religious "worship," that they felt conformed to Christian ideals, such as poverty, humility, sobriety, and public fiestas dedicated to their gods. Their early research on history and mythology, tied to religious or cosmological notions, reflects this search for "commonalities" or for indigenous concepts that could successfully translate or stand in for European religious and theological concepts. This approach would inevitably influence the Nahua colonial culture and religiosity. For a classic discussion of the problems this approach entailed, see Burkhart (1989).

4. For more historical context (apart from Alva Ixtlilxochitl's texts) on Fernando Cortés Ixtlilxochitl's relationship to the Tetzcoca rulership before, during, and after the conquest, see Lee (2016, 136–42).

5. Note that the date but not the manner of death is mentioned in the *Relación del señorío de Teotihuacan* (Pérez-Rocha and Tena 2000a, 388).

6. Münch (1976, 9) calls him Manahuatzin, not Mamalitzin.

7. Just as the Mexica officially appointed and approved the Tetzcoco rulers, so the Tetzcoco rulers approved the successors to the Teotihuacan rulership. For more information on the political structures of the confederated altepetl, or Nahua ethnic state, see Lockhart (1991, 3–11; 1992, 14–28).

8. It is not clear if this was in fact due to age or if this was just the reason given in the document. Münch simply states that he was "confirmado . . . por la Real Audiencia en todo su señorío, con sus tierras, tributarios y gobierno" (1976, 10; confirmed . . . by the Real Audiencia in all of his estate, with its lands, tribute payers, and government) and therefore it seems to have been an economically and politically motivated request. The *Relación* also makes clear the economic consequences of this royal order. After listing the members of the Audiencia, it states that, "Así pues, el señor don Francisco heredó todos los tributos de este pueblo" (388–89; therefore, the lord don Francisco inherited all of the tributes of this town). In the Nahuatl original, don Francisco is called "in tlatohuani don Francisco" while the archbishop, friar Juan de Zumárraga is called "in tlatohuani obispo," with Pérez-Rocha and Tena's Spanish translation reading "el señor obispo" (389).

9. See Lockhart (1992, 104–10) for a discussion of the "western" region of central Mexico, where the institution was more closely integrated into the calpulli structure. In the calpulli system, the macehualtin held lands independently of those of the teuhctli; they paid tribute to the calpulli head (who was also the teuhctli) but were not considered dependents or retainers (in many cases outsiders) of or on lands that were possessed by the teteuhctin. In practical terms, Lockhart remarks that the distinction seems more abstract than real, being a case of emphasis, as the same teuhctli would be the lord of his patrimonial estate and of the calpulli as a whole, although in some senses the two systems did compete with one another. See also Schroeder (1991, 205–21) for a more nuanced discussion of variations in the altepetl subdivisions or constituent parts, and their relationship to rulership

(and its own subdivisions), and Pedro Carrasco (1994), who also looks at potential regional differences through an examination of the Puebla-Tlaxcala material presented in Alonso Zorita's work, based on the now-lost writing of friar Francisco de las Navas. Carrasco's article supports the view that the calpulli corporate structure was tied into the political structure of the tecalli in essentially the same ways across central Mexico: differences indicated in the descriptions from eastern Puebla-Tlaxcala regions are more apparent than real (77). The article provides a useful overview of the essential uses and definitions of central terms used to indicate Nahua social organization—the teccalli, the *mayeque*, and the *calpoll*.

10. Lockhart concentrates his discussion on social formations. Gruzinski (1989), however, discusses the pilli-macehualli distinction in terms of a Nahua perception of power in which the pipiltin, through ritual penitence and other acts, were regarded as having (or being infused with) greater "divine energy that came to strengthen the life spirit (*tonalli*) of the body." He writes, "Thus, in the course of the rites of enthronement and divinization, the sovereign was literally inundated with that divine and protective energy that his body soon diffused" (20).

11. Schroeder (1991, 209) likewise describes the altepetl as consisting of "people, rulership, and land." Robert Haskett, in his up-close study of postconquest rupture and continuity in forms of rulership in colonial Cuernavaca, *Indigenous Rulers: An Ethnohistory of Town Government in Colonial Cuernavaca*, emphasizes the religious and governmental institutions in his definition, saying that "Altepetl status required the possession of deities and religious structures dedicated to them, a government palace, a market, and a land base. They were complex units made up of a number of equal parts, or districts, called either *tlaxillacalli* or *calpulli*, each with a ruling dynasty" (9). His work shows in great detail for the context of Cuernavaca how the larger elite base of the traditional structures of power managed to survive through the Spanish cabildo system, which was adapted and adjusted to meet colonial realities and conditions. He notes that, under the Spanish and throughout the colonial period—even as the population of non-Indians increased—only the "highest levels of traditional rule were obliterated or usurped by the intruders during the first, unstable years following the conquest" (4).

12. For a particularly poignant example of how difficult this was, see the "Texcoca Accounts of Conquest Episodes" (*Codex Chimalpahin* 1997, 2:201–7).

13. See Ouweneel (1995, 771) and Romero Galván (2003, 31–73) for a discussion of the transition from tlatocayotl to gobernadoryotl. Ouweneel argues that the gobernadoryotl was the clear inheritor of the pre-Hispanic tlatocayotl in the pueblos, as well as the cacique, except that the cacicazgos (with their *terrazgueros* or workers) in general broke up due to the lack of correspondence of pre-Hispanic tradition with Spanish primogeniture. Ouweneel, however, discusses and defines the position of cacique strictly in terms of the economic and social—not religious—relationship it implied with tribute-paying workers of their lands. He does not

NOTES TO PAGES 37-38

discuss the relationship of the caciques to the gobernadores (both derivates of the old altepetl ruling structure) when the two positions do not coincide in the same person. Romero Galván likewise provides an excellent and comprehensive overview of the concept of nobility in the pre-Hispanic period and the changes and gradual decline it experienced in the colonial period, centered on economic considerations as well as political positions and social privileges. Of the transition, he argues that the most serious change concerned the eventual prohibition of lifetime governorships (under the cabildo system):

> Esta innovación significó para la nobleza, e incluso para los macehuales, un profundo y doloroso deterioro de la imagen de las autoridades indígenas, habituadas desde siempre a una continuidad en las funciones de poder que les eran propias. Esta nueva situación contrastaba enormemente con la antigua según la cual sólo la muerte podía terminar con un poder adquirido a través de la herencia o las elecciones y sancionado por complejos ritos de entronización mediante los cuales los gobernantes recibían de la divinidad las potestades necesarias para el ejercicio de su poder. (57)

> For the nobility and even for the macehuales, this innovation implied a profound and painful deterioration of the image of the indigenous authorities, accustomed from ancient times to a continuity in the functions of power which were their own. This new situation contrasted greatly with that of ancient times, according to which only death could put an end to a power acquired by means of inheritance or election and sanctioned by complex rites of enthronement through which rulers received from the deities the powers necessary for the exercise of their rulership.

14. A touchstone work on this topic is Ernst H. Kantorowicz's *The King's Two Bodies: A Study in Mediaeval Political Theology* ([1957] 1997). See especially the section on "Dynastic Continuity" (317–35).

15. See Olko (2007) for more information on the concept and depiction of the *tlacamecayotl* (literally, "human cordage") as a system of conceiving of and recording parentage and succession in Mesoamerican pictorial texts. She argues that although the concept of tlacamecayotl is often seen as reflecting influence of the European idea of a direct line of descent, there is a great deal of evidence for its autonomous creation and use in the preconquest period.

16. This sense of being a representative of the gods is suggested in the description given of the "good" and the "bad" ruler in the *Florentine Codex* (Anderson and Dibble, trans. 1950–1982, 10:15), when it mentions that the "good" tlatoani "serves as proxy, as substitute." The rest of the description highlights the security, unity, and coherence provided by the ruler to the people of the altepetl as well as his (or her) potentially awesome and destructive, possibly occult, powers:

The good ruler [is] a protector; one who carries [his subjects] in his arms,
who unites them, who brings them together. He rules, takes responsibilities, assumes burdens. He carries [his subjects] in his cape; he bears them
in his arms. He governs, he is obeyed. [To him] as shelter, as refuge, there is
recourse. He serves as proxy, as substitute.

The bad ruler [is] a wild beast, a demon of the air, a demon, an ocelot,
a wolf—infamous, deserving of being left alone, avoided, detested as a
respecter of nothing, savage, revolting. He terrifies with his gaze; he makes
the earth rumble; he implants, he spreads fear. He is wished dead.

17. The Tetzcoca rulers are obvious exceptions to this point, as will become clear.
18. The idea was to follow pre-Hispanic practice whereby the larger altepeme (sing.
    altepetl) with more powerful tlatoque received tribute from the smaller, depen-
    dent segments. For more on the Spanish point of view in conflict with traditional
    indigenous organization, see Gibson (1964, 32–37, 194–219).
19. See also Schroeder (1991, 185–86) for a similar conclusion regarding the work of
    Chimalpahin.
20. There is a large bibliography of this incident. Published proceedings of the Inqui-
    sition can be found in the reprint of González Obregón's ([1910] 2009) *Proceso
    inquisitorial del cacique de Tetzcoco*. The incident is intertwined with the produc-
    tion of iconic script texts regarding Tetzcoco's lineage, lands, and history as well as
    the careful manner in which they were composed with Christian and indigenous
    audiences in mind (Douglas 2010, 26, 93, 163).
21. While some of the texts Lesbre (1995, 169–70, 172–83) mentions were brought to
    light along with Alva Ixtlilxochitl's early manuscripts in the volumes of the Bible
    Society library, others have disappeared and remain missing. All of these materi-
    als, however, constituted important source material (along with the mid-sixteenth
    century pictorial texts such as the *Codex Xolotl*) for much of the early seventeenth-
    century work on Acolhua history, notably the histories of Torquemada and Alva
    Ixtlilxochitl. Dating from the mid-sixteenth century, as Lesbre notes (175–79),
    these alphabetic texts included detailed accounts of Tolteca and Chichimeca his-
    tory, the life history of Nezahualcoyotl and Nezahualpilli, and the role of Fernando
    Cortés Ixtlilxochitl in the conquest and Tetzcoco's assistance in the missionary
    projects, all while downplaying Tetzcoco's resistance to the Spanish under Cohua-
    nacochtzin [Coanacochtzin]. Susan Schroeder included the Tetzcoco materials of
    the Bible Society manuscripts not written by Alva Ixtlilxochitl in her edition of the
    works of Chimalpahin found therein. See "Don Gabriel de Ayala's Year Count" in
    volume 1 of the *Codex Chimalpahin* (1997, 1:221–37), as well as "Unsigned Nahuatl
    Materials and A Letter by San Juan de San Antonio of Texcoco" in volume 2 (1997
    2:185–239).
22. Baudot's (1995, 175–85) reconstruction of the thematic organization of Olmos's

Suma (a summary of his *Tratado*) culled from Torquemada's work and other histories suggests some correspondences with Alva Ixtlilxochitl's histories: Chichimeca origins, the gods Tezcatlipoca and Quetzalcoatl and their relationship, the doubts of Nezahualcoyotl and Nezahualpilli regarding the divinity of their deities, etc. Motolinía's *Memoriales* (which served as a source for López de Gómara's history of Mexico) reflects the influence of the Tlaxcalteca sources from the tramontane region on the colonial reconstructions of the history of pre-Hispanic settlement of central Mexico. These sources, either directly or filtered through Torquemada, likely made an imprint on Alva Ixtlilxochitl's later works, as we will see.

23. This topic deserves further study, especially the *Codex of San Juan Teotihuacan* that tells the tale, described in Aguilar-Moreno (2007, 273). Gerónimo de Mendieta's *Historia ecclesiástica indiana*, book 3, chapter 59, presents an overview of the events, which Gamio (1922, 2:560–65) uses to interpret the codex itself, suggesting that the motive for the refusal of Augustinian oversight was largely economic, given the order's penchant for constructing sumptuous churches and monasteries (479, 561, 564). Clearly, however, the townspeople, including its ruler, put up a fierce and costly resistance in terms of human life and the town's assets in the community reserve, finally abandoning the pueblo altogether until the authorities relented. These documents, along with the testamentos of Alva Ixtlilxochitl's parents (O'Gorman 1975–1977, 338–42, 346–49), provide glimpses into the complex economic and social ties and tensions between the family and the town through the generations. Gamio's (1922, 2:489–521) discussion of the economic activities, land tenure, and tribute obligations of the region helps to put that information into a broader context. Also pertinent is the latter's presentation of the early religious history of the region (465–81). This includes a section on the persistence of idolatry and the church's concern with the pyramids of the sun and the moon (where Archbishop Zumárraga is said to have ordered the final destruction of the remnants of idols still lying on and around the pyramids [468–72]) and a concluding description of the early and fervent adoption of the cult of the Virgen of Guadalupe in San Juan Teotihuacan (479–81).

24. See also Lee (2016, 123–29), who points out that the marriage was accompanied by the division of the cacicazgo into two parts, one of them directly related to Ana Cortés. For Lee, Alva Ixtlilxochitl's primary motivation for writing his histories is to gain and protect family assets, which causes him to distort and hide contrary claims or visions of rulership, ignoring his Teotihuacan ties in favor of the Tetzcoca in order to avoid fueling challenges to the former and advance claims on the latter. I certainly do not dispute Alva Ixtlilxochitl's "biased" historiography but would point out, however, that it has roots in preconquest forms (like the marriage itself). The extent and nature of his corpus, moreover, make it difficult for me to assume a principally economic motivation for his writing. Certainly Alva Ixtlilxochitl had a clear understanding of pre-Hispanic land tenure and its distribution of lands in the context of the tlatoque, pilli, and macehualli relationships, as indicated

in his description of Nezahualcoyotl's restitution of estates to the deposed nobility after the defeat of the Tepaneca (1975–1977, 2:90–91). This vision, however, is not an individualist or self-seeking one. His work disregards Teotihuacan, moreover, because it was always an allied subordinate, in his vision of history, to the great Tetzcoca lineage from which it emanated. It is this latter lineage, with its ancient Chichimeca heritage—underrepresented in the theretofore published Spanish accounts and histories (except for Torquemada's)—with which Alva Ixtlilxochitl identifies and that he is most interested in preserving.

25. Torquemada ([1723] 1975, 1:147) substantiates this claim, writing that Nezahual-coyotl's son-in-law, Quetzalmamalitzin, ruler of Teotihuacan, served as one of the thirteen "Grandes" of the Tetzcoca realm, and was his military "Captain General," only fighting in battle himself in extreme circumstances.

26. Lee (2016, 129–31), however, argues that Quetzalmamalitzin fought against Ixtlilxochitl I and Nezahualcoyotl but was later allowed to keep his post, so long as he agreed to pay the requisite tributes of submission and accept a Tetzcoca wife (thus starting a new dynastic line in Teotihuacan, as a Tetzcoca dependency). According to Münch, even though many other notables of the Tetzcoca altepetl chose to surrender, "para no dar lugar a que sus súbditos padecieran las calami-dades y persecuciones que causaba la guerra," Huetzin, Quetzalmamalitzin's father, died defending Tetzcoco from the Tepaneca (1974, 9; so that his subjects wouldn't have to suffer the calamities and persecution caused by war). Upon the death of Huetzin, he writes, Quetzalmamalitzin, "sufrió las mismas desgracias y triunfos que sufriera el ilustre rey de Tetzcoco, Nezahualcoyotl" (suffered the same mis-fortunes and triumphs of the illustrious king of Tetzcoco, Nezahualcoyotl). Then, when Nezahualcoyotl recovered the rulership, he restored Quetzalmamalitzin to his post and, in reward, gave him one of his daughters in marriage. Lee's larger point about different factions within the Teotihuaca and Tetzcoca nobility (those upheld by the Tepaneca usurpers and those aligned with the "legitimate" Tetzcoca ruling line) is excellent perspective for balancing Alva Ixtlilxochitl's sweeping por-trayal of Tetzcoco and its allies as pro-Spanish. Certainly Alva Ixtlilxochitl was not interested in having the legitimacy of his noble lineage called into question. In either case, moreover, it is clear that the preconquest scenario provided a template for Francisco Verdugo Quetzalmamalitzin's marriage and his alliance with Tetz-coco in favor of the Spanish.

27. For a key reference on the larger topic of death and dying in the colonial doctrinal context, see Burkhart's "Death and the Colonial Nahua" (2004), which also pro-vides an excellent discussion of and bibliography on the topic of testamentos. As she points out, preconquest Nahuas did not share European Christianity's dualist sense of the self as divided between an immortal, immaterial "soul" and a despised body destined for decay; Nahuas perceived various "animic entities" related to the self and housed in the body, entities which, she writes, "did not belong to another world, but were part of this world, manifested in visible, natural phenomena" (30).

28. According to Torquemada ([1723] 1975, 1:60–61), the Chichimeca custom was to burn the dead. Before describing Xolotl's obsequies, he writes that, "Todas las naciones de el mundo, han tenido modos particulares, de enterrar los cuerpos de sus difuntos (como en otro lugar se dice) pero el que estos Chichimecas usaron, fue quemarlos" ([1723] 1975, 1:60; All the peoples of the world have had their particular ways of burying the bodies of their dead [as discussed in another context] but the one used by these Chichimeca, was to burn them). Torquemada's general discussion of burial rites and beliefs in the afterlife occurs in book 13, especially chapters 45–48, which ends with a description of the land of the sun, where warriors reside, and of the connection between warriors and birds ([1723] 1975, 2:530). In his history ([1723] 1975, 1), Nopaltzin (68), Tloltzin (72), and Ixtlilxochitl (113) are all cremated, while no mention is made of the manner of rites that were observed upon the death of Ixtlilxochitl's predecessor, Techotlala (108). The Tepaneca ruler Tezozomoc is likewise cremated (119). The exception to this rule seems to occur with the obsequies of Tlaltecatzin (Quinatzin), who, according to Torquemada, was after his death disemboweled and sewn back up, with his body dressed with regalia and placed on a royal throne in a great hall, such that he seemed to be alive. In front of him was an eagle, "rica, y preciosamente labrada" (rich, and finely crafted), and behind him a "tigre ferocísimo" (87; fierce jaguar). Torquemada writes that this burial rite was not used with his predecessors,

> aunque lo común que hicieron con los pasados, fue llorarle quarenta días, y a los ochenta, quemaron su cuerpo, y enterraron sus cenizas, con grande solemnidad, en una cueva, que está junto de la ciudad de Tezcuco: y este emperador, fue el primero que hizo sepulcro de reyes, en este lugar, en el cual se enterraron después otros.

> even though the common practice among his predecessors was to mourn them for forty days and upon the eightieth day to burn the body, and, with great reverence, bury the ashes in a cave that is next to the city of Tetzcoco: and this emperor was the first that was given the burial of kings in this place, in which later others were interred.

29. As Douglas (2003, 294, 306n72) has observed, Alva Ixtlilxochitl's insistence on this fact does not coincide with the Mapa Quinatzin, wherein Quinatzin (who establishes Tetzcoco over Tenayuca as the seat of the altepetl) is the first. Douglas attributes the discrepancy to a misreading of the *Codex Xolotl* on the part of Alva Ixtlilxochitl. If this was the case, it was a very convenient mistake, given the important relationship between this figure, and his namesake, Fernando Cortés Ixtlilxochitl, in Alva Ixtlilxochitl's histories. Regarding the importance of the transition from Chichimeca to Tolteca lifeways as a theme in the painted histories from Tetzcoco, see Douglas (2003, 292–94; 2010). In Alva Ixtlilxochitl's works, the

transition is most deliberately and clearly marked or thematized in the *Historia de la nación chichimeca* and the *Sumaria relación de la historia general*.

30. Chichíquil, he writes,

> viendo a su señor en el campo como si fuera el más vil hombre del mundo, compadecido y lleno de dolor, con otros que venían con él, cogieron su cuerpo y le pusieron sus insignias reales, y lo quemaron con todos los ritos y ceremonias, que ellos usaban, y le hicieron las honras de su entierro allí en un lugar y rinconada de aquel arroyo, que era antes del alba. ([1975–1977] 1985, 1:341)

> full of compassion and pain at seeing his lord lying in the field, as if he were the most common man in the world, he, along with others in his company, took the body and placed upon it his royal emblems, and burned it with all of the rites and ceremonies that they practiced, according it all of the burial honors right there in that place in the curve of the brook, before dawn.

In the *Historia de la nación chichimeca*, Alva Ixtlilxochitl tells a very similar version of the impromptu rites, except that he specifies that, "Ixtlilxochitl fue el primer emperador chichimeca que se enterró con semejantes exequias, que es conforme a los ritos y ceremonias de los tultecas" (1975–1977, 2:49; Ixtlilxochitl was the first Chichimeca emperor that was buried with similar obsequies, in accordance with the rights and ceremonies of the Tolteca).

31. After placing Tezozomoc's seated body (which was wrapped in seventeen fine mantles with a portrait of Tezcatlipoca on the outer one and his face covered with a turquoise mask) over a platform and undertaking four days of "ciertos sacrificios" (certain sacrifices), they took him (on day five) to the great temple, dedicated to Tezcatlipoca, "porque se habían cumplido los cuatro días naturales según la ley de Topiltzin" ([1975–1977] 1985, 1:351; because the four natural days established by the law of Topiltzin had come to an end). Alva Ixtlilxochitl then describes how his body was burned in the temple patio alongside the sacrifice of slaves, whose hearts were thrown into the fire, and notes how, after Tezozomoc's body had finished burning, the priests took his ashes and threw them into the chest along with some of his hair that they had cut, a statue made in his likeness, and all of his royal emblems, placing everything alongside Tezcatlipoca's altar (352).

32. "Y de estas honras y entierro servirá para los señores que murieron después, aunque en lo que era el sacrificio de los hombres, después fue con abundancia, como adelante lo declararé en las honras de Nezahualcoyotlzin y su hijo Nezahual-piltzintli" ([1975–1977] 1985, 1:353; And these honors and burial will be used for the rulers that died afterward, although with respect to human sacrifice, afterward this was [practiced] abundantly, as I will declare later about the rites of Nezahual-coyotzin and his son Nezahualpiltzintli).

33. The rites were performed, he writes,

de la misma manera que se le hicieron a su padre, que fue quemarle el cuerpo ataviado con muchas joyas de oro, plata y pedrería, y mucha diversidad de penachos y plumería; sacrificando en sus honras doscientos esclavos y cien esclavas; y sus cenizas fueron guardadas en una arca de oro y llevada a su sepulcro, que estaba en el templo mayor que había en la ciudad de Tetzcuco, que era el del ídolo Huitzilopochtli. (1975–1977, 2:188; emphasis mine)

in the same fashion as was done for his father, which was to burn his body regaled with lots of gold, silver, and stone jewels, and with a great variety of plumed headdresses and featherwork; sacrificing in his rites two-hundred male slaves and one-hundred female slaves; and his ashes were stored in a gold coffer and taken to a tomb, which was in the great temple in the city of Tetzcoco dedicated to the idol Huitzilopochtli.

34. "y cuando murió Nezahualpiltzintli, le quemaron el cuerpo como a su padre, y asimismo quemaron con él mucho oro, plata, joyas, chalchihuites y penachos, y doscientos indios varones y esclavos, y cien esclavas" ([1975–1977] 1985, 1:386; and when Nezahualpiltzintli died, they burned his body as they had done with his father, along with a lot of gold, jewelry, jade and feather headdresses, and two hundred male Indian slaves, and one hundred female slaves).

35. The Spanish "tigre" *could* refer to any number of large cats, however, in this context, and others that I interpret herein, I am assuming that the most certain translation would be "jaguar," given the animal's mythological and cultural importance in the Nahua (and Mesoamerican) world, and its clear association with rulership. See Olko (2007, 154–58) for a discussion of the jaguar pelt in indicating rulers' coveted Chichimeca connections in iconic script texts, including the *Codex Xolotl*.

36. Tezcatlipoca's attributes will be discussed in more depth in chapter 3.

37. The "madre tierra" (mother earth) is identified with a complex of female deities, including Cihuacoatl, Coatlicue, Tlazolteotl, etc., who are connected to (and through) the body of the earth monster or Tlalteuchtli (torn apart by Tezcatlipoca and Quetzalcoatl to separate earth from sky) and with Chicomoztoc, the seven-lobed cave of origins in Nahua migration myths. The curved or twisted candles resemble the double-helix structure of the *malinalli* or twisted grass, which iconographically implied the transit and communication (of deities or terrestrial messengers) between terrestrial and nonterrestrial planes. And, finally, the fire of the candles evokes the divine fire of the gods (similar to the eternally burning pyres in pre-Hispanic temples/rulers' palaces) while the smoking incense (a ubiquitous aspect of pre-Hispanic ritual) recalls, as already stated, the invisible omnipresence of Tezcatlipoca, the Smoking Mirror. For more on the earth-mother complex among the Mexica, see Klein (1988). In addition to the obsequies, the issue of the basic difference between Chichimeca and Tolteca religious worldviews is also very insistently demarcated in Alva Ixtlilxochitl's writings. Reiterating the

nonidolatrous character of Xolotl's branch of Chichimeca, who worshipped the sun and the earth without human sacrifice and deity bundles, he abets his construction of his Tetzcoca ancestors as protomonotheists. Whatever the truth value of the claim, one notes that the acceptance of the Tolteca gods implied a reckoning of the sun-and-earth-focused cosmogony of the Chichimeca with the predominance of the sun/night sun opposition (or astral focus) of the Tolteca cosmogony. For more on the differing Mesoamerican creation accounts, see Miller and Taube (1993, 68–71).

38. The Tolteca accounts of the *Sumaria relación de todas las cosas* are based on a now-lost pictorial history (Whittaker 2016). Alva Ixtlilxochitl's major source for the later Chichimeca-Tolteca encounter is the *Codex Xolotl*, which also distinguishes the dress of the Tolteca and Chichimeca (Olko 2007). See Dibble's (1951, 17–29) explanation of the first plate of this document. Alva Ixtlilxochitl's sources for Tolteca history in the later two works, however, seem to appropriate more significantly from the Tlaxcalteca tradition.

39. Without an honorific suffix, the name Huemac appears to connect this Quetzalcoatl figure to the astrologer and sage Huemantzin or Huema of Alva Ixtlilxochitl's early history of the Tolteca in the *Sumaria relación de todas las cosas*. It is a curious innovation, because this late account and that of the *Sumaria relación de la historia general* seemingly take their new approach from sources derived from Eastern Nahuas of the Tlaxcala-Puebla regions (Motolinía, López de Gómara, Muñoz Camargo, and Torquemada), where Huemac is (affiliated with) Tezcatlipoca as rival to Quetzalcoatl. Indeed, even in the *Sumaria relación de todas las cosas*, while Huemantzin is an ally of the Tolteca he is also the sage who predicts their certain demise. In all of Alva Ixtlilxochitl's accounts, Topiltzin plays the role of the last Tolteca ruler before the destruction of the empire.

40. See Dibble's (1951, 24) reading of the first plate of the *Codex Xolotl*, where the figure of the deity Quetzalcoatl appears in association with Cholula in the context of the text's depiction of the Chichimeca (under Nopaltzin and his father, Xolotl) exploration of the valley and demarcation of the boundaries of their new lands, the Chichimecatlalli (27–29).

41. An opening reference to a great author is standard fare for the early modern history in general; it is not a case of Alva Ixtlilxochitl imitating Torquemada, though his contrasting choice of authors is significant. All quotes from the *Monarquía indiana* found herein I have taken from the Porrúa edition, modifying its orthography, as well as some of its punctuation, to reflect current usage.

42. Cañizares-Esguerra (2001), however, points out that the humanist friars actually held a much more positive view of these sources than their Enlightenment successors, arguing that Mignolo overstates his arguments as to the power of the "literary" colonization of the New World. While Cañizares-Esguerra's perspective is an important one, I do not think that it necessarily undermines or even debilitates the essence of Mignolo's conclusions about the tight interconnection

between language and empire, which goes to the heart of the power to define and categorize—to determine the grounds upon which "the Other" is regarded. In this regard, Rolena Adorno's discussion of Alva Ixtlilxochitl (1989), which begins with an incisive comparison between Todorov and Certeau, is instructive.

43. For a discussion of the placement of the "Prólogo" and "Dedicatoria," see note 25 in the introduction.

44. In fact, the attributions of songs (or poetry) to rulers in colonial-period manuscripts and ethnohistorical writing in general seems to suggest a pre-Hispanic precedent for rulers' artistic engagement. There is, however, much discussion about this point. See especially Bierhorst (1985, 2009), Lee (2008, 151–89), and Lockhart (1991, 141–57). It should not escape our attention, moreover, that, according to Alva Ixtlilxochitl (1975–1977, 2:32), the Tlailotlaque brought the art of writing books *as well as* the deity Tezcatlipoca to Acolhuacan.

CHAPTER TWO

1. Anthony Aveni (2000) notes that while all cultural conceptualizations and abstractions of time derive from the observations and experiences of and in the natural world (its patterns and rhythms), patterns of cause and effect and ideals of progress associated with the European Gregorian calendar effectively separated or "erased" human life and culture from the cosmic picture, alienating human beings from the cyclical processes of the natural world, the interconnectedness of life and death.

2. Of course there were different theories about the degree of divinity the world reflected or contained. For the Renaissance period, see, for example, Arthur O. Lovejoy's classic work, *The Great Chain of Being: The Study of the History of an Idea* (1936).

3. As indicated by the discussion published in *Current Anthropology*, Graulich's (1981) thesis was at first regarded by some scholars as a sweeping oversimplification of the material it addressed and launched a debate over the historicity of Nahua accounts of the Tolteca past. Olivier's more recent work on Tezcatlipoca has been criticized along the same lines (e.g. Oudijk 2005). The fundamental notion of the patterned, repetitive nature of Nahua historiography, however, the quality of the mythic imprint on the reconstruction of the Tolteca past (and its similarity to accounts of the downfall of the Triple Alliance) is not questioned. For a slightly different perspective, see Susan Gillespie, *The Aztec Kings* (1989, especially xxii–xxxv). For another description of the paradigm of the Nahua moral history of the universe and its dialogue with the Christian vision, see Burkhart (1989, 74–79).

4. Douglas's analysis of the *Codex Xolotl* focuses on the spatial organization of the history of the Acolhua settlement.

5. This is not to deny or downplay Alva Ixtlilxochitl's clear interest in preserving the indigenous histories of *all* of the regions of Anahuac, evident in this comment on

the Mexica tradition he collects (for presentation to the viceroy) in the *Relación sucinta en forma de memorial*:

> Hay tanta variedad en lo que es los señores de México, porque dicen tantas fábulas y patrañas, y no me espanto de esto, que lo mismo es en los demás señores de esta tierra, principalmente de su origen y descendencia; y lo que a mí más me espanta, que los que menos saben son sus descendientes, porque unos dicen que vinieron los señores con los mexicanos del Nuevo México; otros, que de ultramar, otros no saben más que son descendientes o nietos de Moteczuma sin saber más fundamento ([1975–1977] 1975, 1:408)

> There is such a variety of opinions about the lords of Mexico, because they tell so many fables and yarns, and this doesn't worry me as it is the same with the rest of lords of this land, especially regarding their origins and lineage; what worries me most is that those who know the least are their descendents, because some say they descend from the lords of New Mexico; others from across the sea, and others only know that they are descendents and grandchildren of Moteczuma without any further information on which to base their claims.

6. For an incisive discussion of the Crown's censorship of writing in and on indigenous languages, and the importance of the author's manner of framing or filtering their representations of the indigenous/exotic for a Spanish audience, see Adorno (2007, 205–14).
7. See Serna (2000) for an overview of the ancient and medieval cosmographical heritage that the New World historians were responding to (15–25), and for a discussion of their various perspectives (26–101).
8. See, for example, the myths describing the birth of the Mixcoa, Quetzalcoatl, and of the making of sacred bundles in Bierhorst's edition of the *Annals of Cuauhtitlan* and the *Legend of the Suns* (1992, 23, 28–29, 152–52). For one discussion of their variants and the structure of the wider context, see López Austin (1973, 145–47).
9. This is the same general scheme and order set out in Motolinía's work, including the earliest version of the *Carta proemial*, published by Georges Baudot (1985, 99–102) in a footnote in his edition of the *Historia de los indios de la Nueva España*.
10. Torquemada's account of the creation of the sun here is similar to that found in the description of the creation of the fifth sun in the *Legend of the Suns* (Bierhorst 1992, 148) and to a small part of the account of the cosmogony of the four ages in the *Sumaria relación de todas las cosas*, where a mosquito bites the sun to get it to move ([1975–1977] 1985, 1:264), but with specific elements that *perhaps* point toward a Tetzcoca provenance. These elements include the protagonism of the god Xolotl, rather than his alter-ego Quetzalcoatl (Miller and Taube 1993, 190–91; Gillespie 1989, 154–55), as bone-collector and knife-bearing deity sacrificer for

the creation of the sun, and the addition of a completely different cosmogony of human origins, which Torquemada says was recorded by friar Olmos from a Tetzcoca elder named Don Lorenzo. This latter creation story, an etiological tale from the pueblo of Acolman, mentions nothing of the myths relating Xolotl's powerful acts of creation through sacrifice, but is (apparently) so sexually explicit that Torquemada (following Mendieta) provides only enough information to allow his readers to finish the story in our heads: "Y preguntados, como había engendrado aquel hombre, pues él no tenía cuerpo entero? Dijeron un desatino, y suciedad, que no es para aquí" (Torquemada [1723] 1975, 2:79; And when asked how the man had procreated, since he didn't have a complete body [he had only the upper half], they said something erroneous, and filthy, that is not fit for placing here).

11. For more on this matter, see especially Michael Palencia Roth, "Enemies of God: Monsters and the Theology of Conquest" (1996).

12. The first part of the (truncated) narrative of Muñoz Camargo's *Historia de Tlaxcala* ([1892] 1972, 5–6) discusses Tezcatlipoca Huemac's persecution of Quetzalcoatl and how he eventually came to rule over many provinces, namely, Cholula and Quauhquecholla, Izúcar and Atlixco, as well as Tepeyacac, Tecamachalco, Quecholac, and Teohuacan. Later, it describes the Olmeca and Xicalanca as the first (pre-Chichimeca) explorers and settlers of Tlaxcala in the region:

> Donde está ahora el pueblo de Santa María de la Natividad, y en Huapalcalco junto a una hermita que llaman de Santa Cruz, que los naturales llaman Texoloc, y Mixco, y Xiloxochitecatl y Tenayacac donde están dos hermitas a poco trecho una de otra que se llaman de San Miguel y de San Francisco. (20, 23–24)

> Where the town of Santa María de la Natividad is now, and in Huapalcalco beside a chapel that is called Santa Cruz, which the people call Texoloc, and Mixco, and Xiloxochitecatl and Tenayacac, where there are two chapels very close to each other called San Miguel and San Francisco.

> There are also distinct similarities (although not perfect coincidence) between Alva Ixtlilxochitl's cosmogonies and the cosmogonic portion of the *Codex Ríos*, which Quiñones Keber (1996, 207–8) notes may reflect a Puebla-area variant of the story.

13. Douglas's (2010, 50–51) reading of the first plate of the *Codex Xolotl* also shows how the notion of ethnic encounter (conceived as a diphrasistic metaphor) was a primary concern of the painters of Tetzcoca Chichimeca history. These painters, he writes, "cast the Chichimecs, the Toltecs, and their respective realms as ontological reverses, and as such they become agents and places of history. The Xolotl's first map is thus a spatial metaphor for as well as a pictorial history of the genesis of the Nahua ethnic groups and polities—products of Chichimec-Toltec

interactions—of the late Postclassic period" (30). More specifically, he treats the initial map's rendition of Nopaltzin's journey, beginning and ending in Xoloc (the Chichimecas' point of arrival to the region), and with a significant stopping point on top of a mountain (possibly Mt. Tlaloc or Tetzcotzinco) that precedes his exploration of the eastern valley (47–48), as well as a likely depiction of an earlier Tolteca presence at the Cholula pyramid temple with its likely associated date of construction in a year Thirteen Rabbit, which directly precedes a One Reed year (50).

14. For more on this topic related to colonial Cuauhquechollan (formerly part of Tepeaca), see Mysyk (2012). Her argument overall is very apropos of what I am arguing for Alva Ixtlilxochitl's text. She writes (117), "I suggest that, in the post-conquest period, those who represented themselves as speaking for the indigenous nobility of Tenochtitlan, Tlaxcallan and Tetzcoco used particular versions of the departure of Quetzalcoatl to lay claim to their political boundaries and authority, if not legitimacy, over them, both past and present."

15. There is a distinct juxtaposition in the narrative of the eastern arrivals with the arrival of the Tolteca from the west, coming from the region "donde es ahora la California por la Mar del Sur" and landing at Huatulco but then eventually crossing to Tochtépec on the opposite coast and finally arriving at Tulancingo and settling in Tula (1975–1977, 2:10; which is now California along the Southern Sea).

16. The ball court is often associated with the change of rulership and also has cosmological associations with the underworld (Olivier [2003] 2008, 141–42).

17. At the end of chapter 83, which begins the narrative of Cortés's conquest of Cempoala and Tlaxcala, Alva Ixtlilxochitl writes:

> En este capítulo y los que se siguen que tratan de las cosas de la señoría de Tlaxcalan, no sigo los autores que han escrito la historia de la conquista, sino la que escribió Tadeo de Niza de Santa María, natural de la cabecera de Tetícpac, por mandato de la señoría, siendo gobernadora de ella don Alonso Gómez, que la dio al padre fray Pedro de Osorio para que la llevase a España a su majestad, la cual se escribió en el año de 1548; y los autores que se hallaron presentes a todo lo sucedido en ella, como testigos de vista, fueron Miguel Tlachpanquizcatzin regidor perpetuo y natural de Quiahuiztlan, Toribio Tolinpanécatl, don Antonio Calmecahua, don Diego de Guzmán, don Martín de Valencia Coyolchichiyuhqui, y otros que no se ponen aquí sus nombres y habría treinta y un años que entró Cortés a esta tierra, y es la más cierta y verdadera de cuantas están escritas, pues fue hecha con tanto acuerdo y de quien tan bien lo sabía. (1975–1977, 2:212–13)

> In this chapter and the succeeding ones that discuss the things of the pueblo [altepetl] of Tlaxcala, I don't follow the authors that have written the history of the conquest, but the one that Tadeo de Niza from Santa María, the head

town of Tectícpac, wrote on order of the pueblo, the governor of which was don Alonso Gómez, who gave it to the father friar Pedro de Osorio so that he could take it to Spain to his Majesty, [and] which was written in the year 1548; and the authors, who were present at everything that happened in it, as eyewitnesses, were Miguel Tlachpanquizcatzin, permanent councilor and native of Quiahuiztlan, Toribio Tolinpanécatl, don Antonio Calmecahua, don Diego de Guzmán, don Martín de Valencia Coyolchichiyuhqui, and others whose names are not mentioned here, and it was thirty-one years after Cortés entered this land, and it is the most correct and truthful of all [the histories] that are written, because it was done with such agreement and by those who knew it so well.

18. Of Quetzalcoatl, LaFaye writes,

> Ese personaje—hombre, héroe, dios o nigromántico (chamán)— tranquilizaba la conciencia de unos y de otros. Para los indios era la única compensación metafísica del cataclismo de la conquista, y para los españoles era el sello de Dios sobre una aventura inaudita, llave preciosa de una historia desmesurada, si no indescifrable. Quetzalcóatl era el único capaz de colmar el foso histórico que separaba el Nuevo Mundo del Antiguo. Gracias a la profecía de Quetzalcóatl, indios y españoles pensaron que pertenecían a una misma historicidad. . . . Así se echa un puente no sólo sobre el abismo de la metahistoria, sino también sobre la falla juridical de la conquista. ([1977] 1995, 228)

> This personage—man, hero, god, or enchanter (shaman)—soothed the conscience of both. For the Indians it was the only metaphysical compensation for the cataclysm of the conquest, and for the Spanish it was a sign of God about an unprecedented adventure, a precious key to an excessive if not indecipherable history. Quetzalcoatl was the only thing capable of bridging the historical breach that separated the New World from the Old. Thanks to the prophecy of Quetzalcoatl, Indians and Spanish thought that they belonged to the same historicity. . . . Thus a bridge was created not only over the abyss of metahistory, but also over the conquest's judicial breaches.

19. Note that the use of the word "desengañar" in the Spanish original reinforces the sense of Cortés's character as a trickster, of his construction and placement between the poles of deception and revelation of the truth, depending on the narrative point of view.

20. At one point, Alva Ixtlilxochitl (1975–1977, 2:223–24) explains how Fernando Cortés Ixtlilxochitl and Cohuanacochtzin trick and capture their Mexica-allied brother Cacama before he can exact revenge for Motecuhzoma's capture and the

death of his brother Nezahualquentzin, and of Quauhpopocatzin. At another point he explains how Fernando Cortés Ixtlilxochitl and his brother Tecocoltzin aided Cortés with supplies and troops during the final conquest (259). However, these are the longest passages dedicated to praising Texcoco's role in the wars of conquest.

21. See Lesbre (2010) for an exhaustive study of the slowly evolving idea of Nezahual-coyotl's "monotheism" and the idea of his spiritual exceptionalism.

22. For a discussion of this text and its cross, identified as a tree, and of the first crosses of the conquistadores described in the Tlaxcalteca historical tradition more broadly, see Martínez Baracs's *La secuencia tlaxcalteca* (2000, especially 83–129).

23. I discuss this concept (vis-à-vis Burkhart [1988]) more fully in the conclusion, although detailed work on the extent, nature, and influence of typology in Alva Ixtlilxochitl's writing (and that of his sources) remains to be done. Here, I wish point out the way in which Cortés is a *repetition* of Quetzalcoatl (with Nezahual-coyotl as a hinge that deepens this relationship), and that this repetition is cogent within both Nahua and Christian historicities or ways of conceiving of history and/or the events of the past as they relate to each other.

CHAPTER THREE

1. As such, they prove themselves heirs of the Tolteca. Earlier in the *Sumaria relación de todas las cosas*, Alva Ixtlilxochitl describes the Tolteca gods, noting the important presence of "Tonacateuhtli" and "Tlálotl" and commenting that "Estos falsos dioses fueron los más principales y antiguos de más de dos mil años de los tultecas, y Tezcatlipuca y Huitzilopochtli, y otros dioses, fueron después acá ciertos caballeros muy valerosos que colocaron asimismo por dioses, y aun se halla que Tezcatlipuca fue un gran nigromántico, y fue causa de las grandes persecuciones de los tultecas, aunque es verdad que esta gente fueron grandísimos idólatras, no sacrificaban hombres ni hacían los supersticiosos sacrificios que los mexicanos después usaron, sino era a Tláloc, sacrificándole cada año, con seis doncellitas de poca edad" ([1975–1977] 1985, 1:272–73; These false gods were the most important and ancient ones of the Tolteca, from more than two thousand years ago, and afterward Tezcatlipoca and Huitzilopochtli and other gods were certain very worthy gentlemen that they thus placed as gods, and one still finds that Tezcatlipoca was a great sorcerer, and was the cause of the terrible calamities of the Tolteca; even though it is true that these people were great idolaters, they did not sacrifice people or engage in the superstitious sacrifices that the Mexica practiced afterward, unless it was to Tlaloc, sacrificing six young maidens to him every year). In summing up their greatness, he then writes that the Tolteca were "Nigrománticos, hechiceros, brujos, astrólogos, poetas, filósofos, y oradores de suerte que usaban de todas las artes, así buenas como malas" (Sorcerers, wizards, witches, astrologers, poets, philosophers and orators and thus they practiced all of the arts, good as well as bad).

2. For more on the presence of Tlaloc in relationship to representations of Acolhua nobility, particularly in the discourse of don Carlos Ometochtzin, see José Contel's (2016, 75–106) article entitled, "Don Carlos Chichimeca tecuhtli Ometochtzin, ¿último heredero de la tradición tezcocana? Ensayo sobre la influencia ejercida por Tlalloc entre los nobles acolhuas."

3. The *Sumaria relación de todas las cosas de la Nueva España* mentions the arrival of Tezcatlipoca with four groups of Tolteca peoples (including Mexica, Colhuaque, Huitznahuaque, and Tepaneca) who came from "de delante de Xalisco" (in front of Xalisco): "Trajeron consigo muchos ídolos, ritos y ceremonias, entre los cuales fueron Tezcatlipuca, ídolo principal de Tezcuco y Tlatlauhquitezcatlipuca" [Alva Ixtlilxochitl [1975–1977] 1985, 1:323–24; They brought with them many idols, rites and ceremonies, among them Tezcatlipoca, principal idol of Tetzcoco and Tlatlauhquitezcatlipuca). Note that this early history also describes the presence of Tolteca religiosity during the rule of Quinatzin, in the same relación in which it mentions the arrival of Tlailotlaque who, it says, came from "de adelante de la Misteca" (from in front of the Mixteca) (315). At the end of the relación, Alva Ixtlilxochitl notes that "Este Quinatzin fue el cuarto que empezaron con él los tultecas mexicanos a quererle enseñar sus idolatrías, ritos y ceremonias; pero jamás pudieron con él; siempre se los contradijo y no quiso creer en cosa ninguna, en lo que le industriaban" (320; This Quinatzin was the fourth whom the Mexican Toltecas tried to teach their idolatries, rites, and ceremonies; but they were never successful; he always rejected them and refused to believe in anything that they presented for him). In the *Relación sucinta en forma de memorial*, Alva Ixtlilxochitl notes Tezcatlipoca's arrival with the Tlailotlaque (402) but does not mention the arrival of other idols. The *Compendio* likewise remarks on the deity's arrival with the Tlailotlaque (from the Mixteca) (430), and also mentions the arrival of other idols, in particular Huitzilopochtli, with the four groups of late-arriving Tolteca (Mexica, Colhuaque, Huitznahuaque, and Tepaneca) who migrated to Tetzcoco under the rule of Techotlalatzin (432–3). The *Historia de la nación chichimeca* describes the arrival of Tezcatlipoca under the rule of Quinatzin with the Tlailotlaque, who were from the Mixteca and were "consumados en el arte de pintar y hacer historias, más que en las demás artes" (Alva Ixtlilxochitl 1975–1977, 2:32; masters in the art of painting and making histories, more than in the other arts). It also notes the later arrival of Huitzilopochtli and Tlaloc and many other "ídolos a quienes adoraban" (idols whom they worshipped) with the four groups of Tolteca under the rule of Techotlalatzin, Quinatzin's heir (35). Alva Ixtlilxochitl writes that Techotlalatzin, having been raised by a nanny from Colhuacan, officially adopted the Nahuatl language and other customs such as "el uso de las pinturas y otras cosas de policía" (34; the use of the paintings and other things of good government) and allowed the public practice of Tolteca religious rites: "Era tan grande el amor que Techotlalatzin tenía a la nación tulteca, que no tan solamente les consintió vivir, y poblar entre los chichimecas, sino que también les dio facultad para hacer sacrificios públicos a sus ídolos y dedicar los templos, lo que no había

consentido ni admitido su padre en sus ritos y ceremonias" (35; So great was the love that Techotlalatzin had for the Tolteca nation that he allowed them to practice public sacrifices to their idols and to dedicate their temples, something that his father never allowed in their rites and ceremonies). The *Sumaria relación de la historia general* focuses on political history and makes no mention of Tezcatlipoca whatsoever. Bautista Pomar ([1891] 1975, 13)does not mention his arrival with the Tlailotlaque, only with the Huitznahuaque. The archeological record on the origins of Tezcatlipoca in the pre-Hispanic period is discussed extensively by Olivier ([2003] 2008, 85–124) and Smith (2015, 7–40).

4. Torquemada ([1723] 1975, 2:20–22) offers this mistaking of humans (usually ancestors or powerful sorcerers) for gods as the explanation of New World idolatry, using Titlacahuan (another name for Tezcatlipoca) and Quetzalcoatl as examples. He then notes that such an error was also common in Old World contexts.

5. While there is no room to disagree with Lesbre's (2010, 28) sense that the Acolhua historians produced a version of their history that ended up being close to "fiction" and that deformed the reality of pre-Hispanic Acolhua religiosity (i.e., by suppressing their own acts of human sacrifice and scapegoating the Mexica for them), it is worth paying close attention to the pathways that the historians' reconciliation between the Tetzcoca and Christian tradition took, in other words, to the nature of the work of "fiction" (or "history") that evolved and influenced Mexico's national historical narrative, in large part thanks to Alva Ixtlilxochitl.

6. In "Nouvelles considérations sur la prétendu monothéisme tezcocan" (2010), Lesbre suggests that, despite Pomar's use of Tezcatlipoca's epithets in naming the "single" god worshipped by Nezahualcoyotl, he (and hence also Alva Ixtlilxochitl) would have been following convention, unaware of their original referent (2010, 22–24). It seems, however, that much more research on the role of Tezcatlipoca in pre-Hispanic, colonial, and contemporary Nahua culture and religious life, and therefore in terms of his status or role in Nahua historicity, needs to be undertaken. See, for example, Nicholas J. Saunders, "A Dark Light: Reflections on Obsidian in Mesoamerica" (2001, 226–29), which mentions the incorporation of obsidian disks into early colonial atrial crosses in Mexico. In his description of the city of Tetzcoco, moreover, Torquemada unequivocally states that Tezcatlipoca was worshipped at the principal temple of Tetzcoco, which was larger than the templo mayor of Mexico ([1723] 1975, 1:305).

7. In "Nezahualcoyotl entre historia, leyenda y divinización" (2000), Lesbre attempts to disaggregate the historical Nezahualcoyotl from his posterior representations, including that of the *Codex Xolotl* and the histories of Alva Ixtlilxochitl and Torquemada, in which he becomes an invincible hero of myth and legends (protected by or descended from the gods), and even a deified the object of a (possibly still ongoing) cult at Tetzcotzingo. Near the end of the study, he suggests the connection between Nezahualcoyotl and Tezcatlipoca, but states the need for further study of the subject.

8. For more on the common features of Quetzalcoatl and Tezcatlipoca and their status as "twins," see Olivier (2015).

9. Torquemada's account does not comment on the birth; with respect to his early years, it places emphasis on his genealogical link to the ruling line of the Mexica ([1723] 1975, 1:116).

10. In Torquemada's version of this scene, there is no ravine, and no leave-taking but rather a treacherous assassination that Ixtlilxochitl's protectors arrive too late to prevent. Nezahualcoyotl's escape to the treetops takes place as they are in flight from the perpetrators ([1723] 1975, 1:112–13).

11. Note that in Torquemada's version Nezahualcoyotl listens to the proclamation in disguise but is not situated on top of a hill (Cuauhyacac). Torquemada states that far from being afraid of being identified, he was going about "como león rabioso" (like an angry lion) looking for vengeance and had to be calmed by a friend named Huitzitziltetl. A Mexica gentleman and captain, however, is seen standing on top of what Torquemada identifies as a "Templo de los Toltecas" (Tolteca temple). Instead of ordering Nezahualcoyotl's death, he announces that no one should harm "nuestro hijo" (our son). This gave Nezahualcoyotl freedom to go about as he wished, writes Torquemada, but it did not free him from the danger posed by Tezozomoc: "que como era heredero de el reino, era fuerza que temiese la mudanza de las cosas; y que en alguna ocasión se trocasen, y él perdiese, en ella, lo ganado" (([1723] 1975, 1:114–15; because as he was heir to the throne, it was only natural that he be afraid that things would change, that at some moment they would reverse course [once again] and he would lose what had been gained). For a description of the scene in the *Codex Xolotl*, from plate 8, see Dibble (1951, 99–100), and also Offner (2016, 86–88). Offner notes that the temple on which the Tepaneca herald (or captain) stands seems to be abandoned and also associated with the Tolteca reed glyph, which would have reinforced symbolically the legitimacy of the (new) Tepaneca rulership. Moreover, he writes that it is significant that Alva Ixtlilxochitl retains the name of the hill upon which he stands—Cuauhyacac—as this is the place where, according to the Mapa Tlotzin, the first Chichimeca (identified therein as Amacui, Nopal, and Tlotli) settled before moving on to the towns of Coatlichan, Huexotla, and Oztoticpac. Thus, there is a specific and intentional identification of Nezahualcoyotl with the initial place of the Chichimeca settlement in the valley region. Offner also notes that the *Codex Xolotl* corroborates Alva Ixtlilxochitl's statement that the Tepaneca ruler delivers his commands to the Acolhuaque in both Nahuatl and "Chichimeca" and that it emphasizes the superior position of the Tepaneca captain through his position *above* Nezahualcoyotl and his companion. He identifies the companion as Nezahualcoyotl's *tutor*, not his servant, as in Dibble's version, moreover, glossing his name as Tehuitzilihuitl, and points out that both are weeping. Perhaps Nezahualcoyotl's presence at Cuauhyacac, in suggesting his connection to this original home of the Chichimeca immigrants, also alludes to his status as the rightful Chichimecatecuhtli, legitimate (*Chichimeca*)

ruler of the Acolhua region. I comment on the importance of the tutor's role and association with Tezcatlipoca's attributes in note 17, below.

12. In Torquemada's version, Nezahualcoyotl indeed murders the pulque seller, but wisely escapes before anyone can detain him for his actions ([1723] 1975, 1:117).

13. Torquemada describes the dream and Nezahualcoyotl's role in it, but mentions a lion and not a "tigre" (tiger or jaguar) and refrains from any mention of a transformation into the heart of the mountains ([1723] 1975, 1:117). For a description of Tepeyollotl and his relationship to Tezcatlipoca, see especially Olivier's (2008, 94–106) discussion of the jaguar.

14. Torquemada's account provides a similar phrase during Tezozomoc's funeral, from which Nezahualcoyotl is seen escaping. Here, Maxtla argues that there will be plenty of opportunities to kill Nezahualcoyotl, who is not, after all, invisible and who, unless he were to jump into the fire or the water or under the earth, would eventually be caught ([1723] 1975, 1:119). The *Historia de la nación chichimeca* does not relate an escape scene with the funeral, switching directly to discussing the controversies over the succession of Tezozomoc and the imprisonment of the Mexica ruler Chimalpopoca.

15. The scene is similarly described in Torquemada, but without the reference to the allegorical or figurative sense of the words ([1723] 1975, 1:125).

16. A similar escape takes place in Torquemada's version ([1723] 1975, 1:126–27). And indeed the trope seems to be a popular one in the tales beyond the Tetzcoca region: earlier in Torquemada's account the Mexica, warned of imminent danger by Huitzilopochtli, escape from Maxtla through a wall made of reeds (122). In this sense, it is a broadly used trope for signifying power in the Mesoamerican context.

17. This escape through water channels is only the first of many manifestations of his (and Nezahualpilli's) privileged connection to water. Other manifestations include the portrayal of the gardens at Tetzcotzinco, his construction of the aqueduct from Chapultepec for the Mexica, the description of Nezahualpilli's palaces, and his intervention to stop the flooding of the Acuecuexatl for Mexica ruler Ahuitzotl. Lesbre (2001, 335) has described Alva Ixtlilxochitl's re-creation of Tetzcotzingo as a garden worthy of Renaissance lords and ladies, noting his erasure of religious elements such as ritual hunting, human sacrifice, and the visible reminders of its connections to Tlaloc and other fertility deities. Yet the preponderance of scenes in which the Acolhua rulers manifest their ability (a superior ability vis-à-vis the Mexica rulers) to channel and control the natural forces of water remain clearly demarcated in his narrative and form part of the symbolic subtext that characterizes them. Although Olivier (2008, 94–100) describes major connections between Tepeyollotl and Tlaloc, there is nothing in the narrative itself that links the two aspects of the rulers' identities.

With respect to Torquemada's account of this scene, there is no reference to Nezahualcoyotl's use of a double to escape Maxtla's plot to trap him in a celebration. It does relate the scene of his escape through the hole in the wall behind the throne, although it is a much more condensed version of the story than what is provided in the *Historia de la nación chichimeca*, fitting for the most part in a single chapter ([1723] 1975, 1:133–34). It is also important to note that Huitzilihuitl, Nezahualcoyotl's tutor (who tipped him off to Maxtla's plot), appears a bit later on in Alva Ixtlilxochitl's narrative. Having been sent to recruit support from Chalco, the tutor is taken prisoner, tortured, and almost sacrificed on the temple of Camaxtli in Tetzcoco by Maxtla's cousin, Yancuiltzin, temporary ruler of the city. Before he is sacrificed, however, a windstorm arises and miraculously transports him to safety (1975–1977, 2:73). The entire sequence of events described in chapter 28, as well as Huitzilhuitzin's other roles in the narrative, deserve more exploration for their strong suggestion of ties to sorcery and the deity Camaxtli, who is associated with Tezcatlipoca. The windstorm recalls the disappearance of Quetzalcoatl at Cholula from the first chapter of the *Historia de la nación chichimeca*. The episode of the tutor's near-sacrifice from chapter 28 can be found described by Dibble (1951, 113–14, 117) from plates 9 and 10 of the *Codex Xolotl*, where he notes that the text does not indicate that Huitzilihuitl escaped his capture (117). In Torquemada's account, he is tortured and killed for refusing to confess. There is a connection with Cholula (and therefore wind or a windstorm) in Torquemada's version, moreover, in that Nezahualcoyotl receives the bad news shortly after being told by messengers from Cholula that he could count on their help to overthrow Maxtla. Very pleased with this news, he notes their ancient ties and apologizes for not being able to visit the city in person at that moment ([1723] 1975, 1:134–35).

18. Important work also remains to be done explicating Alva Ixtlilxochitl's detailed descriptions of Nezahualcoyotl's palaces. The work of Lesbre (2007) and Douglas (2010) constitute essential jumping off-points for such a discussion.

19. This episode has a parallel in Torquemada's description of the great celebration held by Nezahualcoyotl upon completing construction of his palaces ([1723] 1975, 1:156). It is a much shorter description and does not include any mention of ropes or beams. However, the story does include a note that Torquemada (or another first-person narrator!) saw them before they were torn down by the Spanish to make use of the materials. It ends, moreover, with a song text centered on the ephemerality of all rulerships, similar to the story told in the *Historia de la nación chichimeca* in that it is associated with the birth of Nezahualpilli to Nezahualcoyotl's stolen wife, and to the songs described with respect to the opening of the temple to Huitzilopochtli (discussed below in this chapter), from Alva Ixtlilxochitl's (1975–1977, 2:119–20) account.

20. Interestingly, it also seems to have engendered problems for Nezahualpilli, the illicit couple's second heir, who executed one of his concubines (the daughter of the Mexica ruler Axayacatl) for adultery and murder. Alva Ixtlilxochitl concludes his narrative of this event by making a connection to Nezahualcoyotl's case: "Y si bien se notase esta traición y trabajo que al rey [Nezahualpilli] le vino en su casa,

no fue sin misterio, porque parece que él pagó casi por los mismos filos, la extraña manera y modo con que el rey su padre alcanzó a la reina su madre" (1975–1977, 2:165; And if one thinks about it, this betrayal of Nezahualpilli in his own house contained an element of mystery in that it seems he almost paid in this way for the strange manner and method that his father managed to marry his mother, the queen).

21. Indeed, Nezahualcoyotl's most direct link with Tezcatlipoca lies in his name, which ties him to the coyote. Although more famous as a trickster in the North American context, the coyote plays an important role in Mesoamerica, as well. Olivier (1999) sets out the many strong parallels that exist in the literature between Tezcatlipoca and Huehuecoyotl, an important Otomí deity, including an (apparently very ancient) association with music, the sun, discord and war, fire, and sexual virility and transgression. As Olivier notes (116), when Nezahualcoyotl took refuge in the allied Otomí town during his escape from the Tepaneca, the drum in which he was hidden was more than likely a *huehuetl*, which was a vertical drum with a top made of coyote skin. In another scene, Alva Ixtlilxochitl (1975–1977, 2:130) presents a story similar to one discussed by Olivier ([2003] 2008, 32–33) from the *Florentine Codex*. In it, a grateful hunter kills a coyote he finds in a cave eating a turkey and presents it to Nezahualcoyotl. Olivier (1999, 119–21) notes the association between coyotes and warriors on the one hand and turkeys and captive warriors for sacrifices on the other. He also discusses both the coyote and the turkey as nahuales or doubles of Tezcatlipoca ([2003] 2008, 32–33). López Austin (1984, 422) likewise comments on Tezcatlipoca's role as a great transformer or nahual who would often appear as a coyote and in other guises.

22. Bierhorst (2009, "Introduction") suggests the possibility that this comment could refer to those songs in the collection entitled *Romances de los señores de la Nueva España*, preserved with the *Relación* of Juan Bautista Pomar, and which "may have been intended as an adjunct" to that text. The handwriting of both is from the seventeenth century. Many of the songs, moreover, directly discuss Tetzcoca rulers, and Alva Ixtlilxochitl may have used song XXII as a source (if indeed he is not the copyist and/or glossator of the text).

23. It is interesting to consider Tezcatlipoca's nocturnal character in light of Alva Ixtlilxochitl's description of the temple that he claims Nezahualcoyotl built to thank the "dios incognito" (unknown god) for the victory over the Chalca and the birth of Nezahualpilli. This temple, he writes, had a tenth level that on the outside was "matizado de negro y estrellado, y por la parte interior estaba todo engastado en oro, pedrería y plumas preciosas . . . sin ninguna estatua ni formar su figura" (1975–1977, 2:127; shaded with black and starred, and on the inside was all set in gold, stone and precious feathers . . . without any statue or forming of its figure). In a tower or chapel on the ninth level, moreover, were housed musical instruments, most importantly a "chililitli" (a metal percussion instrument or gong), but also "cornetas, flautas, caracoles y un artesón de metal que llamaban tetzilácatl que

servía de campana ... y uno a manera de atambor que es el instrumento con que hacen las danzas, muy grande" all of which were played four times a day (ibid.; cornets, flutes, conchs, and a metal chamber called a *tetzilácatl* that was used as a bell ... and a very large one shaped like a drum that is the instrument with which they accompany the dances).

24. The scene described in Torquemada is void of any mention of sacrifices and prayers and incense, mentioning only that Nezahualcoyotl was sleeping in his palace retreat at Tetzcotzinco when his guards heard a voice call to them from outside. Upon exiting the palace, they see a "mancebo, bien dispuesto" (nice looking young man) who predicts Axoquentzin's feats and the victory over the Chalca. At the end of the brief story, Torquemada notes that "quien haya sido este Mancebo, no se dice" ([1723] 1975, 1:153–54; it does not say who this young man was).

25. The only reference to this prophesy in Torquemada's narrative is the song text already discussed above in note 19. It occurs in the context of a discussion of the inaugural ceremonies held for Nezahualcoyotl's palaces and royal houses.

26. Under this "paradigmatic" or "mythical" reading of Nahua historiography, the prophecy that Ixtlilxochitl would "destroy" his own people, and Nezahualpilli's refusal to put him to death for it, should not come as a surprise. On the contrary, it should be completely expected. The connection between Quetzalcoatl, Nezahualcoyotl (or Acolhua rulership as a whole especially compared to the Mexica), and Cortés is reinforced in prophecies spoken by Nezahualcoyotl's heir Nezahualpilli, for example, when the latter is told to kill his son Ixtlilxochitl because he would befriend strangers and help to defeat his own people. Nezahualpilli refuses, of course, telling his advisors that "era por demás ir contra lo determinado por el Dios criador de todas las cosas, pues no sin misterio y secreto juicio suyo le daba tal hijo al tiempo y cuando se acercaban las profecías de sus antepasados, que habían de venir nuevas gentes a poseer la tierra, como eran los hijos de Quetzalcóatl que aguardaban su venida de la parte oriental" (1975–1977, 2:75; it was useless to go against what God the creator of all things had determined, since not without his mystery and secret judgment did he give him such a son at that moment in time when the prophecies of his ancestors were approaching, that new peoples were to come to possess the lands, as they were the sons of Quetzalcoatl whose arrival from the east they were awaiting). Torquemada's account of the lead-up to the meeting between Motecuhzoma and Cortés states that despite the appearance of Tezcatlipoca to his messengers sent to convince the Spanish to turn back, Motecuhzoma decides to resist until the end: "Ya yo estoy determinado ... de poner el pecho a todo lo que se ofreciere ... no pensemos que gloria Mexicana ha de perecer aquí" ([1723] 1975, 1:447; I am now determined ... to face head on whatever may come ... we must not think that Mexico's glory will die here).

27. The *Sumaria relación de la historia general* mentions Quetzalcoatl as the apostle-like figure of the third age who disappears and promises to return in the year ce acatl; however, it does not link Nezahualcoyotl to the prophecy and a knowledge of

the cross ("la cruz a que llamaron dios de las lluvias y de la salud" [the cross they called the god of the rains and of health]) that he brought with him to the region ([1975–1977] 1985, 1:529–30).

28. O'Gorman duly notes that an "alarming" ("*desconcertante*") reference in the work of Vetancurt, "relativa al número de albañiles que se ocuparon en la reconstrucción de México" (regarding the number of construction workers involved in the reconstruction of Mexico) could perhaps have been taken from a complete version of the *Historia de la nación chichimeca* ([1975–1977] 1985, 1:217). This, along with the close relationship, observed by O'Gorman, between the *Sumaria relación de todas las cosas de la Nueva España* and the *Compendio*, seems to hint that a complete version of the *Historia de la nación chichimeca* could have included this scene as well ([1975–1977] 1985, 1:230–31).

CHAPTER FOUR

1. For a study of Francisco de Monzón, see Fernández Travieso (2010).

2. Although it may seem an unlikely mirror for princes, Laurie K. Hohwald (1999), in "The *Psalms* as 'Mirror of Princes' in the *Siglo de Oro*" discusses the work of Montemayor as important specimens of the genre and provides an interesting window through which to regard the oft-noted parallels in Alva Ixtlilxochitl's work between the life of Nezahualcoyotl and the Old Testament David.

3. It is not clear that Alva Ixtlilxochitl was himself familiar with Ribadeneyra, but the latter's intensive engagement with the question of God's role in history, or the providentialist pragmatism described above, which he is forced to grapple with after the defeat of the Spanish Armada in 1588, provides an interesting angle from which to view Alva Ixtlilxochitl's own providentialist approach to explaining the *defeat/conquest* of his pagan ancestors, which he regarded as a kind of (foreseen and acquiesced) spiritual victory.

4. The *Monarquía indiana* is full of references to the necessary qualities of the good (Christian) prince, but directly addresses the topic in book 11, especially chapter 10, where he cites various authors (in particular Giles of Rome) and argues that the best type of rule is that of the single (prudent) monarch, over and above an oligarchy and a democracy [1723] 1975, 2:324–25). Later, in chapter 26, he writes that Tetzcoco was ruled by wise monarchs (especially Nezahualcoyotl and Nezahualpilli) and with a system of laws and courts (353–56).

5. Gibson (1964) notes the disastrous environmental decisions made by the Spanish as precipitating factors for the flooding. Not only did they silt up the lake bed by cutting down the surrounding forest, they built over it.

6. The latter episode is represented in various sources, both Mexica and Acolhua. It is clear that, in keeping with his usual style, Alva Ixtlilxochitl has historicized the religious and ritual implications of the scene. The *Historia de la nación chichimeca* turns Nezahualpilli into an engineer who wades into the water with construction

materials in order to plug the leak (1975–1977, 167): "él mismo por su persona entró dentro de él y con ciertos artificios que hizo atajó el agua, y la metió dentro de una fuerte caja y cerca de argamasa, de manera que con esto se cerró el ojo y el agua se fue secando; y volvió por la ciudad de México en donde visitó al rey Ahuixotzin y le consoló de sus trabajos, el cual quedó muy agradecido, y reparó su ciudad" (he himself entered into it in person and with certain tricks that he used stemmed the [flow of] the water and channeled it into a strong box and mortar fence, such that only in this way was the spring closed and the water began to dry; and he returned via the city of Mexico where he visited the ruler Ahuixotzin and consoled him about his troubles, for which he was very grateful, and he returned to his city).

7. The importance of the history and context of the Spanish efforts to build (or not) the great desagüe or "Tajo de las Desgracias" (trench of misfortunes) can be more clearly seen in the work of Vera S. Candiani, *Dreaming of Dry Land* (2014), which lays out the ecology of the region (especially its tendency to accumulate water) and the pre-Hispanic and colonial responses to the challenges and opportunities of living within it. Of particular note is her emphasis on the Crown's reliance on the Franciscans as letrados-engineers and as overseers of the advantageously cheap indigenous labor (as well as that of prisoners) used to build it, despite their efforts to curtail the power of the orders (81–83, 99–103). Torquemada was involved in oversight of engineering projects aimed at remediating the flooding of the city, and two Franciscans, one from the province of the Santo Evangelio in Mexico City (friar Luís Flores) and, after his retirement, the guardian from the monastery at Tetzcoco (friar Bernardino de la Concepción), were named superintendants of the project and had extraordinary powers to summon repartimiento labor in the face of many other demands for workers and of its real dangers and meager compensation (102–3). She suggests that the Crown relied on the orders in part because of their long history of building projects with and oversight of indigenous communities, which involved efforts to assuage the workers with spiritual compensation; for the desagüe, in one case they even produced a portable chapel dedicated to Saint Anthony for on-site masses and devotions (103). With respect to flooding in the Teotihuacan region, O'Gorman notes the 1604 construction of the Presa del Rey on the river of San Juan Teotihuacan, forming the (artificial) lake at Acolman, "que alteró notablemente la región y destruyó ese pueblo" ([1975–1977] 1985, 1:22; that significantly altered the region and destroyed that town). And, as mentioned earlier, Alva Ixtlilxochitl's father was employed by the cabildo (or council) of Mexico City as maestro de obras or overseer of all of its construction projects (Townsend 2014, 3). I am grateful to Nicanor Domínguez for bringing Candiani's book to my attention.

8. Candiani (2014) notes that the decision to stop work on the desagüe and allow the waters of the Cuauhtitlan River to revert to their natural course was a "risky experiment" by Gelves motivated by two factors. First, the Crown's desire to simply move the capital to the west, out of danger (a decision not supported by its wealthy

and heavily invested residents); and, second, his interest in assuring the food supply, or, as she puts it: "the viceroy's weighing of the welfare of the city against the
costs of its flood-control measures on Indian and non-Indian cultivators." Of this
latter point, she goes on to note that "although it is not clear that the measures
contributed to the 1624 flood that triggered rioting in the city and Gélvez's own
demise, they did lead to much rejoicing by rural indigenous populations, who not
only would be freed from Desagüe repartimientos but also recover their traditional usage of land and water" (78).

9. Pérez de la Serna also became directly involved in Gelves's dispute with Varáez,
   when the latter took sanctuary in the Dominican monastery. See Bancroft, *The
   History of Mexico* (1883, 3:23–97) for a detailed, blow-by-blow recapitulation of
   the events based on exhaustive documentation (which came from all sides of the
   matter).

10. It seems that Gelves, like Nezahualcoyotl, was well known for going undercover
    in order to spy on his subjects, to verify whether they were fulfilling their duties
    according to the law.

11. According to Richard Boyer,

> While Pérez de Varáez was clearly a worthy target for Gelves' reform
> program it is hard to understand why he did nothing when the capital's
> supplies of grain were cornered and prices were systematically raised by
> a single supplier. Poor people, made desperate by the squeeze, petitioned
> Gelves to regulate prices, the usual procedure during times of scarcity, but
> the viceroy refused to act on grounds that the year's harvests had been
> plentiful and too expensive for the government to stockpile enough maize
> to force prices down. This was an unpopular decision and gave Archbishop
> Pérez de la Serna the opportunity to intervene by excommunicating the cul-
> prit and demanding control of prices. The residents of Mexico City viewed
> the ensuing quarrel between the viceroy and the archbishop as a struggle
> between a secular defender of monopolists and the priestly defender of the
> poor. (1977, 468)

12. Boyer argues the same thing:

> The imperial government's dual program to restrict Mexico's influence and
> extract more revenue was, of course, charged to the viceroys. They became
> targets of a Mexican opposition, therefore, which was most evident in the
> period 1612 to the 1640s. . . . Able ecclesiastical leaders were natural figures
> to coalesce colonial opposition to unpopular Crown policies for which
> viceroys, not the king, always were blamed. As leaders of the Church they
> commanded resources, disbursed patronage, and embodied prestige and
> authority. While they affirmed loyalty to the Crown, they could oppose

viceroys by appealing to the interests of corporations and groups in New Spain. (1977, 470)

CONCLUSION

1. In *Épica náhuatl: divulgación literaria* (1945), Garibay identifies a Tetzcoca epic cycle dedicated to Ixtlilxochitl I, but not to his namesake, Fernando Cortés Ixtlilxochitl.

References

Adorno, Rolena. (1986) 2000. *Guaman Poma: Writing and Resistance in Colonial Peru.* Austin: University of Texas Press.

———. 1989. "Arms, Letters, and the Native Historian in Early Colonial Mexico." In *1492/1992: Re/Discovering Colonial Writing*, edited by René Jara and Nicholas Spadaccini, 201–24. Minneapolis, MN: The Prisma Institute.

———. 1994. "The Indigenous Ethnographer: The 'Indio Ladino' as Historian and Cultural Mediation." In *Implicit Understandings: Observing, Reporting, and Reflecting on the Encounters between Europeans and Other Peoples in the Early Modern Era*, edited by Stuart Schwartz, 378–402. Cambridge: Cambridge University Press.

———. 2007. *The Polemics of Possession in Spanish American Narrative.* New Haven, CT: Yale University Press.

———. 2011. *Colonial Latin American Literature: A Very Short Introduction.* New York: Oxford University Press.

Aguilar-Moreno, Manuel. 2006. *Handbook to Life in the Aztec World.* New York: Oxford University Press.

Alva Ixtlilxochitl, Fernando de. 1977. Vol. 2 of *Obras históricas.* Edited by Edmundo O'Gorman. Mexico City: Instituto de Investigaciones Históricas, Universidad Nacional Autónoma de México, 1975–1977.

———. (1975–1977) 1985. Vol. 1 of *Obras históricas.* Edited by Edmundo O'Gorman. Mexico City: Instituto de Investigaciones Históricas, Universidad Nacional Autónoma de México, 1975–1977.

Anderson, Arthur J. O., and Charles E. Dibble, trans. 1961. *The People.* Vol. 10 of the *Florentine Codex.* Salt Lake City: University of Utah Press, 1950–1982.

———, trans. (1969) 2012. *Rhetoric and Moral Philosophy.* Vol. 6 of the *Florentine Codex.* Salt Lake City: University of Utah Press, 1950–1982.

Anderson, Arthur J. O., and Susan Schroeder, eds. and trans. 1997. *Codex Chimalpahin: Society and Politics in Mexico and Tenochtitlan, Tlatelolco, Texcoco, Culhuacan, and other Nahua Altepetl in Central Mexico.* 2 vols. Norman: University of Oklahoma Press.

Araguás, Icíar Alonso. 2015. "Nobles y mestizos como intérpretes de las autoridades en el México colonial (ss. XVI–XVII)." In *Identidad en palabras: nobleza indígena novohispana*, edited by Patrick Lesbre and Katarzyna Mikulska. 303–22. Mexico City: Universidad Nacional Autónoma de México; Toulouse: Universidad de Toulouse II-Le Mirail; and Warsaw: Universidad de Varsovia.

Aveni, Anthony. 2000. *Empires of Time: Calendars, Clocks, and Cultures.* London: Tauris Parke Paperbacks.

Bakhtin, Mikhail. 1981. "Discourse and the Novel." In *The Dialogical Imagination: Four Essays*, edited by Michael Holquist and translated by Michael Holquist and Caryl Emerson, 259–422. Austin: University of Texas Press.

Bancroft, Hubert Howe. (1883) 1887. *History of Mexico: 1600–1803.* Vol. 11 of *The Works of Hubert Howe Bancroft.* San Francisco: The History Company, 1874–1890.

Baudot, Georges. 1995. *Utopia and History in Mexico: The First Chroniclers of Mexican Civilization (1520–1569).* Translated by Bernard R. Ortiz de Montellano and Thelma Ortiz de Montellano. Niwot: University Press of Colorado.

Bautista Pomar, Juan. (1891) 1975. *Relación de Texcoco.* Edited by Joaquín García Icazbalceta. Mexico City: Biblioteca Enciclopedica del Estado de México.

Benton, Bradley. 2014. "The Outsider: Alva Ixtlilxochitl's Tenuous Ties to the City of Texcoco." *Colonial Latin American Review* 23 (1): 37–52.

Bierhorst, John, trans. 1985. *Cantares mexicanos: Songs of the Aztecs.* Palo Alto, CA: Stanford University Press.

———, trans. 1992. *The History and Mythology of the Aztecs: The Codex Chimalpopoca.* Tucson: University of Arizona Press.

———, trans. 2009. Introduction. *Ballads of the Lords of New Spain: The Codex Romances de los señores de la Nueva España.* Austin: University of Texas Press.

Bireley, Robert. 1990. *The Counter-Reformation Prince: Anti-Machiaveillianism or Catholic Statecraft in Early Modern Europe.* Chapel Hill: University of North Carolina Press.

Blanco, Mónica, and María Eugenia Romero Sotelo. 2004. *La Colonia.* Colección Historia Económica de México 2. Mexico City: Universidad Nacional Autónoma de México.

Boletín. "El Gobierno de México Recupera el *Códice Chimalpopoca*." September 17, 2014. http://www.inah.gob.mx/en/boletines/3555-el-gobierno-de-mexico-recupera-el -codice-chimalpahin.

Boone, Elizabeth Hill. 1998. "Pictorial Documents and Visual Thinking in Postconquest Mexico." In *Native Traditions in the Postconquest World*, edited by Elizabeth Hill Boone and Tom Cummins, 149–99.Washington, DC: Dumbarton Oaks.

———. 2000. *Stories in Red and Black: Pictorial Histories of the Aztecs and Mixtecs.* Austin: University of Texas Press.

———. 2008. *Cycles of Time and Meaning in the Aztec Books of Fate.* Austin: University of Texas Press.

Boone, Elizabeth Hill, and Walter Mignolo, eds. 1994. *Writing without Words: Alternative Literacies in Mesoamerica and the Andes.* Durham, NC: Duke University Press.

Boyer, Richard. 1977. Mexico in the Seventeenth Century: Transition of a Colonial Society. *Hispanic American Historical Review* 57 (3): 455–78.

Brading, David A. 1991. *The First America: The Spanish Monarchy, Creole Patriots, and the Liberal State, 1492–1867.* Cambridge: Cambridge University Press.

Brian, Amber. 2007. "Dual Identities: Colonial Subjectives in Seventeenth-Century New Spain, Don Carlos de Sigüenza y Góngora and Don Fernando de Alva Ixtlilxochitl." PhD diss. University of Wisconsin, Madison.

———. 2010. "Don Fernando de Alva Ixtlilxochitl's Narratives of the Conquest of Mexico: Colonial Subjectivity and the Circulation of Native Knowledge." In *The Conquest All Over Again: Nahuas and Zapotecs Thinking, Writing, and Painting Spanish Colonialism*, edited by Susan Schroeder, 124–43. Portland, OR: Sussex Academic Press.

———. 2014a. "The Alva Ixtlilxochitl Brothers and the Nahua Intellectual Community." In Lee and Brokaw, *Texcoco*, 201–18.

———. 2014b. "The Original Alva Ixtlilxochitl Manuscripts at Cambridge University." *Colonial Latin America Review* 23 (1): 84–101.

———. 2016. *Alva Ixtlilxochitl's Native Archives: The Circulation of Knowledge in Colonial Mexico.* Nashville, TN: Vanderbilt University Press.

Breisach, Ernst. (1983) 1994. *Historiography: Ancient, Medieval, Modern.* Chicago: University of Chicago Press.

Burkhart, Louise M. 1988. "The Solar Christ in Nahuatl Doctrinal Texts of Early Colonial Mexico." *Ethnohistory* 35 (3): 234–56. http://www.jstor.org/stable/481801.

———. 1989. *The Slippery Earth Nahua-Christian Moral Dialogue in Sixteenth-Century Mexico.* Tucson: University of Arizona Press.

———. 2004. "Death and the Colonial Nahua." In *Death and Life in Colonial Nahua Mexico*, vol. 1 of Nahuatl Theater, edited by Barry Sell and Louise Burkhart, 29–54. Norman: University of Oklahoma Press.

Candiani, Vera S. 2014. *Dreaming of Dry Land: Environmental Transformation in Colonial Mexico City.* Palo Alto, CA: Stanford University Press.

Cañizares-Esguerra, Jorge. 2001. *How to Write the History of the New World: Histories, Epistemologies, and Identities in the Eighteenth-Century Atlantic World.* Palo Alto, CA: Stanford University Press.

Castañeda de la Paz, María. 2011. "Historia de una casa real. Origen y ocaso del linaje gobernante en México-Tenochtitlan." *Nuevo Mundo Mundos Nuevos.* http://nuevomundo.revues.org/60624.

Carrasco, Pedro. 1994. "The Provenience of Zorita's Data on the Social Organization of Ancient Mexico." In *Chipping Away on Earth: Studies in Prehispanic and Colonial Mexico in Honor of Arthur J. O. Anderson and Charles E. Dibble*, edited by Eloise Quiñones Keber, 73–79. Lancaster, CA: Labyrinthos.

———. 1974. "Sucesión y alianzas matrimoniales en la dinastía de Teotihuacan." *Estudios de Cultura Nahuatl* 11: 235–41.

Chimalpahin Cuauhtlehuanitzin, Domingo Francisco de San Antón Muñón. 2006.

Annals of His Time. Edited and translated by James Lockhart, Susan Schroeder, and Doris Namala. Palo Alto, CA: Stanford University Press.

Códice Chimalpahin. Digitalized Manuscripts. 3 vols. Mexico City: Biblioteca Nacional de Historia y Antropología. http://www.codicechimalpahin.inah.gob.mx/.

Contel, José. 2015. "Don Carlos Chichimecatecuhtli Ometochtzin, ¿último heredero de la tradición tezcocana? Ensayo sobre la influencia ejercida por Tlalloc entre los nobles acolhuas." In *Identidad en palabras: nobleza indígena novohispana*, edited by Patrick Lesbre and Katarzyna Mikulska, 75–106. Mexico City: Universidad Nacional Autónoma de México; Toulouse: Universidad de Toulouse II-Le Mirail; and Warsaw: Universidad de Varsovia.

Cornejo Polar, Antonio. 1999. "Para una teoría literaria hispanoamericana: a veinte años de un debate decisivo." *Revista de Crítica Literaria Latinoamericana* 25 (50): 9–12.

———. 2005a. "Indigenismo and Heterogeneous Literatures. Their Double Sociocultural Statute." In *The Latin American Cultural Studies Reader*, edited by Alicia Ríos, Abril Trigo, and Ana del Sarto. Translated by Christopher Dennis, 100–115. Durham, NC: Duke University Press.

———. 2005b. "Mestizaje, Transculturation, Heterogeneity." In *The Latin American Cultural Studies Reader*, edited by Alicia Ríos, Abril Trigo, and Ana del Sarto. Translated by Christopher Dennis, 116–19. Durham, NC: Duke University Press.

———. 2011. *Escribir en el Aire: ensayo sobre la heterogeneidad socio-cultural en las literaturas andinas*. Lima: Latinoamericana Editores.

Dibble, Charles, ed. 1951. *Codex Xolotl*. Mexico City: Universidad Nacional Autónoma de México.

dos Santos, Eduardo Natalino. 2007. "Los ciclos calendáricos mesoamericanos en los escritos siglo XVI: de la función estructural al papel temático." In Levin Rojo and Navarrete, *Indios, mestizos y españoles*, 225–62.

Douglas, Eduardo J. de. 2010. *In the Palace of Nezahualcoyotl: Painting Manuscripts, Writing the Pre-Hispanic Past in Early Colonial Period Texcoco, Mexico*. Austin: University of Texas Press.

———. 2003. "Figures of Speech: Pictorial History in the 'Quinatzin Map' of about 1542." *The Art Bulletin* 85 (2): 281–309.

Dubrow, Heather. 1982. *Genre*. London: Methuen.

Elliot, J. H. 2006. *Empires of the Atlantic World: Britain and Spain in America, 1492–1830*. New Haven, CT: Yale University Press.

Feijoo, Rosa. 1964. "El tumulto de 1624." *Historia Mexicana*. 14 (1): 42–70. http://historiamexicana.colmex.mx/index.php/RHM/article/view/1001/892.

Fernández Travieso, Carlota. 2010. "La erudición de Francisco de Monzón en Libro Segundo del Espejo del perfecto príncipe cristiano." *Bulletin of Hispanic Studies* 87 (7): 743–54.

Florescano, Enrique. 1994. *Memory, Myth, and Time in Mexico: From the Aztecs to Independence*, translated by Albert G. Bork and Kathryn R. Bork. Austin: University of Texas Press.

Frost, Elsa Cecilia. 1983. "El plan y la estructura de la obra." In vol. 7 of Torquemada, *Monarquía indiana*, 69–86. http://www.historicas.unam.mx/publicaciones /publicadigital/monarquia/volumen/07/miv7006.pdf.

Gamio, Manuel. 1922. *La población del Valle de Teotihuacan*. 3 vols. Mexico City: Dirección de Talleres Gráficos, Secretaria de Educación Pública.

García Loaeza, Pablo. 2006. "Estrategias para (des)aparecer: la historiografía de Fernando de Alva Ixtlilxochitl y la colonización criolla del pasado pre-Hispánico." PhD diss. Indiana University.

———. 2007. "La historia al servicio de la patria: el patriota mexicano Carlos María de Bustamante (siglo XIX) edita al historiador novohispano Fernando de Alva Ixtlilxóchitl (siglo XVII)." *Colonial Latin American Historical Review* 15 (1): 37–64.

———. 2009. "Saldos del criollismo: el Teatro de virtudes políticas de Carlos de Sigüenza y Góngora a la luz de la historiografía de Fernando de Alva Ixtlilxochitl." *Colonial Latin American Review* 18 (2): 219–35.

———. 2010. "Fernando de Alva Ixtlilxochitl's Texcocan Dynasty: Nobility, Genealogy, and Historiography." In Lee and Brokaw, *Texcoco*, 219–42.

———. 2014. "Deeds to be Praised for All Time: Alva Ixtlilxochitl's *Historia de la nación chichimeca* and Geoffrey of Monmouth's *History of the Kings of Britain*." *Colonial Latin American Review* 23 (1): 53–69.

Garibay, Ángel María. 1945. *Épica náhuatl: divulgación literaria*. Mexico City: Ediciones de la Universidad Autónoma.

———. 1953. *Historia de la literatura náhuatl*. 2 vols. Mexico City: Editorial Porrua.

Gibson, Charles. 1964. *The Aztecs under Spanish Rule: A History of the Indians of the Valley of Mexico, 1519–1810*. Palo Alto, CA: Stanford University Press.

———. 1975. "Prose Sources in the Native Historical Tradition." In *Guide to Ethnohistorical Sources*, edited by Howard F. Cline. *Handbook of Middle American Indians* 15, 311–21. Austin: University of Texas Press. 1964–1976.

Gillespie, Susan D. 1989. *The Aztec Kings: The Construction of Rulership in Mexica History*. Tucson: University of Arizona Press.

Goldthorpe, Rhiannon. 1991. "Ricoeur, Proust and the Aporias of Time." In *On Paul Ricoeur: Narrative and Interpretation*, edited by David Wood, 84–101. London: Routledge.

González Obregón, Luís, ed. [1910] 2009. *Proceso inquisitorial del cacique de Tetzcoco*. Facsimile of the first edition, with an introduction by Víctor Jiménez. Mexico City: Congreso Internacional de Americanistas, AC.

Graulich, Michel. 1981. "The Metaphor of the Day in Ancient Mexican Myth and Ritual." *Current Anthropology* 22 (1): 45–60.

———. 1998. "La Royauté sacrée chez les aztèques de Mexico." *Estudios de Cultura Nahuatl* 28: 197–217.

Gruzinski, Serge. 1989. *Man-Gods in the Mexican Highlands: Indian Power and Colonial Society, 1520–1800*. Translated by Eileen Corrigan. Palo Alto, CA: Stanford University Press.

———. (1999) 2002. *The Mestizo Mind: The Intellectual Dynamics of Colonization and Globalization*. Translated by Deke Dusinberre. New York: Routledge.

———. (1991) 2007. *La colonización de lo imaginario: Sociedades indígenas y occidentalización en el México español. Siglos XVI–XVIII*. Translated by Jorge Ferreiro. Mexico City: Fondo de Cultura Económica.

Gurría Lacroix, Jorge. 1978. *El desagüe del valle de México durante la época novohispana*. Mexico City: Universidad Nacional Autónoma de México.

Hampton, Timothy. 1990. *Writing from History: The Rhetoric of Exemplarity in Renaissance Literature*. Ithaca, NY: Cornell University Press.

Hanke, Lewis. 1970. *Aristotle and the American Indian: A Study in Race Prejudice in the Modern World*. Bloomington: Indiana University Press.

Haskett, Robert. 1991. *Indigenous Rulers: An Ethnohistory of Town Government in Colonial Cuernavaca*. Albuquerque: University of New Mexico Press.

Heyden, Doris. 1997. "La muerte del tlahtoani: costumbres funerarias en el México antiguo." *Estudios de Cultura Nahuatl* 27: 89–109. http://www.historicas.unam.mx /publicaciones/revistas/nahuatl/pdf/ecn27/518.pdf.

Hohwald, Laurie K. 1999. "The Psalms as 'Mirror of Princes' in the Siglo de Oro." *Caliope* 2: 44–54.

Holquist, Michael. (1990) 2002. *Dialogism: Bakhtin and his World*. London: Routledge Press.

Inoue Okubo, Yukitaka. 2007. "Crónicas indígenas: una reconsideración sobre la historiografía novohispana temprana." In Levin Rojo and Navarrete, *Indios, mestizos y españoles*, 55–94.

Irving, Leonard. (1949) 1992. *Books of the Brave: Being an Account of Books and of Men in the Spanish Conquest and Settlement of the Sixteenth-Century New World*. Edited by Rolena Adorno. Berkeley: University of California Press.

Jiménez, Nora Edith. 2001. *Francisco López de Gómara: escribir historias en tiempos de Carlos V*. Michoacán and Mexico City: Colegio de Michoacán, Conaculta, and INAH.

Kantorowicz, Ernst H. (1957) 1997. *The King's Two Bodies: A Study in Mediaeval Political Theology*. Princeton: Princeton University Press.

Kauffmann, Leisa. 2014. The Re-Invented Man-God of Colonial Texcoco: Alva Ixtlilxochitl's Nezahualcoyotl. In Lee and Brokaw, *Texcoco*, 243–59.

Klein, Cecelia. 1988. "Rethinking Cihuacoatl: Aztec Political Imagery of the Conquered Woman." In *Smoke and Mist: Mesoamerican Studies in Memory of Thelma D. Sullivan*, edited by Kathryn Josserand and Karen Dakin, 237–77. Oxford: British Archaeological Reports.

Kobayashi, José María. 1974. *La educación como conquista: la empresa franciscana en México*. Mexico City: El Colegio de México.

Israel, Jonathan. 1974. "Mexico and the 'General Crisis' of the Seventeenth Century." *Past and Present* 63: 33–57.

LaFaye, Jacques. (1977) 1995. *Quetzalcóatl y Guadalupe: la formación de la conciencia nacional en México*. Translated by Ida Vitale y Fulgencio López Vidarte. Mexico City: Fondo de Cultura Económica.

Lee, Jongsoo. 2003. "Westernization of Nahuatl Religion: Nezahualcoyotl's Unknown God." *Latin American Indian Literatures Journal* 19 (1): 19–48.

———. 2008. *The Allure of Nezahualcoyotl: Pre-Hispanic History, Religion, and Nahua Poetics*. Albuquerque: University of New Mexico Press.

———. 2016. "Colonial Writings and Indigenous Politics in New Spain. Alva Ixtlilxochitl's Chronicles and the Cacicazgo of San Juan Teotihuacan." In *Fernando de Alva Ixtlilxochitl and His Legacy*, edited by Galen Brokaw and Jongsoo Lee, 122–49. Tucson: University of Arizona Press.

Lee, Jongsoo, and Galen Brokaw, eds. 2014. *Texcoco: Pre-Hispanic and Colonial Perspectives*. Boulder: University of Colorado Press.

Lee, Raymond L. 1947. "Grain Legislation in Colonial Mexico, 1575–1585." *The Hispanic American Historical Review* 27 (4): 647–60.

León Portilla, Miguel. (1969) 1975. "Introduction." In Torquemada, *Monarquía indiana*, vii–xxxi. Mexico City: Editorial Porrúa.

———, ed. 1983a. Vol. 7 of Torquemada, *Monarquía indiana*. Mexico City: Universidad Nacional Autónoma de México. 1975–1983. http://www.historicas.unam.mx /publicaciones/publicadigital/monarquia/index.html.

———. 1983b. "Biografía de fray Juan de Torquemada." In vol. 7 of Torquemada, *Monarquía indiana*, 13–48. http://www.historicas.unam.mx/publicaciones /publicadigital/monarquia/volumen/07/miv7003.pdf.

———. 1983c. "Fuentes de la Monarquía indiana." In vol. 7 of Torquemada, *Monarquía indiana*, 93–128. http://www.historicas.unam.mx/publicaciones/publicadigital /monarquia/volumen/07/miv7008.pdf.

———, ed. 1983d. "Volúmen VII. Tablas de análisis de las fuentes de todos los capítulos de los Veintiun libros." In vol. 7 of Torquemada, *Monarquía indiana*, 129–266. http:// www.historicas.unam.mx/publicaciones/publicadigital/monarquia/volumen/07 /mi_vo107.html.

———. 2010. "Presentación." vol. 7 of Torquemada, *Monarquía indiana*. Mexico City: Instituto de Investigaciones Históricas, UNAM. 1975–1983. http://www.historicas .unam.mx/publicaciones/publicadigital/monarquia/volumen/01/prelim.html.

———. 1999. "Ometeotl, el supremo dios dual, y Tezcatlipoca "Dios principal." *Estudios de Cultura Náhuatl* 30, 133–52.

Lesbre, Patrick. 1995. "Premiers chroniqueurs Acolhuas." In *La quête du cinquième soleil*, edited by Jacqueline de Durand-Forest and Georges Baudot, 167–227. Paris: Èditions L'Harmattan.

———. 1999a. "Oublis et censures de l'historiographie acolhua coloniale: Nezahualcoyotl." *Caravelle* 72: 11–30.

———. 1999b. "Mapa Quinatzin: las vigas del tecpan de Tetzcoco ¿escritura o figuración?" *Thule* 6/7: 119–37.

———. 2000. "Nezahualcóyotl, entre historia, leyenda y divinización." In *El héroe entre el mito y la historia*, edited by Federico Navarrete Linares and Guilhem Olivier. Mexico City: Centro de Estudios Mexicanos y Centroamericanos. http://books.openedition.org/cemca/1319.

———. 2001a. "El Tetzcutzinco en la obra de Fernando de Alva Ixtlilxóchitl: realeza, religión prehispánica y cronistas coloniales." *Estudios de Cultura Nahuatl* 32: 323–40.

———. 2001b. "Chant de Teanatzin: traditions préhispaniques acolhua et chroniques coloniales." *Caravelle* 76/77: 213–22. http://www.jstor.org/stable/40854961.

———. 2004. "Écrits de Chimalpahin et d'Alva Ixtlilxochitl: des sources interdépendents? L'exemple des annals acolhua." In *Le Mexique préhispanique et colonial: Hommages à J. de Durand-Forest*, edited by Patrick Lesbre and Marie-José Vabre, 247–67. Paris: L'Harmattan.

———. 2010. "Nouvelles considérations sur le prétendu monothéisme tezcocan." *Studi e Materiali di Storia delle Religioni* (Sapienza, Rome) 76 (2): 1–33.

———. 2012. "Le Mexique central à travers le *Codex Xolotl* et Alva Ixtlilxochitl: entre l'espace préhispanique et l'écriture coloniale." *E-Spania: Revue interdisciplinaire d'études hispaniques médiévales et modernes*. http://e-spania.revues.org/22033.

Levin Rojo, Danna, and Federico Navarrete, eds. *Indios, mestizos y españoles: interculturalidad e historiografía en la Nueva España*. Mexico City: Instituto de Investigaciones Históricas.

Lienhard, Martin. 1991. *La voz y su huella: escritura y conflicto étnico-social en América Latina 1492–1988*. Hanover, NH: Ediciones del Norte.

Lockhart, James. 1991. *Nahuas and Spaniards: Postconquest Central Mexican History and Philology*. Palo Alto, CA: Stanford University Press.

———. 1992. *The Nahuas after the Conquest: A Social and Cultural History of the Indians of Central Mexico, Sixteenth through Eighteenth Centuries*. Palo Alto, CA: Stanford University Press.

López Austin, Alfredo. 1973. *Hombre-dios: Religión y política en el mundo náhuatl*. Mexico City: Instituto de Investigaciones Históricas, Universidad Nacional Autónoma de México.

———. 1976. "El fundamento mágico-religioso del poder." *Estudios de Cultura Nahuatl* 12: 197–240.

———. 1984. *Cuerpo humano e ideología: las concepciones de los antiguos nahuas*. Vol. 1. Mexico City: Universidad Nacional Autónoma de México.

———. 1985. "La construcción de la memoria." In *La memoria y el olvido. Segundo simposio de Historia de las Mentalidades*. 75–79. Mexico City: Instituto Nacional de Antropología e Historia.

———. 1993. *The Myths of the Opossum: Pathways of Mesoamerican Mythology*. Translated by Bernard R. Ortiz de Montellano and Thelma Ortiz de Montellano. Albuquerque: University of New Mexico Press.

———. 1997. "El Árbol cósmico en la tradición Mesoamericana." *Monografía Jardín Botánico de Córdoba* 5: 85–98.

Lovejoy, Arthur O. 1936. *The Great Chain of Being: A Study of the History of an Idea.* Boston: Harvard University Press.

Maravall, José Antonio. 1944. *La teoría española del estado en el siglo xvii.* Madrid: Instituto de Estudios Políticos.

Marcus, Joyce. 1992. *Mesoamerican Writing Systems: Propaganda, Myth, and History in Four Ancient Civilizations.* Princeton, NJ: Princeton University Press.

Martínez Baracs, Rodrigo. 2015. "Manuscritos mexicanos peregrinos." Under "Aproximaciones." *Códice Chimalpahin.* Mexico City: Biblioteca Nacional de Antropología e Historia. http://www.codicechimalpahin.inah.gob.mx/aproximaciones /Manuscritos_mexicanos.pdf.

———. 2000. *La secuencia tlaxcalteca: orígenes del culto a Nuestra Señora de Ocotlán.* Mexico City: Instituto Nacional de Antropología e Historia.

Martínez, María Elena. 2008. *Genealogical Fictions: Limpieza de Sangre, Religion, and Gender in Colonial Mexico.* Stanford: Stanford University Press.

———. 2004. "The Black Blood of New Spain: Limpieza de Sangre, Racial Violence, and Gendered Power in Early Colonial Mexico." *William and Mary Quarterly* 61 (3):479–520.

Mazzotti, José Antonio. 1996. *Coros mestizos del Inca Garcilaso: resonancias andinas.* Lima: Fondo de Cultura Económica.

McCaa, Robert. 1995. "Was the 16th Century a Demographic Catastrophe for Mexico? An Answer using Non-quantitative Historical Demography." http://www.hist.umn .edu/~rmccaa/noncuant/index0.htm.

McDonough, Kelly S. 2014. *The Learned Ones: Nahua Intellectuals in Post-conquest Mexico.* Tucson: University of Arizona Press.

Megged, Amos. 2010. *Social Memory in Ancient and Colonial Mesoamerica.* Cambridge: Cambridge University Press.

Mendieta, Gerónimo de. (1980) 1999. *Historia eclesiástica indiana.* Edited by Joaquín García Icazbalceta. Alicante: Biblioteca Virtual Miguel de Cervantes. http://www .cervantesvirtual.com/nd/ark:/59851/bmczs2p6.

Mikulska Dabrowska, Katarzyna. 2010. "'Secret Language' in Oral and Graphic Form: Religious-Magic Discourse in Aztec Speeches and Manuscripts." *Oral Tradition.* 25 (2): 325–63.

Miller, Mary, and Karl Taube. 1993. *An Illustrated Dictionary of the Gods and Symbols of Ancient Mexico and the Maya.* London: Thames & Hudson.

Mignolo, Walter. 1995. *The Darker Side of the Renaissance: Literacy, Territoriality, and Colonization.* Ann Arbor: University of Michigan Press.

———. 1992a. "Nebrija in the New World: The Question of the Letter, the Colonization of Amerindian Languages, and the Discontinuity of the Classical Tradition." *L'homme* (32) 3–4: 185–207.

———. 1992b. "On the Colonization of Amerindian Languages and Memories: Renaissance Theories of Writing and the Discontinuity of the Classical Tradition." *Comparative Studies in Society and History* 34 (2): 301–30.

Miranda, José. [1952] 1980. *El tributo indígena en la Nueva España durante el siglo XVI.* Mexico City: El Colegio de México.

Mörner, Magnus. 1967. *Race Mixture in the History of Latin America.* Boston: Little, Brown and Company.

Motolinía, fray Toribio de Benavente. 1985. *Historia de los indios de la Nueva España,* edited by Georges Baudot. Madrid: Editorial Castalia.

Münch Galindo, Guido Germán. 1976. *El Cacicazgo de San Juan Teotihuacan durante la colonia, 1521–1821.* Mexico City: Instituto Nacional de Antropología e Historia.

Muñoz Camargo, Diego. (1892) 1972. *Historia de Tlaxcala.* Edited by Alfredo Chavero. Facsimile, Guadalajara: Biblioteca de Facsimiles Mexicanos.

Mysyk, Darlene. 2012. "Quetzalcoatl and Tezcatlipoca in Cuauhquechollan (Valley of Atlixco, Mexico)." *Estudios de Cultura Nahuatl* 43: 115–38.

Navarrete Linares, Federico, and Guilhem Olivier, eds. (2000) 2013. *El héroe entre el mito y la historia.* Mexico City: Universidad Nacional Autónoma de México and Centro de Estudios Mexicanos y Centroamericanos. doi: 10.4000/books.cemca.1302.

Nicholson, H. B. 1971. "Pre-Hispanic Central Mexican Historiography." In *Investigaciones contemporáneas sobre historia de México: memorias de la tercera reunión de historiadores mexicanos y norteamericanos,* Oaxtepec, Morelos, 4–7 noviembre, 38–81. Austin: University of Texas Press.

———. 1975. "Middle American Ethnohistory: An Overview." In *Guide to Ethnohistorical Sources,* edited by Howard F. Cline. *Handbook of Middle American Indians* 15, 487–505. Austin: University of Texas Press. 1964–1976.

Nogales Rincón, David. 2006. "Los espejos de príncipes en Castilla (siglos XIII–XV): Un modelo literario de la realeza bajomedieval." *Medievalismo* 16: 9–39.

Offner, Jerome. 2014. "Improving Western Historiography of Texcoco." In Lee and Brokaw, *Texcoco,* 25–61.

O'Gorman, Edmundo. (1975–1977) 1985. "Introduction." In Alva Ixtlilxochitl, *Obras históricas,* 1:1–257.

———, ed. (1975–1977) 1977. "Apéndice documental." In Alva Ixtlilxochitl, *Obras históricas,* 2:265–402.

Okubo, Inoue. 2007. "Crónicas indígenas: una reconsideración sobre la historiografía novohispana temprana." In Levin Rojo and Navarrete, *Indios, mestizos y españoles,* 55–95.

Olivier, Guilhem. 1999. "Huehuecoyotl 'Coyote Viejo', el músico transgresor: ¿Dios de los otomíes o avatar de Tezcatlipoca?" *Estudios de Cultura Nahuatl* 30: 113–32. http://www.ejournal.unam.mx/ecn/ecnahuatl30/ECN03005.pdf.

———. (2003) 2008. *Mockeries and Metamorphoses of an Aztec God: Tezcatlipoca, "Lord of the Smoking Mirror."* Translated by Michel Besson. Boulder: University of Colorado Press.

———. 2015. "Enemy Brothers or Divine Twins?" In *Tezcatlipoca: Trickster and Supreme Deity,* edited by Elizabeth Baquedano, 59–82. Boulder: University of Colorado Press.

Olko, Justyna. 2007. "Genealogías indígenas del centro de México: raíces prehispánicas de su florecimiento colonial." *Itinerarios* 6: 141–62. http://itinerarios.uw.edu.pl/wp -content/uploads/2014/12/07_Olko.pdf.

———. 2010. "Alphabetic Writing in the Hands of the Colonial Nahua Nobility." *Contributions in New World Archeology* 7: 177–98. http://www.cnwajournal.org/wp -content/uploads/2015/07/Alphabetic-writing-in-the-hands-of-the-colonial -Nahua-nobility1.pdf.

Oudijk, Michel R. 2005. Review of "Mockeries and Metamorphoses of an Aztec God: Tezcatlipoca, 'Lord of the Smoking Mirror'" by Guilhem Olivier. *Ethnohistory* 52 (3): 656–58.

———. 2008. "De tradiciones y métodos: investigaciones pictográficas." *Desacatos* 27: 123–38. http://desacatos.ciesas.edu.mx/index.php/Desacatos/article/view/552.

Ouweneel, Arij. 1995. "'Tlahtocayotl' to 'gobernadoryotl': A Critical Examination of Indigenous Rule in 18th Century Central Mexico." *American Ethnologist* 22 (4): 756–85.

Pagden, Anthony. 1986. *The Fall of Natural Man: The American Indian and the Origins of Comparative Ethnology.* Cambridge: Cambridge University Press.

Palencia-Roth, Michael. 1992. "Quarta Orbis Pars: Monologizing the New World." *Comparative Civilizations Review* 26 (Spring): 4–42.

———. 1996. "Enemies of God: Monsters and the Theology of Conquest." In *Monsters, Tricksters and Sacred Cows: Animal Tales and American Identities*, edited by A. James Arnold, 23–50. Charlottesville: University Press of Virginia.

Pérez-Rocha, Emma and Rafael Tena, eds. 2000a. *La nobleza indígena del centro de México después de la conquista.* Mexico City: Instituto Nacional de Antropología e Historia.

———. 2000b. Introduction to *La nobleza indígena de México después de la conquista*, edited by Emma Pérez-Rocha and Rafael Tena, 11–72. Mexico City: Instituto Nacional de Antropología e Historia.

Phelan, John Leddy. 1956. *The Millennial Kingdom of the Franciscans in the New World: A Study of the Writings of Gerónimo de Mendieta.* Berkeley: University of California Press.

Quiñones Keber, Eloise. 1996. "Creating the Cosmos: The Myth of the Four Suns in the *Codex Vaticanus A.*" *Latin American Indian Literatures Journal* 12 (2):192–211.

Ramírez López, Javier Eduardo. 2014. "La iglesia en el siglo XVI: Tezcoco cuna de la evangelización en la Nueva España." In *Evangelización, educación y cultura en Texcoco, siglos XVI al XVIII*, edited by Javier Eduardo Ramírez López, 17–51. Texcoco: Diócesis de Texcoco, Centro de Estudios Hisótricos y Sociales de Texcoco 'Lorenzo Boturini Benaduci.'

Read, Kate Almere. 1998. *Time and Sacrifice in the Aztec Cosmos.* Bloomington: Indiana University Press.

Rebhorn, Wayne. 1992. "'The Emperor of Men's Minds': The Renaissance Trickster as *Homo Rhetoricus.*" In *Creative Imitation: New Essays on Renaissance Literature In*

Honor of Thomas M. Greene, edited by David Quint, Margaret W. Ferguson, G. W. Pigman III, and Wayne A. Rebhorn, 31–65. Binghamton: Center for Medieval and Early Renaissance Studies.

Restall, Matthew. 1997. "Heirs to the Hieroglyphs: Indigenous Writing in Colonial Mesoamerica." *The Americas* 54 (2): 239–67.

Restall, Matthew and Susan Kellog. 1998. Introduction to *Dead Giveaways: Indigenous Testaments of Colonial Mesoamerica and the Andes*, edited by Matthew Restall and Susan Kellog, 1–11. Salt Lake City: University of Utah Press.

Restrepo, Luís Fernández. 2002. "Narrating Colonial Interventions: Don Diego de Torres, Cacique of Turmequé in the New Kingdom of Granada." In *Colonialism Past and Present: Reading and Writing About Colonial Latin America Today*, edited by Gustavo Verdesio and Álvaro Félix Bolaños, 97–117. Albany: State University of New York Press.

Ricoeur, Paul. (1984) 1990. *Time and Narrative*. Vol. 1. Translated by Kathleen McLaughlin and David Pellauer. Chicago: University of Chicago Press.

Romero Galván, José Rubén. 2003. *Los privilegios perdidos: Hernando Alvarado Tezozomoc, su tiempo, su nobleza, y su crónica Mexicana*. Mexico City: Instituto de Investigaciones Históricas, Universidad Nacional Autónoma de México.

Rucquoi, Adeline and Bizzarri, Hugo Oscar. 2005. "Los espejos de príncipes en Castilla; entre Oriente y Occidente." *Cuadernos de historia de España* 79: 7–30.

Ruwet, Wayne. 1997. "Physical Description of the Manuscripts." In Anderson and Schroeder, *Codex Chimalpahin*, 1:17–24.

Saunders, Nicholas J. 2001. "A Dark Light: Reflections on Obsidian in Mesoamerica." *World Archaeology* 33 (2): 220–36.

Schroeder, Susan. 1991. *Chimalpahin and the Kingdoms of Chalco*. Tucson: University of Arizona Press.

———. 1997. Introduction to Anderson and Schroeder, *Codex Chimalpahin*, 1:3–13.

———. 2006. "Writing Two Cultures: The Meaning of 'Amoxtli' (Book) in Nahua New Spain." In *New World, First Nations: Native Peoples of Mesoamerica and the Andes under Colonial Rule*, edited by David Cahill and Blanca Tovías, 13–35. Brighton: Sussex Academic Press.

Schwaller, Frederick. 1994a. "Don Bartolomé de Alva, Nahuatl Scholar of the Seventeenth Century." In *Chipping Away on Earth: Studies in Prehispanic and Colonial Mexico in Honor of Arthur J. O. Anderson and Charles E. Dibble*, edited by Eloise Quiñones Keber, 95–103. Lancaster, California: Labyrinthos.

———. 1994b. "Nahuatl Studies and the 'Circle' of Horacio Carochi." *Estudios de Cultura Nahuatl* 24: 387–98.

———. 1999. "Don Bartolomé de Alva, Nahuatl Scholar of the Seventeenth Century." In *A Guide to Confession Large and Small in the Mexican Language, 1634*, edited by Barry D. Sell and John Frederick Schwaller, 3–15. Norman: University of Oklahoma Press.

———. 2014. "The Brothers Fernando de Alva Ixtlilxochitl and Bartolomé de Alva." In

Indigenous Intellectuals: Knowledge, Power, and Colonial Culture in Mexico and the Andes, edited by Gabriela Ramos and Yanna Yannakakis, 39–59. Durham, NC: Duke University Press.

Serna, Mercedes. 2000. Introduction to *Crónicas de Indias: Antología*, edited by Mercedes Serna, 15–112. Madrid: Cátedra.

Serna Arnaiz, Mercedes and Bernat Castany Prado. 2014. Introduction to *Historia de los indios de la Nueva España*, by fray Toribio de Benavente, "Motolinía." Edited by Mercedes Serna Arnaiz and Bernat Castany Prado, 9–104. Madrid: Real Academia Española.

Simpson, Lesley Byrd. (1941) 1966. *Many Mexicos*. Berkeley: University of California Press.

Smith, Michael. 2015. "The Archeology of Tezcatlipoca." In *Tezcatlipoca: Trickster and Supreme Deity*, edited by Elizabeth Baquedano, 7–40. Boulder: University Press of Colorado.

Tang, Frank. 1996. "Machiavelli's Image of the Ruler: Il principe and the Tradition of the Mirror for Princes." In *Machiavelli: Figure-Reputation*, edited by Joep Leerssen and Menno Spiering, 187–200. Amsterdam: Rodopi.

Torquemada, fray Juan de. (1723) 1975. *Monarquía indiana*. Edited by Miguel León Portilla. 3 vols. Mexico City: Editorial Porrúa.

Townsend, Camilla. 2014. "Introduction: The Evolution of Alva Ixtlilxochitl's Scholarly Life." *Colonial Latin American Review* 23 (1): 1–17.

Townsend, Camilla. 2016. *The Annals of Native America: How the Nahuas of Colonial Mexico Kept Their History Alive*. Oxford: Oxford University Press.

———. 2003. "Burying the White Gods: New Perspectives on the Conquest of Mexico." *The American Historical Review* 108 (3): 659–87.

Vásquez Galicia, Sergio Ángel. 2013. "La identidad de Fernando de Alva Ixtlilxochitl a través de su memoria histórica. Análisis historiográfico." PhD diss., Universidad Autónoma Nacional de México.

Velazco, Salvador. 2003. Visiones de Anáhuac. *Reconstrucciones historiográficas y etnicidades emergentes en el México colonial: Fernando de Alva Ixtlilxóchitl, Diego Muñoz Camargo y Hernando Alvarado Tezozómoc*. Guadalajara, Universidad de Guadalajara.

Villella, Peter B. 2014. "The Last Acolhua: Alva Ixtlilxochitl and Elite Native Historiography in Early New Spain." *Colonial Latin American Review* 23 (1): 18–36.

———. 2016. *Indigenous Elites and Creole Identity in Colonial Mexico, 1500–1800*. New York, NY: Cambridge University Press.

Vizenor, Gerald. 1994. "Trickster Discourse: Comic and Tragic Themes in Native American Literature." In *Buried Roots and Indestructible Seeds: The Survival of American Indian Life in Story, History, and Spirit*, edited by Mark A. Lindquist and Martin A. Zanger, 67–84. Madison: University of Wisconsin Press.

Ward, Thomas. 2011. "Alva Ixtlilxochitl, Civilization, and the Quest for Coevalness." *Studies in American Indian Literatures* 23 (1): 96–125.

Whittaker, Gordon. 2014. "The Signature of Fernando de Alva Ixtlilxochitl." *Mexicon*
    36: 69–71.

———. 2016. "The Identities of Fernando de Alva Ixtlilxochitl." In *Fernando de Alva
    Ixtlilxochitl and His Legacy*, edited by Galen Brokaw and Jongsoo Lee, 29–76. Tuc-
    son: University of Arizona Press.

Whitehead, N. L. 2003. Introduction to *Histories and Historicities in Amazonia*, edited by
    Neil L. Whitehead, vii–xxi. Lincoln, University of Nebraska Press.

Wood, Stephanie. 1997. "Matters of Life and Death: Nahuatl Testaments of Rural Women,
    1589–1801." In *Indian Women of Early Mexico*, edited by Susan Schroeder, Steph-
    anie Wood and Robert Haskett, 165–82. Norman: University of Oklahoma Press.

———. 2003. *Transcending conquest: Nahua Views of Spanish Colonial Mexico*. Norman:
    University of Oklahoma Press.

Zárate Toscano, Verónica. 1996. Los conflictos de 1624 y 1808 en la Nueva España. *Anu-
    ario de estudios americanos* (3) 2: 35–50.

Index

Page numbers in italic text indicate illustrations.

tlatoque, tlatoani. See rulers

Tlaxcala, 108, 118–20, 241n12

Tlazolyaotzin, Juan, 32

Tolteca, 12, 39, 100, 110; adopting traditions of, 52; arrival of, 244n3; arrival of groups of, 245n3; attire of, 60–62; Chichimeca ties with, 111; creation story of, 105–8; cultural attributes of, 58–60; destruction of, 206–7, 214n15; heirs of, 244n1; history of, 217n23; structuralist interpretation of, 47; writing associated with, 77

Topiltzin, 28, 47, 153–54, 203; death of, 54–55, 206; fate of, 110; funeral rites of, 52–56; as man-god, 61

Torquemada, Juan de, 23–25, 45, 166–67, 234n25, 247nn9–16; on burial rites, 235n28; Carta Nuncupatoria (dedication letter) by, 195–201; celebration description by, 249n19, 251n25; on creation of sun, 240n10; idolatry explanation of, 246n4; plagiarism and, 15; questions addressed by, 65–66; on Quetzalcoatl, 94–95; spiritual exceptionalism and, 126–27; Tezcatlipoca described by, 131; theory presented by, 72; true protagonists of, 92–93; vision of history in New Spain, 15–17; works inherited by, 47. See also *Veintiun libros rituales y Monarquía indiana*

totalidad contradictoria (contradictory totality), 20

Townsend, Camilla, 47, 54, 63, 220n27, 220nn29

tradition, 5–6; adoption and acceptance of, 52; culture absorbed from, 77; of nobles, 49; rupture with, 62; of song, 208; understanding indigenous, 41–42. See also Nahua tradition

tragedy, sense of in the *Comentarios reales,* 19–20

transculturation, 25, 76, 84, 225n41

transgression, 135, 141, 145–50

translatio imperii, 84

translation, 69, 75, 78

Tratado de antigüedades mexicanas (Olmos), 47, 232n22

trees, cosmic, 126, 136

tribute goods, 22

tribute payments, 39–40, 152, 181, 185–86

trickster, 20, 22, 243n19; irony of, 147; power of, 120–21; traits of, 25; various kinds of, 200. See also Tezcatlipoca

Triple Alliance, 50, 116, 118, 151, 174

trust (*pialli*), 6, 9–10

truth, 64, 169; alternate expressions of, 103; authors and, 67–69, 79; Christianity definition of, 150; histories and, 73–75, 102

universal history, 102, 106; genre of, 14, 23, 31, 47; presence of, 64–65

Urbina, Andrés de, 4

usurpations, 36, 230n11

Valeriano, Antonio, 16

Vega Carpio, Lope de, 12–13

Veintiun libros rituales y Monarquía indiana (Monarquía indiana) (Torquemada), 14–17, 64, 195, 202, 223nn35–36, 238n41; analyzing of, 24, 31; cosmic time in, 94; cosmography in, 97–102; *Historia de la nación chichimeca* comparisons with, 94–97; organization of, 91; prologue of, 70–71; sequences of civilizations in, 93; theory presented in, 72; trajectory of events, 135

Venegas, Alejo, 72